# EVERYTHING
## You Were Taught About The Civil War Is Wrong
## Ask a Southerner!

# BOOKS BY LOCHLAINN SEABROOK

A Rebel Born: A Defense of Nathan Bedford Forrest - Confederate General, American Legend
(winner of the 2011 Jefferson Davis Historical Gold Medal)

Nathan Bedford Forrest: Southern Hero, American Patriot - Honoring a Confederate Icon and the
Old South

The Quotable Nathan Bedford Forrest: Selections From the Writings and Speeches of the
Confederacy's Most Brilliant Cavalryman

Give 'Em Hell Boys! The Complete Military Correspondence of Nathan Bedford Forrest

Everything You Were Taught About the Civil War is Wrong, Ask a Southerner! - Correcting the
Errors of Yankee "History"

Honest Jeff and Dishonest Abe: A Southern Children's Guide to the Civil War

Abraham Lincoln: The Southern View - Demythologizing America's Sixteenth President

The Unquotable Abraham Lincoln: The President's Quotes They Don't Want You To Know!

Lincolnology: The Real Abraham Lincoln Revealed in His Own Words - A Study of Lincoln's
Suppressed, Misinterpreted, and Forgotten Speeches and Writings

The Quotable Jefferson Davis: Selections From the Writings and Speeches of the Confederacy's First
President

The Quotable Alexander H. Stephens: Selections From the Writings and Speeches of the
Confederacy's First Vice President

The Quotable Robert E. Lee: Selections From the Writings and Speeches of the South's Most Beloved
Civil War General

The Old Rebel: Robert E. Lee As He Was Seen By His Contemporaries

The Constitution of the Confederate States of America: Explained

The Quotable Edward A. Pollard: Selections From the Writings of the Confederacy's Greatest
Defender

Encyclopedia of the Battle of Franklin - A Comprehensive Guide to the Conflict that Changed the
Civil War

Carnton Plantation Ghost Stories: True Tales of the Unexplained from Tennessee's Most Haunted
Civil War House!

The McGavocks of Carnton Plantation: A Southern History - Celebrating One of Dixie's Most Noble
Confederate Families and Their Tennessee Home

The Caudills: An Etymological, Ethnological, and Genealogical Study - Exploring the Name and
National Origins of a European-American Family

The Blakeneys: An Etymological, Ethnological, and Genealogical Study - Uncovering the Mysterious
Origins of the Blakeney Family and Name

Britannia Rules: Goddess-Worship in Ancient Anglo-Celtic Society - An Academic Look at the United
Kingdom's Matricentric Spiritual Past

UFOs and Aliens: The Complete Guidebook

Christmas Before Christianity: How the Birthday of the "Sun" Became the Birthday of the "Son"

The Book of Kelle: An Introduction to Goddess-Worship and the Great Celtic Mother-Goddess Kelle,
Original Blessed Lady of Ireland

The Goddess Dictionary of Words and Phrases: Introducing a New Core Vocabulary for the Women's
Spirituality Movement

Aphrodite's Trade: The Hidden History of Prostitution Unveiled

*Thought Provoking Books For Smart People*
**www.SeaRavenPress.com**

# *Did You Know That . . .*

- American slavery got its start in the North
- the American abolition movement began in the South
- most Southern generals did not own slaves, and many, like Robert E. Lee, were abolitionists
- many Northern generals, like Ulysses S. Grant, owned slaves and said they would not fight for abolition
- according to the 1860 U.S. Census a mere 4.8 percent of Southerners owned slaves, 95.2 percent did not
- Abraham Lincoln was a white supremacist who said publicly that he wanted to send all blacks "back to Africa"
- Jefferson Davis adopted a black boy during the War and freed Southern slaves before the North did
- Lincoln was not against slavery, he was against the spread of slavery
- Lincoln's Emancipation Proclamation did not free a single slave
- true slavery was never practiced in the South
- Lincoln was a big government liberal, Davis was a small government conservative
- in the 1860 and 1864 elections less than 50 percent of Americans voted for Lincoln
- there were tens of thousands of both black and Native-American slave owners
- Lincoln started the Civil War, not the South
- the North said it fought to "preserve the Union," not to abolish slavery
- the South said it fought to "uphold the Constitution," not to maintain slavery
- the Northern armies were racially segregated, the Southern armies were racially integrated
- after emancipation 95 percent of all blacks voluntarily remained in the South
- it would have cost ten times less to simply free America's slaves than to go to war
- as many as 1 million African-Americans fought for the Confederacy
- Europe would have supported the South but she was scared off by Lincoln's war threats
- Northern prisons had higher death rates than Southern ones
- the original Ku Klux Klan was an anti-Yankee, social-welfare organization with thousands of black members
- "Reconstruction" was a dismal failure, which is why the South is still recovering from the War

If you weren't aware of the above information it's probably because *Everything You Were Taught About The Civil War Is Wrong*. In this book, popular Southern historian and award-winning author Lochlainn Seabrook uncovers the Truth that has for so long been neglected, dismissed, glossed over, twisted, rejected, mishandled, and suppressed by enemies of the South. Today they're trying to ban this information more vigorously than ever before! However, there are some, like Mr. Seabrook, who are taking back control of Southern history, and who will no longer allow the facts about America's "Civil War" to be obscured. Read the sensational bestselling book that everyone's talking about—the book that blows the lid off Yankee mythology—and learn the Truth for yourself.

# PRAISE FOR

*Everything You Were Taught About The Civil War Is Wrong, Ask a Southerner!*

"I have often told my students that the 'History' studied in American Public (Government) Schools is as bogus as what the children in the previous Soviet nations were taught by their Russian tutors. Lochlainn Seabrook takes an objective giant step in seeking to restore accuracy and integrity in our understanding of the American experience of The U.S. War to Prevent Southern Independence (called 'Civil War' by northerners). This is an important step in correcting the obnoxious myths and lies widely promoted by the U.S. court historians." — **TIMOTHY D. MANNING**, Executive Director of *The Southern Partisan Reader*

"From the time that our nation was formed until the time of the War Between the States, many complicated issues within the republic that had remained unresolved finally exploded in a tragic trial by combat. Many of the volatile issues that led to that bloody crucible as well as many that emerged from it, along with the manner in which those issues and connected personages are now portrayed, are addressed in this thought-provoking narrative." — **SCOTT BOWDEN**, five-time award-winning historian and author of *Last Chance for Victory: Robert E. Lee and the Gettysburg Campaign* and *Robert E. Lee at War*

Confederate troops resisting Lincoln's illegal Yankee invasion at Fredericksburg, Virginia.

# EVERYTHING

## You Were Taught About the Civil War Is Wrong
## Ask A Southerner!

*Correcting the Errors of Yankee "History"*

# LOCHLAINN SEABROOK

WINNER OF THE JEFFERSON DAVIS HISTORICAL GOLD MEDAL

Foreword by Nelson W. Winbush

*Third Printing, Revised*

SEA RAVEN PRESS, FRANKLIN, TENNESSEE, USA

EVERYTHING YOU WERE TAUGHT ABOUT THE CIVIL WAR IS WRONG,
ASK A SOUTHERNER!

Published by
Sea Raven Press, P.O. Box 1054, Franklin, Tennessee 37065-1054 USA
www.searavenpress.com • searavenpress@nii.net

First edition, first printing: December 2010 • First edition, second printing: January 2011
First edition, third printing, revised: January 2012

ISBN: 978-0-9827700-7-8
Library of Congress Catalog Number: 2010936513

Everything You Were Taught About the Civil War is Wrong, Ask a
Southerner! - Correcting the Errors of Yankee "History"/by Lochlainn
Seabrook. Foreword by Nelson W. Winbush. Includes bibliographical
references and index. (Portions of this book have been adapted from the
author's other works.)

Front and back cover design, interior design and layout, by Lochlainn Seabrook
Front cover image: Robert E. Lee, March 1864, Library of Congress
Confederate Battle Flag photo front cover, by Lochlainn Seabrook
Flag courtesy Craig Eilermann, Flag World, Franklin, TN
Title page photo: black Confederate soldier, 1913, Library of Congress
Typography: Sea Raven Press Book Design
Sketch of the author on "Meet the Author" page copyright © Tracy Latham

The views on the American "Civil War" documented in this book are those of the publisher.

The paper used in this book is acid-free and lignin-free. It has been certified by the Sustainable Forestry
Initiative and the Forest Stewardship Council and meets all ANSI standards for archival quality paper.

PRINTED & MANUFACTURED IN OCCUPIED TENNESSEE, FORMER CONFEDERATE STATES OF AMERICA

Matthew 7:12

# Dedication

To everyone who loves the South—and the Truth.

# Epigraph

"The real war will never get in the books."

Walt Whitman (1819-1892)

# CONTENTS

Southern hero, Confederate President Jefferson Davis

# FOREWORD

## by Nelson W. Winbush

Nelson W. Winbush stands in front of the Confederate Battle Flag that draped the coffin of his grandfather, black Confederate soldier Private Louis Napoleon Nelson. Mr. Winbush, who is wearing a Nathan Bedford Forrest button and a Sons of Confederate Veteran lapel pin, holds the reunion uniform and kepi Louis wore to thirty-nine Confederate Veteran reunions. Photo © courtesy Nelson W. Winbush.

My grandfather, Louis Napoleon Nelson, was a Confederate soldier, who in his later years related many of his war experiences to me. At age fourteen he accompanied his master's two sons, Sidney and E.R. Oldham, as members of the 7th Tennessee Cavalry, Company M, to Shiloh.

When they arrived at Shiloh they discovered there was no chaplain for the camp, and Louis was made temporary chaplain. Later, at Lookout Mountain, his position was made official, making him the only known black Confederate chaplain.

He told me that when he was conducting services, it was not uncommon for Confederates and Yankees to worship together. When the service was over soldiers returned to their respective sides to resume firing at each other.

At Lookout Mountain my grandfather said the Yankees would start up the mountainside in long lines. When they were en route, the Confederate troops would open fire with small field pieces. A cannon ball would strike the first Yankee and continue down the mountainside killing several soldiers in the single-file line. He stated they were not smart enough to break this long line while trying to make it up the mountainside.

Though initially he was E.R.'s bodyguard, Private Nelson did end up firing at the Yankee invaders. At Lookout Mountain he kind of did double duty. There, during heavy exchanges of gunfire and under the cover of darkness, he would sneak past the Yankee lines, kill a jenny mule, remove a hindquarter, strap it to his back and make his way back up the mountainside. He always smiled when he said "when you don't have anything else, mule meat tastes pretty good." From there they ended up at Brice's Crossroads in Mississippi. Early one morning, all hell broke loose as cannons were firing from both sides. They were in a cornfield and there was a low-hanging cloud of black gun smoke. So they lay between the rows of corn. Mid-afternoon, when the firing ceased, corn stalks that had been taller than eight feet had been cut to nubbins of only about three to five feet tall by the hail of artillery exchange. If anyone had taken the chance to stand up or run they would have been killed. From there the Confederates chased the Yankees back to Memphis.

Vicksburg was a different story. Bodies from both sides were strung as far as he could see. Confederate and Yankee dead lay beside and across each other, along with the wounded. The Oldham brothers and my grandfather surrendered and were marched to Gainesville, Alabama. Eventually they were released and they walked back to Lauderdale County, Ripley, Tennessee. None of the three suffered any injuries, and lived to attend many Confederate Veteran reunions together.

Louis Napoleon Nelson, grandfather of Nelson W. Winbush, poses in his reunion uniform at a Confederate Veteran reunion. Chaplain Nelson was just one of hundreds of thousands of African-Americans who fought for the Confederacy and self-determination. Photo © courtesy Nelson W. Winbush.

History has a strange way of recording things. "To the victor go the spoils." But in the War Between the States there was no real winner. There was tragic destruction of lives and property. This was the result of staged activity by the Yankees that blew up into a full fledged war between the Southern States that had seceded from President Lincoln and the Northern States.

As Mr. Seabrook's book shows, the true story of this occurrence is not fully recorded. Contrary to what history has presented, the war was not about "slavery," but was about states' rights. During this conflict there were persons of color serving as members of the Confederacy. Not just as teamsters, cooks and body guards, but in every military capacity. One of them was my grandfather Private Louis Napoleon Nelson, 7th Tennessee Cavalry, Company M.

Nelson W. Winbush
Kissimmee, Florida
November 2010

# Notes to the Reader

*Third printing, revised 2012 Civil War Sesquicentennial Edition*

As I heartily dislike the phrase "Civil War," for the reasons given in Chapter 1, its use as part of the title of this book deserves an explanation.

Today America's entire literary system refers to the conflict of 1861 using the Northern term the "Civil War," whether we in the South like it or not. Thus, as *all* book searches by readers, libraries, and retail outlets are now performed online, and as *all* bookstores categorize works from this period under the heading "Civil War," book publishers and authors who deal with this particular topic have little choice but to use this term themselves. If I were to refuse to use it, as some of my Southern colleagues have suggested, few people would ever find or read my books.

Add to this the fact that scarcely any non-Southerners have ever heard of the names we in the South use for the conflict, such as the "War for Southern Independence"—or my personal preference, "Lincoln's War." It only makes sense then to use the term "Civil War" in most commercial situations.

We should also bear in mind that while today educated persons, particularly educated Southerners, all share an abhorrence for the phrase "Civil War," it was not always so. Confederates who lived through and even fought in the conflict regularly used the term throughout the 1860s, and even long after. Among them were Confederate generals such as Nathan Bedford Forrest,[1] Richard Taylor,[2] and Joseph E. Johnston,[3] not to mention the Confederacy's vice president, Alexander H. Stephens.[4] Even the Confederacy's highest leader, President Jefferson Davis, used the term "Civil War,"[5] and in one case at least, as late as 1881—the year he wrote his brilliant exposition, *The Rise and Fall of the Confederate Government*.[6]

In any study of the "Civil War" it is vitally important to understand that the two major political parties were then the opposite of what they are today. As is explained in Chapter 10, the Democrats of the mid 19th Century were conservatives, akin to the Republican Party of today, while the Republicans of the mid 19th Century were liberals, akin to the Democratic Party of today. Thus the Confederacy's Democratic president, Jefferson Davis, was a conservative (with libertarian leanings); the Union's Republican president, Abraham Lincoln, was a liberal (with socialistic leanings).

Above, the Confederate Monument at Arlington National Cemetery, Arlington, Virginia, original site of Gen. Robert E. Lee's home, Arlington House—before it was stolen and ruthlessly plundered by the Yanks. Note the man second from the right: not merely a black slave or a body servant, but a real armed black Confederate soldier, marching proudly side-by-side with his white Confederate brothers. The memorial was designed by Southern artist Moses Ezekiel, one of 12,000 Jewish Confederate soldiers who routinely witnessed thousands of blacks in the Rebel armed forces firsthand—which is why, after all, he included an African-American in this typical Civil War scene as experienced by Southerners. About the time this monument was erected, in 1908, the North began suppressing the truth about the reality of black Confederate soldiers because it exposed the supreme lie of Lincoln's War; namely, that it had been fought to "free the slaves" in the "evil slave-ridden South." Contrary to this contrived Yankee nonsense, slavery was still being practiced in the North in 1861, the very birthplace of American slavery (in Massachusetts in 1641). What is more, of the South's 4,000,000 blacks, at least 300,000 served as combatants in the Confederate army and navy, far more than went North and fought for Lincoln (many who did so with great regret). At least 95 percent of the remaining 3,700,000 Southern blacks stayed in their homeland, Dixie (ignoring Lincoln's fraudulent and illegal Emancipation Proclamation), where they supported the Confederacy in a myriad of ways—as the Arlington Confederate Monument, there for all to see, silently and stubbornly attests.

# INTRODUCTION

## OUR GLORIOUS HERITAGE
### by Lochlainn Seabrook

DON'T MESS WITH SOUTHERN HISTORY

The title of this book, *Everything You Were Taught About the Civil War is Wrong, Ask A Southerner!*, may sound humorous, but it's not meant to be. Here in the South we traditional Southerners don't take kindly to the distortion and suppression of our history. In fact, we view it as a serious offense.

As a Southern writer and historian I take this crime more seriously than most, for being a traditionalist I feel it's my responsibility to both tell and preserve the Truth from the South's perspective. In 1906 my cousin Confederate General Stephen Dill Lee asked all authentic Southerners and lovers of liberty to remember that "it is your duty to see that the true history of the South is presented to future generations."[7] The "true history" General Lee is referring to here pertains to the facts about what we call the "War for Southern Independence," and what Yanks wrongly call the "Civil War."

Southerners raised in traditional homes are the most likely to already know our true history, hence the title of this book. Yet, since 99 percent of all books written on this topic are authored and published by extremely biased, and often hopelessly South-illiterate enemies of Dixie, the odds are extremely good that no matter where you're from, you don't know *all* the facts. This is especially true if you're not from the South, or if you were born to Southern parents whose political stance leans to the liberal left.[8]

THE TYPICAL VIEW OF THE CIVIL WAR

Ask the average person to give a brief synopsis of the American "Civil War" and their answer will invariably go something like the following.

In the mid-1800s the abolitionist North began pressuring the pro-slavery South to give up slavery. Believing the institution to be God-ordained and essential to their economy, Southerners stubbornly resisted.

The brewing conflict finally boiled over with the election of the famous abolitionist Abraham Lincoln in November 1860. The belligerent South was so angry at the thought that slavery would now be taken away from her that she unlawfully split from the hated Union in order to try and form her own country, after which she aggressively and needlessly started a war with the North at Fort Sumter in April 1861.

Lincoln immediately freed the slaves and every single Southern black fled North to fight against the Rebels and preserve the Union. Because the South was in the wrong, and because secession was illegal, God was on Lincoln's side, and within four years the North easily destroyed the Confederacy.

The South, still upset because it could no longer practice its "peculiar institution," continued to rebel, and so "Reconstruction" was inaugurated in order to drive out whatever remained of the innate Southern love of slavery. The rebellious Southern states, now duly chastised and repentant, finally gave up, gladly rejoining the Union.

Our nation's most illustrious abolitionist, "Honest Abe," was crowned the "Great Emancipator" for destroying slavery and for finally recognizing the civil rights of African-Americans. For this, and for "preserving the Union," Lincoln will rightly forever be known as the greatest and best president in U.S. history.

GATEKEEPING IN MODERN AMERICA

There is only one problem with this view: not a single one word of it is true! Why? Because it's the *Northern* version. Many people are not even aware that there is a Southern view of the War, and that it is this perspective that's the correct and historically accurate one of the two.

Despite the Northern view's many falsehoods, this is the version of the "Civil War" that is still being taught in schools and in the media, not only in the U.S., but around the world. The reason is simple enough: it's the victor in war who writes the history. And it is the descendants (both biological and ideological) of the victors of our "Civil War" who have become the modern gatekeepers of American history. As this book represents the Southern view, it's obvious they'd rather you not read it, which is why they've been suppressing this information for the past 150 years.

Just who specifically are today's information gatekeepers?

They're the people in charge of who reads what, particularly when it comes to the "Civil War." These would include the liberal elite who run most of our public and private schools, colleges, and universities, along with the thousands of left-wing, politically correct book editors and publishers, newspaper editors, magazine editors and publishers, bookstore owners, librarians, textbook writers, museum directors, Civil War site directors, and historical house directors across the U.S.

Most of America's information gatekeepers are Democrats, of a liberal, or even socialistic, Marxist, or communist frame of mind, and each one is hellbent on keeping the Truth from you at all costs. For liberals are, generally speaking, speech tyrants and literary dictators, the kind of Big Brother folks who only want one side to be heard: their own.

As an author of pro-South books I've experienced liberal censorship firsthand, and I can tell you unequivocally that it's alive and well in the land of free speech. Thanks to the PC thought police, who have taken over our schools both South and North, your children, for instance, will probably never see a single

South-friendly book from the day they enter kindergarten to the day they graduate from high school. It's a stone-cold guarantee that the book you now hold in your hand will probably never be allowed in any high school in Dixie, and this is exactly how the anti-South gatekeepers who run our schools want it.

What your children *will* end up reading are carefully selected, handpicked books written from the Northern point of view, all guaranteed to cast the South in the worst light possible. Liberals generously call this "getting an education." We traditional Southerners call it what it really is: the slanted anti-South propaganda of uneducated pro-North revisionists.

Not all gatekeepers want to prevent you from knowing the Truth about the so-called "Civil War." There are a few rare individuals and organizations, mainly Republicans, conservatives, libertarians, and Tea Party members, who are dedicated to disseminating the facts about America's bloodiest and most senseless military conflict, despite incredible pressure and resistance. We salute these honorable men and women.

The main culprits are South-hating Yankees[9] and South-hating Southerners, the latter South-illiterate turncoats known as "scallywags" here in Dixie. These people would probably prefer to give up their first-born child rather than have you find out that slavery started in the North, abolition began in the South, Abraham Lincoln was a rabid white racist, Jefferson Davis adopted a black child, 95 percent of Southern blacks supported the Confederacy, and the Yanks started the War, a conflict that was illegal from start to finish.

But try as they might, no amount of censorship can keep the Truth from finally coming out. And in this book it will do just that.

THE ANTI-SOUTH MOVEMENT
The publication of *Everything You Were Taught About the Civil War is Wrong, Ask A Southerner!*, is well-timed: as part of the near universal anti-South movement, Dixie and her people are being increasingly subjected to public ridicule, slander, harassment, destruction of private property, the complete perversion of their history, and even death threats.

In some cases these threats have spilled over into actual murder, such as when, on January 14, 1995, a white Kentuckian, nineteen-year-old Michael Westerman (a new father of twins), was chased across two states by three carloads of teens, then shot dead. Why? Because in honor of his Southern heritage he had been flying a Confederate flag from his pickup truck.[10]

Along with such horrors the South's traditional flags have been banned from public squares (and even from NASCAR, a *Southern* business), her traditional songs have been prohibited from college sporting events, statues of her heroes are routinely defaced, and organizations trying to preserve Southern culture are persecuted, denigrated, defamed, and even sued. One of the latest outrages against Dixie is the removal of Colonel Reb, the universally beloved former sporting mascot of the University of Mississippi (apparently he was too "Old South" for the school's politically correct authorities).

But Ole Miss is far from being the only educational institution making war on America's wonderful Southern heritage. Schools throughout the U.S. now regularly ban the wearing or display of any Confederate symbol, such as flags, lapel pins, bumper stickers, clothing, pictures, and posters, and pro-South books are prohibited from school libraries by their PC administrators. In these attempts to both silence and eventually obliterate authentic Southern history we learn much more about the meddlesome anti-South movement than we do about the South herself, a region that has traditionally not only respected the rights of others (even when they disagree with her), but has always only asked one thing of liberal do-gooders like political twins Abraham Lincoln and Barack Obama: leave us alone![11]

## YANKEE CIVIL WAR MYTHS BEGAN WITH LINCOLN

The real question is this: why is there so much hatred toward the South, not only from Northerners, but from many misguided Southerners themselves? The many anti-South lies fabricated by Lincoln's wartime propaganda machine explains much of this. But how do we explain the Yankee detestation of the South long prior to Lincoln's War?

This loathing dates back to the very first European settlers in America, at which time enormous differences between Southern and Northern colonists were already manifesting. By the start of the "Civil War," South and North were like two completely different civilizations, wholly incompatible and mutually antagonistic.

Between 1861 and 1865 Lincoln, a former newspaper editor who well knew how to manipulate the populace using the written word,[12] and who once said that someone who can mold public opinion is more powerful than someone who can make statutes,[13] played up these sharp differences in order to curry votes, maintain support for his War, and attract wealthy benefactors. In the process of trying to portray Dixie as unfavorably as he could, Lincoln buried the Truth about the South amid an avalanche of deception, ridiculous accusations, and intentional fraud, a villainous scheme that resulted in a gargantuan historical coverup of the facts.

But the facts about the Old South are ornery stubborn things. Thankfully they don't cease to exist or simply go away because liberals and progressives wish them to, or because they've been hidden from view, ignored, or suppressed.

The North engaged in and continues to engage in what has been called "cultural genocide": the indiscriminate effort to obliterate the true history and traditions of an entire society, in this case the traditional South.[14] Is it any wonder that the world knows little or nothing about what really happened before, during, and after the "Civil War"; that it's familiar only with the Northern version, one founded almost completely on invented folklore?

The first casualty of war is indeed the Truth.

## JUSTIFYING AN ILLEGAL WAR

All of this begs the question: why is the anti-South movement so desperately committed to covering up the facts about the War for Southern Independence?

Established by the Declaration of Independence, carried forward by the Articles of Confederation, and protected by both the U.S. Constitution and the Bill of Rights, secession was perfectly legal in the 1860s.[15] This makes the Confederacy a legally formed nation, Lincoln's War illegal, and Lincoln himself a war criminal. As for the millions (of all races) who were injured, killed, or turned into homeless refugees, these were nothing less than the needless victims of Northern political treachery.

In order to justify its unlawful invasion of the South, the mindless destruction of Southern homes, businesses, schools, libraries, hospitals, factories, and entire towns, and the wanton death of thousands (many of them innocent noncombatants), the North has had to suppress the truth, then create a fantasy history to replace it; a vast Yankee mythology that supplants every fact with fiction in favor of the North. It is thus due to Lincoln and his contemporary and modern worshipful followers that the Truth about the "Civil War" has been blotted out, substituted by "facts" skewed to represent the Northern point of view—one that paints the North as the moral power, the South the immoral one. I call this the Great Yankee Coverup, a vast anti-South conspiracy to hide the North's many crimes between 1861 and 1877.

## REINSTATING THE FACTS

Thanks to the diligent work of thousands of anti-South historians, propagandists, authors, and mythographers, we are already overly familiar with so-called "Southern racism" and the alleged horrors of Southern slavery, the atrocities of Southern soldiers, the "illegality" of secession, the sorry condition of Confederate prisons, the heinous crimes of the KKK, the many cruelties of Southern slave owners, the purported "innate ignorance, brutality, and laziness" of the Southern people, and the "inferiority" of the Confederate government and her statesmen, politicians, and military officers.

In order to correct this one-sided distortion of history, this book will focus on the other side of the coin, namely: the Northern origins of slavery and the slave trade, Northern racism, the legality of secession, Lincoln's many war crimes, the atrocities of Northern soldiers, the innate arrogance, greediness, and megalomania of many 19th-Century Northerners, the pitiful state of Yankee prisons, the Northern origins of the KKK, the realities of Reconstruction, and the superiority of our Confederate leader, President Jefferson Davis, among many other items and issues.

In the process we'll demolish many of the errors, pseudo histories, asinine frauds, intentional fabrications, preposterous tall tales, and literal libraries of disinformation spewed out by the Northern/New South propaganda machine over the past 150 years. After all, this is a book about the *Southern* view of the War, a perspective that has not been written about, read, or discussed nearly enough, as Mr. Winbush's wonderful foreword illustrates.

Is my book biased, subjective, slanted toward the South, Confederate-friendly, and pro-Dixie? Absolutely and unapologetically yes. And this is as it should be. After being destabilized by centuries of South-hating literature and mythology, it's high time that a more holistic, realistic, more balanced, and factual portrait of our nation's great intra-fratricidal conflict be disseminated. Indeed, as all objective historians now agree: *A complete understanding of America's "Civil War" is impossible without a thorough knowledge of the South's point of view.*

## THE SELF-SERVING PRACTICES OF SOUTH-HATERS

When Southern writers try to correct the mistakes of Northern writers by carefully sifting their way through the vast mountains of Yankee-slanted material, they're labeled "revisionists," their method of research "cherry picking." When Southern historians pen their own histories of Lincoln's War they're called "polemic" and "biased." Pro-South books in general are labeled mere "Southern propaganda," their authors "racists."

Yet when anti-South authors completely rewrite authentic "Civil War" history they're respectfully called "brilliant" and "objective." When anti-South historians cherry pick around the facts and invent South-negative myths out of thin air, they're called "scholarly," their arguments "lucid," their statements "authoritative," their opinions "thoughtful," their books "well-written." Pro-North books in general are called "impartial treatments" or "brilliant expositions," their authors lavished with praise and literary awards.

In short, what we in the South call the Truth the North calls a "lie," and what we Southerners call setting the record straight Northerners call "revisionism." This is nothing less than politically-charged language, pure and simple, meant to shut down all dialogue, justify Lincoln's War, demean the South, and continue to keep her in a state of economic, cultural, political, and psychological subordination to the North.

## WHY THE TRADITIONAL SOUTH DEFENDS THE TRUTH

Thankfully the push to extinguish what General Stephen Dill Lee termed the South's "true history" has been slowed, and is even reversing in some cases with books like this one. Southerners, and even a few enlightened non-Southerners, are now standing up for the truth about the War. Not the North's "truth," but the South's Truth, long buried under a century and a half of Yankee fairy tales.

Being of Southern heritage, a cousin of General Robert E. Lee, and the 2nd, 3rd, and 4th great-grandson of numerous Confederate soldiers (at least one who was illegally murdered by Yankees while on furlough in Kentucky), naturally I embrace the Southern view of Lincoln's War.

Why is it so important that authentic Southerners and lovers of the U.S. Constitution everywhere stand up for the Truth about the "Civil War"? On January 2, 1864, Confederate General Patrick R. Cleburne answered the question this way. Addressing his fellow Southerners, the Irish officer stated unequivocally:

> [If we lose the War to the North] . . . we can give but a faint idea when we say it means the loss of all we now hold most sacred . . . It means that the history of this heroic struggle will be written by the enemy; that our youth will be trained by Northern school teachers; will learn from Northern school books their version of the war; will be impressed by all the influences of history and education to regard our gallant dead as traitors, our maimed veterans as fit objects for derision. It means the crushing of Southern manhood . . .[16]

Though he didn't know it at the time (a year before the War ended), General Cleburne would turn out to be all too correct. Following the Confederacy's capitulation at Appomattox in April 1865, the result was all but inevitable: Northern liberals—many who are still not interested in living in a true democracy, but prefer that the world conform to their progressive, often socialistic, even totalitarian ideals—immediately set out to make the South into an exact copy of the North, just as Lincoln had planned from the beginning.[17]

## REVEREND SMITH'S DREAM

A half century later, in 1907, another Southerner spoke out; this time against the very Northernization process that Cleburne predicted. It was in that year that former Confederate Reverend James P. Smith—a staff member of one of the South's greatest heroes, my cousin General Stonewall Jackson—wrote eloquently about the trashing of Southern history, heritage, and culture, and about preserving Southern Truth for future generations. After the War for Southern Independence, Smith penned,

> . . . there emerged as the years went by a condition and a necessity which had not been anticipated. With utmost difficulty the schools of the South had been re-established, and seminaries and colleges had been re-opened, in the faithful effort to preserve the intelligence and character of the generation of sons and daughters rising up through the land.
>
> It was discovered with a shock of pain and indignation that the great body of the youth of the land were being fed with a literature created by alien authors. Histories, biographies, readers, issued by publishers whose one purpose was to secure the great market now opening in every school district far and wide over the South, were found to be replete with error and misrepresentation. Consciously or unconsciously, the aims of the people of the South, and of their State

governments were falsified, and the characters of great and good men were belittled and defamed.

The poison of unjust accusation was carried to the minds of all the children of the Southland, and already a generation was growing up with conceptions of the motives of their fathers, and the causes of the war between the sections which were not only mistaken, but altogether dishonorable. The youth of the whole South were being stealthily robbed of an heritage glorious in itself and elevating and ennobling to themselves and all who came after them.

It was a condition and a process which could not be consented to for a moment. There was no surrender at Appomattox, and no withdrawal from the field which committed our people and their children to a heritage of shame and dishonor. No cowardice on any battlefield could be as base and shameful as the silent acquiescence in the scheme which was teaching the children in their homes and schools that the commercial value of slavery was the cause of the war, that prisoners of war held in the South were starved and treated with a barbarous inhumanity, that Jefferson Davis and Robert E. Lee were traitors to their country and false to their oaths, that the young men who left everything to resist invasion, and climbed the slopes of Gettysburg and died willingly on a hundred fields were rebels against a righteous government.

The State Camp of Virginia of Confederate Veterans rose promptly and vigorously to resist another invasion, which would have turned the children against their fathers, covered the graves of patriots and heroes with shame and made the memory of the Confederacy and its sacrifices and struggles a disgrace in all coming history. The camps throughout the South had a new task given them. They were to meet the threatening evil at the door of every school house in the land.

All that was, or is now, desired [by the South] is that error and injustice be excluded from the text-books of the schools and from the literature brought into our homes; that the truth be told, without exaggeration and without omission; truth for its own sake and for the sake of honest history, and that the generations to come after us be not left to bear the burden of shame and dishonor unrighteously laid upon the name of their noble sires.[18]

It is hoped that this book will play a role in fulfilling Reverend Smith's dream. I share it.

Lochlainn Seabrook, recipient of the Jefferson Davis Historical Gold Medal
Franklin, Tennessee, USA
November 2010

DONT TREAD ON ME

# THE SO-CALLED "CIVIL WAR"

**WHAT YOU WERE TAUGHT:** The "Civil War," and the "War Between the States," are the most grammatically, politically, and historically accurate names for America's War of 1861.

**THE TRUTH:** No two names could be more inappropriate for this conflict.

The word "civil," as it is used here, implies a conflict between states belonging to the same nation, or one in which the contestants are fighting to control the same government. The term "between the states" has the same intended meaning. Neither applies in any way to our nation's bloody intra-fratricidal struggle.

When Yankee President Abraham Lincoln committed his first official war crime against the South on April 12, 1861, she was already a separate, free, and sovereign nation by the name of the Confederate States of America (C.S.A.). It had been symbolically formed with the secession of the first Southern state, South Carolina, on December 20, 1860, while it was constitutionally formed just two months later, on February 4, 1861, when the provisional Confederate government was set up.[19] Additionally, the C.S.A. was never officially made nonexistent and is still considered a region under Northern occupation by knowledgeable Southerners. Thus the War was legally and truly a battle between two individual countries.

For self-serving political reasons Lincoln continually chose to downplay and even deny this fact, calling the South's secession a "rebellion"[20] and its inhabitants "rebels,"[21] "disloyal citizens,"[22] "insurgents,"[23] and "treacherous associates."[24] But these labels do not make it untrue. Quite the opposite: Lincoln's duplicitous actions and his endless repetition that the Confederacy was merely a rebellious American neighbor instead of a separate warring nation, only further emphasized the reality that the War was between two autonomous countries.

That the term "Civil War," coined by the North and repeated endlessly by Lincoln in his speeches and letters,[25] has become the standard phrase by which this conflict is known, must be counted as the single greatest achievement of Yankee mythologists. For this erroneous phrase was purposefully designed to mislead the public and obfuscate the truth, and so it has for 150 years.

Its net effect has been to define the War as one between neighboring regions of the same nation, one righteous (the North)—which fought against the "rebels"; the other evil (the South)—which fought against the "sacred Union" to gain control of the U.S. government. This overt falsehood in turn forces history to disregard the constitutional legitimacy of the Confederacy and its creation upon the Founding Fathers' idea of states' rights. This, of course, was the original intention of this deceitful Yankee phrase to begin with.

As history has proven, the War was between two independent nations, the C.S.A. and the U.S.A., the former which fought to maintain states' rights—that is, to preserve Thomas Jefferson's original constitutional, agrarian republic, "the Confederacy,"[26] the latter which fought to destroy states' rights—so it could install Henry Clay's new democratic, industrial empire, the "American System." As such the "Civil War" was patently not a true civil war, which Webster defines as "a war between opposing groups of citizens of the *same country*," a meaning that dates back to the 1400s, 400 years before Lincoln's War.[27]

What is the correct name for this conflict then?

The South could only win by claiming and maintaining independence; the North could only win by forcing the South to forfeit its independence and return to the Union. Thus from the Southern point of view the most accurate name for the conflict is the *War for Southern Independence*, while from the Northern perspective the most applicable name would be the *War to Prevent Southern Independence*. The North has never used either because by doing so the horrendous realities of its illegal war on Dixie would be exposed. By using "Civil War" instead, the North has found a convenient way to suppress the truth while casting the South as the villain.

The phrases Civil War and War Between the States should not then be used, for they make a mockery of both the Constitution and the legal existence of the Southern Confederacy while masking the North's unlawful actions and war crimes.

Dozens of other Southern-appropriate names have been coined for the conflict, my own favorite being "Lincoln's War." For if not for liberal Lincoln and his megalomaniac political aspirations, the violent carnage he instigated against the Southern people (beginning at Fort Sumter in 1861) would never have occurred. Instead, Dixie would have been allowed to secede peacefully, as Lincoln's predecessor President James Buchanan—and millions of other Northerners—had wanted, and the many differences between the Confederacy and the Union would have eventually been resolved amicably, diplomatically, and legally.

**WHAT YOU WERE TAUGHT:** The South is still fighting the Civil War. Why can't Southerners accept that they lost and move on?

**THE TRUTH:** The South is indeed still fighting. But it is not the "Civil War." She is still fighting for the ideas that her ancestors died for in that conflict to begin with; namely, strict constitutionality, states' rights, a small limited central government, conservative Jeffersonian political ideals, free trade, capitalism, fiscal responsibility, and traditional family and religious values.

All of these are being slowly eroded and replaced by the liberal, nationalistic, industry-based, Hamiltonian, big-government-loving, Federalist North, a process leftover from Lincoln's campaign to destroy the Old South and northernize her by remaking her in the image of the northeastern states—the last thing any red-blooded Southerner would ever want. Thus the South fights on. Not the War itself, but for the ideals over which her ancestors fought and perished.

In point of fact it would be more accurate to say that it is the North who is still fighting the War. Each year hundreds of books are published on Lincoln's War. Nearly all of them slanted toward the Northern perspective; nearly every one overflows with Yankee mythology, lies, slander, misinformation, and disinformation; nearly every one is authored by politically correct non-Southerners and (traitorous) New South Southerners, both who are ignorant of our true history, and who thus misunderstand and revile Dixie.

Yet when a Southerner attempts to defend his homeland and heritage against this avalanche of ludicrous and often purposefully hurtful fiction, he or she is reprimanded for "still fighting the Civil War." An apt analogy would be for a person to provoke a rattlesnake into attacking by repeatedly stepping on it, then shooting it for trying to protect itself.

A rattler only wants to be left alone to live in peace. So with the average Southerner.[28] But interfere with his or her way of life, and you will have a fight on your hands, even though the defense will usually be made with pen and paper, from behind a pulpit, or at a computer keyboard.

The South, at heart still very much a leisurely, peace-loving agrarian society,[29] is *not* still fighting the War. It did not want it to begin with, and certainly has no desire to continue what the North illegally began so many years ago. However, it is true that the South is still sensitive about the "late unpleasantness"—and with good reason.

Lincoln's War took place on Dixie's soil, in her front and backyards, in her gardens, on her farmland, on her roads and bridges, in her cemeteries, in her shops, and in her houses, farm buildings, schools, and churches. These are considered sacred places in the South. Yet all still bear the scars of Lincoln's illicit invasion after a century and a half.

During this violent and irrational intrusion, most of Dixie's people were displaced, turning millions of once placid, innocent farming families into terrified, wandering, homeless refugees. Along with this her infrastructure was destroyed, her telegraph lines cut, railroads torn up, granaries leveled, houses robbed, farms demolished, factories razed, churches torn down, businesses of every kind wrecked,[30] and her females beaten and often raped in their own plundered homes.[31]

Even Dixie's schools, universities, libraries, and hospitals were not spared the Yankee torch,[32] for incredibly, Lincoln had ordered everything in the South to be destroyed by fire, particularly in Virginia.[33] Thus in Lexington, U.S. troops, for example, wantonly burned down the Virginia Military Institute, along with all of the homes of the school's teachers. They were preparing to torch Washington College (now Washington and Lee University) as well, but thankfully were restrained at the last moment.[34]

Why were such atrocities and acts of terrorism waged upon noncombatants? Normally, civilized nations at war do not destroy these kinds of structures, for it is both immoral and unnecessary to do so. Why then did Lincoln insist on setting fire to the South, even as the first of the Geneva Conventions was adopted in 1863, midway through his War?

This is not all.

Between 1861 and 1865 across the Confederacy pets were sadistically and needlessly killed and farm animals were stolen by Yanks and used in the fight against their own owners. Animals that could not be impressed and taken away were shot down on the spot before the eyes of anguished families, many in poverty with only a single skeletal mule or horse to their name.[35]

Likewise, food and provisions were brazenly pilfered, even from Southern households already starving after months under the brutal and illegal Yankee naval blockade. That which could not be carried off was summarily burned (under Lincoln's orders), as fathers, mothers, children, and grandparents begged for mercy from a merciless invader.

Many Southern homes were commandeered for use by Yankee forces. This is not unusual in wartime. What *was* unusual is that under the Yankee policy of coercion, Southern families were often forced from their homes at bayonet point, even in the dead of winter, with nowhere to go, no place to take shelter. Newborn infants were treated with the same callousness as adults, women the same as men, seniors the same as children.

The family's house would then be searched from top to bottom for valuables.  In the process, cruel and unthinking Yanks tore beds and linens apart, overturned cabinets, chairs, and tables, broke mirrors, shattered windows, sliced beautiful framed paintings to tatters with Bowie knives, smashed family heirlooms to pieces, threw dishes, plates, and cups against walls, stripped watches from men, and tore rings from the hands of frightened girls, angry women, and trembling grandmothers.

Neither were the South's black servants exempt from the inexplicable wrath of the Federal militia.  Strangely, though after the issuance of the Emancipation Proclamation on January 1, 1863, the North was alleged to be the "friend of the Negro"—sent South to free them from their inhuman bondage under "Cracker rule"—blacks were among the primary targets of white Northern soldiers.  Incidents of harassment, beating, torture, rape, and even the murder of Southern blacks by Yankees, were all duly recorded in the diaries, letters, and journals of both black and white Southerners.

After using a Confederate family's house for their purposes—usually to rest, eat, and plan their next move—Union forces sometimes allowed families to remove cherished objects that had managed to survive the initial Yankee savagery, and set them out on the front road.  The house was then burned to the ground, often to the heartless laughter of Lincoln's soldiers.

Entire communities were treated in this fashion, with some cities utterly disappearing before the onslaught of Yankee boots (Union footwear was often steel-toed in order to expedite mayhem and destruction).  Northern war hero General William T. Sherman liked to brag that Southern maps would have to be re-drawn after he and his troops passed by.  He literally wiped towns like Meridian, Mississippi, off the face of the earth.

So wonderfully and completely did Lincoln's minions "make the South howl" that the region has not fully recovered yet, even after 150 years.  Indeed, as of 2012, Dixie is only starting to catch up and, in some areas, surpass the North.  Hundreds of Civil War cemeteries dot the landscape, and homes and buildings whose walls are filled with bullet holes remain, mute but overt testimony to the blizzard of remorseless violence and carnage that was spread across the South by the North during those terrible years.  Illinoisan and Lincoln apologist Carl Sandburg, certainly no friend of the South, correctly called the War's affect on Dixie a "human slaughterhouse."[36]  Southern diarist Mary Chesnut put it this way: ". . . our world, the only world we cared for, [was] literally kicked to pieces."[37]

In contrast, few Northerners had their world "kicked to pieces." Very few Northern cities were touched by the War and, in fact, most Northern states were completely spared and would not have had any reason to think that a major military conflict was raging across North America, except for newspaper reports.

More to the point, most of the North's citizens never saw the horrors of the War on their doorstep; never had to flee from an approaching army; never had to watch their home being torn down; never had their nostrils filled with the pungent smoke of the battlefield and the stench of rotting bodies; never heard the screams of loved ones who had been shot or bayoneted; never had to defend themselves against an enemy who robbed, torched, raped, pillaged, and blasted its way through their communities; and never received a government letter saying that their son, brother, or father had been tortured, then intentionally starved to death in a Southern military prison (as nearly 6,000 Rebel soldiers were at Lincoln's notorious Camp Douglas in Chicago).

Most Northerners also never saw their schools, churches, hospitals, and libraries senselessly blown apart; never saw their factories demolished, their railroads ripped up, their crop fields set ablaze; never witnessed their pets and livestock being tortured, killed or stolen; never saw their businesses torn down, every structure turned to rubble, or their entire countryside laid waste.

But nearly every Southern citizen experienced one or more of these things in the twelve years between 1861 and 1877, from the beginning of Lincoln's War to the year so-called "Reconstruction" ended.

The memories of this period of savage, pointless, and sadistic Yankee cruelty have been transferred from generation to generation across the South. There is our oral memory, passed from adult to child; our literary memory, passed from writer to reader; and our genetic memories, passed through blood from parent to offspring.

Is the South still fighting the Civil War, as Yankee myth attests? Hardly. Why would it want to repeat, or even relive, twelve years of Hell on earth, an infernal period instigated by a dictatorial enemy of the South?

What the South and her people *are* doing is trying to maintain the freedoms we once enjoyed under the original U.S. Confederacy (1781-1789), when the torch of freedom, Jeffersonianism, small government, and self-determination burned brightly. General Lee later mournfully regretted "surrendering" at Appomattox. Dixie will not make the same mistake again.

**WHAT YOU WERE TAUGHT:** The Civil War did not do nearly as much physical damage to the South as Southerners claim.

**THE TRUTH:** In total the War cost America about $150 billion, most of this expense accrued in the South.[38] Entire Southern towns were wiped from the face of the earth by Yankees like Sherman, never to be rebuilt, with only a memorial stone to mark their original existence today.

Even during Lincoln's War the devastation was considered appalling, as the only evidence of many Southern villages were lone-standing chimneys, once attached to beautiful family homes and thriving businesses. In some cities, later called "Chimneyvilles," street after street contained nothing but fire-smoked chimneys, inevitably to become known as "Sherman's Sentinels." One of the best known Chimneyvilles was Jackson, Mississippi, put to the torch by none other than the South-loathing general himself.[39]

**WHAT YOU WERE TAUGHT:** Only 329,000 Confederate soldiers died during the Civil War,[40] hardly what one would call a bloodbath compared to the millions that died during conflicts like World War II.
**THE TRUTH:** This is a purely Northern figure, and as such inaccurate. For one thing it does not include noncombatants like Southern European-American seniors, women, and children. It also does not include Southern African-American servants (men, women, and children). The practice of omitting these losses from the total has long been employed by Yankee and scallywag historians to artificially keep down the number of Southern dead.

According to we traditional Southern historians, an estimated 2 million Southerners died during Lincoln's War: 1 million whites (out of 8 million) and probably as many as 1 million blacks (out of 4 million).[41] This is a stunning 16 percent of Dixie's total white and black population (of 12 million). There is no record of how many Southern Asians, Native-Americans, and Hispanics also died in the conflict, but we can be sure these deaths easily numbered in the thousands.

In short, 12.5 percent of all Southern whites died, while 25 percent of all Southern blacks died as a direct result of Lincoln and his War. This is what we Southerners call a bloodbath.

**WHAT YOU WERE TAUGHT:** The Civil War was necessary.
**THE TRUTH:** No conflict was ever more unnecessary. Not only was secession legal, but Lincoln did not preserve the *voluntary* union created by the Founding Fathers,[42] nor did he end slavery, which was only finally abolished eight months after he died under the Thirteenth Amendment.[43]

Of course, ending slavery was not one of Lincoln's original goals to begin with, as he himself stated in his First Inaugural Address.[44] Our sixteenth president may have been mentally unstable, but he was not stupid: freeing the slaves then compensating Southern slave owners for their financial losses would have cost the U.S. ten times less than what it cost to go to war.[45] The War, from any viewpoint, was unnecessary.

**WHAT YOU WERE TAUGHT:** The Civil War was unavoidable and

inevitable.

**THE TRUTH:** We Southerners are all too familiar with Yankee William H. Seward's monstrous fable that the War was an "irrepressible conflict," for pro-North historians have forced this phrase into all of our textbooks and history books.[46] What they conveniently leave out is the fact that Lincoln's secretary of state twisted the truth to benefit the North.

The South only wanted peace and, before the War, did everything in her power to maintain it. As threats of violence began to come from Washington, D.C. in early 1861, Confederate President Jefferson Davis sent one peace commission after another to the U.S. White House in an attempt to prevent bloodshed. During the War he did everything in his power to draw the conflict to a close as soon as possible.[47]

Lincoln, in contrast, actively sought war then created one illegally, all in pursuit of his personal liberal agenda: big government, a national bank, protectionism, and government subsidies (which he called "internal improvements").[48] Along the way he spurned all attempts, both by his cabinet members and by his Northern constituents, to end the War and allow the South to go her own way in peace. Had differences been settled legally in court, or at least diplomatically—as they should have been, and as the South repeatedly tried to do, the entire tragedy could have easily been prevented.

The "Civil War" was not irresistible, inevitable, or "America's destiny," as many Northerners saw it—and still see it. This is just another Yankee folktale designed to justify Lincoln's many crimes against the South, against the Northern people, and against the Constitution.

**WHAT YOU WERE TAUGHT:** The U.S.A. won, which means that the North was right and that its cause was just. Thus the loser, the C.S.A., was wrong and the South's cause was unjust.

**THE TRUTH:** This is the cry of every victor in every conflict. But is it true? Throughout its history the U.S. has participated in numerous conflicts that ended in a standoff or in which it actually lost. Among these are the War of 1812, the Korean War, and the Vietnam War. If winning is the sole criteria for judging whether a warring nation is in the right or not, then based on the outcomes of these particular conflicts, America's participation in them must be judged immoral and dishonorable. Obviously this is not the case.

Every soldier, every army, and every nation goes into battle believing that God and justice are on their side. The Confederate and Federal armies were no exception: both held that God was with them and only them, and pastors on both sides freely mixed religion and politics each Sunday in an effort to convince their soldiers of this notion.[49]

Nearly 100 years later the same sentiment was still current. During World War II, for example, Hitler's Nazi soldiers wore belt buckles with the inscription: *Gott mitt uns* ("God is with us"). American and European soldiers were of the same opinion, however. During Lincoln's War, a similar belief was proclaimed across the South. According to Mary Chesnut, one of the most common statements made in Dixie was that "God is on our side . . . [for] He hates the Yankees!"[50] Is God a Southerner? At the time the majority of Southerners thought so—and most of us still do!

After the battle ends and the smoke clears away only one side can be counted the winner. The question is this: is the winner always right? Is God always on the winner's side? Is the Devil always on the loser's side? Does "might make right"? Here is how Napoleon I answered these questions: "God favors the side with the biggest battalions." The South agrees.

And so it was with the North (which had by far the biggest battalions) and the South (which had one third the men, money, resources, and supplies). According to Napoleon's maxim then, losing the Civil War certainly does not automatically make the South wrong and the North right.

And what of ethics, morality, and patriotism? Here Jefferson Davis and the Confederacy were surely in the right, for they stood for all that was truly American: family values, spirituality, faith, religious belief, tradition, capitalism, conservatism, localism, a free market economy, and an authentic dirt-under-the-fingernails love of agriculture, animals, and the land.

What did Lincoln and the North represent? Commercial values, materialism, skepticism, agnosticism, progress, socialism, liberalism, nationalism, a controlled market economy, and a get-rich-quick love of industry and money. After Lincoln, America did indeed begin to travel down this, the *Northern* road. But at the time these were clearly not the ideals that Founding Fathers like Thomas Jefferson (an old-fashioned, conservative Southern farmer) had in mind for the future of the U.S.

We must also consider the legal question. Here the South also scores on the side of right. In 1861 secession was a legal Constitutional right,[51] while instigating war without congressional approval against a foreign nation, as Lincoln did, was illegal and thoroughly unconstitutional. And while President Jefferson Davis allowed and even encouraged civil rights in the South during the War, President Abraham Lincoln restricted and actually destroyed civil rights in the North.[52]

It is plain that Lincoln and his Northern constituents denigrated and eroded our longstanding American laws and traditions by illegitimately initiating a war, subverting the Constitution, curtailing civil liberties, illegally invading a sovereign nation, meddling in foreign affairs, despoiling that nation's land, destroying her infrastructure, and maiming, imprisoning, torturing, starving, raping, and killing as many as 2 million of Dixie's people.[53] All for what purpose? To realize liberal Lincoln's enigmatical obsession with big government and "preserving the Union," a union that its very founders based on small government and the right of secession, and which they purposefully designed to be impermanent, malleable, and open.[54] Lincoln changed all that on April 9, 1865, at Appomattox, Virginia, making the Union permanent, inflexible, and closed.[55]

The North may have won. But she was wrong. This is why, to this day, the Southern battle for the constitutional (Confederate) government of the Founding generation continues so vigorously south of the Mason-Dixon Line.

# WHO STARTED THE WAR?

**WHAT YOU WERE TAUGHT:** The South started the War by firing the first shot at Fort Sumter, South Carolina, on April 12, 1861.

**THE TRUTH:** It is true that the South fired the opening volley that day. But this does not also mean that she launched the conflict. In fact, there is indisputable evidence showing the opposite; that it was the North who instigated hostilities, marking the beginning of the War.[56]

In the winter of 1860 Fort Sumter was still a small U.S. garrison on a small island strategically located in Charleston Harbor, South Carolina.[57] By the spring of 1861, however, it had become one of the last Federal outposts that had not been seized by the new Confederacy, and was considered a great prize.[58]

On April 11, 1861, Yankee Major Robert Anderson[59] and his troops were stationed at Fort Sumter, hoping to keep it in Union hands. As they had been there since December 26, 1860 (six days after South Carolina seceded), it was believed that they were in need of food and provisions.

Actually, Confederate General P. G. T. Beauregard had allowed Anderson and his troops to purchase groceries in Charleston up until April 5. Additionally, every day "the people of Charleston sent to Sumter a boat load of food supplies, fresh meats, fowls, fruits, vegetables, etc."[60] The Union soldiers on the island were thus well-stocked with victuals and were in no way "starving," as some Northern newspapers had been telling their eager readers.[61]

Should the "starving" fort be "reprovisioned"? Lincoln claimed so, but his cabinet, including the attorney general and the secretaries of the interior, war, navy, and state, all advised against it.[62]

Abolitionists, Northern members of the opposing party, and Union military brass from across the U.S. were nearly all of the same mind. Horace Greeley's newspaper, the New York *Tribune*, called on Lincoln to avoid the use of force and allow the Southern states to secede in peace, while Illinois Democrat Stephen A. Douglas said that "Anderson and his gallant band should be instantly withdrawn."[63]

On March 28 the greatly respected Yankee General Winfield Scott had advised his president to not only evacuate Fort Sumter, but the nearby Union-held garrison Fort Pickens, as well.[64] "Abandon these forts. They're militarily useless to us, and such action would politically benefit the U.S.," Scott wisely urged Lincoln. According to Simon Cameron, Lincoln's secretary of war: "All the officers within Fort Sumter . . . [also] express this opinion . . .," including Anderson himself, still awaiting orders there.[65] Caleb B. Smith, Lincoln's secretary of the interior, agreed. "If you send in provisions it will trigger a civil war."[66]

What his cabinet did not seem to realize was that this is exactly what Lincoln wanted. And the "starving fort" tale was the very trigger mechanism Lincoln needed to initiate it.

On April 12, against the advice of his own cabinet and the sentiment of most of the Northern people, Lincoln sent a provisions supply ship to Fort Sumter. Accompanying it were several armed warships bristling with heavily armed troops.[67] Lincoln had meticulously planned out every detail and knew what was about to happen.

Seeing the Federal fleet moving through Charleston harbor toward Fort Sumter, Confederate troops let loose their cannon. For a full thirty-six hours they bombarded the island, expecting at any moment to receive enemy fire. But the expected Yankee response never came. Why? Because Lincoln had ordered his men not to. It was all a hoax, one meant to goad the Confederacy into firing the first shot.

Shrewd as he was, Lincoln cannot claim credit for the idea of pranking the Confederates; only for perpetrating the hoax.[68] It had originated with his secretary of the navy, Gideon Welles,[69] who slyly advised the president that "it is very important that the Rebels strike the first blow in the conflict."[70]

Lincoln's assistant secretary of the navy, Gustavus Fox, then took Welles' idea and worked out the details of the plan. Writing to Montgomery Blair (soon to be Lincoln's postmaster general) on February 23, 1861, Fox had said:

> I simply propose three tugs, convoyed by light-draft men-of-war.
> . . . The first tug to lead in empty, to open their fire.[71]

Fox's plan never materialized, however, because the Rebels, having been grossly misled and lied to, went ahead and bombed and captured the fort first. But either way, the end result was still what Lincoln had intended: the South appeared to the world to be the instigator.[72] Now the onus of initiating war lay with the Confederacy.

On May 1, 1861, three weeks after his heinous deed at Sumter had been committed, Lincoln acknowledged the devilish connivance in a letter to Fox. While Fox was disappointed that his and Welles' plan had not come off exactly as planned, Lincoln was elated:

> I sincerely regret that the failure of the attempt to provision Fort Sumter should be the source of annoyance to you . . . [73]
>
> You and I both anticipated that the cause of the country would be advanced by making the attempt to provision Fort Sumter even if it should fail; and it is no small consolation now to feel that our anticipation is justified in the results. [74]

What "results?" The inauguration of a war he so desperately wanted! Even Lincoln's own authorized biographers, John G. Nicolay and John Hay, admitted that:

> When the President determined on war, and with the purpose of making it appear that the South was the aggressor, he took measures . . . [75]

Lincoln's so-called "measures" were nothing more than pure evil trickery.

As the public too soon learned, the entire Fort Sumter event turned out to be a cleverly calculated conspiracy—as one Northern newspaper described it—to incite the South into shooting first. In this way the Confederacy was seen as the aggressor, a hot-headed rebel who had fired on Old Glory[76] and tried to prevent food from reaching "starving" U.S. soldiers. [77]

Here then was the perfect justification for invading the South. [78] For with the "Rebel attack on the U.S. flag," as Lincoln told Congress,

> no choice was left but to call out the war power of the Government, and so to resist force employed for its destruction by force for its preservation. [79]

In 1867, six years later, Southern fire-eater Edward A. Pollard wrote of this flashpoint in American history:

> The point of the [Lincoln] government was to devise some artifice for the relief of Fort Sumter, short of open military reinforcements, decided to be impracticable, and which would have the effect of inaugurating the war by a safe indirection and under a plausible and convenient pretence. The device was at last conceived. [80]

On April 14, Anderson, now out of ammunition, surrendered. The Union flag was lowered and the Confederate flag was raised. Fort Sumter was now official Confederate property.[81] Instead of being taken prisoner, Anderson and his small unit were allowed to leave for New York immediately, for the South had not declared war, and had no intention of declaring war.[82] In the minds of Southerners, the conflict was over and all was well.

Amazingly, no one on either side was killed in the melee. But the perception that the South had made a "vicious attack" on a small group of bedraggled Yankee soldiers and an unarmed Union supply vessel, whipped Northerners into a fever pitch of anti-Dixie hatred. Millions of Northern citizens who, before April 12, had been for peaceful secession or who had been sitting on the fence, now fell squarely in behind Lincoln, demanding retribution against the South for "attacking the U.S."[83]

Lincoln, who had preplanned the entire scheme, wasted no time granting their wish. On April 15, 1861, the day after a humiliated Anderson (a Southerner who had joined the Union ranks and was very much against going to war with Dixie)[84] turned Sumter over to the South, Lincoln issued a proclamation calling for 75,000 U.S. troops to invade the South and crush the so-called "rebellion."[85]

The War was on, a conflict that would eventually kill 10 percent of the U.S. population, or some 3 million of the 30 million Americans then living: 2 million white and black Southerners, 1 million northerners, the former completely innocent; guilty of nothing more than defending their constitutionally formed nation, the Confederate States of America.

Let us note here that this is the modern equivalent of our current president killing 30 million Americans (10 percent of our present day population of 300 million).[86] Would we revere him, annually vote him our "favorite president," and carve his face into Mount Rushmore? No. He would be arrested, tried, convicted, and put to death for war crimes, his name and legacy forever blackened in the pages of history. Though Lincoln was in fact responsible for the deaths of the modern day equivalent of 30 million Americans—more people than were killed by Joseph Stalin (12 million)[87] and Adolf Hitler (16 million)[88] combined—he continues to be apotheosized, idolized, and worshiped like a Pagan god. We in the South say this is wrong.

Four years later, in his Second Inaugural Address, on March 4, 1865, Lincoln was still trying to keep up the pretense before the public. Here he had the nerve to say that both the South and the North had tried to avoid bloodshed,

> but one of them would *make* war rather than let the nation survive, and the other would *accept* war rather than let it perish; and the war came.[89]

The idea that the war simply "came," and that this was due to the aggressive actions of those he preposterously called "insurgents,"[90] is absurd and an insult to all intelligent people. Yet it was in this exact way that the South has been held criminally responsible for a war it did not begin—or want.[91] Let us bear in mind, as President Jefferson Davis said:

> He who makes the assault is not necessarily he that strikes the first blow or fires the first gun.[92]

How true.

In the end, as Pollard notes:

> The battle of Sumter had been brought on by the Washington Government by a trick too dishonest and shallow to account for the immense display of sentiment in the North that ensued. The event afforded indeed to many politicians in the North a most flimsy and false excuse for loosing passions of hate against the South that had all along been festering in the concealment of their hearts.[93]

Yes, the South fired the first shot. But the North intentionally and guilefully tricked her into it, launching a full-scale war based solely on deception and a tiny skirmish in which not a single person was even injured. Thus, as Confederate army chaplain Robert Lewis Dabney so aptly observed, the "Civil War was conceived in duplicity, and brought forth in iniquity."[94]

# CAUSE OF THE WAR

**WHAT YOU WERE TAUGHT:** The North fought to abolish slavery.

**THE TRUTH:** Not according to the man who inaugurated it. "We did not fight the South in order to abolish slavery . . ." Lincoln repeated endlessly to abolitionist politicians and his antislavery friends. But they refused to listen. Even when they did, they would not accept his reasoning. Still Lincoln continued to hammer the point home: "We didn't go into the war to put down slavery . . ."[95]

Indeed, from the very beginning of his first presidential term Lincoln made it clear that he had no interest in slavery whatsoever; not in abolishing it; not even in tampering with it. On March 4, 1861, for example, a little over a month before the start of the War, he gave his First Inaugural Address, a speech that included these now famous words:

> Apprehension seems to exist among the people of the Southern States, that by the accession of a Republican administration, their property, and their peace, and personal security, are to be endangered. There has never been any reasonable cause for such apprehension. Indeed, the most ample evidence to the contrary has all the while existed, and been open to their inspection. It is found in nearly all the published speeches of him who now addresses you. I do but quote from one of those speeches when I declare that 'I have no purpose, directly or indirectly, to interfere with the institution of slavery in the States where it exists. I believe I have no lawful right to do so, and I have no inclination to do so.' Those who nominated and elected me did so with full knowledge that I had made this, and many similar declarations, and had never recanted them.[96]

If Lincoln believed, as was true, that he had no legal right to meddle with the institution, *and* he actually promised not to meddle with it, both just five weeks prior to the War, it is obvious that for the man who started the conflict, it was not about slavery.

In this same March 4 speech, as he was planning his coming war (over a month before the Battle of Fort Sumter), he stated absolutely clearly that his one and only issue with the Southern states was money. My main purpose, he declared in his First Inaugural Address, is

> to collect the duties and imposts; but beyond what may be necessary for these objects, there will be no invasion—no using of force against or among the people anywhere.[97]

Strangely, just as many today refuse to accept Lincoln's actual statements, many in his own time also did not seem to be able to take the man at his word. One of these was abolitionist Reverend Charles Edward Lester, who was immovable on the subject: the focus of the War must be on abolition, he preached unwaveringly. In the summer of 1861, after impatiently revoking an attempt by one of his officials to emancipate slaves (just one of at least five known times the president would do this),[98] Lincoln took Lester aside and scolded him and other Northern abolitionists who were pushing for emancipation. Said "Honest Abe" sternly:

> I think [Massachusetts Senator Charles] Sumner, and the rest of you, would upset our apple-cart altogether, if you had your way. . . . We didn't go into the war to put down Slavery, but to put the flag back, and to act differently at this moment, would, I have no doubt, not only weaken our cause, but smack of bad faith; for I never should have had votes enough to send me here, if the people had supposed I should try to use my power to upset Slavery. Why, the first thing you'd see, would be a mutiny in the army. No! We must wait until every other means has been exhausted. This thunderbolt will keep.[99]

We will note here Lincoln's clear assertion that the Northern people would have never elected him, and that Northern soldiers would have mutinied, if he had tried to "use his power to upset slavery."

On August 22, 1862, in his now famous public reply to abolitionist Horace Greeley (who had vigorously attacked the president in the press for delaying emancipation), Lincoln restated his purpose for making war on the South, this time even more succinctly:

> As to the policy I "seem to be pursuing," as you say, I have not meant to leave any one in doubt. I would save the Union. I would save it the shortest way under the Constitution. The sooner the

national authority can be restored, the nearer the Union will be
"the Union as it was." If there be those who would not save the
Union unless they could at the same time save slavery, I do not
agree with them. If there be those who would not save the Union
unless they could at the same time destroy slavery, I do not agree
with them. My paramount object in this struggle is to save the
Union, and it is not either to save or destroy slavery. If I could save
the Union without freeing any slave, I would do it; and if I could
save it by freeing all the slaves, I would do it; and if I could save it
by freeing some and leaving others alone I would also do that.
What I do about slavery, and the colored race, I do because I
believe it helps to save the Union; and what I forbear, I forbear
because I do not believe it would help to save the Union.[100]

Lincoln could not have been any more plain speaking than this.

If he did not initiate an illegal war against the South to end slavery,
why then did he do it?

As the above reply to Greeley shows, his public claim was that it was
to "save the Union." But this was just a smokescreen for his true covert agenda:
the inauguration of his American System plan, in which the government was to
be changed from Thomas Jefferson's conservative confederation (a weak
decentralized government supported by small, but strong, self-sufficient nations
called "states"), into Henry Clay's liberal federation (a strong central
government ruling over weak subservient states). Like nearly all liberals,
Lincoln wanted desperately to enlarge both the Federal government and the
powers of the president, neither which he could fully do if the South seceded.

There were other reasons as well.

Lincoln did not want to lose the South's prosperous seaports,
riverways, and farmland, nor her 8 million white citizens and their numerous
electoral votes. But he had no hope of keeping the South within the Union
unless he could destroy the idea of state's rights in Dixie. To do this, he
reasoned, he had to eradicate the South's political will and psychologically
exhaust its people through militarily conquering the region.

Why did the South fight? To sustain states' rights and, of course, to
protect its new nation from the invasion of Northern forces. It had little choice
in the matter. At Fort Sumter Lincoln had ordained the course the South would
have to take over the next four years: kill or be killed.

Confederate diplomats who, during the early stages of the War, went
to Europe seeking formal recognition, made sure that Europeans understood the
true causes of the War. It was obvious, they told the English and French courts,
that the Yankees had no interest in abolishing slavery. They had entered into
war against the South because, having formed a despotism under Lincoln, and

having lost the wealth of the Southern states, they needed to force Dixie back into the U.S. in order to re-subjugate her. This Lincoln called "preserving the Union"![101]

But the Confederate diplomats had, at that particular time (1861 and 1862), little trouble convincing Europe that the War was not about slavery, for Europeans themselves saw no connection between abolition and the conflict. Why? Because Lincoln had not sided with the abolitionists, had not proposed emancipation, had promised not to interfere with the slavery, and had in fact definitively stated that his sole goal was to "restore the proper practical relations between the seceded states and the Union."[102]

In short, we are dealing with two Yankee myths in one here. First, that the South went into battle against Lincoln to preserve slavery, and second, that the North fought to preserve the Union. Both are equally false. In his monument to the Confederacy, *The Rise and Fall of the Confederate States*, Jefferson Davis accurately put the matter like this:

> . . . the war was, on the part of the United States Government, one
> of aggression and usurpation, and, on the part of the South, was for
> the defense of an inherent, unalienable right.[103]

What was that right? The right of self-determination as laid out in the Declaration of Independence, the Articles of Confederation, the Bill of Rights, and the Constitution itself. Where then does slavery fit into the picture?

We know slavery was not the cause of or even a contributing factor of the War, not only because of what Lincoln himself said and did, but also because:

1. The South knew the institution was doomed long prior to the War, and had made many attempts, under Southerners like Thomas Jefferson, to abolish it since the earliest history of the U.S.[104] Indeed, the American abolition movement began in the South.[105] Abolitionist Jefferson himself, a Founding Father from Virginia, had included a clause in the original draft of the Declaration of Independence that would have permanently banned the slave trade. Unfortunately, as Jefferson observed, it was later removed because, in part, it offended wealthy Northern merchants whose livelihoods depended on both the Yankee slave trade and Southern slavery.[106]

2. The vast majority of Northerners and Southerners simply did not care enough about the issue of slavery to die over it. In the North, where according to European visitors like Alexis de Tocqueville, white racism was far worse than in the South[107] (one of the main reasons the North abolished slavery before the South did),[108] most Yankees were positively hostile toward the idea of fighting for abolition, preferring to keep their distance from blacks altogether

(just one of the reasons many Northerners both *wanted* the South to secede and were against abolition).[109]

3. In the South only a tiny fraction, less than five percent, of the populace owned slaves.[110] The other 95.2 percent had no stake in the institution and therefore cared little about its outcome. Even the 4.8 percent of the Southern population that did own servants were fully aware that the institution was going extinct, and most were quite happy about it.[111]

The South's hesitation to abolish slavery was never about whether it should be done or not. It was about how and when it should be done.[112] Unfortunately, Lincoln took this choice away from Southerners by force, even though just a few decades earlier the North had granted itself unlimited time to abolish slavery in its own region. All this being true, what then would be the average Southerner's motivation for going to war over slavery?

As for the Northern soldiery, Lincoln's own men made it clear during and after the War that they would have never even joined the military, let alone fought, if they had thought the battle was an abolitionary one. Most of Lincoln's military officers were of the same mind. The cigar-chomping Yankee General Ulysses S. Grant, for example, an Ohioan who kept his wife's slaves until eight months *after* the War was over[113] (and only set them free because he was forced to by the ratification of the Thirteenth Amendment on December 6, 1865),[114] spoke for nearly all Federal soldiers when he said:

> The sole object of this war is to restore the union. Should I be convinced it has any other object, or that the government designs using its soldiers to execute the wishes of the Abolitionists, I pledge to you my honor as a man and a soldier, I would resign my commission and carry my sword to the other side.[115]

The same sentiment was expressed by nearly all Rebel officers and soldiers, as well. Here is how Confederate Major Robert Stiles, who served under General Robert E. Lee, put it in 1910:

> What now of the essential spirit of these young [Confederate] volunteers? Why did they volunteer? For what did they give their lives? We can never appreciate the story of their deeds as soldiers until we answer this question correctly.
>
> Surely it was not for slavery they fought. The great majority of them had never owned a slave and had little or no interest in the institution. My own father, for example, had freed his slaves long years before; that is, all save one, who would not be "emancipated,"—our dear "Mammy" who clung to us when we moved to the North and never recognized any change in her

condition or her relations to us. The great conflict will never be
properly comprehended by the man who looks upon it as a war for
the preservation of slavery.[116]

In great part, white Southerners were apathetic toward slavery because
so few possessed slaves: as mentioned, less than 5 percent owned black servants,
even at the peak of the institution in 1860. No rational Southerner was about
to risk his life, his family, his business, or his homeland, for a handful of slave
owners. Slave owners themselves would have far preferred giving up their
servants rather than die to keep them. Consider the following words from
Confederate General Randolph H. McKim, penned in 1918:

> Stonewall Jackson never owned but two slaves—a man and a
> woman—whom he bought at their earnest solicitation. And he
> kept account of the wages he would have paid for white labor, and
> when he considered himself reimbursed for the purchase money
> gave them their freedom. [Confederate] Gen. Joseph E. Johnston
> never owned a slave, nor did Gen. A. P. Hill, nor Gen. Fitzhugh
> Lee. Gen. J. E. B. Stuart, the famous cavalry leader, never owned
> but two, and he rid himself of these long before the war.
>     To these facts as to the attitude of the leaders and
> commanders of the Confederacy, should be added the testimony of
> the rank and file of the Southern armies. With one voice they
> avowed then, with one voice they avow now, that they were not
> marching and fighting and suffering and dying for slavery but for
> the right of self-government. Old soldiers, known to the writer,
> declare they never met a Southern soldier who had drawn his
> sword to perpetuate slavery. What they had at heart was the
> preservation of the supreme and sacred right of self-government.
> They had the same pride in their cause as [General Robert E.] Lee
> had when he expressed his absolute belief in its nobility and justice,
> and his resolute determination to fight for it so long as there was
> any possibility of success. To use his own words, "Let each man
> resolve that the right of self-government, liberty and peace, shall
> find in him a defender."
>     And what was true of the soldiers of the South was true
> also . . . of the soldiers of the North. Slavery was not the issue in
> their minds. As a general rule, at least, they were not fighting to
> free the slaves but to preserve the Union.[117]

Put simply, slavery was never more than an ancillary matter in the
South and in the North. What Yankee myth misleadingly calls the "slavery
issue" was actually the *states' rights issue*: in accordance with the Constitution the

Southern people merely wanted to be able to choose the manner and time in which to dismantle slavery and emancipate their slaves.[118] No one likes to be told what to do, particularly by an aggressive, meddlesome, despotic foreigner, which is exactly how Southerners viewed Lincoln at the time, the man they rightly called "the Military Dictator at Washington."[119]

So what was really behind Lincoln's total war against Dixie? It was fought, like all wars, over money, power, ego, greed, and politics—though today's Yankee/scallywag PC thought police do not want you to know this.

Nonetheless, Lincoln, his cabinet, and his military officers were, as we have just seen, publicly clear on at least one thing: the War was not over slavery, it was over the preservation of the Union. Lincoln maintained this falsehood until literally the last day of his life. On April 11, 1865, at the White House, four days before his death, and just as "Reconstruction" was beginning, the president gave his last public speech. The Emancipation Proclamation was already over two years old. Still Lincoln once again reiterated:

> We all agree that the seceded States, so called, are out of their proper practical relation with the Union, and that the sole object of the government, civil and military, in regard to those States, is to again get them into that proper practical relation.[120]

No talk here of slavery, of abolition, of civil rights for African-Americans, of incorporating blacks into American society. Just preserving the Union. This was Lincoln's mantra at the start of the War, during the War, and after the War. As he literally says in the above quote, it was his "sole object."

Why then do Yankees and New South Southerners continue to maintain that it was about slavery? The answer is that secession was legal,[121] making abolition the only possible defense (to Yankees and scallywags anyway) for the North's illegal invasion of the South and the needless deaths of nearly three million Americans.

However, this Yankee myth, no matter how well it is gussied up, can never and will never justify what the North did between 1861 and 1865.

**WHAT YOU WERE TAUGHT:** We know the Civil War was fought over slavery because on several occasions Lincoln asserted, or at least implied, that it was.

**THE TRUTH:** It is true that Lincoln made a number of such comments, like the following from his December 1, 1862, Message to Congress: "Without slavery the rebellion never could have existed; without slavery it could not continue." On January 31, 1865, he referred to slavery as "the original disturbing cause." And there is his famous remark, on March 4, 1865, that "all knew that the slavery interest was, somehow, the cause of the war."[122] Such comments, however, completely contradict those we examined in the previous entry, in which Lincoln repeatedly and clearly states that he went to war with the South to "preserve the Union." Why the two opposing views?

The ultimate demagogue, Lincoln always carefully crafted his words to fit the moment and his audience. This suited the devilish bureaucrat, whose ambiguous speech, obfuscationary tricks, passivity, prevarication, stall tactics, secrecy, shady back-room dealings, deception, pseudo-religiosity, opportunism, do-nothing policies, and political double-talk kept him out of prison and got him elected twice with under 50 percent of the American vote.[123]

Illinois Senator Stephen A. Douglas put Lincoln's stupendous talent for duping the American people this way: "He has a fertile genius in devising language to conceal his thoughts."[124] This is, of course, why, as Douglas also once said: "Lincoln is to be voted in the south as a proslavery man, and he is to be voted for in the north as an Abolitionist . . . [for] he can trim his principles any way in any section, so as to secure votes."[125]

The truth of the matter is that *privately*, as opposed to *publicly*, Lincoln never once wavered about what lay behind the conflict. His *public* statements concerning slavery as the "cause" of the War were meant strictly for Northern abolitionists, whose votes and financial backing he always desperately needed.

**WHAT YOU WERE TAUGHT:** The War saved the Union.

**THE TRUTH:** A union is, by definition, a *voluntary* association. An example of this is Western marriage: the voluntary union of two people. Western law would thus consider a marriage performed under coercion invalid.

The original United States Confederacy (designated by the Founders as such from 1781 to 1789) was designed in the same manner as a civil marriage: as a voluntary union.[126] This "wedding" formalized the affiliation between its weak decentralized government and the thirteen-member group of powerful, self-governing, independent nation-states.[127] The Articles of Confederation, and its later replacement, the U.S. Constitution, both upheld the idea of accession and secession. That is, a state could join or leave the Union voluntarily. As in a marital union, one must be able to leave volitionally what one has entered volitionally, which is why both marriage and divorce are legal in the U.S.

In 1861 the South "divorced" the North legally and constitutionally. What Lincoln and his War did was to force, at the end of a rifle barrel, the South to "remarry" the North, in essence voiding their earlier separation. But far from preserving the Union this illegal "shotgun wedding" destroyed it. How? By forcing one group, against its will, to form an association with

another. In the West there is no such thing as a *legal* involuntary union, civil or
political. Like Lincoln's act to "preserve the Union" by force, it is an
oxymoron. Even the liberals among the Founding Fathers understood this
elementary concept. In 1788, seventy-three years before the American "Civil
War," for instance, arch anti-Jeffersonian, Alexander Hamilton said insightfully:

> It has been observed, to coerce the States is one of the maddest
> projects that was ever devised. A failure of compliance will never
> be confined to a single State. This being the case, can we suppose
> it wise to hazard a civil war? Suppose Massachusetts, or any large
> State, should refuse, and Congress should attempt to compel them,
> would they not have influence to procure assistance, especially
> from those States which are in the same situation as themselves?
> What picture does this idea present to our view? A complying
> State at war with a non-complying State; Congress marching the
> troops of one State in to the bosom of another; this State collecting
> auxiliaries, and forming, perhaps, a majority against its Federal
> head. Here is a nation at war with itself. Can any reasonable man
> be well disposed towards a Government which makes war and
> carnage the only means of supporting itself—a Government that
> can exist only by the sword? Every such war must involve the
> innocent with the guilty. This single consideration should be
> sufficient to dispose every peaceable citizen against such a
> Government. But can we believe that one State will ever suffer
> itself to be used as an instrument of coercion? The thing is a
> dream; it is impossible.[128]

Unfortunately for the American people, Lincoln turned what Hamilton
called an "impossible dream" into a possible nightmare: a government that exists
"only by the sword"—the opposite of that intended by the Founding generation.

**WHAT YOU WERE TAUGHT:** The South fought to preserve slavery.
**THE TRUTH:** According to the president of the Confederate States of
America, Jefferson Davis, this was not at all the reason the South went to War
against the North. And who would know this better than the South's chief
executive, its highest leader? According to Davis:

> The truth remains intact and incontrovertible, that the existence of
> African servitude was in no wise the cause of the conflict, but only
> an incident. In the later controversies that arose, however, its
> effect in operating as a lever upon the passions, prejudices, or
> sympathies of mankind, was so potent that it has been spread like
> a thick cloud over the whole horizon of historic truth.[129]

# SOUTH & NORTH

**WHAT YOU WERE TAUGHT:** Nineteenth-Century North and South had more similarities than differences, and in fact, their inhabitants were the same people, Americans, all descended mainly from common European ancestors. The South therefore had no reason to secede.

**THE TRUTH:** In the mid 1800s no two parts of the U.S. were more unalike than the South and the North. The distinctness between the C.S.A. and the U.S.A. actually has ancient roots, profound dissimilarities that long predate even the birth of America in 1776.

Already in that year the two regions were manifesting sharp cultural, religious, social, and political differences. They were like two distinct nations, two nations that some believe would have been better off not uniting to begin with. Indeed, their differences only became more evident when the Southern and the Northern colonies combined, forming Jefferson's American Confederacy in 1781, later to be known as the United States of America.[130] Southern historian Frank Lawrence Owsley rightly called this merger the union of two completely different business and societal models, two opposing civilizations, in fact.[131]

Far from the Yankee myth that the South and North were equals, homogenous, compatible, even interchangeable, the two were actually separated by a deep cultural chasm that few today, particularly in the North, appreciate. Many modern Southerners too, now accustomed to Northern accents (thanks to the contemporary "Second Yankee Invasion" of the South) have forgotten how divergent the two regions once were.

Prior to the "Civil War" the North was primarily industrial, institutional, urban, nationalistic, liberal, radical, conformist, agnostic, Catholic, progressive, business oriented, and publicly schooled. To the Yankee mind the Union was a purely commercial entity, a single monolithic democracy by which that region could profit through tariffs, bounties, and "sectional aggrandizement."

In contrast to this worldview, known as "Yankeeism" in the South, Dixie was mainly agricultural, personal, rural, localistic, conservative, Constitutional, individualistic, highly religious, Protestant, traditional, family oriented, and home-schooled. To the Southern mind the Union was a moral social order, a "friendly association" of states held together by "good faith," the "exchanges of equity and comity," and the concept of states' rights.[132]

There were a number of other social and cultural differences, however. As the South saw it, Northerners were discourteous and reserved, while they themselves were well mannered and emotional. Northerners were greedy, shrewd, and materialistic, while Southerners were generous, hospitable, and spiritual. Northern society was prim, proper, and fast-paced, Southern society was relaxed, informal, and leisurely.[133]

*Pro tem* president of South Carolina's secession convention, David F. Jamison, spoke for most Southerners when, in 1861, he referred to what he saw as the "jealousy," "aggressions," "cupidity," and "avarice of the Northern people . . ." Tired of Yankee meddling, overtaxation, and annoying insults, and violently resenting the North's constant attempt to interfere with local and state affairs, Jamison said: "As there is no common bond between us, all attempts to continue as united will only prove futile."[134]

One example in particular aptly illustrates the broad gulf partitioning South from North at the time: the U.S. Constitution does not contain the word God. The C.S. Constitution, however, not only mentions God, it calls Him "Almighty God." The general lack of authentic religiosity and humanitarianism among white Victorian Northerners was no idle Southern fable. It was well-known at the time, even by apostate Yankees like Ralph Waldo Emerson (who gave up his Christian faith and helped launch the Hindu-inspired Transcendentalist movement),[135] that industrialism and the rank capitalism of the North put making money above everything else.[136]

Even major religious denominations experienced a South-North schism over Lincoln's election in 1860 and the secession of the Southern states. The Presbyterian Church, for instance, split in 1861, not reuniting until 1983. The Methodists also broke apart on a South-North axis, with Dixie's branch being called the "Methodist Episcopal Church, South," and the Yankee one becoming known as the "Methodist Episcopal Church." One Christian denomination found the differences between South and North so disagreeable that it fractured even long before Lincoln's War: in 1845 Southern and Northern Baptists went their separate ways, the former taking the name "Southern Baptists," the latter calling itself "American Baptists." The two sides have still not reconciled their differences and to this day remain two distinct branches of the same faith.[137]

Could any two regions have been more culturally, politically, religiously, psychologically, spiritually, and socially opposite one another?

There are indications that the Old South and the Old North were also divided by ethnicity, primarily Gaelic versus Anglo-Saxon.[138] Dixie, which later designed its Confederate Battle Flag primarily on Scotland's Saint Andrew's Cross and on Ireland's Saint Patrick's Cross, had a noticeable Celto-cavalier flavor,[139] while the upper Northeast, steeped in centuries of Anglo-Puritanism, was more English in color, and is indeed still called "New England." Even the Confederate army was more like a gathering of clans headed by great warrior-chieftains than a standard military force headed by a single commander-in-chief. It could be said then that Lincoln's War was waged, to some extent, between Gaelic Southern cavaliers and Anglo Northern Puritans.[140]

The animosity between the Celtic nations (Ireland, Scotland, and Wales,) and England are well-known and have existed for centuries right into the present day.[141] This ethnic animus was already quite evident in America in the 1700s and 1800s, the time period in which the freedom-loving, independent-thinking Southern "redneck" has his roots.[142]

The Old South also had a far greater ethnic homogeneity than the Old North, with less the 1 percent of her white citizens being born outside the U.S. At the same time the North was noted for its large foreign born population. Religiously the South was not only nearly completely Protestant, but also almost wholly evangelical, quite rare in Yankeedom. Dixie also had a common ideology lacking at the North: a deep and abiding belief in self-determination, an idea that would one day spawn the states' rights movement. All of these attributes gave the South a sense of national unity that did not exist in the North in the late 1700s to mid 1800s.

In essence, while Northerners considered themselves Americans, Southerners considered themselves Southerners. This purely Southern sense of identity, combined with the sectional strife with their Yankee neighbors, eventually developed into what would come to be called the "Confederate Cause": Southerners' desire to maintain their own way of life, traditional American values founded upon the principles of the Declaration of Independence, penned by Southern hero and Founding Father Thomas Jefferson (a school of thought known today as Jeffersonianism, which combines aspects of conservatism, paleoconservatism, traditionalism, libertarianism, and Tea Partyism).

In the Old South then one was either pro-South and anti-North or pro-North and anti-South. There was no middle ground. For as a traditionally conservative people there could be no compromise with Middle America, which Dixie saw as the embodiment of a despised, alien society; Yankee society, that is. By the mid 1800s the South had developed into a true counterculture, one adhering to the "original faith," while the North was a mainstream culture, an infidel that had abandoned the Church of Jeffersonianism.[143]

Added to these built-in differences was the fact that the North had long been forcing high tariffs on the South, all which unduly benefitted the North's financial and commercial groups.[144] Why? Because tariffs discourage and even impede the import of foreign goods, at the time making this type of taxation a boon to the largely manufacturing North.[145]

But these same tariffs hurt Southern farmers. Why? Because Dixie was primarily an agrarian, consumerist region. Northern-imposed tariffs raised the prices the South had to pay for finished, imported goods,[146] especially manufactured goods purchased from the North. Because of her own tariff protection, the North was able to charge the South greatly inflated prices.[147] High protective tariffs, for example, reduced the price of cotton (by imposing a 20 percent tax on the profits of Southern planters), while raising both the income and the profits of Yankee labor and manufacturers.[148]

This sectional shell game, for decades wholly dominated by the North, prompted many Southerners, like Thomas Cooper, the president of South Carolina College, to ask whether or not it was worth it for the South to remain in the Union when the North continued to act like a master requiring tributaries of its slaves (that is, Southerners).[149]

By 1860 the Southern states had come to feel that they were now mere colonies of the empirical North, just as by 1775 the early American colonies came to feel they were living under the thumb of the British Empire and her insufferably unfair taxes. Little wonder that the South saw her relationship with the North, not as a sociopolitical one, but as a purely legal one, as a sort of business relationship that had gone sour.[150]

This economic tyranny of one section over another, however, was only one small part of a much larger political worldview that the North was seeking to impose on Dixie, one that liberal slave owner Henry Clay called the "American System." It was this idea, later fully implemented by President Abraham Lincoln, that would forever divide South from North—still, despite modern Yankee encroachment, two of the most distinctly different civilizations to have ever existed on the same continent. This is why Southerners like Robert E. Lee always impersonally referred to Northerners as "those people."[151] To those from Dixie, Yankees seemed like creatures from another world. For many in the North the feeling was mutual.

To summarize the innate social, cultural, and religious differences between South and North, we can do no better than to compare the U.S. Pledge of Allegiance with the Confederacy's own pledge, had it chosen to have created one. The original U.S. version, written in 1892 by Northern socialist

Francis Bellamy, read:

> I pledge allegiance to my Flag and to the Republic for which it
> stands, one nation, indivisible, with liberty and justice for all.[152]

No mention here by the liberal New Yorker of the words "United States" or
even "under God," which were added later, in 1923 and 1954 respectively.

Even the 1954 version of the U.S. oath, the one we use today, is
stunningly different than what Confederate leaders would have written. It
reads:

> I pledge allegiance to the flag of the United States of America and
> to the republic for which it stands, one nation under God,
> indivisible, with liberty and justice for all.

While the Confederacy had no Pledge of Allegiance, if it had designed
one it would go something like the following oath—created by the author:

> I pledge allegiance to the flag of the Confederate States of America
> and to the republic for which she stands, thirteen nation-states
> under Almighty God, divisible, with liberty and justice for all.[153]

The references to "nation-states," "Almighty God," and a "divisible"
republic were key components in the original Southern worldview, which was
quite religious in character and wholly dedicated to the idea of confederation
(that is, anti-federation): a small, weak central government supported by all-
powerful, sovereign nation-states whose foundation was states' rights—which
includes the right of secession.

Today's progressive, socialist-based Pledge of Allegiance would have
certainly delighted big government liberal Abraham Lincoln. Yet it would have
horrified small government conservative Jefferson Davis—just as it appalls
modern day traditional Southerners. Just another example of the great divide
that continues to separate the two regions a century and a half after the "Civil
War."[154]

# ★ 5 ★

# SECESSION

**WHAT YOU WERE TAUGHT:** Secession was (and is) illegal. Therefore the Southern states had no right to break away from the United States and form their own nation. Lincoln then had every right to send troops into Dixie in an effort to "preserve the Union."

**THE TRUTH:** Secession was (and still is) perfectly legal, which makes Lincoln's War on the South illegal and everything that the North inflicted on the Southern people between 1861 and 1877 (the year "Reconstruction" ended) a war crime.

To begin with, secession is one of the rights of states, and states' rights are assured and openly declared in the Declaration of Independence, penned by Southern hero and Founding Father Thomas Jefferson. The Declaration of Independence, issued by the U.S. Congress on July 4, 1776, could literally be called a "states' rights document," for from beginning to end it speaks of almost nothing else, as the following excerpt illustrates:

> When, in the course of human events, it becomes necessary for one people to dissolve the political bands which have connected them with another . . . a decent respect to the opinions of mankind requires that they should declare the causes which impel them to the separation.
>
> We hold these truths to be self-evident, that all men are created equal, that they are endowed by their Creator with certain unalienable rights, that among these are life, liberty and the pursuit of happiness. That, to secure these rights, Governments are instituted among men, deriving their just powers from the consent of the governed; that, whenever any form of government becomes destructive of these ends, it is the right of the people to alter or to abolish it, and to institute new government, laying its foundation on such principles, and organizing its powers in such form, as to them shall seem most likely to effect their safety and happiness.
>
> . . . We, therefore, the representatives of the United

> States of America, in general Congress assembled . . . do, in the name, and by the authority of the good people of these colonies, solemnly publish and declare, that these united colonies are, and of right ought to be, free and independent states . . . and that as free and independent states, they have full power to levy war, conclude peace, contract alliances, establish commerce, and to do all other acts and things which independent states may of right do.[155]

It is true that the Declaration of Independence was meant as a document officially separating the American colonies from Britain. However, its focus on states' rights and the concomitant right of secession was carried forward by the U.S. Confederacy (1781-1789) into the Articles of Confederation—proposed by Congress November 15, 1777, and ratified March 1, 1781. Here, in Article Two, the concept of states' rights is plainly laid out:

> Each state retains its sovereignty, freedom, and independence, and every power, jurisdiction, and right, which is not by this Confederation expressly delegated to the United States, in Congress assembled.[156]

For various reasons the colonies eventually found the Articles of Confederation wanting.[157] Subsequently this led to the creation of the Constitution of the United States of America—proposed by Convention September 17, 1787, and made effective March 4, 1789. Again the Founders did not neglect the issue of states' rights. In fact they considered it important enough to include it as a separate amendment in the Bill of Rights (the first ten Amendments), which went into effect in 1791.[158] Indeed, the Tenth Amendment is, in its entirety, devoted solely to states' rights[159]:

> The powers not delegated to the United States by the Constitution, nor prohibited by it to the States, are reserved to the States respectively, or to the people.[160]

In other words, the national government was only allowed to exercise those powers bestowed on it by the people. What are these powers? They are explicitly defined in Article Four, Section Four:

> The United States shall guarantee to every state in this Union a republican form of government, and shall protect each of them against invasion; and on application of the Legislature, or of the executive (when the Legislature cannot be convened), against domestic violence.[161]

As laid out here in essence the only power originally granted to the national government by the people was the power to protect them against the formation of state dictatorships, foreign invasion, and internal disturbances (for example, riots). Outside of these three obligations (basically, the defense of lives, rights, and property), all sovereign power was to remain in the hands of the people.[162]

President James Madison put it this way:

> The powers delegated by the proposed constitution to the Federal Government are few and defined; those which are to remain in the State governments are numerous and indefinite; the former will be exercised principally on external objects, as war, peace, negotiation, and foreign commerce—with which last the powers of taxation will, for the most part, be connected. The powers reserved to the several States, will extend to all the objects which, in the ordinary course of affairs, concern the lives, liberties, and properties of the people, and the internal order, improvement, and prosperity of the State.[163]

In his First Inaugural Address in 1801 President Thomas Jefferson spoke plainly about the states' right of secession:

> If there be any among us who would wish to dissolve the Union or to change its republican form, let them stand undisturbed as monuments of the safety with which error of opinion may be tolerated where reason is left free to combat it.[164]

In 1839 President John Quincy Adams, though an anti-Jeffersonian Federalist, gave a passionate speech at the fiftieth anniversary celebration of George Washington's inauguration, in which he said:

> To the people alone is then reserved, as well the dissolving as the constituent power; and that power can be exercised by them only under the tie of conscience, binding them to the retributive justice of heaven. With these qualifications, we may admit the same right to be vested in the people of every State in the Union, with reference to the general government, which was exercised by the people of the United colonies with reference to the supreme head of the British Empire, of which they formed a part; and, under these limitations, have the people of each State in the Union a right to secede from the Confederated Union itself. Thus stands the right. But the indissoluble link of union between the people of the several States of this confederated nation is, after all, not in the

right, but in the heart. If the day should ever come (may heaven avert it!) when the affections of the people of these States shall be alienated from each other—when the fraternal spirit shall give way to cold indifference, or collisions of interest shall fester into hatred—the bands of political association will not long hold together parties no longer attracted by the magnetism of conciliated interests and kindly sympathies; and far better will it be for the people of the disunited States to part in friendship from each other, than to be held together by constraint.[165]

On March 11, 1861, seventy years after the Bill of Rights went into effect, the Constitution of the Confederate States was issued. Patterned on the U.S. Constitution it began with the following preamble:

We, the people of the Confederate States, each State acting in its sovereign and independent character, in order to form a permanent federal government, establish justice, insure domestic tranquillity, and secure the blessings of liberty to ourselves and our posterity—invoking the favor and guidance of Almighty God do ordain and establish this Constitution for the Confederate States of America.[166]

Then, in Article Six, the Confederate Constitution uses the exact wording of the United States Constitution in its proclamation of states' rights, only substituting the words United States with Confederate States:

The powers not delegated to the Confederate States by the Constitution, nor prohibited by it to the States, are reserved to the States, respectively, or to the people thereof.[167]

Though at the time Lincoln was not among them, a truly stunning number of Northerners agreed with both the U.S. Constitution and the "Cotton States" (that is, the South) that secession was indeed lawful, and that, under the circumstances, it was entirely appropriate for the South to part company with the Union. One of these was Yankee abolitionist and New York *Tribune* owner Horace Greeley, who, in the November 10, 1860, issue, wrote:

And now, if the Cotton States consider the value of the Union debatable, we maintain their perfect right to discuss it. Nay, we hold with Jefferson to the inalienable right of communities to alter or abolish forms of government that have become oppressive or injurious; and if the Cotton States shall decide that they can do better out of the Union than in it, we insist on letting them go in peace. The right to secede may be a revolutionary one, but it exists nevertheless; and we do not see how one party can have a right to do what another party has a right to prevent. We must ever resist the asserted right of any State to remain in the Union and nullify or defy the laws thereof; to withdraw from the Union is quite another matter. And whenever a considerable section of our Union shall deliberately resolve to go out, we shall resist all coercive measures designed to keep it in. We hope never to live in a republic, whereof one section is pinned to the residue with bayonets.[168]

In short, based on the preceding, if the individual states of the U.S. were intended to be sovereign nation-states, as these documents clearly assert they were, and are, then the rights of both accession (joining) and secession (leaving) are legal.

As mentioned, the original function of the Federal government was merely "protection" (from invasion and domestic violence). All other powers were to remain with the states. This system, part of what is known as the "separation of powers," was intentionally built into the U.S. Constitution to prevent the very type of tyranny that Lincoln would later institute in 1861.

States' rights then, which include secession, were legal across the U.S.A., in the mid-1800s, for they are clearly elucidated in the Declaration of Independence, the Articles of Confederation, and the United States Constitution. These rights rest, not on the authority of the national government, but on the authority derived from the will of the people, as noted in the Constitution's Preamble and in Article Seven.[169]

According to Thomas Jefferson, the man who authored the Declaration of Independence, rebellion, resistance to tyranny, and secession are as natural as air and sunshine. In fact, he often said, patriots should never allow their rulers to get too comfortable, their governments to get too powerful. If they do there is always a remedy, as he described in a 1787 letter to Colonel William S. Smith:

What country before ever existed a century and a half without a rebellion ? And what country can preserve its liberties, if its rulers are not warned, from time to time, that its people preserve the spirit of resistance? Let them take arms. The remedy is to set them right as to facts, pardon and pacify them. What signify a few lives lost in a century or two? The tree of liberty must be refreshed, from time to time, with the blood of patriots and tyrants. It is its natural manure.[170]

In June 1816, now a former U.S. president, Jefferson wrote a letter to William Crawford that read in part:

> If any state in the Union will declare that it prefers separation to a
> continuance in the Union, I have no hesitation in saying, "Let us
> separate."[171]

When, beginning in 1860, the South began acting on this principal, of legal, peaceful "separation," and the resumption of "the powers of government," it was disdainfully called a "rebellion" by Lincoln, its participants "insurgents."[172] However, here is what Jefferson, writing from Paris, France, to James Madison on January 30, 1787, said on this subject:

> I hold it that a little rebellion now and then is a good thing, and as
> necessary in the political world as storms in the physical.[173]

After decades of interference from the Northern states, the South finally decided to exercise her Constitutional right to foment "a little rebellion," a Jeffersonian act of secession that was both correct and legal under every official document created by the U.S. government up until the election of Abraham Lincoln.

In the end, Lincoln's assertion that the act of secession was nothing more than a "rebellion" against the Union was both false and technically inaccurate. For as Jefferson Davis pointed out, the Southern states were "the sovereign parties to the compact of union," and thus they "had the reserved power to secede from it whenever it should be found not to answer the ends for which it was established."[174] In other words, sovereigns cannot rebel because there is nothing to rebel against. They are free entities, with the power to come and go as they please, when and how they please.[175]

Like dictators before and after him, Lincoln preferred to live in an *involuntary* Union in which its separate states were "pinned to the residue with bayonets," as Greeley put it. The South preferred to live in a *voluntary* Union where states' rights were honored and maintained, allowing for the free and unimpeded ingress and egress of the separate states.

Which side was in the right?

According to the U.S. Constitution, the South. For secession was, and still is, entirely legal. This is what makes Lincoln's War, the "Civil War," illegal, and it is what makes Lincoln a war criminal.[176]

**WHAT YOU WERE TAUGHT:** The Southern people could not wait to secede from the Union.

**THE TRUTH:** The Southern people loved the Union and did everything in their power to avoid having to leave it. Almost every Southerner of note at the time was a unionist, not a disunionist, and was violently against the idea of breaking up the U.S.

Such men included everyone from President Jefferson Davis, Vice President Alexander H. Stephens, Robert E. Lee, and Nathan Bedford Forrest, to John S. Mosby, Stephen R. Mallory, Robert A. Toombs, and even the Yankee loathing Edmund Ruffin. After all, the American Union had been formed primarily by their own Southern ancestors,[177] and thus was for them a sacred institution, one that Southerner Thomas Jefferson revealingly said was meant to be "a lasting Confederacy."[178]

This passionate love for the Union is one reason why, during the initial construction of the new Southern Confederacy, Southerners were so adamant about creating a national flag that retained elements of the U.S. flag. It was only after several months of War against a despotic, aggressive, cruel, and meddlesome U.S. that they began to change their minds and demand a flag that was as dissimilar to the Star Spangled Banner as possible.[179]

The fact is that the South did not rebel against the Union. It rebelled against Lincoln's perverse and self-deluded concept of the Union: a big government controlled socialistic democracy, with a dictator-like president acting as "king," the dream of every Federalist (liberal) dating back to monarchist Alexander Hamilton.

If Dixie had been against the Union itself she would have left it in the 1850s, or even earlier. Instead, the Southern states did not begin to secede until immediately *after* Lincoln was elected. The result? "Honest Abe," our nation's first sectional (pro-North, anti-South) president,[180] did not receive a single vote from the South in 1860.[181]

**WHAT YOU WERE TAUGHT:** The belligerent Southern states were the first to consider seceding from the Union.
**THE TRUTH:** At least a half century earlier, belligerent New England was already seriously discussing the idea. And her states were the first to do so.

Yankee secessionist sentiment was born of infuriation over several legislative actions by then U.S. President Thomas Jefferson (who served two terms, from 1801 to 1809). These included the Louisiana Purchase (1803), the Embargo Act—which placed restrictions on Yankee merchants and exporters (1807), and the War of 1812 (caused, in part, by the embargo). These actions, and others that were felt to negatively impact the North, launched the fourteen-year New England Secession Movement, led by Massachusetts Senator Timothy Pickering, George Washington's former adjutant general,[182] and later President John Adams' secretary of state.[183]

In a March 4, 1804, letter to fellow New Englander Rufus King—like most other Yankees, both a Federalist (big government liberal) and an advocate of black colonization[184]—Jefferson-hating Pickering discussed the proposed secession plan of the Northern states:

> I am disgusted with the [Southern] men who now rule us and with their measures. At some manifestations of their malignancy I am shocked. . . . I am therefore ready to say 'come out from among them and be ye separate.' . . . Were New York detached (as under . . . [Aaron Burr's] administration it would be) from the Virginian influence, the whole Union would be benefitted. [President] Jefferson would then be forced to observe some caution and forbearance in his measures. And, if a separation should be deemed proper, the five New England States, New York, and New Jersey would naturally be united. Among those seven States, there is a sufficient congeniality of character to authorize the expectation of practicable harmony and a permanent union, New York the centre. Without a separation, can those States ever rid themselves of negro Presidents and negro Congresses, and regain their just weight in the political balance? . . . As population is *in fact* no rule of taxation, the negro representation ought to be given up. If refused, it would be a strong ground of separation; tho' perhaps an earlier occasion may occur to declare it.[185]

The brewing issue finally culminated in the Hartford Convention, a secession conference held in December 1814 and January 1815.[186] Here, twenty-six big government Federalist delegates met secretly to not only propose amendments that would lessen the influence of the small government South,[187] but to discuss leaving the Union in order to form a new and separate confederacy, the "New England Confederacy," as they called it, one they hoped would eventually include New York, Pennsylvania, and even Nova Scotia.[188]

A furious, anti-South Pickering—who once called Southern hero Thomas Jefferson a "revolutionary monster," and accused him of cruelty, cowardice, turpitude, corruption, and baseness[189]—spoke for the convention's members:

> I will rather anticipate a new [Northern] Confederacy, exempt from the corrupt and corrupting influence of the aristocratic Democrats of the South. There will be—and our children at farthest will see it—a separation. The white and black population will mark the boundary. The British Provinces, even with the assent of Britain, will become members of the Northern confederacy. A continued tyranny of the present ruling sect will

precipitate that event.[190]

With congressional ratification of the Treaty of Ghent on February 15, 1815, the War of 1812 soon came to an end.[191] New England then decided against secession—though only for economic reasons.[192]

While New England would try at least three times to secede from the Union during the early 1800s,[193] Massachusetts did so on four different occasions, all—it should be noted—without any resistance from the Southern states, or any other state for that matter.[194]

Why then, in 1860, when the Southern states decided to begin exercising their right of secession as well, did the North put a bloody and violent stop to it?

As we will see in Chapter 10, the answer can be encapsulated in two words: Abraham Lincoln.

# RACE RELATIONS
# IN 19th-CENTURY AMERICA

**WHAT YOU WERE TAUGHT:** White racism was always far worse in the South than it was in the North.

**THE TRUTH:** Alexis de Tocqueville was not the first, but only one of many, who noted that in early America white racism was far more severe in the North than in the South. During his tour of the states in 1831 the French aristocrat summed up his impressions this way:

> Whosoever has inhabited the United States must have perceived that in those parts of the Union in which the negroes are no longer slaves, they have in no wise drawn nearer to the whites. On the contrary, the prejudice of the race appears to be stronger in the States which have abolished slavery than in those where it still exists; and nowhere is it so intolerant as in those States where servitude never has been known.
>
> It is true that in the North of the Union marriages may be legally contracted between negroes and whites; but public opinion would stigmatize a man who should connect himself with a negress as infamous, and it would be difficult to meet with a single instance of such a union. The electoral franchise has been conferred upon the negroes in almost all the States in which slavery has been abolished; but if they come forward to vote, their lives are in danger. If oppressed, they may bring an action at law, but they will find none but whites among their judges; and although they may legally serve as jurors, prejudice repulses them from that office. The same schools do not receive the child of the black and of the European. In the theatres, gold can not procure a seat for the servile race beside their former masters; in the hospitals they lie

apart; and although they are allowed to invoke the same Divinity as the whites, it must be at a different altar, and in their own churches with their own clergy. The gates of Heaven are not closed against these unhappy beings; but their inferiority is continued to the very confines of the other world; when the negro is defunct, his bones are cast aside, and the distinction of condition prevails even in the equality of death. The [Northern] negro is free, but he can share neither the rights, nor the pleasures, nor the labour, nor the afflictions, nor the tomb of him whose equal he has been declared to be; and he can not meet him upon fair terms in life or in death.

In the South, where slavery still exists, the negroes are less carefully kept apart; they sometimes share the labour and the recreations of the whites; the whites consent to intermix with them to a certain extent, and although the legislation treats them more harshly, the habits of the [Southern] people are more tolerant and compassionate. In the South the master is not afraid to raise his slave to his own standing, because he knows that he can in a moment reduce him to the dust at pleasure. In the North the white no longer distinctly perceives the barrier which separates him from the degraded race, and he shuns the negro with the more pertinacity, since he fears lest they should some day be confounded together.

Among the Americans of the South, Nature sometimes reasserts her rights, and restores a transient equality between the blacks and the whites; but in the North pride restrains the most imperious of human passions. The American of the Northern States would perhaps allow the negress to share his licentious pleasures if the laws of his country did not declare that she may aspire to be the legitimate partner of his bed; but he recoils with horror from her who might become his wife.

Thus it is, in the United States, that the prejudice which repels the negroes seems to increase in proportion as they are emancipated, and inequality is sanctioned by the manners while it is effaced from the laws of the country. But if the relative position of the two races which inhabit the United States is such as I have described, it may be asked why the Americans have abolished slavery in the North of the Union, why they maintain it in the South, and why they aggravate its hardships there? The answer is easily given. It is not for the good of the negroes, but for that of the whites, that measures are taken to abolish slavery in the United States.[195]

In the 1840s, English writer James Silk Buckingham wrote that "the prejudice of colour is not nearly so strong in the South as in the North."[196] Here is how Robert Young Hayne, a South Carolina senator, described the treatment of those few Southern blacks who fled to the North:

> . . . there does not exist on the face of the whole earth, a population so poor, so wretched, so vile, so loathsome, so utterly destitute of all the comforts, conveniences, and decencies of life, as the unfortunate blacks of Philadelphia, and New York and Boston. Liberty has been to them the greatest of calamities, the heaviest of curses. Sir, I have had some opportunities of making comparison between the condition of the free negroes of the North, and the slaves of the South, and the comparison has left not only an indelible impression of the superior advantages of the latter, but has gone far to reconcile me to slavery itself. Never have I felt so forcibly that touching description, 'the foxes have holes, and the birds of the air have nests, but the Son of Man hath not where to lay his head,' as when I have seen this unhappy race, naked and houseless, almost starving in the streets, and abandoned by all the world. Sir, I have seen, in the neighborhood of one of the most moral, religious and refined cities of the North, a family of free blacks driven to the caves of the rocks, and there obtaining a precarious subsistence from charity and plunder .[197]

Only a few years later, in 1835, Virginian James Madison met with English author Harriet Martineau and regaled her with stories about how the Northern states erected numerous barriers in an attempt to thwart Negro emigration.[198] In 1841, after traveling through Philadelphia, an English Quaker, Joseph Sturge, met with former Illinois Governor Edward Coles. Writes Sturge:

> In the course of conversation, the Governor spoke of the prejudice against colour prevailing here as much stronger than in the slave States [the South]. I may add, from my own observation, and much concurring testimony, that Philadelphia appears to be the metropolis of this odious prejudice, and that there is probably no city in the known world, where dislike, amounting to hatred of the coloured population, prevails more than in the city of brotherly love![199]

After a visit to New York City, English writer Edward Dicey recorded his observations concerning Yankee racism and Northern blacks. In the North, Dicey noted:

> Everywhere and at all seasons the coloured people form a separate

community. In the public streets you hardly ever see a coloured
person in company with a white, except in the capacity of servant.
. . . On board the river steamboats, the commonest and homeliest
of working [white] men has a right to dine, and does dine, at the
public meals; but, for coloured passengers, there is always a
separate table. At the great [Northern] hotels there is, as with us
[in England], a servants' table, but the coloured servants are not
allowed to dine in common with the white. At the inns, in the
barbers' shops, on board the steamers, and in most hotels, the
servants are more often than not coloured people. . . . White
[Northern] servants will not associate with black on terms of
equality. . . . I hardly ever remember seeing a black employed as
shopman, or placed in any post of responsibility. As a rule, the
blacks you meet in the Free [that is, Northern] States are shabbily,
if not squalidly dressed; and, as far as I could learn, the instances of
black men having made money by trade in the North, are very few
in number.[200]

When Connecticut landscape architect Frederick Law Olmsted
traveled through Virginia in the early 1800s,[201] he was shocked by the
incongruity of what he had been taught about the South's racist "African slavery"
system and the reality of Southern servitude: all of the slaves he saw working in
the fields were either whistling or singing.[202] In his book *The Cotton Kingdom*,
the Yankee racist wrote of a "scandalous" experience he had during a train ride
through the Old Dominion State:[203]

I am struck with the close cohabitation and association of black and
white—negro women are carrying black and white babies together
in their arms; black and white children are playing together . . .;
black and white faces are constantly thrust together out of the
doors, to see the train go by. . . . A fine-looking, well-dressed, and
well-behaved coloured young man sat, together with a white man,
on a seat in the cars. I suppose the man was his master; but he was
much the less like a gentleman of the two. The railroad company
advertise to take coloured people only in second-class trains; but
servants seem to go with their masters everywhere. Once, to-day,
seeing a [white] lady entering the car at a way-station, with a family
behind her, and that she was looking about to find a place where
they could be seated together, I rose, and offered her my seat,
which had several vacancies round it. She accepted it, without
thanking me, and immediately installed in it a stout negro woman;
took the adjoining seat herself, and seated the rest of her party
before her. It consisted of a white girl, probably her daughter, and
a bright and very pretty mulatto girl. They all talked and laughed

together; and the girls munched confectionary out of the same
paper, with a familiarity and closeness of intimacy that would have
been noticed with astonishment, if not with manifest displeasure,
in almost any chance company at the North.[204]

This scene, however, would have "astonished" or "displeased" very few white
Southerners, nearly all who were accustomed to, and enjoyed, the company of
blacks, as this incident clearly shows.

In his 1918 book *American Negro Slavery*, Ulrich B. Phillips writes:

Fanny Kemble [famed white British actress], in her more vehement
style, wrote of the negroes in the North: "They are not slaves
indeed, but they are pariahs, debarred from every fellowship save
with their own despised race, scorned by the lowest white ruffian
in your streets, not tolerated even by the foreign menials in your
kitchen. They are free certainly, but they are also degraded,
rejected, the offscum and the offscouring of the very dregs of your
society. . . . All hands are extended to thrust them out, all fingers
point at their dusky skin, all tongues, the most vulgar as well as the
self-styled most refined, have learned to turn the very name of their
race into an insult and a reproach." Marshall Hall expressed himself
as "utterly at a loss to imagine the source of that prejudice which
subsists against him [the Negro] in the Northern states, a prejudice
unknown in the South, where the domestic relations between the
African and the European are so much more intimate." Olmsted
recorded a conversation which he had with a free colored barber on
a Red River steamboat who had been at school for a year at West
Troy, New York: "He said that colored people could associate with
whites much more easily and comfortably at the South than at the
North; this was one reason he preferred to live at the South. He
was kept at a greater distance from white people, and more
insulted on account of his color, at the North than in Louisiana."
And at Richmond Olmsted learned of a negro who after buying his
freedom had gone to Philadelphia to join his brother, but had
promptly returned. When questioned by his former owner this
man said: "Oh, I don't like dat Philadelphy, massa; an't no chance
for colored folks dere. Spec' if I'd been a runaway de wite folks
dere take care o' me; but I couldn't git anythin' to do, so I jis
borrow ten dollar of my broder an' cum back to old Virginny." In
Ohio, John Randolph's freedmen were prevented by the populace
from colonizing the tract which his executors had bought for them
in Mercer County and had to be scattered elsewhere in the state; in
Connecticut the citizens of New Haven resolved in a public
meeting in 1831 that a projected college for negroes in that place

would not be tolerated, and shortly afterward the townsmen of Canterbury broke up the school which [Quaker] Prudence Crandall attempted to establish there for colored girls.[205] The legislatures of various Northern states, furthermore, excluded free immigrants as well as discriminating sharply against those who were already inhabitants. Wherever the negroes clustered numerously, from Boston to Philadelphia and Cincinnati, they were not only browbeaten and excluded from the trades but were occasionally the victims of brutal outrage whether from mobs or individual persecutors.[206]

On August 15, 1862, a black Massachusetts justice of the peace, John S. Rock, made the following remarks about white racism there. According to Rock the Bay State did not compare favorably with Southern states, such as South Carolina:

> The masses seem to think that we [blacks] are oppressed only in the South. This is a mistake; we are oppressed everywhere in this slavery-cursed land. Massachusetts has a great name, and deserves much credit for what she has done, but the position of the colored people in Massachusetts is far from being an enviable one. While colored men have many rights, they have few privileges here. . . . The educated colored man meets, on the one hand, the embittered prejudices of the whites. And on the other the jealousies of his own race. . . . You can hardly imagine the humiliation and contempt a colored lad must feel by graduating the first in his class, and then being rejected everywhere else because of his color.
>
> No where in the United States is the colored man of talent appreciated. Even in Boston, which has a great reputation for being anti-slavery, he has no field for his talent. Some persons think that, because we have the right of suffrage [in Massachusetts] . . . there is less prejudice here than there is farther South. In some respects this is true, and in others it is not true. We are colonized in Boston. It is five times as difficult to get a house in a good location in Boston as it is in Philadelphia, and it is ten times more difficult for a colored mechanic to get employment than in Charleston [South Carolina]. . . . if we don't like that state of things, there is an appropriation to colonize us.[207]

Sadly for Northern blacks, white Northern abolitionists were often among the most racist of an already overwhelmingly racist population.

White antislavery advocates, for example, often told former slave, black civil rights leader, and lecturer, Frederick Douglass, that he should try not to appear overly intellectual before his white audiences. "People won't believe that you ever were a slave, Frederick, if you keep on this way," said one. "Better have a little of the plantation speech than not; it is not best that you seem too learned," said another abolitionist.[208] (All this despite the fact that Douglass was half-white,[209] and that he was then a well respected educator whose second wife was a white woman.)[210] According to Douglass, due to the color of his skin, as late as the late 1830s he could still not get a job as a caulker in New Bedford, Massachusetts.[211]

Many Northern white abolitionists liked to refer to blacks, as Lincoln often did, using the "n" word,[212] and comments about their "ni**erly odour"[213] and "woolly heads" were not uncommon at Yankee antislavery meetings.[214] These were terms one never heard at Southern abolition meetings, which were attended by whites *and* blacks.

Even Northern Quakers, allegedly the most ardent of the abolitionists, often displayed overt prejudice: blacks were regularly denied membership, Quaker meeting halls were segregated, and many Quakers belonged to Lincoln's favorite organization, the Northern-founded American Colonization Society, whose main objective was to "free the U.S. of the presence of the black race."[215] Such attitudes underscore the fact that the constitution of the American Anti-Slavery Society, an organization established in Philadelphia, Pennsylvania, in 1833, did not even mention social equality as one of its goals.[216]

It was because of this nearly ubiquitous white Yankee racism that Southern Congressmen enjoyed comparing

> the happy, well-fed, healthy, and moral condition of the southern
> slaves, with the condition of the miserable, vicious, and degraded
> free blacks of the North.[217]

Such are the facts of what Northern mythologists and South-haters still deceptively refer to as the "abolitionist North."

This is the same region that barred blacks from voting, jury duty, holding political office, interracial marriage, hotels, restaurants, theaters, stagecoaches, trains, schools, steamboats, churches, lecture halls, hospitals, and even cemeteries, right up to and beyond the "Civil War."[218] Even African-Americans who risked their lives for the Union, such as black Yankee officers, were repeatedly denied first-class railroad accommodations across the North.[219]

Why was the white North so much more racist than the white South? It was due, in great part, to a lack of familiarity with blacks.

In the South whites intermingled with both free and servile blacks on a daily basis, developing strong, lasting, and affectionate bonds,[220] especially with their own personal African servants.[221] This intimate association helped banish both white and black racism, while nurturing warm even loving relationships that often endured for life.[222]

There was indeed a human dimension to Southern servitude ("slavery") that was completely lacking in Northern free labor: Northern black employees, for example, could be fired and made penniless and homeless at a moment's notice, and often were.[223] Southern black servants, however, were assured permanent employment, *and* their every need was provided for by their "owners" (employers)—including food, clothing, housing, and health care—from cradle to grave.[224]

In reality, at the time it was much harder for most blacks to live free, which is why, when given a choice, many actually preferred bondage in the South over "liberty" in the North.[225]

Why are such facts left out of our history books? It is because they do not fit in with the great anti-South agenda: in order to justify Lincoln's illegal war on Dixie, his illicit slaughter of millions, and the permanent emotional scar he left across the Mason-Dixon Line, the South and her people must always be made to look as terrible as possible, in every way possible.

It is a testament to humanity's innate love of Truth that so many people, both North and South, and even foreigners, are now standing up to this outrageous cultural attack, one meant to erase all traces of authentic Southern history and replace them with anti-South propaganda, liberal disinformation, Yankee myth, and New South fairy tales.

# SLAVERY

**WHAT YOU WERE TAUGHT:** Southern slavery was rightly called the "Peculiar Institution."

**THE TRUTH:** Actually there was nothing "peculiar" whatsoever about slavery, and neither was it a specifically Southern institution, for it was once a worldwide phenomenon dating back to prehistoric times.[226]

An institution that has been found on every continent and among nearly every civilization from earliest recorded history right into present-day America can hardly be considered "peculiar."[227] In fact, as the following entries show, it would be more appropriately and accurately called the "standard institution."[228]

**WHAT YOU WERE TAUGHT:** Slavery was an invention of Southern whites.

**THE TRUTH:** This statement would certainly amaze the thousands of Africans who were practicing slavery on each other millennia before the first European slave ships visited West Africa.[229]

No one knows who actually invented slavery of course, but we do know that it dates from prehistory, was once universally accepted around the world, and that at one time it was found on every continent, in every single nation, and among every people, race, religion, and ethnic group. As such it must certainly be counted as one of humanity's most ancient social institutions, and an essential feature of both society and economics.[230]

In short, this makes slavery a natural byproduct of human culture,[231] placing it alongside our other oldest human social institutions: hunting and gathering, religion, marriage, warfare, puberty rites, funerary rites, and prostitution.[232] Indeed, some anthropologists consider slavery not an indication of barbarity, but an early sign of civilization: its emergence meant that humans had begun to enslave rather than kill one another.[233]

From its appearance in the prehistoric mists of time, slavery went on to be employed by the Mesopotamians (ancient Iraqis), Indians, Chinese, ancient Egyptians, Hebrews, Greeks, and Romans. In the pre-Columbian Americas slavery became an integral part of such Native-American peoples as the Maya, Aztec, and Inca, who depended on large scale slave labor in warfare and farming.[234]

Other Indian peoples who once practiced slavery include the Cherokee, Iroquois, Navaho, Seminole, Choctaw, Creek, Chickasaw, Cheyenne, Natchez, Comanche, Arapaho, Kiowas, Paiute, Chinook, Yuchie, Pima, Nootka, Papago, Carib, Halchidhoma, Guarani, Shasta, and Klamath. Some of the forms of slavery employed were particularly brutal, involving torture and even cannibalistic rituals. It is said that slavery was as economically important to many of these Native-American tribes as it was to European-American slavers prior to the "Civil War."[235]

After the fall of Rome and the establishment of Christianity as the dominant religion in Europe, the Christian Church also accepted slavery, though in a less harsh system known as serfdom. Islam recognized slavery, as did all of Arabia and Europe, with the Portuguese initiating the European-African slave trade in the year 1444, after which they monopolized human trafficking for over a century.[236]

Since the master-slave relationship predates human history, American Southern whites were obviously not the inventors of American slavery. In fact, Southern whites adopted the institution very late in the game, many thousands of years after it had been practiced in Africa, Asia, the Middle East, and Europe.

Indeed, as both the American slave trade[237] *and* American slavery began in New England,[238] the South was actually the *last* region in America to adopt slavery, and it is this fact that has helped contribute to the Yankee myth that she is the one responsible for inventing it. Memories are short and propaganda is long, particularly *Yankee* propaganda.

The reality is that slavery is a ubiquitous worldwide phenomenon, one that stubbornly persists into modern times, and which dates far back into the fog of prehistory on all continents, and among all races, ethnic groups, religions, societies, and peoples.[239] All of us then, no matter what our race, color, or nationality, have ancestors who were once in bondage. *We are all descendants of slaves.*

**WHAT YOU WERE TAUGHT:** American enslavement was especially painful for African-born blacks, who in their entire history had never known slavery or any other kind of bondage or captivity.
**THE TRUTH:** Africans were practicing slavery on themselves for thousands of years before the arrival of Europeans, at least back to the continent's Iron Age some 2,200 years ago.[240] Along with slavery, servitude, vassalage, and

serfdom were also practiced among pre-European Africans, whose kingdoms routinely engaged in the mass subjugation of neighboring tribes. Among the early African peoples who practiced slavery were the Yoruba of western Nigeria, the Fon of Dahomey, and the Fanti and Asante (or Ashanti) of Ghana. Entire African civilizations were built on and maintained by slavery, using some of the world's cruelest and most inhumane forms of bondage known.[241]

This reality led many Southerners and Northerners to view American slavery as benign in comparison. In 1854, for example, Southerner George Fitzhugh spoke for many white Americans when he wrote that Africans were actually better off being slaves in the U.S. than being slaves in their native land, Africa, where there existed a type of slavery infinitely worse.[242]

However much we may condemn slavery today, Fitzhugh was correct.

**WHAT YOU WERE TAUGHT:** Native Africans were hunted down in the wilds of Africa by white American slavers before being shackled and loaded aboard slave ships.

**THE TRUTH:** What Yankee historians, New South professors, and the liberal media will not tell you is that Africans were never actually hunted down and captured directly by the crews of visiting slave ships. Rather they were captives who had already been taken during intertribal raids and then enslaved by enterprising African kings, who quite eagerly traded them to non-African slavers for rum, gunpowder, and textiles.[243] Wars were often started on purpose by greedy African chiefs in order to obtain slaves, a practice that eventually became "endemic" across many parts of the continent.[244]

Thus, every one of the Africans brought to America on Yankee slave ships had already been enslaved in their home country by fellow Africans, after which they were sold to white slavers by fellow Africans.[245] This means that whites played no role in the actual enslaving process that took place in the interior, and thus had no idea what went on beyond the coastal areas.[246] Even our nation's most notorious anti-abolitionist, President Abraham Lincoln, admitted as much, saying:

> . . . the African slave trader . . . does not catch free negroes and bring them here. He finds them already slaves in the hands of their black captors, and he honestly buys them at the rate of about a red cotton handkerchief a head. This is very cheap, and it is a great abridgement of the sacred right of self-government to hang men for engaging in this profitable trade![247]

In 1908 J. Clarence Stonebraker wrote:

Slave dealers only obtained their slaves by one tribe conquering another and delivering same into the hands of the slave dealers, or by the consent of parents, getting up their children and selling them. The very false stories that a vessel's crew could go into the jungles and drive out as many negroes as they wished is grossly vile, and was hatched along with many others by the unconscionable and incorrigible prejudice of [Northern] partisans, and for an equally vile purpose. Such things are still being taught and believed to an extent in the frigid [Yankee] section of our country . . .[248]

In short, it was African chiefs who first enslaved other Africans,[249] and it was African slave dealers who then carried them to the coast and sold them to Arabs, Europeans, and eventually Yankees.[250] And it was on this walk to the coast, forced violently along by their African owners, that most African slaves died—not on the infamous Middle Passage to the Americas, as Yankee mythology has long maintained.[251]

It is obvious that Africa herself must be held accountable for taking part in the enslavement and forced deportation of some 10 million of her own people between the 16th and the 19th Centuries.[252]

**WHAT YOU WERE TAUGHT:** White Europeans were the first people to enslave Africans.

**THE TRUTH:** As the previous entry discloses, Africans were the first to enslave themselves. Indeed, indigenous African slavery existed long before whites and blacks even knew the other existed. Much later, thousands of years later, Arabs became the first Caucasian people to enslave Africans. White Europeans were the *last* foreign people to enslave Africans.

We will note here that 21st-Century Africa is still deeply involved in the "peculiar institution": some 200,000 African children alone are enslaved each year by Africans, then sold through the African slavery system to other Africans.[253]

**WHAT YOU WERE TAUGHT:** The first Africans brought to America's shores came as slaves.

**THE TRUTH:** The first blacks to step foot in North America were not slaves, for true slavery was unknown in the earliest North American colonies. They were indentured servants, a type of legal status in which one contracts himself to work under another in exchange for travel expenses, room, board, and general maintenance, or an apprenticeship.[254] But blacks were not the only ones to emigrate to what was to become the United States of America as bonded workers.

The vast majority of white immigrants who arrived in America's original thirteen English colonies—at least two-thirds[255]—came as white servants.[256] In fact, *white indentured servitude*, being much preferred over African slavery (Africans were considered "alien" by early white colonialists),[257] *was the institution that paved the way for black slavery in America*.[258] Two of the signers of the Declaration of Independence arrived in the U.S. as indentured servants,[259] and at least two future U.S. presidents began their adult life as white servants: Millard Fillmore and Andrew Johnson.[260]

President Martin Van Buren's third great-grandfather, Cornelius Maesen Van Buren, emigrated from the Netherlands to New York as an indentured servant.[261] Henry Wilson, President Ulysses S. Grant's second vice president and a cofounder of the Free-Soil party, worked as an indentured slave for eleven years, from age ten to twenty-one.[262] Even one of Lincoln's ancestors, an early relation who was part of the Massachusetts Bay Colony, came to America as an indentured servant.[263]

**WHAT YOU WERE TAUGHT:** All of the South's 3.5 million slaves were cruelly purchased in Africa and dragged in manacles to America aboard slave ships.

**THE TRUTH:** Contrary to this popular Northern myth, of the South's 3.5 million black servants, only 14 percent—or about 500,000 individuals—were imported from Africa *by Yankee slavers* between the settling of Jamestown, Virginia, and 1861. The other 3 million (86 percent), all American-born, were the result of natural reproduction.[264] Most of the South's 500,000 free blacks probably also derived from the latter group.

**WHAT YOU WERE TAUGHT:** Slavery is a racist business predominated by whites.

**THE TRUTH:** Slavery is a business, period, one that has nothing to do with race. As we have seen, Africans, Native-Americans, Europeans, Asians, and Middle-Easterners, all peoples and races, in fact, were enslaving their own kind long before they discovered that there were colors and varieties of humans different than themselves.

Let us take an example, Western slavery, which has its roots among Caucasians. Besides the overwhelming evidence of white-on-white slavery across ancient and Medieval Europe, any doubts about its Caucasoid origins vanish when we examine the etymology of the word slave itself: slave derives from the word "Slav," from the name of a European people, the Slavs,[265] today the largest European ethnic and language group inhabiting central and eastern Europe, as well as Siberia. (All 225 million speak one of the Slavonic languages.)[266]

The word Slav became synonymous with slavery due to the enslavement, by other Europeans (mainly Celts),[267] of thousands of Slavic individuals during Europe's early history.[268] As their names indicate, the Slovenes (of Slovenia), the Slovaks (of Slovakia), and the Yugoslavians (of Yugoslavia), are the modern (white) descendants of the ancient Slavs.

Whites were enthusiastically still enslaving one another right into the 20th Century and beyond. Soviet dictator Joseph Stalin, for example, enslaved some 18 million Caucasians during his reign of terror in the 1930s[269] (thus Stalin owned 14.5 million more *white* slaves than the American South owned *black* slaves),[270] while between 1941 and 1945 nearly 8 million Caucasians were enslaved across Europe under Nazi Germany, including children as young as six years of age (4.5 million more than Dixie).

Under socialist leader Adolf Hitler, white European families were routinely separated and forced to work in factories, fields, and mines, where they were dehumanized, beaten, whipped, and starved by their German overlords.[271] White Nazi slavery was the largest revival of the institution in the 20th Century, and one of the fastest and most monumental expansions of slavery in world history.[272] This appalling event occurred a mere sixty-five years ago, demolishing the Yankee/New South myth that slavery is a white racist institution.

**WHAT YOU WERE TAUGHT:** The American slave trade got its start in the South. Thus, Southerners were "America's slave traders" and Dixie is the region responsible for bringing the first slaves to North American soil.
**THE TRUTH:** The only slave ships to ever sail from the U.S. left from Northern ports, and all were commanded by Northern captains and funded by Northern businessmen, and all operated under the auspices of the U.S. flag.[273]

The South, on the other hand, did not own slave ships and never traded in slaves,[274] which is one of the reasons it banned the foreign slave trade in the Confederacy's new Constitution, penned by the Confederate Founding Fathers in 1861.[275]

As proof consider the following: the only American ever tried, convicted, and executed for slaving was a Northerner: Captain Nathaniel Gordon of New York was put to death for the crime on February 21, 1862, by Lincoln's personal order.[276] In addition, the last American slave ship to be captured by the U.S. government was a Northern one: the *Nightingale*, also from New York, confiscated on April 21, 1861. At the time of its seizure, this vessel, from the so-called "abolitionist North," had nearly 1,000 manacled Africans on board.[277] It was doing "business as usual" up until the first few weeks of the "Civil War."[278]

Why did American slave ships sail to and from the North and not the South? The answer is simple. It was the North, and more specifically Massachusetts, that was, from the very beginning, America's first slave trading region:[279] Boston began importing African slaves in 1638, when Captain William Pierce brought New England's first shipload of Africans from the West Indies aboard the Salem vessel *Desire*.[280] By 1676 Boston slavers were routinely coming home with shiploads of human cargo from East Africa and Madagascar.[281] By the 1700s Massachusetts had 5,000 black slaves and 30,000 bondservants.[282]

By 1639 Connecticut had slaves,[283] and by 1645 New Hampshire had them as well. The largest slave concentrations in New England were in Rockingham County, New Hampshire; Essex, Suffolk, Bristol, and Plymouth Counties, Massachusetts; New London, Hartford, and Fairfield Counties, Connecticut; and Newport and Washington Counties, Rhode Island. Let us bear in mind that most of the Southern states had not even been formed yet.

There were so many slaves in the Narragansett area of Rhode Island that they made up half the population. The slavers of Rhode Island and those of Massachusetts combined to make New England the leading slave trading center in America and slavery "the hub of New England's economy."[284] Two-thirds of Rhode Island's fleets and sailors alone were devoted to the trade. Even the region's state governors participated in it, Yankee politicians such as Jonathan Belcher of Massachusetts and Joseph Wanton of Rhode Island. It was well-known that slavery was so integral to New England's economy that without it she would have collapsed into financial ruin.[285]

Many notable New England families owe their present-day wealth and celebrity to slavery.[286] Among them: the Cabots (ancestors of Massachusetts Senators Henry Cabot Lodge, Sr. and Henry Cabot Lodge, Jr.), the Belchers, the Waldos (ancestors of Ralph Waldo Emerson), the Faneuils (after whom Boston's Faneuil Hall is named), the Royalls, the Pepperells (after whom the town of Pepperell, Massachusetts, is named), the DeWolfs (at least 500,000 descendants of their slaves are alive today),[287] the Champlains (after whom Lake Champlain is named), the Ellerys, the Gardners (after whom Boston's Isabella Stewart Gardner Museum is named), the Malbones, the Robinsons, the Crowninshields (after whom Crowninshield Island, Massachusetts, is named), and the Browns (after whom Rhode Island's Brown University is named).[288]

The slave trading Royall family, who made millions from their slave plantations in Antigua, donated money and land to what would become the Harvard Law School. The educational center still uses a seal from the Royall family crest.[289]

At least one half of the land in Brookline, Massachusetts, was once in the possession of slave owners, while in the town of Concord, Massachusetts, 50 percent of its government seats were occupied by slave owners.[290] In this quaint New England borough, where slavery continued well into the 1830s (decades after the official "abolition" of slavery there), those blacks fortunate enough to be freed were then, unfortunately, exiled to the woods surrounding Walden Pond, where they struggled for survival in fetid squatter camps.[291]

So great were the profits made by slave traders at Newport, Rhode Island,[292] that it has been said that the city was literally constructed over the graves of thousands of Africans.[293] By 1790, when Liverpool had become England's primary slave port, her only serious competition was from the Yankee slave ship owners of Bristol[294] and Newport, Rhode Island.[295] Rhode Island's state flag still bears a ship's anchor, an apt reminder of her days as the nation's largest slave trader, one that imported 100,000 African slaves—20 percent of all those brought into the U.S.[296]

It was not just slave trading that Rhode Island was involved in. The state also possessed thousands of crop and cattle plantations which depended almost exclusively on slave labor, many of them located in the town of Providence.[297] In fact, due to the number of plantations that once dotted the Renaissance City, to this day the official name of the state of Rhode Island is "Rhode Island and Providence Plantations,"[298] a carryover from the 1600s when the slavery-loving colony was first named.[299]

Even after slavery was abolished in the North, both Rhode Island and Massachusetts continued to amass huge profits from the slave trade,[300] the same profits that would later help Lincoln fund his "Civil War" on the South.[301]

Like our nation's capital city, Washington, D.C.,[302] Baltimore, Maryland, and Philadelphia, Pennsylvania,[303] were also great slave ports.[304] Baltimore in particular was one of the nation's most important slave trade centers: her slave ships were said to be packed "like livestock" with black human cargo, with mortality rates reaching as high as 25 percent.[305] Another Maryland city, Annapolis, also became one of America's most prosperous towns due to its thriving slave trade. It was a Northern slave ship that brought Kunta Kinte, the lead character in Alex Haley's saga *Roots*, to Annapolis from West Africa in 1767. The city still goes by the nickname the "sailing capital of the world."

It was New York City, however, that eventually came to be the main port of exit and entry for America's slave ships.[306] This is why, by 1720, New York had become one of the largest slaveholding states in the North, with 4,000 slaves against a white population of only 31,000. The situation was unbearable to the North's few abolitionists, resulting in the nation's first antislavery essay: *The Selling of Joseph*, penned in Massachusetts by the famed Yankee judge who presided at the Salem witch trials, Samuel Sewell.[307]

By 1756 New York state possessed some 13,000 adult black slaves, giving it the dubious distinction of having the largest slave force of any Northern colony at the time. That same year slaves accounted for 25 percent of the population in Kings, Queens, Richmond, New York City, and Westchester, making these areas the primary bastion of American slavery throughout the rest of the colonial period.[308]

What Northern and New South historians will not tell you is that there is only one reason that New York City is today America's largest and wealthiest municipality: for centuries it served as the literal heart of North America's slaving industry.[309] Many of the most famous New York names, in fact—names such as the Lehman Brothers, John Jacob Astor, Junius and Pierpont Morgan, Charles Tiffany, Archibald Gracie, and many others—are only known today because of the tremendous riches their families made from the town's "peculiar institution."[310]

New York City, the center of America's cotton trade as early as 1815, was so deeply connected to the Yankee slave trade and to Southern slavery that it opposed all early attempts at abolition within its borders,[311] and, along with New Jersey, was the last Northern state to resist the passage of emancipation laws.[312]

Later, in December 1860, when the Southern states began seceding, New York City's mayor Fernando Wood advocated that his city secede as well, for it was primarily King Cotton that was keeping it economically stable.[313] Little wonder that when Lincoln's War finally erupted, New York was one of the last states to recruit African-Americans: the state's governor, Horatio Seymour, refused to enlist them until he was forced to by the U.S. War Department.[314]

The fact is that it was the North's heavy dependence on the Yankee slave trade and on selling slaves to the South, that helped precipitate the "Civil War": in March 1861 the Southern Confederacy adopted its Constitution, which included a clause banning slave trading with foreign nations. "Foreign nations," of course, included the U.S. The North panicked, deciding it was better to beat the South into submission than allow her to cut off one of the Yankees' primary streams of wealth.[315] Big government liberal Abraham Lincoln, the only 1860 presidential candidate who promised *not* to interfere with slavery,[316] and who was put into office by Northern industrialists using profits from the Northern slave trade, launched the "Civil War" in April, just a few weeks later.[317]

**WHAT YOU WERE TAUGHT:** American slavery began in the South.

**THE TRUTH:** Like the American slave trade (which is distinct from American slavery), American slavery also got its start as a legal institution in the North. Its birthplace was, of course, none other than Massachusetts, the very *first* of the thirteen original states (colonies) to legalize it in 1641.[318] In contrast, the *last* of the thirteen colonies to legalize slavery was a Southern one, Georgia, which officially sanctioned it in 1749.[319]

Even the second, third, and fourth states to legalize slavery were all Northern ones: New Hampshire had slaves by 1645 and Delaware by the mid-1640s,[320] while Connecticut legalized slavery in 1650. It was not until 1661, twenty years after Massachusetts adopted slavery, that the first Southern state, Virginia, legalized the institution (becoming the fifth colony to do so).

A complete time table for the states is as follows:
The first colony to legalize slavery was Massachusetts, in 1641.
The second colony to legalize slavery was New Hampshire, in 1645.
The third colony to legalize slavery was Delaware, mid 1640s.
The fourth colony to legalize slavery was Connecticut, in 1650.
The fifth colony to legalize slavery was Virginia, in 1661.
The sixth colony to legalize slavery was Maryland, in 1663.
The seventh colony to legalize slavery was New York, in 1664.
The eighth colony to legalize slavery was New Jersey, in 1664.
The ninth colony to legalize slavery was South Carolina, in 1682.
The tenth colony to legalize slavery was Pennsylvania, in 1700.
The eleventh colony to legalize slavery was Rhode Island, in 1700.
The twelfth colony to legalize slavery was North Carolina, in 1715.
The thirteenth and last colony to legalize slavery was Georgia, in 1749.

In short, the Northern states are the ones responsible for launching both the American slave trade (in 1638) and American slavery (in 1641), not the Southern states.[321]

**WHAT YOU WERE TAUGHT:** The Northern states hated the inhumanity of slavery and could not wait to abolish it. This is why the North emancipated its slaves before the South.

**THE TRUTH:** Slavery was officially extinguished in the Northern states first, not because the always materialistic Victorian Yankee began to feel shame or guilt, but because it became unprofitable.[322] And it only became unprofitable due to the North's largely rocky sandy soil and short cold summers, which made the region unsuitable for large-scale farming.[323]

Another factor, of course, was Northern white racism: most 18th- and 19th-Century Yanks simply preferred to live in an all-white society,[324] free from what white supremacist Lincoln called the "natural disgust" engendered in whites at the mere thought of the two races mixing.[325] And so the Northern states "abolished" slavery in the late 1700s and early 1800s, though the institution continued illegally, with the tacit approval of the U.S. government, until after the "Civil War."

Proof that the North was not truly an abolitionist region was that while it abolished slavery in its own backyard, it did not want to end slavery in the South, for New England's textile mills, and the New York industrialists who owned them, were still making vast fortunes from Southern cotton, picked and ginned by millions of Southern slaves. Thus, a full scale Northern effort began to keep Southern slavery alive, and even strengthen and enlarge it. It was in this way that when the white North grew tired of dealing with blacks and slavery, she pushed the institution southward on a mostly unwilling populace, one that had been trying to abolish it since the 1700s.[326]

Among those Northerners most interested in the continuation of slavery were New York's "Wall Street Boys,"[327] that is, the Northern business establishment,[328] which had bankrolled Lincoln's first (and later his second) presidential campaign using money they had made primarily from the Yankee slave trade.[329] There was also the Boston elite, who made it known that they were quite willing to make huge concessions to the South in the interest of making money.[330]

Is it any wonder then that in his First Inaugural Address, March, 4 1861, Lincoln promised not to disturb slavery,[331] or that American slavery did not come to a final end until December 6, 1865 (eight months after Lincoln's death), with the passage of the Thirteenth Amendment?[332] Here we have more proof, if more is needed, that the "Civil War" was not a contest over slavery. It was a Northern contest over slavery money, a Southern contest over constitutional rights (that is, self-determination).[333]

**WHAT YOU WERE TAUGHT:** The type of black bondage practiced by the Old South was called "slavery."

**THE TRUTH:** This chestnut is perhaps Yankeedom's oldest and most enduring anti-South myth. The only problem is that it happens to be false.

Edward A. Pollard, Virginian, staunch Confederate, and editor of the pro-South Richmond *Examiner* during the War, said it best: there was never such a thing as "slavery" in the Old South. What North and New South writers conveniently and slanderously call Southern "slavery" was actually, Pollard rightly asserts, a "well-guarded and moderate system of negro servitude."[334]

As mentioned previously, the first blacks brought to British North America (in 1619) were not regarded as slaves, but as indentured servants, laborers with the same rights as white indentured servants.[335] Though this status would eventually change from voluntary servitude to involuntary servitude, most Southerners, unlike Northerners, correctly continued to refer to bonded blacks as "servants" (not "slaves") right up to and after Lincoln's War. As such, Southerners seldom used the phrase "African slavery." Like Jefferson Davis they used the term "African servitude."[336] To this very day, unlike most Yankees, traditional Southerners still refer to the bonded blacks of 19th-Century America as "servants" rather than "slaves."[337]

What is the difference between slavery and servitude?

Slavery is the state of working under the control, ownership, or absolute dominion of another, without pay, and often for life. Additionally, slaves have almost no rights of any kind, are generally debased and disenfranchised, and cannot purchase their freedom. In short, a true slave is seen by his or her owner as little different than a cow or a horse, just another piece of livestock to be owned and worked.[338]

Servitude, on the other hand, is for a limited duration, the individual is not "owned" (his boss is not his "owner" or "master," but rather his employer), he is paid a wage, and he may hire himself out to work for others. Servants also possess a wide variety of personal and civil rights that are both recognized and protected by society and tempered by religious sentiment. In this way, under servitude a person's right to comfort and happiness are taken for granted and he or she is treated with common respect and decency.[339] Finally, servants have the right and the power to buy their freedom.[340]

Among the more famous of those black servants who purchased their liberty (or had it purchased for them) are Northern slave Frederick Douglass,[341] black racist-militant Denmark Vesey,[342] travel adventurer Gustavus Vassa,[343] and Lincoln's own modiste, Elizabeth Keckley (who purchased her freedom with money she made hiring herself out as a dressmaker).[344] Slightly lesser known are Lott Cary, Hiram Young, Free Frank McWorter, Venture Smith, Amos Fortune, John Parker, Samuel Berry, and Paul Jennings (one of President James Madison's servants).

Tens of thousands of others could be named. If any of these individuals had lived under authentic slavery they would have remained in bondage for life. The reality is that by the late antebellum period (1850-1860), most manumissions were the result of free blacks buying their own relatives then freeing them.[345]

It is clear from these facts alone that the South practiced servitude, not slavery.

The use of the injurious and false word "slavery" instead of "servitude" for the type of bondage that was practiced in the Old South has been forced on us by Northern propagandists and by New South liberals. For this word, like the equally fallacious and deleterious Northern terms "copperhead," "rebel," "pro-slavery," and "slave state," all help to justify Lincoln's unjust war.

Sadly for Dixie, much of the outside world—misled by anti-South language like this—has never fully understood the true nature of so-called "Southern slavery." But those Southerners who lived through this period, and those today who have researched the institution objectively, understand that it was, in all actuality, a form of servitude not slavery. This fact is overtly preserved in the Latin words for servant, the Western form of "slave": *servus* (male), *serva* (female).[346] So-called Southern "slaves" then were actually servants, not slaves in the legal, or even stereotypical, sense.

In short, there was no such thing as "slavery" or a "slave state" in the Old South. This politicized nomenclature is an invention of enemies of Dixie, whose aim has been to defile the South in the eyes of the world and, as noted, to excuse Lincoln's unholy war on the Confederacy.

The truth is that Southerners who were labeled "proslavery" and Southern states that were labeled "slave states," were merely pro-states' rights. For, as we are about to discuss in more detail, only a tiny minority of Southerners actually owned servants (less than 4.8 percent in 1860).[347] The South's ultimate goal was always the preservation of the right of self-determination (self-government), not the continuation of black servitude, no matter what the North chooses to believe or what name New South scallywags choose to call the institution.

In point of fact, if one were to take Northern history books and replace every instance of the word "slavery" with the word "servitude," the word "pro-slavery" with "pro-states' rights," the phrase "slave state" with "slavery optional state," and the term "free state" with "slavery prohibited state," one would have a much more accurate and honest portrait of the South-North conflict.

**WHAT YOU WERE TAUGHT:** Southern slaves had no rights.

**THE TRUTH:** As touched on above, the South's servants had numerous rights, which is why they were not true slaves. As such, because having basic civil rights is one of the things that separates servants from slaves, 19th-Century Southerners generally referred to their bondsmen and bondswomen as "servants," not "slaves."

Among the many civil and legal rights possessed by Southern servants were the right to own private property, the right to marry, the right to sue another and to give evidence in court (in special cases), the right to have days off, the right to hire themselves out to others, the right to write up and sign their own work contracts, the right to practice religion and receive religious instruction, and the right to be supported by their temporary "owners" from birth to death, including in times of sickness and in old age. Female servants had the additional right to apply for domestic service and could not be forced into doing heavy labor.[348]

In particular, all servants had the right to be treated justly and fairly. Violations of any and all of these laws and rights was prohibited by legal statute in *all* of the Southern states.[349] Then as today, possessing such rights are what differentiate true servants from true slaves—the latter group which have no rights whatsoever.

**WHAT YOU WERE TAUGHT:** Only white Americans owned black slaves.
**THE TRUTH:** Liberal historians carefully hide the fact from the general public, but the reality is that there were tens of thousands of black slave owners in early America, most who were not counted in the U.S. Census.

One of the very first slave owners in the American colonies was a black man by the name of Anthony Johnson. The Virginia slaver from Angola (Africa), who owned both black *and* white slaves,[350] actually helped launch the American slave trade by forcing authorities to legally define the meaning of "slave ownership."[351]

In 1830, in the Deep South alone, nearly 8,000 slaves were owned by some 1,500 black slave owners (about five slaves apiece). In Charleston, South Carolina, as another example, between the years 1820 and 1840, 75 percent of the city's free blacks owned slaves. Furthermore, a stunning 25 percent of all free American blacks owned slaves, South and North.[352]

As we are about to discuss, in 1861 the South's 300,000 white slave owners made up only 1 percent of the total U.S. white population of 30,000,000 people.[353] Thus, while only one Southern white out of every 300,000 owned slaves (1 percent), one Southern black out of every four owned slaves (25 percent). In other words, far more blacks owned black (and sometimes white) slaves than whites did: 25 percent compared to 1 percent!

Wealthy blacks bought, sold, and exploited black slaves for profit, just as white slave owners did. The well-known Anna Kingsley, who began life as a slave in her native Africa, ended up in what is now Jacksonville, Florida, where she became one of early America's many black plantation owners and slaveholders.[354]

Some, like the African-American Metoyers, an anti-abolition family from Louisiana, owned huge numbers of black slaves; in their case, at least 400.[355] At about $1,500 a piece,[356] their servants were worth a total of $600,000, or $20,000,000 in today's currency.[357] This made the Metoyers among the wealthiest people in the U.S., black or white, then or now. Louisiana's all-black Confederate army unit, the Augustin Guards, was named after the family patriarch, Augustin Metoyer.[358]

Black slavery was also common among America's 19th-Century Indians, who bought and sold African chattel right alongside black and white slave owners.[359] In fact, one of the many reasons so many Native-Americans sided with the Southern Confederacy was that it promised to enforce the fugitive slave law in Indian Territory, making it a legal requirement to return runaway slaves to their original Indian owners.[360]

While the average white slave owner owned five or less slaves (often only one or two),[361] the average Native-American slaveholder owned six. One Choctaw slaver owned 227.[362] Again, it was *non-white* slave owners who individually owned the most slaves, not whites.[363]

**WHAT YOU WERE TAUGHT:** Slavery was the cornerstone of the Confederacy, as its own vice president declared.

**THE TRUTH:** Few statements have ever been more garbled and misunderstood by enemies of the South than the one made by Confederate Vice President Alexander H. Stephens on the eve of Lincoln's War. Here are his exact words, uttered on March 21, 1861, during a speech at Savannah, Georgia:

> [The Confederacy's] cornerstone rests upon the great truth, that the negro is not equal to the white man; that slavery, subordination to the superior race, is his natural and normal condition.[364]

First, let us compare these words with those of Yankee President Abraham Lincoln, delivered publicly on July 17, 1858, at Springfield, Illinois:

> My declarations upon this subject of negro slavery may be misrepresented, but cannot be misunderstood. I have said that I do not understand the Declaration [of Independence] to mean that all men were created equal in all respects. . . . Certainly the negro is not our equal in color—perhaps not in many other respects . . .[365]

A few months later, on September 18, 1858, at Charleston, Illinois, Lincoln made the following statement:

> I will say then that I am not, nor ever have been, in favor of bringing about in any way the social and political equality of the white and black races—that I am not, nor ever have been, in favor of making voters or jurors of negroes, nor of qualifying them to hold office, nor to intermarry with white people ; and I will say in addition to this that there is a physical difference between the white and black races which I believe will forever forbid the two races

living together on terms of social and political equality. And inasmuch as they cannot so live, while they do remain together there must be the position of superior and inferior, and I as much as any other man am in favor of having the superior position assigned to the white race.[366]

Our point here is that Vice President Stephens' racism was no different than President Lincoln's. Both men were products of a 19th-Century white society that saw blacks as an "inferior race," as Lincoln *always* referred to African-Americans.[367] Thus, if critics of the South wish to avoid being called hypocrites, Northerner Lincoln must be denounced just as heartily as Southerner Stephens.[368] As the "Great Emancipator" Lincoln himself said of "nearly all white people" living in America at the time:

There is a natural disgust in the minds of nearly all white people, to the idea of an indiscriminate amalgamation of the white and black races . . .[369]

While the deeply held lifelong white supremacy in Lincoln's speeches is obvious for all to see, the racism displayed in Stephens' speech turns out to be far less vicious and entrenched, as a closer examination reveals.

There were indeed a few Southerners who claimed that slavery was necessary for the operation of the Confederacy, and that this was the reason the Yankee government was determined to abolish it. However, there was never a period in Southern history when more than 5 percent of Southerners owned slaves. As such, it is clear that the South did not need slavery to survive, making Stephen's claim both ludicrous and illogical.

The reality is that the Union was no threat to Southern slavery, for not only had Lincoln promised not to interfere with it,[370] but slavery was still fully legal across the entire U.S. in 1861, the year Stephens gave his "cornerstone" speech. At the time Southern slavery was actually in more danger from the Southern abolitionist majority than the much smaller Northern abolitionist minority.

Why then did some Southerners, like the Rebel vice president, make such patently absurd comments?

Those few who declared that slavery was the "cornerstone" of the South were engaging in a clever but reckless political ploy, one used to try and agitate other Southerners in the tariff conflicts with the North.[371] There were so few slave owners in the South in the early 1860s, that in an attempt to gain their support it is not surprising that the traditional political tactics of exaggeration, fear-mongering, and hyperbole were sometimes employed by

Confederate leaders like Stephens, just as they are still used by politicians today.

We must also consider the fact that if slavery had truly been the "cornerstone of the Confederacy," not to mention the cause of the "Civil War," then the conflict would have ended with Lincoln's Final Emancipation Proclamation on January 1, 1863.[372] Instead, it dragged on for over two more bloody years, not ending until Confederate abolitionist General Robert E. Lee reluctantly stacked arms at Appomattox on April 9, 1865.

Afterward, Southerner Lyon Gardiner Tyler, the son of America's tenth President, John Tyler,[373] put the matter this way:

> The emancipation of slaves [on January 1, 1863] by the late war is the best evidence that the South never fought for slavery, but *against a foreign dictation and a sectional will.* Within the Union slavery was probably secure for many years to come. The war was nothing more than the outcome of a tyranny exerted for seventy-two years by the North over vital interests of the South.[374]

In summary, it would be far more accurate to say that *slavery was the cornerstone of the Union,* for as we have seen, not only would New England have gone bankrupt without it,[375] it was the North's Wall Street Boys (Yankee financiers, merchants, and industrialists) who made the most money from the institution and who were thus the most interested in keeping it alive.[376]

Indeed, it was this very group, keen to put anyone into the Oval Office who would maintain the lucrative Northern slave trade and the equally lucrative business of Southern slavery, that got Lincoln elected president. For he was the only candidate who promised to do just that.[377] Later, these same backers rewarded "Honest Abe" by donating millions of dollars from their slave profits to fund his War against the South and get him reelected in 1864.[378]

**WHAT YOU WERE TAUGHT:** Southern slavery was an un-Christian, cruel, cold, impersonal, and despicable labor system that wasted and destroyed the lives of slaves and alienated the races.

**THE TRUTH:** Southern servants were legally registered as literal members of the families of their white, black, red, or brown owners, and, in nearly all cases, delicately cared for throughout their entire lives, very much as if they were the adopted children of their owners.[379] Little wonder that many blacks did not welcome emancipation, preferring servitude instead![380] As Dr. Henry A. White, history professor at Washington and Lee University, wrote in 1900:

> The [Southern slavery] system produced no paupers and no orphans; food and clothing the negro did not lack; careful attention

he received in sickness, and, without a burden [care] the aged servants spent their closing days. The plantation was an industrial school where the negro gradually acquired skill in the use of tools. A bond of affection was woven between Southern masters and servants which proved strong enough in 1861-'65 to keep the negroes at voluntary labour to furnish food for the armies that contended against [Lincoln's] military emancipation.[381] In the planter's home the African learned to set a higher value upon the domestic virtues which he saw illustrated in the lives of Christian men and women; for, be it remembered, the great body of the slave-holders of the South were devotees of the religious faith handed down through pious ancestors from Knox, Cranmer, Wesley, and Bunyan. With truth, perhaps, it may be said than no other economic system before or since that time has engendered a bond of personal affection between capital and labour so strong as that established by the institution of slavery.[382]

**WHAT YOU WERE TAUGHT:** While few in the North ever owned slaves, nearly every Southerner was once a slave owner. The Confederacy was a nation of slaveholders.

**THE TRUTH:** We have already seen that American slavery got its start in the North, and that many thousands of Yankee farmers owned slaves while thousands of Yankee businessmen funded and operated the slave trade. As for slave ownership in the South, far from being "a nation of slaveholders," the reality is that this group made up only a tiny fraction of Southern whites.

Land and slaves were costly in the 1800s, so invariably slavery was a rich man's business. Nearly all 19th-Century Southerners were poor farmers, however. Thus very few Southerners could afford to own slaves, even if they had wanted them (most, like General Robert E. Lee and Stonewall Jackson, did not want them). It was not possible then for there to be a "slave owning majority," a phrase that anti-South writers enjoy using. Quite the opposite. The large slaveholding families of the South, those with over twenty slaves, numbered only about 10,000.[383] This was only 0.6 percent of the 1.5 million families who lived across the South in 1860.[384]

According to the U.S. Censuses during the mid 1800s, slightly less than 5 percent of all Southerners owned slaves, and most of these owned less than five.[385] In 1850 specifically, for example, the Census shows that of the total population of 8,039,000 white Southerners, only 384,884 owned slaves: just 4.7 percent. Of these same whites that year only 46,274 owned twenty or more servants (0.5 percent of the total white population), only 2,500 owned thirty or more (0.03 percent),[386] and a mere handful, 2,300, owned 100 or more (0.02 percent).[387] This last group, the extremely wealthy "Aristocratic

Planters," the only group that anti-South writers focus on, actually made up only one-half of 1 percent of the total population of the South. [388]

Ten years later, in 1860, now with a white population of 7,215,525, little had changed in the way of white slave ownership. According to the U.S. Census, that year only 4.8 percent (or 385,000) of all Southerners owned slaves, the other 95.2 percent did not. [389] Of those that did, most owned less than five. [390] Correcting for the mistakes of Census takers—which would include counting slave-hirers as slave owners and counting more than once those thousands of slave owners who annually moved the same slaves back and forth across multiple states—this figure, 4.8 percent, is no doubt too large. Either way, Southerners themselves believed that only about 5 percent of their number owned slaves, which is slightly high, but roughly accurate. [391]

In 1860 there were still only 2,300 Aristocratic Planters (those who owned 100 or more slaves), just 0.03 percent of the total white population, while only 8,000 owned as many as fifty slaves (0.11 percent). Of the total white Southern population in 1860, just 46,000 individuals met the criteria for actual planter status (that is, owning large acreage and twenty or more slaves), a mere 0.06 percent of Dixie's populace. [392]

With only around 5 percent of Southern whites as slave owners, what about the other 95 percent? They were non-servant owning, yeoman farmers, small landholders who operated without labor assistance, [393] and who thus had no need for outside workers and no interest in the institution of slavery. [394] In fact, there had been enormous tension between slaveholders and non-slaveholders from the very beginning, for the latter group resented the very existence of black servant labor in the South. [395] Northern slave owner, and later U.S. president, General Ulysses S. Grant, admitted that:

> The great bulk of the legal voters of the South were men who owned no slaves; . . . [thus] their interest in the contest [to abolish slavery] was very meagre . . . [396]

Even Lincoln himself acknowledged that "in all our slave States except South Carolina, a majority of the whole people of all colors are neither slaves nor masters." [397] Southern scholar Shelby Foote correctly calls this group "the slaveless majority," a phrase never heard, discussed, or even acknowledged in Yankee and scallywag "history" books. [398] Yet it made up the foundational majority of the Old South.

Agriculturalists maintain that a farmer would need at least twenty laborers to achieve a decent level of "economies of scale" on a large farm. By this standard there were actually very few planters and plantations in the Old South. [399] In other words, slave owning Southern whites were in the vast minority, non-slave owning Southerners were in the vast majority.

**WHAT YOU WERE TAUGHT:** Contrary to the claim made by Southerners, Confederate General Robert E. Lee was indeed a slave owner, for he makes numerous references to them in his writings.

**THE TRUTH:** It is true that there were black servants in the Lee household, and the South has never denied this. The question is, did they belong to General Lee?

The answer is, they did not.[400] They belonged to the family of his wife, Mary Anne Randolph Custis. More specifically, they were the property of Mary's father, George Washington Parke Custis. General Lee had no choice but to "adopt" Mr. Custis' servants when he married his daughter in 1831, who, in the tradition of wealthy Southerners, had been given some of the family servants as a wedding gift.

As for General Lee himself, I can find no records of him ever purchasing or selling slaves. In fact, as has been widely known across the South for generations, the General's so-called "slaves" were merely an assortment of black servants he had involuntarily inherited from other family members, such as Mr. Custis. All were treated humanely, fairly, and, as was the popular custom in Dixie, like members of the Lee family, particularly the house servants.

In the Fall of 1862, five years after Mr. Custis' death on October 10, 1857, General Lee, who had been made the executor of Mr. Custis' will, immediately set about emancipating the Custis family servants, as was requested of him in that document. Thus it is clear that not only did the General *not* personally own slaves, but that the entire Lee clan was discussing personal abolition in their household at least five years before the start of Lincoln's War. We will note here that this was the same period in which Lincoln was most enthusiastically promoting the idea of deporting all blacks out of the U.S., his lifelong obsession.

In short, abolitionist General Lee emancipated the Custis servants four months *before* black colonizationist Lincoln issued his fake and illegal Final Emancipation Proclamation on January 1, 1863. Slave-hating Lee was no slave owner.[401]

**WHAT YOU WERE TAUGHT:** There were no Northern slaves and thus no Northern slave owners.

**THE TRUTH:** This statement is obviously false because both the American slave trade and American slavery got their start in the northeastern United States (the former in 1638,[402] the latter in 1641).[403] This automatically makes

Northerners not only slave traders and slave owners, but the *first* white American slaver traders and slave owners.

Official records show that as of the year 1800 there were 36,505 black slaves in the North, working on farms and plantations in a myriad of occupations, from agricultural to mechanical.[404]  As most slaves were not counted in the Census, we know that this number was actually much higher.

In fact, statistics from the time period reveal that in the early 1700s, 42 percent of all New York households owned slaves, and that the share of slaves in both New York and New Jersey was larger than that of North Carolina.[405]  By 1690, in Perth Amboy, New Jersey, as just one example, nearly every white inhabitant owned one or more black slaves.[406]  This means that nearly 100 percent of the whites in some Northern cities were slaveholders.

Based on mathematics alone it is clear that many Yankees were far more enthusiastic slavers than Southerners: not only did most Southern towns have no slaves or slave owners at all, but the percentage of overall Southern slave owners never went above 5 percent (it usually hovered between 3 and 4 percent).

Exactly how many slaves and slave owners were there in the North as a whole?  We know that blacks were in North America as early as 1526.[407]  Unfortunately, the U.S. Census did not start until 1790, so we have no hard data for the number of Northern slaves in the intervening 264 years.  During that period we can be sure, however, that many millions lived, worked, and died in the North, the majority unrecorded, their names unchronicled, their births, lives, descendants, and deaths completely unknown.

This unfortunate dearth of information regarding Northern slavery has long helped the North avoid acknowledging that it once possessed millions of African slaves, and that it alone is responsible for launching the U.S. slave trade and instigating American slavery.  But authentic history cannot be ignored, suppressed, or rewritten.  The record stands clear, defiant, and intractable: the North and African slavery were once inextricably bound together, a deeply symbiotic relationship that was finally only torn asunder by the passage of the Thirteenth Amendment on December 6, 1865, nearly a year *after* Lincoln died.[408]

It was only in the late 1700s, when Northerners finally found slavery to be unprofitable (due to their generally poor soil and cold climate) and uncomfortable (due to rampant white Northern racism),[409] that they began to slowly abolish the institution.[410]  Nonetheless, nearly 100 years later, in 1860, near the start of the "Civil War," historian Dr. Clement Eaton believes there were at least 500,000 black slaves still left in the North,[411] while Southern historian Don Hinkle maintains that their number was closer to 1 million.[412]

Taking the higher number, 1 million slaves, and an average ownership of two slaves apiece, we get 500,000 Northern white slave owners, 2.5 percent of the 20 million white Northerners in 1860.[413] Numbered among these were many famous Yanks, including, as we have observed, General Ulysses S. Grant,[414] as well as General Winfield Scott, Admiral David G. Farragut, General George H. Thomas, and the family of Lincoln's wife, Mary Todd.[415]

Literally millions of slaves lived and died in the Northern states between the 1600s and 1865. If all their names had been recorded, it would be enough to fill several volumes.[416] An abbreviated list of some of the better known Northern slaves whose names *were* recorded includes:

Crispus Attucks (Massachusetts)
Frederick Douglass (Maryland)
Sojourner Truth (New York)
Harriet Tubman (Maryland)
Amos Fortune (Massachusetts)
James Derham (Pennsylvania)
Prince Whipple (New Hampshire)
Daniel Coker (Maryland)
Theophilus Thompson (Maryland)
Richard Pierpoint (New York)
Quock Walker (Massachusetts)
Lisette Denison Forth (Michigan)
Amanda Smith (Maryland)
Briton Hammon (Massachusetts)
Samuel Green (Maryland)
Jane Johnson (Washington, D.C.)
Phillis Wheatley (Massachusetts)
Josiah Henson (Maryland)
Seymour Burr (Connecticut)
James Roberts (Maryland)
Prince Estabrook (Massachusetts)
Cynthia Hesdra (New York)
Venture Smith (Connecticut)

Francis Burns (New York)
Anthony Bowen (Maryland)
Ayuba Suleiman Diallo (Maryland)
Henry Highland Garnet (Maryland)
Pyrrhus Concer (New York)
Felix Holbrook (Massachusetts)
Leonard Black (Maryland)
John Jea (New York)
Charles Ball (Maryland)
William S. Crowdy (Maryland)
Peter Salem (Massachusetts)
Mary Edmonson (Maryland)
Emily Edmonson (Maryland)
Elizabeth Freeman (New York)
Lewis Charlton (Maryland)
Elijah Abel (Maryland)
Richard Allen (Pennsylvania)
Decatur Dorsey (Maryland)
Benjamin Bradley (Maryland)
Molly Williams (New York)
Solomon Bayley (Delaware)
John Edward Bruce (Maryland)
James H. Bronson (Pennsylvania)[417]

**WHAT YOU WERE TAUGHT:** There is no evidence, especially physical evidence, for Northern slavery. Therefore it did not exist.

**THE TRUTH:** If evidence for Northern slavery is scarce it is because, in great part, liberals and other enemies of the South have suppressed it for fear that the Truth about Lincoln and his War will be revealed—as it has in this very book. However, there is another more practical reason: time.

In the late 1700s and early 1800s the white North pushed slavery South, accomplishing two goals simultaneously: it rid itself of the "dangerous presence" of blacks (as Lincoln referred to it),[418] while maintaining the institution in order to continue reaping its huge financial profits. As *unofficial* abolition began in the North nearly 100 years before the South (as we have seen, *official* Northern abolition came after Southern abolition), it was largely forgotten as attention was transferred to the South, the most recent region in the U.S. to practice slavery.

Not only this, but scientifically speaking this means that archaeological evidence of Southern slavery is more recent, closer to the earth's surface, and thus easier to discover, while physical evidence of Northern slavery, being older, lies deeper in the ground, and its artifacts are less well preserved and more difficult to find.

Despite this problem, archaeological proof of Northern slavery is being brought to light like never before. Near Salem, Massachusetts, for example, scientists have uncovered traces of a 13,000 acre plantation once owned by a Yankee named Samuel Browne. Near Browne's farm, one that traded its products for Caribbean rum and molasses, a massive slave cemetery was discovered, the final resting place of some 100 African-American slaves who worked there between the years 1718 and 1780.[419]

An 8,000 acre plantation was also recently found at Shelter Island, Long Island, New York. The enormous homestead which supplied products for slave plantations in Barbados itself used slave labor: some twenty black servants lived in bondage here in the late 1600s.[420]

More and more Northern plantations like these are being discovered and excavated each year, making it more and more difficult for the anti-South movement to hide the Truth about the "Civil War."

**WHAT YOU WERE TAUGHT:** If Northern slavery existed there would still be cultural traces of it.

**THE TRUTH:** For those who care to look, cultural vestiges of the North's "peculiar institution" are still obvious to this day, particularly in New England. One of the more conspicuous of these is the pineapple symbol, commonly seen decorating front doors, gates, store fronts, street signs, and driveways.

Though the emblem of the pineapple is now seen as a "welcome" sign across the Northeast, this is an intentional corruption to mask its original meaning: when New England slave traders returned from their ocean expeditions to the tropics to pick up slaves, they would impale a pineapple on their fencepost to let everyone in town know that they were "welcome" to come in and shop for slave products, as well as for slaves themselves.[421]

We will note that the pineapple motif, that great symbol of Yankee slavery, is still commonly seen all over the U.S., not just in the North, but in the South as well. Here, scallywags and transplanted Yankees have convinced many of the unsuspecting inhabitants of Dixie that the pineapple is an innocent emblem of friendship and hospitality. All who read this now know the truth.

**WHAT YOU WERE TAUGHT:** Millions of Southern slaves were saved by the Underground Railroad, which allowed them to flee North and escape the horrors of the South's "peculiar institution."
**THE TRUTH:** Though the Underground Railroad functioned throughout most of the War, only about 4,000 total (just 1,000 Southern slaves a year) out of 3.5 million availed themselves of it—a mere 0.11 percent of the total.[422] The rest voluntarily stayed at home, defending both their owners' farms, and the owners themselves, from marauding Yanks.[423]

**WHAT YOU WERE TAUGHT:** The horrible racist Black Codes were an invention of Southerners.
**THE TRUTH:** This is one of the most deeply cherished of all the Yankee myths. But it happens to be untrue.

Naturally, the Black Codes, laws meant to restrict the movements, freedoms, and rights of African-Americans, began in that part of the United States where not only both the American slave trade and American slavery got their start, but more importantly where racism was most severe.[424] And that region, in the 1800s, was the North, as foreign visitors, Southerners, and even Northerners themselves repeatedly observed.[425]

**WHAT YOU WERE TAUGHT:** Southern slavery was less efficient than Northern free labor.
**THE TRUTH:** Southern slavery was actually more efficient than Northern free labor. Even when all of slavery's attendant problems are taken into account, such as the high start-up costs, the care of slaves too young or too old to perform labor, and runaways and death, slavery paid and paid well in the Old South.[426]

Plantations that used slave labor, for example, were 50 percent more efficient than those that used free labor, giving the South an enormous advantage: her farms were 35 percent more productive than slave-free farms in the North.[427] Indeed, Southern slavery became more productive, and thus more lucrative, right up to the time of Lincoln's War.[428]

**WHAT YOU WERE TAUGHT:** The South should be ashamed of itself for practicing slavery.
**THE TRUTH:** The white South does feel shame for its involvement in slavery,

and it has apologized for it repeatedly over the years—and continues to do so, at every opportunity.[429]

What the South wants to know is why the North has not also apologized for its role in the "peculiar institution"? After all, it was Northerners (in Massachusetts) who first introduced the slave trade to the American colonies in 1638;[430] it was Northern ship builders who constructed America's first slave ships; it was Northern businessmen who financed these ships; it was these Northern slave ships which first sailed to Africa; it was Northern ports that harbored the first American slave ships;[431] it was a Northern state (the colony of Massachusetts) that first legalized slavery in 1641;[432] it was Yankee businessmen who owned and operated the entire American slave trading business; it was the North that first prospered from slavery; and finally, it was the North that sold its slaves to the South when it finally found them to be both disagreeable and unprofitable.[433]

An apology for African slavery in America is also due from the thousands of descendants of early slave owning African-Americans, Native-Americans, and Latin-Americans, as well as from Africa herself: Africa not only practiced slavery long prior to the arrival of Europeans, but greatly expedited and even encouraged Europeans in developing the Atlantic slave trade.[434]

**WHAT YOU WERE TAUGHT:** Southern slave owners whipped their slaves on a daily basis.

**THE TRUTH:** Whipping was extremely rare on Southern plantations, and for good reason. Not only was it bad for morale, it also increased the cost of labor while reducing the value of those slaves it was used on (whip marks indicated a recalcitrant individual), which is why *all* early plantation manuals strongly advised against the practice.[435] Additionally, the majority of Southerners considered those who used the whip to be inhumane, and those who wielded it against their servants were often reported by neighbors to the authorities for cruelty.

Far from being a common item on Southern plantations, most slave owners permanently banned the whip from their property,[436] which is why Confederate President Jefferson Davis could honestly say that when it came to the alleged "sadistic" treatment of Southern slaves, it "probably exists to a smaller extent [here] than in any other relation of labor to capital" in the world.[437]

Southerners hated unmerciful slave owners and the use of the whip was widely regarded as unneeded and indefensible.[438] According to one white plantation owner's "Rules in the Management of a Southern Estate":

> I will most certainly discharge any overseer for striking any of my
> negroes with a club or the butt of his whip, or in any way injuring
> one of my negroes. My negroes are not to be abused or injured in
> any way; and, at the same time, they must be kept under strict
> discipline, which can be accomplished by talking to them . . .[439]

What is more, the violence, unethical treatment, and immorality
portrayed between black slaves and their masters and mistresses in fantasy
fiction books like *Uncle Tom's Cabin*, was not only uncommon but was a
punishable crime in the South.[440] In fact, by the early 1800s *all* Southern states
had passed anti-cruelty laws that provided fines, imprisonment, and even
execution for those who mistreated their servants, and more than one sadistic
slaver died at the business end of a lawman's gun.[441]

The reality is that whipping was not a corrective tool created especially
for the institution of Southern slavery, as the North and New South teaches.
From the 1600s to the 1800s it was the standard form of punishment in the U.S.
for misdemeanors; and it was applied to lawbreakers of every kind, whether
male or female, whether black, white, brown, or red.[442] As such, far more
American whites were whipped by the local sheriff than American blacks.[443]

From New England to the Deep South the whipping post was the
centerpiece of the village green in hundreds of towns and cities across early
America. The standard punishment for horse thieves, for example, nearly all
who were white, was "three good whippings," each one consisting of thirty-nine
lashes.[444]

Whipping was the standard military punishment at the time as well.
During the Revolutionary War, while the "father of the nation," George
Washington, served as General of the Continental Army, he had his white
soldiers regularly whipped for a host of offences ranging from drunkenness to
desertion.[445] The future first president's whippings were so ferocious that
Congress had to intervene and place a limit on the number of lashes that could
be doled out.[446]

During the "Civil War" white farmers in the South risked being
whipped by Confederate authorities for violating the government's ban on
growing cotton instead of food.[447] Yankee troops whipped Southern
noncombatants as readily as they whipped Rebel soldiers. In Screven County,
Georgia, for instance, a white citizen who was found armed was given 200
lashes by a Union officer.[448]

It is well-known that both white and black Yankee soldiers used the
whip on "stubborn" captured Southern blacks between 1861 and 1865.[449]
"Insubordinate" black Yankee soldiers were sometimes whipped by their white
superiors as well.[450] Black Union soldiers were known to whip white civilians

during the War.[451]

It is true that aboard Yankee slave ships unruly black slaves on their way from Africa to the Americas were sometimes whipped during the infamous Middle Passage. But what Northern mythology always leaves out is the fact that on these same slave runs disorderly white sailors were also whipped. In fact, eyewitnesses described the practice as "constant flogging," with men dying from their wounds on a daily basis, both black *and* white.[452]

During Lincoln's War, Southern cotton plantations were "taken over" (that is, stolen) from their owners and white Yankee officers and Northern businessmen were put in charge. Freed blacks were then transferred to these farms to labor at the same menial jobs they had performed while slaves (Lincoln's idea of "emancipation"). Worse, their white Yankee overseers were often permitted to use the whip. At times the use of the lash became so frequent that it had to be disallowed, but the practice continued behind closed doors.[453]

As Union General Thomas West Sherman reported to his superiors in Washington, "the [freed] Negroes are disinclined to labor and will evidently not work to our satisfaction without . . . the driver and the lash."[454] (What Sherman failed to realize is that 19th-Century African-Americans, far from being lazy, were actually extremely hard working. It was simply that they did not like working for cruel and inhumane Yankees under constant threat of violence.)

Even after Lincoln's War was over Yankees continued to use the whip as a method of punishment across the South during "Reconstruction."[455] Native-Americans too relied on the lash during this period: when freed blacks were caught coming into Indian territory they were soundly flogged.[456] And in the North postwar whites in Massachusetts routinely whipped blacks who overstayed their welcome (the limit a nonresident black could remain in the so-called "abolitionist" Bay State was just two months).[457]

In early America then the whip was the normal penalty for unwanted behavior. Thus it was only natural that it was also used to enforce authority on plantations. In fact, black slaves themselves, such as those who worked in positions of power (for example, mammies, overseers, drivers, and managers), regularly used the whip on other black slaves when the situation warranted it[458] (contrary to Yankee myth, some 70 percent of white Southern plantations were managed by blacks).[459] And we will note that *black* slave owners—of which there were tens of thousands across the South[460]—used it on their black servants as well.[461] As there were far worse penalties (such as being branded with a hot iron or shot before a firing squad), use of the whip was an accepted and recognized form of penalizing not only black servants, but criminals of all colors and social statuses.

At the time, black slave parents often brutally whipped their disobedient offspring (with switches), while black male slaves were known to whip their wives when they felt it was "necessary."[462] In most Western nations this approach to discipline lasted well into the 20th Century, and there are, no doubt, people reading this book who will recall being "whipped" with a belt or spanked with a paddle as a youngster. It is well-known, for example, that President Jimmy Carter was whipped as a child.[463] Even Lincoln's wife Mary Todd Lincoln often whipped their children, as the Yankee president acknowledged in a letter dated October 22, 1846.[464]

Still the innate savagery of the whip offended all thinking Southerners, just one of the many reasons why African-American, Native-American, Latin-American, and European-American slave owners did not use physical coercion on their human chattel unless absolutely necessary.[465] Even in the most severe cases owners were much more likely to rely on traditional methods of punishment, such as withdrawal of privileges, being assigned unpleasant tasks, or temporary confinement.[466]

In the end, actual use of the whip was indeed often unnecessary, for it was mainly seen across early America as a symbol of law and order. Knowing it existed, and that it *could* be used, was usually enough to keep even the most incorrigible citizens, free or enslaved, white or black, in line.[467]

In 1900 Dr. Henry A. White debunked the Yankee myth of the so-called "routine abuse" of Southern servants:

> Self-interest restrained harsh masters from cruelty, and a wholesome public sentiment enforced the practice of kindness toward the quiet wards of the plantation. Cruelty was the exception. Not often was the lash used; not often were negro families separated by sale, except as penalty for misdemeanor, or in the distribution of estates to heirs or to creditors.[468]

**WHAT YOU WERE TAUGHT:** The relationship between slaves and their masters was unhappy, unhealthy, abusive, and exploitive.

**THE TRUTH:** Slave-master relationships were the much same as today's employee-employer relationships: most are good, while only a few are not. As we saw in Chapter 6, the facts are that the majority of Southern owners and their slaves had what can only be called warm relations, in many cases bordering on deep familial love, wherein whites and blacks considered each other "family."

In 1908, Luther W. Hopkins, a former Confederate soldier in Jeb Stuart's cavalry, wrote the following, revealing the true nature of the slave-master relationship across the South in the mid 1800s:

There was a peculiar relationship existing between the slave owner's family and the slaves that the North never did and never will understand. On the part of the white children it was love, pure and simple, for the slave, while on the part of the adult it was more than friendship, and, I might add, the feeling was reciprocated by the slaves. The children addressed the adult blacks as Uncle and Aunt, and treated them with as much respect as they did their blood relatives. It was Uncle Reuben and Aunt Dinah. The adult white also addressed the older colored people in the same way. With but few exceptions, the two races lived together in perfect harmony. If a slave-owner was cruel to his slaves, it was because he was a cruel man, and all who came in contact with him, both man and beast, suffered at his hands. Even his children did not escape. Such men are found everywhere. The old black mammy, with her head tied up in a white cloth, was loved, respected and honored by every inmate of the home, regardless of color.

The following incident will be of interest: Hon. John Randolph Tucker, one of Virginia's most gifted and learned sons, who represented his State in the U.S. Congress, always celebrated his birthday. I remember to have attended one of these celebrations. It was shortly after the close of the war. Mr. Tucker was then between forty-five and fifty years of age. He had grown children. Fun making was one of his characteristics. On these annual occasions, it was his custom to dress himself in a long white gown and bring into the parlor his old black nurse, whom he called "mammy." She sat in her rocking-chair with her head tied up in the conventional snow-white cloth. Mr. Tucker, dressed up as a child in his nightgown, would toddle in and climb up into her lap, and she would lull him to sleep with an old time nursery song, no doubt one of her own compositions. This could not possibly have occurred had the skin of his nurse been white.

When a daughter married and set up her own home, fortunate was she if she took with her the mammy. In many homes the slaves were present at family prayers. The kitchen and the cabin furnished the white children places of resort that were full of pleasure.

This was the relation between white and colored as I remember it from a child in my part of Virginia. And tonight, as I write these lines, while the clock tolls off the hour of eleven, I cannot keep out of my mind the words of that little poem by Elizabeth Akers: "Backward, turn backward, oh time in thy flight, and make me a child again, just for tonight." How anyone could have desired to break up this happy relationship was beyond the conception of the child, and more or less incomprehensible to the adult.[469]

**WHAT YOU WERE TAUGHT:** The American South owes modern day blacks reparations for slavery.

**THE TRUTH:** While some Southerners today may be receptive to this proposal, it would be difficult if not impossible to fulfill it for the following reasons.

First, slavery was legal across the entire U.S. from 1776 to 1865,[470] and was practiced by both by Southerners *and* Northerners. The North was itself the instigator of North American slavery [471] and the epicenter of the American slave trade for decades.[472] Because of this the North would also have to contribute. But why would it after spreading the lie, for the last 150 years, that "the South is totally responsible for American slavery"? By doing so it would be admitting its role in inaugurating and maintaining slavery for several hundred years, something it clearly does not want to do.

Second, European-Americans, as we have seen, were not the only ones who bought, sold, and owned blacks slaves. Tens of thousands of African-Americans, as well as untold scores of Native-Americans, Asian-Americans, and Latin-Americans, were also slave traders and slaveholders.[473] Additionally, most American whites did not own slaves.[474]

Third, reparations for American blacks would, allegedly, be paid by Americans. But it was not Americans who were responsible for the founding of the American slave trade in the Western hemisphere. It was an Italian, one by the name of Cristoforo Colombo, or Christopher Columbus, as we know him in English.[475] If recompense is to be awarded American blacks, should it not then be paid by Italy, his birthplace, and by Spain, the nation that financed his expeditions to the Americas?

Fourth, in 1619 the Dutch were the first to bring blacks (as indentured servants) to North America.[476] Thus the Netherlands would also need to help pay reparations. Portugal too, like Spain, was deeply involved in opening up slave trade routes between Africa and the New World.[477]

Lastly, other racial and ethnic groups in early America besides blacks were also held in various types of bondage, from slavery to servitude, from indenture to involuntary apprenticeship. Among these were European-Americans themselves, the great majority who, like one of Lincoln's ancestors (an early relation who was part of the Massachusetts Bay Colony), came to America as indentured servants.[478]

With these facts in mind, who would decide—and *how* would they decide—which European nations, and which European-Americans, African-Americans, Native-Americans, Asian-Americans, and Latin-Americans are obligated to pay reparations for slavery and who are not?

# THE ABOLITION MOVEMENT

**WHAT YOU WERE TAUGHT:** The American abolition movement started in the North.

**THE TRUTH:** The American abolition movement began in the South. While Northern colonies like Massachusetts were busy legalizing slavery and expanding the slave trade, Southern colonies were busy trying to put a stop to both. Indeed, the very first American colony to attempt to abolish the entire ugly institution was a Southern one: Virginia. Another Southern state, Georgia, was the first to place a prohibition against the importation of slaves into her state constitution.[479]

Among the Virginians who were behind the antislavery movement was America's first president, George Washington, who was so against the institution that he beseeched God to help bring about emancipation in both the South and the North as soon as possible. Said the Southerner:

> Not only do I pray for it on the score of human dignity, but I can clearly foresee that nothing but the rooting out of slavery can perpetuate the existence of our union by consolidating it in a common bond of principle.[480]

Since the American abolition movement got its start in the South, and more specifically in Virginia, we should not be surprised to learn that it was in the Old Dominion State that voluntary emancipation found its greatest success: between 1782 and 1790 some 10,000 black servants were voluntarily freed by white Virginian "slave owners." In contrast, slave owners in many Northern states showed much greater reluctance to give up their black chattel. New Jersey, for example, did not pass its emancipation act until 1804, which is why it still had over 3,500 slaves as late as 1830.[481]

After the American Revolutionary War ended in 1783, though the U.S. government had not yet even given citizenship to blacks, many Southern states were passing laws allowing African-Americans to own property, testify in court, vote, and travel without restrictions.[482]

In 1807, under another Virginian, President Thomas Jefferson, the Southern states enthusiastically voted to end the slave trade by 1808, the year the Constitution had set as the earliest date Congress could decide on the issue.[483] Unfortunately for African-Americans, Northerners, as even Lincoln observed,[484] ignored the ban and continued the trade illegally right through to the end of the "Civil War."[485]

Seventeen years earlier other Virginians were also pushing for abolition. In 1790 Fernando Fairfax drafted his "Plan for Liberating the Negroes within the United States," while six years later, in 1796, St. George Tucker, one of the earliest abolitionists in the U.S., drew up another even more elaborate emancipation system. About the same time another Southerner, James Madison, joined Thomas Jefferson in formulating ideas for permanently ending slavery in Virginia.[486]

Twenty years before that, the Virginia Declaration of Rights—first drafted in 1776 by native son and antislavery advocate George Mason—included the phrase that all men are "born equally free and independent," and are possessed of certain "natural, essential, and unalienable rights."[487]

A myriad of other early Southerners stepped forward to push the abolitionist cause. Among them were Calvin A. Wiley of North Carolina and the Reverend James Lyons of Mississippi. Both men campaigned for legal reforms that would lift the ban on educating slaves, help protect slave marriages, ban the splitting up of slave families, and allow slaves to testify in court.[488] Their efforts were heartily welcomed throughout the abolitionist South. Louisiana, as just one example, eventually prohibited separating servant families,[489] a fact you will read in few American history books.

A friend of Mary Chesnut's, Confederate General James Johnston Pettigrew, wrote an antislavery essay in 1862—the same year Lincoln was trying to figure out how to prevent abolitionists from pressuring him into issuing an emancipation proclamation. A South Carolina slave owner and abolitionist, Mary not only read it but highly approved of Pettigrew's words and ideas, and told him so, much to the officer's pleasure.[490] Sadly the North Carolinian died shortly after the Battle of Gettysburg and never saw the fruition of his dream of ending of slavery in the South.[491]

Of the 130 abolition societies established before 1827 by Northern abolitionist Benjamin Lundy, over 100, comprising four-fifths of the total membership, were in the South.[492] Early North Carolina, as another example, had a number of well-known "forceful" antislavery leaders, such as Benjamin Sherwood Hedrick and Daniel Reaves Goodlow,[493] and in South Carolina the famed Quaker sisters Sarah and Angelina Grimké were just two among millions of Southerners fighting for the cause of abolition.[494]

In the early 1800s Madison and Jefferson were still discussing, and fully expecting, their home state of Virginia to move toward abolishing slavery,[495] and by the mid-1800s the Southern abolition movement was in full swing. In the 1850s Yankee minister Nehemiah Adams traveled through the South and found, contrary to all that he had heard about "racist Southerners," a vast and thriving abolition movement, complete with fiery abolitionist speakers and widely disseminated antislavery tracts. A stunned Adams noted that white Southerners everywhere could not wait to abolish the institution, "till no wrong, no pain, should be the fruit of it which is not incidental to every human lot."[496]

Around the same time, on December 27, 1856, five years before Lincoln's War, here is what one famous antislavery Virginian, Robert E. Lee, had to say about the institution:

> There are few, I believe, in this enlightened age, but what will acknowledge that slavery as an institution is a moral and political evil in any country. It is idle to expatiate on its disadvantages. I think it is a greater evil to the white than to the colored race.[497]

Even before Lee spoke these words white Southerners everywhere were adopting ever more liberal reforms that, along with the forces of industrialization, urbanization, and the Enlightenment, would have inevitably led to eventual abolition and emancipation all across the South. That is, if Lincoln had not interfered by illegally invading what was by then a constitutionally-formed foreign country.[498] After the War started Southerners in their thousands continued to come out against the "peculiar institution." Among them was Lee, who said:

> If I owned the four millions of slaves [in the South], I would cheerfully sacrifice them to the preservation of the Union . . .[499]

The true irony of all this of course is that, as Lee intimated, the North ended up using slavery as justification for its illegal invasion of Dixie, and yet it was the North who sold these same slaves to the South to begin with.[500]

**WHAT YOU WERE TAUGHT:** The North never fully embraced slavery. Only the South.
**THE TRUTH:** Since American slavery got its start in the North, and since the American abolition movement got its start in the South, this statement is

obviously untrue for these two reasons alone. In fact, contrary to Northern mythology, not only did the Old South never fully embrace slavery, it never invited it to begin with.

What our current Northern-slanted history books do not teach is that up until the year 1831—the year meddlesome Yankee abolitionist William Lloyd Garrison began publishing his arrogant, slanderous anti-South newspaper, *The Liberator*—nearly all Southerners were abolitionists.[501] In late 1861 slave owner Mary Chesnut, for example, writes that both she and her husband James Chesnut, Jr. (President Jefferson Davis' aide-de-camp) literally hated slavery.[502] All Southerners detest the institution more than Harriet Beecher Stowe ever could; we abhor slavery, know that it is doomed, and are happy about it, she said. Mary then describes a letter she had written to her husband while he was on their plantation in Mississippi in 1842. It is the most ardent abolitionist document, the diarist noted, one she kept so that the South's allegedly highly educated foes to the North might one day learn the truth about so-called Southern slavery.[503]

So far, 170 years later, few anti-South partisans have shown any interest in becoming "educated" when it comes to the facts about American slavery!

Early Southerners like the Chesnuts, being innately humanitarian, deplored the institution of slavery and felt that they had, quite rightly, unwillingly inherited it from their Northern neighbors, who in turn had inherited it, by force, from Great Britain.[504] Hence, in the early 1800s Virginia's eccentric antislavery advocate, Senator John Randolph, could truthfully say that slavery was foisted on the South, and was never an institution she sought out,[505] while Virginian Senator John Taylor could declare that slavery was an inherited disaster that Southerners would have to endure but never accept.[506] In 1900 Dr. Henry A. White wrote of this monstrous process:

> Unto the ships of New England the slave-carrying-trade was transferred after the [American] Revolution. Even before that war, her [Yankee] skippers had taken cargoes of rum from Cape Cod and Narragansett to exchange for flesh and blood on the coast of Africa. Fresh impetus was now given to this kind of barter. Wealth was rapidly heaped up in Rhode Island through the traffic of her fleet of slave vessels. Gradually the negroes of Northern masters were sent to the Southern markets, and thus were the Southern States filled up with the alien race.[507]

Personally, 17th-Century Southerners, now "saddled" with slavery, would have preferred that it had never come to America's shores to begin with.

This is why both the civil rights movement and the abolition movement began in, and were so strong in, the South from the earliest days of the nation. And this is why the region tried to ban slavery long before the North did. As Southerner and U.S. President Woodrow Wilson writes, nowhere in early America were there more sincere, more openly declared denunciations of the "evil influence" of slavery on both whites and blacks than in the South.[508]

**WHAT YOU WERE TAUGHT:** The Confederacy never tried to, or even wanted to, abolish slavery.

**THE TRUTH:** On November 7, 1864, President Jefferson Davis took his first step toward becoming America's true and only "Great Emancipator" when he asked the Confederate Congress to allow the government to purchase 40,000 slaves with the intention of emancipating them after the War.[509] The non-racist Davis, who—while racist Lincoln was busy trying to convert new members to the American Colonization Society—adopted an orphaned black boy (named Jim Limber) during the War,[510] said to the Confederate Congress:

> The policy of engaging to liberate the negro on his discharge after [military] service faithfully rendered seems to me preferable to that of granting immediate manumission, or that of retaining him in servitude.[511]

(Shortly we will discuss why, unlike the North, the South was, correctly, against immediate emancipation.)

In essence what Davis' proposal amounted to was complete emancipation, only twenty-three months after Lincoln reluctantly issued his Emancipation Proclamation (which purposefully did not free a single slave in the North or South), and over a year before the Thirteenth Amendment finally freed all bonded blacks in the U.S. Thus the South was realistically discussing authentic emancipation for its black soldiers long before the U.S. actually abolished slavery on December 6, 1865. Had not Lincoln interfered, full and complete emancipation of *all* black Southern slaves would have soon followed.

**WHAT YOU WERE TAUGHT:** The North abolished the slave trade before the South did.

**THE TRUTH:** The Rebels put an end to the slave trade long before the Yanks. Section Nine, Clauses One and Two of the Constitution of the Confederate States of America, written up in early 1861, clearly forbids the foreign slave trade. They read:

1) The importation of negroes of the African race from any foreign

country other than the slaveholding States or territories of the
United States of America, is hereby forbidden; and Congress is
required to pass such laws as shall effectually prevent the same.

2) Congress shall also have power to prohibit the introduction of
slaves from any State not a member of, or territory not belonging
to, this Confederacy.[512]

The U.S.A. did not ban the slave trade until December 1865 (with the
ratification of the Thirteenth Amendment), almost five years later.[513]

**WHAT YOU WERE TAUGHT:** There is no good reason why the South
continued to postpone emancipation before and during the War, particularly
after Lincoln's Emancipation Proclamation. For this the South deserves the
eternal condemnation of the world.

**THE TRUTH:** This is strong language coming from the region, namely the
North, that not only founded American slavery *and* became the center of the
American slave trade, but which outlawed slavery in its own time and way (that
is, when the institution became unprofitable and unbearable), postponed
emancipation for as long as possible (finally only relenting under enormous
political pressure), then unfairly turned around and tried to force the South to
abolish slavery before she was ready.[514]

After Lincoln's War, here is how former Confederate soldier Luther
W. Hopkins explained the situation in the South during the 1850s:

Somewhere between childhood and youth we [Southern] children
all learned that there was a race of people up North called
Abolitionists, who were so mean that they sent secret agents
through the country to persuade the colored people to leave their
homes and go North, where they could be free. That these agents
were disguised as peddlers or otherwise, and that they visited the
cabins of the slaves during the late hours of the night, and went so
far as to urge them to rise up in a body and declare their freedom,
and if necessary to murder those who held them as slaves [was
obvious to everyone]. This delusion, if it were a delusion, might
have been dispelled had not [anti-South Yankee abolitionist] John
Brown and his men appeared upon the scene to give an ocular
demonstration of their real intent [popularly known as John
Brown's Raid on Harper's Ferry, it occurred October 16, 1859].
The few men with him may have been the only following that he
had, but the damage had been done. Virginia was fighting mad.
What had been whispered about the abolitionists in secret was now
proclaimed from the housetops. John Brown was an abolitionist,

and all abolitionists were John Browns, so the youths, at least, reasoned. The words abolitionist and Yankee were for the most part synonymous terms; the former being hard to pronounce, the child usually employed the latter. Some of the young children did not know that a Yankee was a human being . . .[515]

It was just this kind of Northern abolitionist pressure on the South, and the inevitable accompanying charge of racism, that delayed emancipation in Dixie.[516] How?

Human nature being what it is, Newton's Third Law of Motion is applicable here: "For every action, there is an equal and opposite reaction." The harder the North pushed the South toward emancipation, the harder the South resisted. Not because she was against abolition—as we have discussed, the American abolition movement got its start in the South—but because 19th-Century Southerners, just like Southerners today, did not like being told what to do, how to do it, why they should do it, and when to do it.

What our Yankee biased history books do not teach is that from the 1700s on, nearly all Southerners desired, and expected, slavery to come to an end naturally. This is why, being a leisurely people, they felt no great urgency to hurry the process along. And this is why thousands of slave owners, like Nathan Bedford Forrest, emancipated their slaves even before Lincoln's War,[517] while others, like Robert E. Lee, liberated their family's servants before the Emancipation Proclamation was issued.[518] Why hold on, such Southerners reasoned, to something that was soon to disappear of its own accord across the U.S. as completely as the American Mastodon?

Jefferson Davis too knew that slavery's days were numbered. The Confederate chief executive understood that the secession of the Southern states would mean the demise of slavery, but he supported the creation of the Confederacy anyway, writing to his wife Varina in February 1861: "In any case [whether we are successful in establishing the Confederacy or not,] our slave property will eventually be lost."[519]

Even Lincoln was fully aware that slavery was soon to end, which is one of the many reasons we know that his War was not over slavery. In fact, according to a speech the Big Brother liberal gave at Columbus, Ohio, on September 16, 1859: "The *whole* country looked forward to the ultimate extinction of the institution [emphasis added]."[520] The "whole country" at that time, of course, included the South.

Why then did Dixie seem to "resist" abolition so intensely after the 1830s? Understanding the answer to this question is vital to an understanding of Southern culture, the Confederacy, and Lincoln's War.

At first the North acknowledged that it had instigated both slavery and the slave trade. And it fully accepted this fact as well—at least up until 1831, the year the loud, Radical Yankee abolitionist and busybody, William Lloyd Garrison, launched his antislavery gazette, *The Liberator*. Though, like Harriet Beecher Stowe, Garrison knew absolutely nothing about either the South or black servitude, he published articles in his paper condemning Southern slavery as a "crime" and Southern slave owners as "criminals." His columns brimmed with misinformation, disinformation, errors, and outright lies regarding the institution, all carefully calculated to whip the North into an anti-South frenzy.[521]

*The Liberator* did cause agitation. But not the kind that would weaken Southern slavery. Instead, Garrison and his paper helped strengthen it, becoming one of the many embers that helped ignite the "Civil War."[522]

This came chiefly through inciting a particularly horrific slave insurrection in Virginia: the notorious Nat Turner Rebellion of 1831,[523] in which some sixty whites (most of them abolitionists and non-slave owners) were butchered in their sleep. (Not even newborn babies were spared Turner's axes.)[524]

An unremorseful Turner and his racist madmen were all caught within a few weeks. Many of the mob, including their psychopathic leader, swung from the hangman's rope. But the bloody mayhem was all for naught. In fact, if Turner was trying to end slavery, he had done the worst thing possible: his "rebellion" not only did not advance the cause of African-Americans, it actually reversed it. For in its aftermath at least 100 blacks were killed,[525] horrified whites passed new exceptionally harsh slave codes, and abolitionist sentiment, once strong across the entire South, was considerably dampened for decades thereafter.[526]

This was a revolutionary change in attitude for white Southerners, who had for so long viewed their black servants as "family" and free blacks as fellow citizens of Dixie. Thus, while nearly every Southerner had once been an abolitionist,[527] after 1831 the idea of emancipation was considered "too dangerous," and blacks everywhere, bonded and free, now began to be viewed with suspicion.[528]

Between Garrison's increasingly vociferous attacks on Dixie and Turner's bloody killing spree, white Southerners had had enough. Now, instead of discussing abolition, they dug in their heels and built up a defensive wall of resentment and fear. No one, especially Yankees, would tell them what to do—particularly when they and their family's lives were at stake.[529]

*How* would the South end slavery? This was her decision. *When* would the South end slavery? It was her right to decide this for herself, as the U.S. Constitution clearly affirmed.[530] Unlike Lincoln, who believed that the Federal government should have the power to force states to adopt doctrines against their wishes, other Northerners were more constitutionally aware, recognizing the South's right of self-determination in this regard. One of them, Illinois Senator Stephen A. Douglas, wisely observed:

> The whole South is rallying to the support of the doctrine that if the people of a Territory want slavery they have a right to have it, and if they do not want it that no power on earth can force it upon them.[531]

State independence from the Federal government. This important states' right was what the conservative South wanted in the 19th Century, and it is what she still wants in the 21st Century.

The South's reaction to the North's constant meddling was particularly strong after Lincoln's dire 1861 predictions of coming Negro insurrections, anarchy, and widespread white deaths across Dixie. At that point Southern antislavery sentiment once again began to rapidly disintegrate, and the South, out of legitimate fear—as well as Southern pride and honor—understandably began to resist the idea of abolition.[532] For in the end, it was not the destruction of slavery that the South was against. She was against the premature, forced destruction of slavery, and that by a foreign power (the Northern states of the U.S.) that had been unmercifully dominating her for decades.[533]

The North no doubt expected the response it got from Dixie, which was part of its original intention to begin with: by constantly pressuring the South to abolish slavery prematurely, the North knew it would be met with stubborn resistance. This allowed Lincoln to paint the South as the "bad guy," which in turn gave him the excuse to later force the issue at the tip of a bayonet. (This only occurred, of course, when on January 1, 1863—the day he grudgingly issued the Final Emancipation Proclamation—it suddenly served his political agenda to underhandedly alter the character of the war from one to "preserve the Union" to one meant to "abolish slavery.")[534]

In a word, the ill will created by Northern abolitionists' indiscriminate accusations against Dixie made it impossible for Southerners to make any immediate movement toward abolition.[535]

Was the South being stubborn? Hardly. It merely expected to be treated with the same respect and dignity that the U.S. government normally accorded any foreign nation. Yet this was something the North seemed incapable of doing where slavery and her neighbor to the South were concerned. Along with the fact that less than 5 percent of Southerners were slave owners,[536] it is obvious then that the South's resistance to abolition was primarily psychological.

But there was an additional reason, one much more practical in nature.

Southerners understood that the abolition of slavery was not something that could be accomplished overnight. It was a complex procedure that had taken other countries years, decades, centuries, to complete, and it would take Dixie just as long, or longer. Time was needed to prepare, from designing laws and rules to regulate the process and readying 3.5 million former slaves for a life of freedom, to finding the capital to compensate former slave owners and establish housing and jobs for freedmen and women.

And so the South had a number of perfectly good reasons for postponing abolition, not one of them having to do with either so-called "Southern racism" or the absurd "slavery was the cornerstone of the Confederacy" theory.

Tragically, the Northern agenda called for the *immediate* destruction of Southern slavery, a contemptuous attitude that only bred further bad blood, stalled Southern abolition, and ultimately helped lead the two nations into war. Of this, the aggressive and violent Northern approach to foreign diplomacy, Mary Chesnut opined:

> We separated North from South because of incompatibility of temper. We are divorced because we have hated each other so. [537]

# ★ 9 ★

# JEFFERSON DAVIS

**WHAT YOU WERE TAUGHT:** Jefferson Davis was rightly called the "Sphinx of the Confederacy" because he was cold, inhumane, and aloof.

**THE TRUTH:** Davis was known as the "Sphinx" because, being a complex man, few fully understood him,[538] not because he was cold, inhumane and aloof. His often contradictory always intricate nature will be more fully revealed in the following entries.

**WHAT YOU WERE TAUGHT:** Davis was not a great man.

**THE TRUTH:** Though South-haters take particular pleasure in deprecating our Confederate president,[539] we of course take the opposite stance. And here is why.

Davis was a West Point graduate, a Mexican War hero, a faithful husband, an outstanding father, an eminent Mississippi senator, a bold defender of the Southern Cause, a talented author, and a fearless and knowledgeable protector of the Constitution.

Also an honest politician and a brave military man who was popular with his soldiers, Davis was an extraordinary leader of the Confederate nation during what was arguably America's most difficult period. In the eyes of the South these things alone make him a great man, and an immortal hero.

**WHAT YOU WERE TAUGHT:** Jefferson Davis was a traitor to the United States for accepting the presidency of a region that broke away from the Union.

**THE TRUTH:** We have seen, and proven, in Chapter 5 that secession was—and remains—a legal right as laid down in the Declaration of Independence (1776), the Articles of Confederation (1781), and the U.S. Constitution (1789). This being so, Davis was no traitor. Quite the opposite: he was an outstanding American patriot!

It was big government progressive Abraham Lincoln who betrayed his country by re-interpreting the Constitution to fit his own agenda (like another liberal, Barack Hussein Obama, who called the Constitution "an imperfect document,"[540] Lincoln once said that he did not like the Constitution as it was written),[541] then illegally invading the lawfully formed Confederate States of America in 1861 (and that without congressional approval).[542] This is why in the traditional South we consider Lincoln the true traitor to the United States.

**WHAT YOU WERE TAUGHT:** Davis could not hold a candle to the Great Emancipator Abraham Lincoln.

**THE TRUTH:** This, of course, is a highly subjective myth, one with which traditional Southerners wholeheartedly disagree. Some in the South (that is, scallywags) have gone as far as siding with the Yanks in granting Lincoln superior status as a war president. However, this too is debatable and, in our estimation, completely untenable.

Lincoln assured a Yankee victory in great part by subverting the Constitution,[543] engaging in political chicanery (such as rigging elections)[544] and countless war crimes (such as arresting and torturing Northern peace advocates,[545] allowing the theft, abuse, rape and murder of countless Southern civilians),[546] disregarding the Geneva Convention (by sanctioning total war on the South),[547] and psychologically and emotionally manipulating the Northern populace.[548]

Davis, on the other hand, helped guarantee Southern defeat by honoring the Confederate Constitution, avoiding political skullduggery, holding his troops to a high standard of behavior, observing the Geneva Convention, discouraging criminal activity among his soldiers, and being honest with the Southern people.[549]

Without regard to who won or lost the War, which one then was the superior war president? It is clear where we in the traditional South stand, but you the reader must judge for yourself.

As far as Lincoln being the "Great Emancipator," we will deal with this in more detail in the next chapter. Suffice it to say that we find this idea to be absurd in the extreme. For Lincoln was what we would today consider a white racist, a white supremacist, and a white separatist.[550] Furthermore, he did not legally or officially free a single American slave during his lifetime[551] (it was eight months after Lincoln's death, in December 1865, that the Thirteenth Amendment finally freed all American slaves).[552]

It was Davis who was the true Great Emancipator, which is why he is known as such by all enlightened Southerners. For it was Davis who began the official, *and* legal, emancipation of slaves over a year earlier, on November 7, 1864,[553] with the recruitment of Southern blacks into the Confederate military.[554]

**WHAT YOU WERE TAUGHT:** Davis was a fault-ridden man with few if any positive traits.

**THE TRUTH:** Like all of us Davis had his weaknesses. But his many wonderful qualities far outweighed them.[555] We would contrast Davis with Lincoln in this area, with Lincoln having more negative characteristics than positive.

But Lincoln's defects are something that pro-North writers and anti-South propagandists refuse to concede. Instead he has been apotheosized, surrounded by an impossibly absurd mythology, and placed in the pantheon of political gods and goddesses where we mere mortals cannot touch him. It is doubtful that even Lincoln himself would approve of what his rabid devotees have done to him. After all, this was a man who, when first approached with the idea of running for the highest office in the land, said:

> I must, in candor, say I do not think myself fit for the Presidency.
> . . .[556] Just think of such a sucker as me as President.[557]

The difference between South and North here is that we are not afraid to acknowledge the faults of our 19th-Century leaders. We readily admit, for example, that to some, particularly to strangers, Davis at times appeared slow and humorless, possessed an overly sensitive degree of dignity and pride, and lacked a systematic approach to handling the War. Frail of health—he suffered from nervousness, neuralgia, and what seems to have been an infection of Herpes II complex in his left eye—making him tense and petulant in social and business situations.[558]

Tightly wound, reserved, and always old-fashioned, Davis struggled to focus on important details, and instead, seemingly unaware of the art of delegation, spread his energies over a wide range of areas, many of which should have been handled by his cabinet, staff, and military officers.[559]

Also to the detriment of the South, he had argumentative relationships with many of his generals (for example, P. G. T. Beauregard and Joseph E. Johnston), and was prone to cronyism: placing friends in positions of power for which they were often not qualified (for example, John Bell Hood, Lucius B. Northrop, John C. Pemberton, and Braxton Bragg),[560] a phenomenon that modern-day Dr. Laurence J. Peter has called "The Peter Principle."[561] To make matters worse, Davis often disregarded his best officers, such as the brilliant General Nathan Bedford Forrest—who, without question, should have been promoted to full general and given greater command.[562]

Possessed of a strongly legalistic and some would say inflexible mind, Davis was not always well-suited to being commander-in-chief, as he had no real background in dealing with the intricacies of running an army in the field, as George W. Randolph once said of the Confederate leader.[563] But how many presidents enter office with this type of experience? In Davis' defense, very few.[564] Lincoln lacked this kind of background completely.[565]

The Rebel chieftain also had little flair for writing memorable speeches, and his dearth of charisma sometimes made it difficult for him whip up enthusiasm for his causes. Unable to relax and overly sensitive to criticism, Davis' own secretary of war, James A. Seddon, called his law-obsessed boss a maddeningly obstreperous man, and often almost impossible to get a long with—an obviously highly subjective view.[566]

Despite his few "difficult" traits, Davis was a superlative individual, and in many ways—particularly in defending the Confederate Cause—was the ideal choice to lead the Southern states, as our next entry illustrates.

**WHAT YOU WERE TAUGHT:** Compared to Lincoln, Davis was a fanatical racist.

**THE TRUTH:** It is true that Davis was somewhat encumbered with the white racism of his day. But we beg to differ when it comes to comparing him with Lincoln in this regard.

While Lincoln was blocking emancipation, black enlistment, and black civil rights, and working day and night on his colonization plan to deport all blacks out of the U.S., Davis was busy trying to figure out a way to end Southern slavery, enlist blacks, initiate black civil rights, and incorporate blacks into mainstream American society.

In the meantime, during the War Davis and his wife Varina (Howell) adopted a young black boy, Jim Limber, who they raised as their own in the Confederate White House.[567] The Davises were widely known as a family who always treated their black servants equitably and with the greatest respect, as part of their family in fact.[568] Not surprisingly, President Davis' first Confederate states marshal was a black man.[569] Lincoln never appointed a black man to any position, let alone U.S. states marshal, and unquestionably he would have never adopted a black child.

After Lee's surrender, during the Davis family's escape southward, their coachman was a "faithful" free African-American.[570] Later, after the War, the one-time Southern leader and his wife sold their plantation, Brierfield, to a former slave.[571] Davis even spoke once of a time when he led a unit of "negroes against a lawless body of armed white men . . .,"[572] something we can be sure that white separatist Lincoln never did.

**WHAT YOU WERE TAUGHT:** It was to the South's benefit that Davis was arrested on May 10, 1865, for his imprisonment finally killed off the spirit of rebellion in Dixie. The North had three times the manpower and three times the supplies, and could have continued the War forever.

**THE TRUTH:** According to none other than Yankee General Ulysses S. Grant, Lincoln's claim that "the contest could have been continued indefinitely"[573] is false. In his 1885 *Memoirs* Grant revealed that if Confederate General Nathan Bedford Forrest's protraction strategy (endorsed by numerous Rebel officers, including General Joseph E. Johnston) had been adopted by the South,[574] the Confederacy would have won the War within one year.[575] (Forrest's plan called for prolonging the conflict—thus exhausting the North—by closing down the Yankees' major supply routes, the Mississippi and Tennessee Rivers).[576] Wrote Grant:

> I think that [this] . . . policy was the best one that could have been pursued by the whole South—protract the war, which was all that was necessary to enable them to gain recognition in the end. The North was already growing weary . . .[577] Anything that could have prolonged the war a year beyond the time that it did finally close, would probably have exhausted the North to such an extent that they might then have abandoned the contest and agreed to separation.[578]

It is clear now why the ingenious Davis wanted to continue the War, even after Lee's "surrender."[579]

**WHAT YOU WERE TAUGHT:** Davis was never brought to trial after the War because he was too sickly and cowardly. This is unfortunate, as he should have been punished for his treasonous crimes against the U.S.

**THE TRUTH:** At the time, Davis was more than healthy and courageous enough to be tried.[580] And in fact, he repeatedly requested a trial. What *is* unfortunate is that he was repeatedly turned down. The U.S. government had asked three different prosecuting attorneys to try him, but all three refused, deeming the case thoroughly unwinnable.[581] Why?

A public trial would have allowed the South's brilliant legal minds, including Davis', to prove the legality of secession *and* expose what I call the Great Yankee Coverup; that is, the concealment of the many illegalities of Lincoln's War. As one of the North's own lawyers stated:

> Gentleman, the Supreme Court of the United States will have to acquit that man under the Constitution when it will be proven to the world that the North waged an unconstitutional warfare against the South.[582]

No wonder that before Davis was captured trying to reorganize his armies,

President Lincoln and General Grant had ardently "wished and hoped" that he would escape unnoticed into the Southern wilderness.[583]

The reality is that it was not Davis who committed treason against the U.S. It was Lincoln. And it was Lincoln who, had he lived, should have been tried.

**WHAT YOU WERE TAUGHT:** The South lost the Civil War, a fact which must be laid at the feet of Jefferson Davis, proving that he was wholly unfit to be the Confederate president.

**THE TRUTH:** Davis possessed a background, along with many sterling traits, that made him well-qualified for the Confederacy's highest office, which is precisely why most of his fellow Southerners selected him for the job.[584]

Born in Kentucky, within one-hundred miles of Lincoln, early on Davis' father Samuel moved the family to the conservative state of Mississippi, where the future Rebel president was raised. Like Confederate Secretary of War John C. Breckinridge and Confederate General Albert Sidney Johnston, Davis attended Transylvania University, at Lexington, Kentucky. Later, he transferred to West Point and served as an officer in the Mexican War.[585]

Almost from the beginning politics was in his blood, and the thin six-foot Southern aristocrat soon found himself serving as a Mississippi senator, then as secretary of war under U.S. President Franklin Pierce. With commanding presence Davis ably helped guide the Pierce administration (1853-1857), and he was, and still is, considered one of the nation's top secretaries of war.[586]

One man who worked under Secretary of War Davis had this to say about his boss:

> He was a kind, social man very considerate and pleasant to serve under. I never heard a complaint from one of the clerks. Socially, he was a most charming man, officially, very pleasant. He was a warm friend . . . . I knew him many years, and as a man I found him a very good friend.[587]

President Davis even got high marks from many of his former Northern enemies. One of them, Yankee General Montgomery C. Meigs, spoke of Davis' time as war secretary under Pierce this way:

> Mr. Davis was a most courteous and amiable man in those days, and I found intercourse with him very agreeable. He was a man, too, of marked ability, and I quite looked up to him and regarded him as one of the great men of the time.[588]

At the Montgomery (Alabama) Convention on February 4, 1861, Davis was unanimously chosen Provisional President of the Confederate States of America, a position he had not sought, but which he accepted as his civic duty.[589] As the chief executive of the Confederacy, Davis' best attributes came into play from the very beginning. A man of true devotion, faithfulness, and honor, he held the Confederate Cause in highest esteem, and would let nothing tarnish its righteousness or glory. His tireless work ethic meant that his already delicate health often suffered. But he pushed on, helping to create both a political revolution and an eternal Southern legacy dedicated to self-determination.[590]

His extreme religiosity sustained President Davis through many difficult times, strengthening his own morale and that of the Southern people. His sense of morality and courage were second to none, which is why he was so willing to make nearly any sacrifice for the Southern Cause, regardless of opposition. And while he was totally devoted to the Confederate Constitution, unlike the more radical fire-eaters in his party, he understood that war sometimes required compromise, particularly regarding civil rights (though here he never sank to Lincoln's level).[591]

Many of Davis' negative characteristics, while sometimes hampering the Southern Cause, also helped it. At the drop of a hat, for example, his legalistic mind could elucidate, in minute detail, the constitutional basis for secession, elucidations that were carefully laid out in his brilliant two-volume defense of the Confederacy, *The Rise and Fall of the Confederate Government*.[592] This awe-inspiring work, along with his *Short History of the Confederate States* (both which should be required reading in every American high school), are still avidly studied by both traditional Southerners and lovers of liberty around the world.

For so ably serving the U.S.A. and the C.S.A. both militarily and politically, for diligently leading and holding together the Confederacy for four long thankless years, for unflinchingly adhering to the South's beloved Jeffersonian ideals, for being willing to carry on the fight after Appomattox, for suffering humiliation in a Yankee prison for several years in order to preserve the honor of the South,[593] for leaving the world the greatest literary defense of the Confederacy, for refusing to request an official "pardon" from the U.S. government, for wanting to end slavery before Lincoln did, for all these things and more, the regal and defiant Jefferson Davis must be counted one of history's most unique and accomplished individuals, one of America's greatest men, and certainly the Confederacy's most articulate and passionate symbol.

We in the South will always applaud, praise, admire, celebrate, toast, acknowledge, commend, appreciate, and honor him.

# ★ 10 ★

# ABRAHAM LINCOLN

**WHAT YOU WERE TAUGHT:** Lincoln was an honorable, law-abiding, trustworthy man who would never even lie, let alone commit a crime. This is why, after all, he's called "Honest Abe."

**THE TRUTH:** Lincoln's nickname "Honest Abe" was bestowed on him as a sarcastic comment on his perfidious behavior, for his dishonest dealings with the American people, not for his alleged "honesty."[594] Thus it would be far more appropriate to call America's sixteenth president "Dishonest Abe," for he not only lied repeatedly, but he committed a truly dazzling number of well chronicled constitutional, civil, political, ethical, social, religious, spiritual, and moral felonies and misdemeanors.

A highly abbreviated list of Lincoln's atrocities includes the following:

- Completely subverting (and perverting) the Constitution.[595]
- Arresting and deporting Yankee anti-war advocates, like Ohio congressman Clement Laird Vallandigham who, though a civilian, was illegally tried by a military court.[596]
- Arbitrarily arresting and trying (by military commission) civilian draft resistors and others suspected of "disloyalty."[597]
- Seizing rail and telegraph lines leading to the capital.[598]
- Suppressing and shutting down over 300 hundred pro-peace Northern newspapers, and arresting their owners.[599]
- Censoring telegraph communications.[600]
- Torturing both Northern soldiers (accused of desertion) and Northern citizens (accused of espousing anti-war sentiment); the preferred methods were "violent cold water torture" and being suspended by handcuffed wrists.[601]
- Illegally suspending the writ of *habeas corpus* across the entire U.S., and for the first time in U.S. history.[602]
- Prohibiting the emancipation of slaves by his cabinet members and Union

military officers, such as General John. C. Frémont,[603] General David
Hunter,[604] John W. Phelps,[605] Jim Lane,[606] and General Simon
Cameron[607] (which proves once and for all, if nothing else does, that
Lincoln did not wage war against the South over slavery).[608]

• Unlawfully ordering a naval blockade of Southern ports (unlawful because
Lincoln never recognized the Confederacy as a separate nation and war
had not yet been declared).[609]

• Declaring all medicines contraband of war (which helped kill countless
thousands of Southerners, both soldiers and civilians, not to mention
thousands of Yankee soldiers held in Confederate prisons).[610]

• Proclaiming Confederate privateersmen "pirates," subject to the death
penalty[611] (privateering, that is, working on an armed privately-owned
vessel, is a legal profession).[612]

• Intimidating judges.[613]

• Closing the post office in an effort to prevent anti-Lincoln, anti-war mail from
being sent or delivered.[614]

• Forcing all Federal employees to contribute 5 percent of their annual income
to his 1864 re-election campaign.[615]

• Refusing to exchange prisoners (which aided in the deaths of thousands of
soldiers, both Confederate and Federal).[616]

• Defying the Supreme Court.[617]

• Instituting the largest number of military drafts in U.S. history.[618]

• Fabricating heretofore unknown offices, such as "military governor," in
conquered Southern states.[619]

• Shutting down the governments of entire Northern states and arresting
members of their state legislatures (usually for suspicion of advocating
peace with the South); one of the more notable of these was the state
of Maryland, which originally had hoped to join the Confederacy.[620]

• Inaugurating America's first federal monetary monopoly.[621]

• Imprisoning some 38,000 to 50,000 Northern civilians (men, women, and
children),[622] without trial, some for as long as four years.[623]

• Incarcerating civilians, like Rebel Vice President Alexander H. Stephens, in
military prisons.[624]

• Levying the first personal income tax, launching what would later become the
Internal Revenue Service (IRS).[625]

• Preventing governmental debate over secession.[626]

• Ordering the first and only mass execution (and that of his own citizens) by
a president in U.S. history.[627]

• Changing the meaning of the "United States" from plural to singular.[628]

• Establishing provisional courts in conquered Southern states (this was illegal

because Dixie's own civilian courts remained open during the War).[629]
- Illegally creating the state of West Virginia from the state of Virginia (Lincoln encouraged the western area of Virginia to secede while he was at war with the South because she had seceded!).[630]
- Rigging Northern elections to skew the outcome in his favor,[631] using such devices as "bayonet votes" (stationing armed Union soldiers at the polls to intimidate voters) and "fictitious states" (inventing states, as mentioned, like West Virginia, in order to accrue more electoral votes).[632]
- Bribing voters, soldiers, and fellow politicians to vote for his party.[633]

Lincoln even signed an order for the arrest of the Supreme Court's Chief Justice Roger B. Taney, simply because Taney had correctly told him that suspending *habeas corpus* was unconstitutional and therefore illegal.[634]

Lincoln later tried to justify his staggering criminal activities with the following bizarre declaration, sounding more like a delusional demented dictator than a U.S. president:

> I felt that measures otherwise unconstitutional might become lawful by becoming indispensable to the preservation of the Constitution through the preservation of the nation. Right or wrong, I assumed this ground and I now avow it.[635]

Believing that he was "preserving" the Constitution when in fact he was destroying it, reveals the true depth of Lincoln's twisted thinking.

It was for such crimes and indecencies that legal and constitutional scholars now maintain that the Lincoln administration was the worst period for civil liberties up until then, ranking it, in fact, as one of the worst in all of American history.[636]

**WHAT YOU WERE TAUGHT:** Lincoln was a devout Bible-believing Christian.

**THE TRUTH:** From his earliest days Lincoln was an avowed atheist, skeptic, "infidel," and agnostic, who declared the Bible a fairy tale and rejected the divinity of Christ, even calling him a "bastard." Lincoln never attended church, never belonged to any religion, scoffed at Christian preachers, and once wrote "a little book" proving that the Bible is not the word of God and Jesus is not the Son of God. Lincoln's closest friends and political associates, even his wife Mary, all later testified to the president's atheism and apathy toward, and even hatred of, religion—particularly Christianity.[637]

**WHAT YOU WERE TAUGHT:** Lincoln was a Republican, and therefore a conservative, right-wing politician.

**THE TRUTH:** It is true that Lincoln was a Republican. What is not true is that he was a conservative, for the Republicans of the mid 19th Century had the same platform as the Democrats of today, while the Democrats of the mid 19th Century had the same platform as the Republicans today.[638] Thus Lincoln was what we would now refer to as a big government liberal Democrat (with socialist leanings), while Jefferson Davis was what we would now call a small government conservative Republican (with libertarian leanings).

The Republicans of Lincoln's day indeed called themselves "liberals,"[639] and the Democrats of that period referred to themselves as "conservatives."[640] One could say then that Lincoln was the 19th-Century's Franklin Delano Roosevelt, Barney Frank, or Barack Hussein Obama, while Jefferson Davis was the 19th-Century's Ronald Reagan, Ron Paul, or Sarah Palin.

In short, while Lincoln was indeed a Republican, it is important to bear in mind that the Republicans (mainly Northerners) of that time period were identical to today's liberal Democrats (and similar to today's socialists), while Lincoln's opposition, the Democrats (mainly Southerners), were identical to today's conservative Republicans (and similar to today's libertarians and Tea Partyists).[641]

The confusion resulting from the 19th-Century party platform reversal has caused a number of modern day Republicans, conservatives, independents, and even libertarians—all who should know better—to reverently cite Lincoln in an attempt to ally themselves with his name.

In reality the only people Lincoln would have anything in common with today are Democrats, liberals, socialists, Marxists, dictators, kings, monarchists, totalitarians, the politically correct, big government advocates, Big Brother proponents, the East and West coast elite, racial separatists, atheists, and those who dislike the Constitution—in particular the First, Second, Ninth, and Tenth Amendments.

**WHAT YOU WERE TAUGHT:** Lincoln espoused democratic ideals; that is, political and social equality for all people.

**THE TRUTH:** Lincoln never once called for equal rights for all American citizens. To the contrary, as he said in a speech on October 13, 1858:

> I have no purpose to introduce political and social equality between the white and black races. There is a physical difference between the two, which, in my judgement, will probably forever forbid their living together upon the footing of perfect equality, and, inasmuch as it becomes a necessity that there must be a difference,

> I . . . am in favor of the race to which I belong having the superior position. I have never said anything to the contrary . . .[642]

Eleven months later, in September 1859, just a year before he was elected president, Lincoln reemphasized his feelings on the matter:

> Negro equality. Fudge! How long in the Government of a God great enough to make and maintain this universe, shall there continue to be knaves to vend and fools to gulp, so low a piece of demagoguism as this?[643]

**WHAT YOU WERE TAUGHT:** As president of the United States Lincoln believed that he was a servant of the people.

**THE TRUTH:** If Lincoln himself ever believed this particular Yankee myth, he certainly never acted like it. His behavior was far more similar to a Roman emperor, a ruthless imperial tyrant who viewed the American people as his docile and malleable subjects, a mass of nameless faceless automatons who existed merely to pay their taxes, flatter his ego, keep him in power, and help fulfill his political agenda. (How different Lincoln's attitude was from Southerners like Thomas Jefferson, who believed in the inherent intelligence and wisdom of the common man and woman. "[It is] the people, to whom all authority belongs," our third president once wisely declared.)[644]

In order to achieve his goal of installing big government in Washington and the northernization of the South, Lincoln quite consciously assumed the role of a consolidating dictator, the head of Henry Clay's American System (what we now call "crony capitalism"). This was, after all, part of the president's dream from the very beginning: just as many liberals do today, Lincoln rejected both the natural rights principles of the Declaration of Independence and the idea of state sovereignty found in the U.S. Constitution.

Believing instead in the supremacy of an all-powerful central government, he sought to totally control the economic and human resources of the American people, along with the nation's banking system and military establishment.[645] Because of this, despots, totalitarians, and dictators, whose chief aim is the total control of nations, came to idolize the socialist-styled president.

One of these, arch socialist Adolf Hitler, head of the National Socialist German Workers Party, was fond of citing Lincoln as a shining example of how to destroy states' rights. In his book *Mein Kampf* ("My Struggle"), Hitler not only denies the fact that the U.S.A. was originally a confederacy,[646] he also repeats Lincoln's fantasy that a union always precedes (and thus creates) its states, and that therefore there is no such thing as state sovereignty.

In 1926 here is how the Führer presented Lincoln's theory: the question is, should Germany be turned into a Confederacy or a Union, and just what is a Confederacy? It is a voluntary union of free and independent states. By this definition, today there are no true confederacies anywhere in the world, Hitler asserted. The least like a confederacy is the United States of America, for her individual states do not have, could not have, and never had, any sovereignty. Why? Because, as he concluded, it was the Union that created the individual states, not vice versa.[647]

In short, Hitler was saying, the idea of "sovereign states" has never existed in America, the same view that Lincoln held from the day he first walked into the Oval House until the day he lost his life at Ford's Theater.

From this example alone there can be little question that Hitler used Lincoln's despotic, unhistorical, inaccurate, and self-serving ideas to justify demolishing states' rights as he rampaged his way across Europe.[648]

The publicly proclaimed white racist who was adored by Adolf Hitler is now on our penny, five-dollar bill, the Illinois license plate, and sacred Mount Rushmore. Is this right? Traditional Southerners think not.

**WHAT YOU WERE TAUGHT:** Lincoln was a red-blooded American capitalist.

**THE TRUTH:** If Lincoln was truly a capitalist we must wonder why so many socialists (like Adolf Hitler) and Marxists (like chief Lincoln scholar Eric Foner)[649] have admired and even worshiped him over the years; or why the Forty-Eighters, an organization made up of progressive European socialists, eagerly supported "Honest Abe's" run for president in 1860.[650]

While Lincoln was not officially a socialist, many of his policies were socialistic. This is precisely why he was so revered by men like Karl Marx—a truly worldwide leftist veneration that Lincoln apologists have never acknowledged.[651] In late November 1864, for example, Karl, the man who literally gave his name to Marxism, wrote Lincoln a letter congratulating him on his "re-election by a large majority." The missive included Marx's sincere hope that Lincoln would "lead his country through the matchless struggle for the rescue of an enchained race and the reconstruction of a social world."[652]

As one who was an economic protectionist, mercantilist, and interventionist who supported the ideas of corporate welfare and a nationalized banking system,[653] as the one who instigated personal income tax and launched what would become the Internal Revenue Service,[654] as one who disliked free trade and preferred that the state own and control the wealth, and as the individual who sought the permanent installation of an all-powerful central government and the destruction of states' rights so that he could dominate the

South economically,[655] it would be difficult, if not impossible to call liberal Lincoln a true capitalist.    It would be more accurate to call him an anticapitalistic, dictatorial-like leader with socialistic progressive tendencies.

**WHAT YOU WERE TAUGHT:** Lincoln was America's greatest abolitionist.
**THE TRUTH:** Far from being an abolitionist Lincoln actually detested the group as a whole,[656] constantly tried to distance himself from it, and always spoke of abolitionists in the negative.[657] Indeed, he considered the very concept of abolition itself a pernicious influence, which is why he often made public comments on how he loathed and distrusted abolitionists and considered its members a public nuisance.[658]    Real abolitionists like Massachusetts-born Lysander Spooner, of course, detested and suspected him in return.[659]

Once when he was asked if he minded having abolitionists in his political party, Lincoln snapped back: "As long as I'm not tarred with the abolitionist brush."[660] For the rest of his life, when speaking of abolitionists, he always referred to them with barely disguised revulsion, and as a group quite distinct and separate from himself.

As early as 1837, while Lincoln was still a young member of his state's legislature, he made it a practice to send anti-abolition statements to the U.S. House of Representatives, as he did on March 3 under the title "Protest in the Illinois Legislature on the Subject of Slavery." Here, the obviously irritated young lawyer wrote that when it came to slavery, "the promulgation of abolition doctrines tends rather to increase than abate its evils."[661] His views on this topic never changed.

Antislavery advocate William H. Herndon, Lincoln's law partner and later his biographer, labored throughout his entire friendship with Lincoln trying to convert him to abolitionism.   But he would not be moved.   This is because the U.S. president equated abolitionism with slavery itself, seeing both as two dangerous sides of the same coin.[662] Eradicating slavery, Lincoln warned once, will produce "a greater evil" than slavery, an evil that is a hazard "even to the cause of human liberty itself."[663]    No other American ever held more extreme anti-abolitionist views than these.

Naturally Lincoln was heartily despised by abolitionists, who, from the very first day of his presidency, were extremely cautious of him.   Why? Because he had not yet called for the immediate end of slavery.   Even in the final months of 1862, two years into his first term, antislavery forces continued to express their unhappiness with Lincoln over his reluctance, even his refusal, to emancipate the nation's slaves.[664] It was just such efforts to hinder abolition that earned him the popular nickname the "tortoise President."[665]

In the end, Lincoln hoped, abolitionists would be condemned, cursed, and hated; or as he put it, "receive their just execration . . ."[666] Our sixteenth president was no abolitionist.

**WHAT YOU WERE TAUGHT:** Lincoln was a proponent of making blacks citizens of the U.S.

**THE TRUTH:** Throughout his political career Illinoisan Lincoln was repeatedly challenged as to whether he was in favor of "negro citizenship," and he repeatedly gave the same answer, as he did at Charleston, Illinois, on September 18, 1858:

> . . . very frankly . . . I am not in favor of Negro citizenship. . . . Now, my opinion is that the different States have the power to make a negro a citizen, under the constitution of the United States, if they choose. . . . If the State of Illinois had that power, I should be against the exercise of it. That is all I have to say about it.[667]

To his last days Lincoln continued to hesitate to give blacks full civil rights, including voting rights and citizenship. Even his postwar "Reconstruction" plans for the nation did not include complete black enfranchisement.[668]

To put a period on this myth once and for all, we have the observable fact that he never once publicly thanked blacks, Northern or Southern, for the countless sacrifices they made for his War, or for the many contributions they had made to American society.[669]

**WHAT YOU WERE TAUGHT:** Lincoln was a warm, open, soulful, sociable, sophisticated individual who was loved by everyone.

**THE TRUTH:** According to many eyewitnesses, Lincoln had no close friends, was mistrusted by his cabinet, had lifelong strained relations with his wife Mary (Todd) Lincoln, and was an intensely private loner who was awkward in social situations.

Constantly struggling with severe depression and perhaps the genetic disorder Marfan Syndrome,[670] Lincoln was uncouth by almost any standard: not only were his clothes tattered and ill-fitting, he was prone to telling obscene jokes at parties (even in front of delicate Victorian ladies), much to the horror of everyone present.[671]

A short list of Lincoln's traits as recorded by his friends, associates, and other observers of the time gives us a better idea of how he was perceived during his lifetime. Lincoln was said to be cruel and bestial,[672] unfeeling and insensitive,[673] churlish, selfish, and curmudgeonly,[674] superficial and materialistic,[675] socially inept,[676] bereft of a sense of propriety,[677] crude and unrefined,[678] unpleasant company,[679] a crafty and dishonest criminal,[680] demagogic,[681] and coarse and unsophisticated.[682]

In 1863, before the U.S. Congress, Yankee Senator Willard Saulsbury of Delaware stood up and, insinuating that the president was an "enemy of the country," boldly spoke the following:

> Thus has it been with Mr. Lincoln—a weak and imbecile man; the weakest man that I ever knew in a high place; for I have seen him and conversed with him, and I say here, in my place in the Senate of the United States, that I never did see or converse with so weak and imbecile a man as Abraham Lincoln, President of the United States. . . . if I wanted to paint a tyrant, if I wanted to paint a despot, a man perfectly regardless of every constitutional right of the people, who's sworn servant, not ruler, he is, I would paint the hideous form of Abraham Lincoln.[683]

Famed Yankee abolitionist William Lloyd Garrison said of him: he may be a giant in height, but he is a midget in intellect.[684] A number of Lincoln's military officers were ill-disposed toward him as well. George B. McClellan had this to say about his commander-in-chief:

> The president is nothing more than a well meaning baboon. He is the original gorilla. What a specimen to be at the head of our affairs now![685]

Southerners were, of course, even less kind. The Charleston *Mercury*, for example, perfectly captured the Southern view of Lincoln in 1860:

> A horrid looking wretch he is, sooty and scoundrelly in aspect, a cross between the nutmeg dealer, the horse swapper, and the night man, a creature 'fit evidently for petty treason, small strategems and all sorts of spoils.' He is a lank-sided Yankee of the uncomeliest visage, and of the dirtiest complexion. . . . It is humiliating, if not disgusting, to see a party in this country putting forward a man for the presidential chair, once occupied by [the likes of] Washington and Jefferson, whose only achievements have been that he split a few hundred rails in his early life, and at a later period vilified the armies of his country while fighting her battles on foreign soil.[686]

Still, most of Lincoln's worst detractors were Yankees, many of them abolitionists. Among them were: Richard H. Dana, Benjamin F. Wade, Thaddeus Stevens, John C. Frémont, David Hunter, John W. Phelps, Frederick

Douglass, Horace Greeley, Theodore Tilton, Wendell Phillips, George B. Cheever, Henry Ward Beecher, William H. Seward, Edwin M. Stanton, Salmon P. Chase, Hannibal Hamlin, Charles Sumner, Lyman Trumbull, and Henry Winter Davis, to name but a few.[687]

Lincoln considered most of these men his friends. Yet all turned out to be some of his worst and most vociferous critics; all denounced him at every opportunity;[688] all made life very arduous for the anti-abolitionist president they frequently referred to as "that damned idiot in the White House."[689]

**WHAT YOU WERE TAUGHT:** Lincoln and the Northern populace loved the Jewish people while Davis and the Southern populace were anti-Semitic.

**THE TRUTH:** The Confederacy's 12,000 loyal Jewish soldiers would be quite surprised to hear that their nation disliked them,[690] as would the Rebel army's twenty Jewish staff officers.[691] There was also Colonel Abraham Myers, a noted Jewish Confederate and West Point graduate after whom Fort Myers, Florida, was named.[692]

Another individual who would have laughed at this statement was Judah Benjamin, a brilliant and enterprising Jew known as the "brains of the Confederacy," handpicked by Davis to be his first attorney general.[693] The famous and well respected Benjamin, who went on to serve as the C.S.A.'s second secretary of war and her third secretary of state, was once referred to by Davis as the most amazing politician he had ever met.[694]

After subduing New Orleans, Yankee officer Benjamin F. Butler said that Southern Jews were the most enthusiastic supporters of the Confederacy, and that they all should be as severely punished as "that Jew Benjamin."[695] No signs of Jewish hatred in the Confederacy here.

Whatever anti-Semitism existed in 19th-Century America was to be found mainly in the North,[696] and most prominently among Lincoln and his military staff, as the following example reveals.

Based on numerous complaints about "illicit trade" among Jews in the Western theater of operations, on December 17, 1862, Yankee General Ulysses S. Grant issued his ill-famed General Order No. 11.[697] It read:

> The Jews, as a class violating every regulation of trade established by the Treasury Department and also department orders, are hereby expelled from the department within twenty-four hours from the receipt of this order. Post commanders will see that all of this class of people be furnished passes and required to leave, and any one returning after such notification will be arrested and held in confinement until an opportunity occurs of sending them out as prisoners, unless furnished with permit from headquarters. No

passes will be given these people to visit headquarters for the purpose of making personal application for trade permits. By order of Maj. Gen. U. S. Grant.[698]

This was no insignificant military order. When Grant says, "All of this class of people," he meant exactly that. *All* Southern Jewish men, women, and children, were to vacate large areas of the South occupied at the time by Union soldiers—and within just one day. The heartless decree applied not only to transient Jewish peddlers, but to everyday law-abiding Confederate Jewish townspeople, living in homes they and their Southern ancestors had inhabited for generations.[699] In essence, it turned every Southern Jew into a criminal.

Grant's order would be truly shocking were it not for the already well-known anti-Semitism of a great many of the Northern people.[700] This is why, for the first year of the War, Lincoln (and the U.S. Congress) prohibited Jews from serving as army and navy chaplains;[701] it is why August Belmont, the American agent for the British Rothschilds (a family of distinguished Jewish investors and bankers), was unfairly accused of aiding and abetting the Confederacy;[702] it is why Grant referred to Jews as "an intolerable nuisance"; and it is why he once ordered Yankee railroad conductors to prevent Jews from traveling south of Jackson, Mississippi.[703]

Though Grant's General Order No. 11 understandably offended thousands of Jewish soldiers and citizens across both the North and the South, the ban remained in effect until January 3, 1863, when Jewish Kentuckian Caesar J. Kaskel went directly to Lincoln to protest it. The president's general-in-chief, Henry W. Halleck, revoked Grant's order the next day, then, a few weeks later (on January 21),[704] he sent Grant the following feeble note explaining Lincoln's actions:

> It may be proper to give you some explanation of the revocation of your order expelling all Jews from your department. The President has no objection to your expelling traitors and Jew peddlers, which, I suppose, was the object of your order; but, as it in terms proscribed an entire religious class, some of whom are fighting in our ranks, the President deemed it necessary to revoke it.[705]

Lincoln definitely had no love for "Jew peddlers."

We wonder today how many displaced innocent Jewish families lost everything in this forced expulsion from their homes, or how long Lincoln would have allowed Grant's ban to stand had Kaskel not paid a visit to the White House.

The order certainly raised no eyebrows among Lincoln's cabinet or party members. Congressman Elihu B. Washburne of Illinois expressed approval of Grant's order to Lincoln himself. Afterward he paid a visit to Halleck, who told Representative Washburne that if Grant had only inserted the word "peddler" after the word "Jew," it would have been "all right," and that "no exception would have been taken" by anyone, including Lincoln.[706]

**WHAT YOU WERE TAUGHT:** Lincoln's Gettysburg Address is rightly considered one of the most honest, historically accurate, and beautiful speeches ever given by a U.S. president.
**THE TRUTH:** Lincoln's most celebrated address, delivered November 19, 1863, at the dedication of the cemetery at Gettysburg, Pennsylvania, was meant to promote his overriding message that the South, by seceding, threatened to obliterate the U.S. government. Even though the South had no such intentions—and, of course, it never came close to occurring—the mendacious allure of his words at Gettysburg has brainwashed six generations of Americans against the South.

To the citizens of Dixie, and to all respecters of the truth, the Gettysburg Address must go down in history as one of the most faithless, cynical, erroneous, and cruelly ironic speeches ever uttered, for in it Lincoln promises to uphold the Constitution, when in fact he did the opposite. He blames the South for the War, when it was a conflict that he not only wanted but that he also wickedly instigated. Finally, he praises America's true political heritage. Yet two years later, on April 9, 1865, at Appomattox,[707] he overturned it, then caused it to "perish from the earth." What was that political heritage? It was our original Jeffersonian Confederate Republic, a constitutional government "of the people, by the people, for the people."[708]

Here is what Maryland journalist H. L. Mencken had to say about Lincoln's most famous declamation: the Gettysburg Address is understandably celebrated for its poetry, beauty, and eloquence. But this is all that can be said for it. In truth, it is a nonsensical piece of bombast. If we approach it objectively, Lincoln is saying that the Union soldiers who were blown to pieces at the Pennsylvania town in early July 1863, gave up their lives so that "government of the people, by the people, for the people, shall not perish from the earth." Actually, Mencken goes on to say, nothing could be further from the truth. Lincoln's armies fought *against* free government, while the Southern Rebels fought *for* it, for the right of the people to determine their own destinies.[709]

British journalist Alistair Cooke concurred, calling Lincoln's Gettysburg Address a classic work of oratory of highly questionable reasoning.[710] As a Southern historian, I agree as well, but I will be more direct. The Gettysburg Address is a malevolent fiction, written by an incorrigible criminal, created for the sole purpose of justifying an unjustifiable war.

Despite the obvious anti-South political propagandizing at the root of this speech, incredibly, it continues to be lauded by thousands of pro-North scholars, authors, and academicians, with hundreds of books being entirely and worshipfully devoted to it.[711] Astounding. And here is the reason we in the traditional South do not trust pro-North books: at their best they are subjective and biased, at their worst they are vindictive and historically inaccurate. Yet it is from these very types of Yankee-slanted works that our children are being taught American history today.

**WHAT YOU WERE TAUGHT:** The public response to Lincoln's Gettysburg Address was overwhelmingly positive, particularly during the speech itself, at which time it was received with rapt attention, constant cheers, tear swollen eyes, and thunderous applause.

**THE TRUTH:** Contrary to this silly Northern myth, Lincoln's own words tell quite a different story. According to his friend Ward Hill Lamon, after the speech Lincoln said to him:

> I tell you, Hill, that speech fell on the audience like a wet blanket. I am distressed about it. . . . It is a flat failure and the people are disappointed.[712]

It is little wonder the Northern public responded this way. Victorian Americans, of course, had not yet been blinded by the anti-South movement's postwar political deification of Lincoln. Instead, at the time most saw him simply as what he really was: a demagogic rhetorician reciting vacuous pro-North nonsense.

**WHAT YOU WERE TAUGHT:** After issuing the Emancipation Proclamation Lincoln kindly gave all freed blacks "forty acres and a mule" as a head start on their new lives of freedom.

**THE TRUTH:** Lincoln never gave freed blacks anything, not even the most basic of human rights. In regard to this particular myth, what he did do was *promise* freed Southern blacks "forty acres and a mule." But as with most of the North's other pledges to blacks, this one too turned out to be a lie:[713] there were no mules,[714] only deprivation, starvation, and vagrancy.[715] And Lincoln's so-called "black land giveaways" were only meant to be temporary[716]—and most of those that were issued ultimately went to rich white Northerners,[717] railroads, land speculators, and lumber companies.[718]

**WHAT YOU WERE TAUGHT:** Lincoln's Emancipation Proclamation included a generous plan to incorporate freedmen and freedwomen into American society.

**THE TRUTH:** The Emancipation Proclamation contains no plans whatsoever for freed blacks, other than a self-serving push to enlist as many black males into the Union army as possible, one of the main purposes for issuing the edict to begin with.[719] Indeed, this is why Lincoln himself referred to it as a "military emancipation," not a "civil rights emancipation."[720]

The tragic fact is that Lincoln had no organized plan to admit freed blacks into American society as equal citizens;[721] nothing to help the elderly, the ill, or orphaned blacks who could not work and who had previously been under the lifelong care of their owners;[722] no education, no loans or grants, no job training, no housing, to ease freedmen and freedwomen into the world of capitalism, competition, and a free, highly skilled, and often hostile labor force. All were merely "liberated" to roam the streets and make their way as best they could; or as Lincoln flippantly put it, to "root, pig, or perish."[723]

After the reality of Lincoln's double-dealing politics sank in, all hope of free land, or anything else, for blacks evaporated.[724] (Lincoln and the U.S. Congress did eventually create the Bureau of Refugees, Freedmen, and Abandoned Lands. But this was in March 1865,[725] over two years after the Emancipation Proclamation and just one month before the War ended—far too late to mitigate the myriad of problems caused by Lincoln's sudden, violent, and unplanned abolition in January 1863.)

Black civil rights leader W. E. B. Du Bois summed up Lincoln's emancipation "plan" this way: former slaves are now free to do whatever they want with the nothing they never had to begin with.[726] Of the Yankee president's "root, pig, or perish" emancipation program, former slave Thomas Hall later spoke for millions of Southern blacks:

> Lincoln got the praise for freeing us, but did he do it? He give us freedom without giving us any chance to live to ourselves and we still had to depend on the Southern white man for work, food, and clothing, and he held us through our necessity and want in a state of servitude but little better than slavery. Lincoln done but little for the negro race and from a living standpoint nothing.[727]

**WHAT YOU WERE TAUGHT:** Today each year Americans correctly vote Lincoln the number one best and most popular U.S. president.

**THE TRUTH:** The only reason for this is that the full truth about Lincoln has been withheld from the world. Those living during his presidency *did* know the truth about him, however, which is why—despite our modern deification of him—during his two terms in office he was extremely disliked in both the North and the South.[728]

Indeed, not only was Ulysses S. Grant far more popular at the time,[729] in the 1860s a large percentage of the general public viewed Lincoln as the worst chief executive up to that time,[730] some even referring to him as "America's most hated president."[731]

**WHAT YOU WERE TAUGHT:** Lincoln was so beloved by Americans that he was voted into the White House both times by a landslide.

**THE TRUTH:** Lincoln won his first election in 1860 with only 39.8 percent of the popular vote,[732] with less than one in seventeen Americans voting for him.[733] This means that in the 1860 election he received nearly one million votes less than his opponents combined. A minority president, he won that year mainly due to the electoral college,[734] and he won that primarily because the Democrats (Victorian conservatives) were in disarray, causing a four-way split that left the door open for a Lincoln victory.[735] But there were other reasons.

In 1909 Judge George L. Christian of Richmond, Virginia, wrote of the 1860 presidential election, affirming that Lincoln

> was only nominated by means of a corrupt bargain entered into between his representatives and those of Simon Cameron, of Pennsylvania, and Caleb B. Smith, of Indiana, by which Cabinet positions were pledged both to Cameron and to Smith in consideration for the votes controlled by them, in the [1860 Chicago] convention, and which pledges Lincoln fulfilled, and, in that way made himself a party to these corrupt bargains.[736]

Lincoln only won the 1864 election because he rigged the polls[737] (he often stationed soldiers at voting stations in order to intimidate and "persuade" voters),[738] restricted free speech (so that pro-peace advocates could not speak out against him),[739] curbed freedom of the press (so that anti-war journalists could not criticize him),[740] and bribed, lied, horse-traded, and cheated his way into office.[741] His 1864 convention managers, who handed out patronage pledges like candy, later admitted that they had promised "anything and everything" to anyone who would vote for him.[742] All of this occurred, of course, under Lincoln's personal supervision.[743]

Though he "won" with a 55 percent majority that year, many of these votes, of course, were garnered dishonestly. Additionally, his win was far from a "landslide": if only 38,111 people, less than 1 percent of the votes cast, had shifted in specific regions, he would have lost to his chief opponent George B. McClellan.[744] If the Southern states had participated in the 1864 U.S. election,

Lincoln would have *lost* by a landslide.[745]

**WHAT YOU WERE TAUGHT:** Lincoln was a humanitarian and a non-racist, and in particular was an admirer and respecter of African-Americans.
**THE TRUTH:** This may be how he is seen by most people today, but this is not how he was perceived during his life. Though Lincoln's own words refute this Yankee myth,[746] let us allow one of Lincoln's so-called "friends," former *Northern* slave Frederick Douglass, to reveal the facts.

When it came to people of color Lincoln's words often lacked "the genuine spark of humanity," Douglass once observed acidly.[747] As for his supposed "love of the black man," Douglass set the record straight for all those willing to read his words: Lincoln was a hypocrite who was only proud of his own race and nationality. Though voted into office as an antislavery liberal, he was actually a prejudiced, black colonizationist, with nothing but contempt and even hatred for the Negro, the black orator stated.[748]

Years later, on April 14, 1876, Douglass elaborated on his feelings about Lincoln in a speech he gave at Washington, D.C. Former Union general, now U.S. President Ulysses S. Grant (today still known in the South, like Lincoln, as a war criminal), was in attendance. The old liberal Yankee warhorse must have cringed as he listened to Douglass utter the following words to his largely black audience:

> It must be admitted, truth compels me to admit, even here in the presence of the monument we have erected to his memory, Abraham Lincoln was not, in the fullest sense of the word, either our man or our model. In his interests, in his associations, in his habits of thought, and in his prejudices, he was a white man.
>
> He was preeminently the white man's President, entirely devoted to the welfare of white men. He was ready and willing at any time during the first years of his administration to deny, postpone, and sacrifice the rights of humanity in the coloured people to promote the welfare of the white people of this country. . . . He came into the Presidential chair upon one principle alone, namely, opposition to the extension of slavery. His arguments in furtherance of this policy had then motive and mainspring in his patriotic devotion to the interests of his own race. To protect, defend, and perpetuate slavery in the States where it existed, Abraham Lincoln was not less ready than any other President to draw the sword of the nation. He was ready to execute all the supposed constitutional guarantees of the United States Constitution in favour of the slave system anywhere inside the slave States. He was willing to pursue, recapture, and send back the

fugitive slave to his master, and to suppress a slave rising for liberty, though his guilty master were already in arms against the Government. The race to which we belong were not the special objects of his consideration. [749]

Contrary to so-called Northern "history," it is clear that "Honest Abe's" attitude toward African-Americans was nothing like we have been taught.

In the South we know and teach the Truth: Lincoln was no abolitionist; [750] hated the entire movement; [751] said abolition was worse than slavery; [752] stalled the Emancipation Proclamation for as long as possible [753]—and then only issued it for military and colonization purposes; [754] was a leader in the American Colonization Society; [755] forced slaves to complete the construction of the White House; [756] implemented extreme racist military policies; [757] used profits from Northern slavery to fund his War; [758] often referred to blacks using the "n" word; [759] said he was willing to allow slavery to continue in perpetuity if the Southern states would come back into the Union; [760] pushed nonstop right up to the last day of his life for the deportation of all American blacks; [761] as a lawyer defended slave owners in court; [762] proposed a proslavery amendment to the Constitution in 1861; [763] and continually blocked black enlistment, black suffrage, and black citizenship. [764]

To hide these facts is criminal, an insult to the South, and a disservice to both authentic American history and posterity.

# ★ 11 ★

# LINCOLN'S NAVAL BLOCKADE

**WHAT YOU WERE TAUGHT:** The Northern naval blockade of Southern ports and waters was perfectly legal.

**THE TRUTH:** There are numerous reasons why this Yankee myth is false.

International law at the time stipulated that for a blockade to be legitimate every mile of coastline had to be patrolled. Knowing that this was impossible the Union never even attempted it, making this particular military action nothing more than a "paper blockade," and as such, unlawful.[765]

A legal blockade also had to be both 100 percent effective and continuous. Lincoln's was anything but.[766] Indeed, the impossibility of barricading every bay, inlet, channel, lagoon, and swamp along the South's 3,550 mile coastline was obvious even to Europeans, who heaped scorn and ridicule upon Lincoln's preposterous plan.[767]

Adding to its ineffectiveness the blockade was often suspended at varying points along the Southern coast.[768] The result in the first year, 1861, was that the rate of Union capture of Rebel ships was only about one in ten vessels.[769] More revealingly, during the entire four years of the War not a single blockade runner commanded by a Confederate navy officer was ever captured by the Yankee navy.[770] We would not call this "effective."

Another problem: the Declaration of Paris of 1856—a set of well established international maritime laws[771] that had been signed by the Confederacy in the summer of 1861, and which was binding upon the United States as a maritime nation—specified that in order for a blockade to be legal, entree beyond the blockaded nation's coastline would have to be rendered completely inaccessible. In the case of the Southern coastline this was clearly not true, for it was never totally blockaded at any time during the War.[772]

There were still other reasons Lincoln's naval blockade was illegitimate.

A nation could not lawfully blockade coastline and waterways within its own borders. It could only blockade coastline and waterways of foreign nations. While it is a fact that the Confederacy was a legally formed separate nation at the time, Lincoln never recognized the Confederacy as such. Throughout the duration of the War he considered the Southern states to be merely belligerents who were out of their "proper practical relation" to the Union.[773]

Finally, a blockade is illegal unless war is formally declared. When Lincoln ordered his blockade on April 19 and 27, 1861, war had not yet been officially announced, either by himself or the U.S. Congress. It was only later, by a convoluted set of self-serving arguments, that the Dixie-hating U.S. Supreme Court was able to convince itself that the blockade was legal because the South's puny April 12th "insurrection" at Fort Sumter (where no one was killed or even injured) did indeed qualify as a full scale "war."[774]

Let us look at these issues a little more closely. We have, for instance, plenty of evidence proving the utter ineffectiveness, and thus the illegality, of the blockade. In the winter of 1861 alone Confederate commissioners in Europe, Ambrose D. Mann, Pierre Rost, James Mason, and William L. Yancey, provided lists of over 450 ships that had successfully run Lincoln's blockade. Also noted was the fact that both they and various British consuls stationed at Confederate ports had reported that the blockade, far from being continuous, was often temporarily closed.[775]

Additionally, as of the spring of 1862, Confederate statesman Judah Benjamin said that at least twenty Southern ports had never seen a Union warship stationed there. These ports, along with many others, were completely open, allowing both the ingress and the egress of Confederate vessels, yet another clear blockade violation of international law and the Declaration of Paris. By the end of the War some 8,250 violations of the blockade had occurred, clearly showing that the blockade was never even close to being 100 percent effective.[776]

Indeed, with the risk of being caught only 16 percent, these 8,250 blockade runners were able to smuggle some $200 million (or in today's currency, about $5 billion) worth of goods into the Confederacy, while exporting 1,250,000 bales of cotton.[777] So inadequate was Lincoln's blockade that not only did inbound capture rates of Confederate vessels actually decline in 1863 and 1864,[778] but even after the War ended and the U.S. had taken over every last Southern port and waterway, blockade running continued.[779]

The truth is that Lincoln never really seemed interested in making his blockade full-proof and legitimate. Always thinking of himself and his reputation before the welfare of the American people, this was no doubt because a perfect blockade would have so injured the entire world economy that the U.S. would have been inevitably drawn into war with other nations, particularly England and France. In addition, a 100 percent effective blockade would have siphoned off valuable Union resources, giving the Confederacy a military and psychological advantage, something Lincoln would not allow to happen—even if it meant committing a war crime (that is, the blockade).[780]

Even though Lincoln knew full well that thousands of Union ships and marines would be needed to make his blockade both legal and successful, he consistently refused to provide the resources that would have made this possible. To Yankee navy Captain Louis Goldsborough, for example, Lincoln only gave thirteen ships to blockade the entire coasts of North Carolina and Virginia.[781]

Lincoln's own navy men, trained leaders who should have known better, often helped make the blockade even more ineffectual and unlawful than it already was. Yankee naval officer Napoleon Collins, for instance, was court-martialed for capturing the great Confederate raider, the *Florida*, in Brazilian waters, an obvious violation of international law.[782]

Despite the naval blockade's weaknesses, most Yankee historians—and in particular, Yankee economists[783]—believe that by demoralizing Southern citizens and weakening Confederate forces, it was a success (at least from the Northern point of view) and was the primary reason the South lost the War.[784] This may be true. However, what they do not mention is that the blockade was wholly illegal, that no one was ever punished for this crime, and that because of it the South did not so much "lose" the war as she had victory illicitly robbed from her.

And there are still people who wonder why Southerners call Lincoln a "war criminal."

**WHAT YOU WERE TAUGHT:** Lincoln's blockade was designed to hurt only the American South. Thus it did not damage any non-American nation, especially Europe.

**THE TRUTH:** Lincoln's blockade had such a negative impact on the world economy that historians are still debating which European country was affected most severely.

As early as October 5, 1861, just six months into Lincoln's War, Confederate European agents William L. Yancey and Pierre Rost sent a report to Richmond notifying President Davis of the effects of the blockade. According to the two men, tobacco and cotton imports had been so profoundly impeded by then that thousands of Europeans were now unemployed, textile companies were operating at half-time, and the blue-collar class as a whole was under extreme duress, particularly the laboring poor of France[785] and England, who were forced into living conditions universally described as "absolutely intolerable."[786]

Lincoln's blockade caused a literal "cotton famine" in Lancashire, England, where its "deadly" effect resulted in massive unemployment. In 1862, as the famine was peaking in France, the cotton producers of the Lower Seine, Rouen, Dieppe, and Harve "suffered terribly," and every last cotton mill had to be closed down, the smaller ones going into foreclosure and bankruptcy.[787]

By the end of that year some 130,000 French men were unemployed. This means that at least 390,000 French (this number includes dependents) were immediately thrown into poverty as a result. Starvation set in, beggars overwhelmed France's cities, and filthy half-naked children were seen roaming the countryside. So widespread was the impact that at least two million Europeans were eventually negatively affected.[788]

Lincoln himself acknowledged the misery he was causing all across Europe. In a January 19, 1863, letter addressed to English cotton workers, he said disingenuously:

> I know and deeply deplore the sufferings which the working-men at Manchester, and in all Europe, are called to endure in this crisis.[789]

What he neglects to apologize for is starting the "crisis" to begin with![790]

# THE EMANCIPATION

# PROCLAMATION

**WHAT YOU WERE TAUGHT:** Lincoln issued the Emancipation Proclamation to free America's slaves.

**THE TRUTH:** While the North has long comforted itself with this picturesque notion, the facts reveal something quite different.

It is well-known to most Southerners today that the Final Emancipation Proclamation, issued January 1, 1863, only freed slaves in the South, and even then, only in specific areas of the South. Lincoln's edict purposefully excluded Tennessee, for example (the entire state had been under Yankee control since the fall of Nashville, February 25, 1862),[791] along with numerous Northern-occupied parishes in Louisiana and several counties in Virginia.[792]

The Final Emancipation Proclamation, in fact, was issued only in areas of the South *not* under Union control. It also did not ban slavery anywhere in the North, where thousands of Yankees still practiced it, including Union officers like General Ulysses S. Grant and his family.[793] As Lincoln states in the proclamation itself, the North and those places exempted "are for the present left precisely as if this proclamation were not issued."[794] Lincoln could not have made the meaning of this sentence more clear: *slavery was to be allowed to continue in the U.S. (that is, the North) and in any areas of the South controlled by the U.S. (that is, by the Union armies).*

The question Southerners have been asking Northerners for the past century and a half is why, if Lincoln was so interested in black equality, did he only abolish slavery in the South where he had no jurisdiction but not in the North where he had full control?

The answer is obvious to most Southerners today, just as it was to a majority of them in 1863. If Northerners had asked themselves this same question at the time, they would have never created the myth of Lincoln the "Great Emancipator" to begin with.

In truth our sixteenth president did not issue the Emancipation Proclamation for the specific purpose of trying to establish black civil rights across the U.S. If that had indeed been his intention he would have also banned slavery in the North and in non-Union occupied areas of the South.

Actually, being the penultimate politician, Lincoln had five primary goals in mind when he wrote out the edict, not a single one of them having anything to do with black equality.

Lincoln revealed the first of these in the proclamation itself by calling it a "war measure," instead of a "civil rights measure,"[795] a connivance he had been developing for many months, perhaps for several years. And what a brilliant idea it was. After all, no one could argue against emancipation—not even the most pro-South Northerners or pro-North Southerners—if Lincoln could prove that freeing the slaves was vital to winning the War.[796] And it would indeed prove to be vital. But not for the reasons Yankee myth has long claimed.

Since the beginning of the conflict Lincoln had been trying to court and maintain support from Europe, mainly Britain and France. For he knew if Europe sided with the South, giving her weaponry, ammunition, ships, clothing, and other types of supplies, the Union would have no hope of winning. Only by keeping Europe on his side could Lincoln achieve his true goal: total conquest of the wealth-producing South and the eradication of states' rights.

In part, the Emancipation Proclamation was calculated to do just that, for as Europe had much earlier abolished slavery herself, Lincoln assumed that she would automatically support the side most dedicated to humanitarian ideals. The edict not only made it appear that the North was the region most interested in abolition, but midway through the War it also transformed the North's purpose for fighting Dixie from "preserving the Union" to that of "ending slavery."[797] The proclamation thus reenforced Lincoln's lie to Europe that "slavery is the basis of the war." I sincerely hope that this fact will "obtain the favor of Europe," he implored deceptively.[798]

But Lincoln's wish utterly failed in this regard. As we will explore in more depth in Chapter 19, Europe repeatedly stated, quite emphatically and clearly, that slavery had nothing whatsoever to do with which side she would support, if either.[799]

The second reason Lincoln had for issuing the Emancipation Proclamation was to incite a massive "slave rebellion" in the South, which he hoped would bring about chaos, destabilize Southern society, and destroy her economy.[800] Thus he states in the proclamation that the Yankee government will do nothing to stop any acts that Southern slaves wish to engage in to attain their freedom.[801]

To every thinking Southerner, Lincoln here was not only breaking the laws of civilized warfare, he was clearly inviting their black servants to insurrection, mayhem, violence, rape, and murder.[802] This was even understood as far away as Europe. In England, for instance, the aristocracy widely regarded both Lincoln's Preliminary Emancipation Proclamation (issued September 22, 1862) and his Final Emancipation Proclamation as nothing less than a naked attempt to incite African-American riots across the South.[803] They were right of course.

Unfortunately for Lincoln, like psychopath John Brown's futile attempt at Harper's Ferry to foment black riots in the South, his own nefarious plan came to naught. There was not a single slave rebellion anywhere in the South after he issued the proclamation,[804] as he himself later grudgingly admitted.[805]

The truth is that of the South's 3.5 million black servants,[806] 95 percent (nineteen out of twenty) maintained their loyalty to Dixie.[807] Ignoring Lincoln's fake proclamation of freedom, they instead pledged their allegiance to their home states, to the South, and to their white families.[808] Remaining at home they ran their owner's farms, grew food, produced provisions for the Confederate military, and protected their master's family and property while he was away on the battlefield.[809]

In an effort to raise money for the Southern war effort many Southern slaves and freemen bought Confederate bonds.[810] Others held bake sales and auctions, while still others donated clothing and other goods in an effort to help support Confederate soldiers.[811] Those untold thousands of African-Americans who marched off to resist Lincoln and his illegal invaders, proudly stood up for "ole Jeff Davis," wearing placards on their hats that read: "We will die by the South."[812] Among them were tens of thousands who served the Confederacy as teamsters, bridge and road builders, musicians, cooks, nurses, carpenters, smithies, couriers, and lookouts.[813]

By most objective estimates at least 300,000 Southern blacks donned Rebel uniforms, marched unhesitatingly onto the battlefield, and fought fearlessly for the Southern Cause.[814] Those who were crack shots served as sharpshooters, helping to bring down thousands of Yankee interlopers.[815] Using Yankee General August Valentine Kautz's definition of a "private soldier,"[816] I believe that as many as 1 million Southern blacks served in one capacity or another in the Confederate military. This means that 50 percent of the South's soldiers were black,[817] and that 80 percent more blacks fought for the Confederacy than for the Union.[818]

Here too Lincoln once again failed in his goal, for far from initiating a full scale slave rebellion in the South, his overt racism and selfish political scheming only turned most Southern blacks further against him, while renewing their love for Dixie.

The third motivation behind Lincoln's Emancipation Proclamation was to provide manpower for his army and navy, both which, after two years of fighting, were quickly diminishing in numbers due to what I call "the four D's": desertion, defection, disease, and death.

His "military emancipation," as Lincoln himself openly called it,[819] would offset these losses by freeing up the South's 3.5 million slaves, all of whom he assumed would speedily come North and gratefully enlist in the Union military effort. Lincoln himself said as much in a letter to Tennessee's Military Governor Andrew Johnson on March 26, 1863, just three months after issuing the Emancipation Proclamation:

> The colored population is the great available and yet unavailed of force for restoring the Union. The bare sight of fifty thousand armed and drilled black soldiers upon the banks of the Mississippi would end the rebellion at once . . .[820]

With racist Lincoln there was always racial reasoning behind his schemes, as he noted on August 26, 1863, in a letter to James C. Conkling:

> I thought that whatever negroes can be got to do as soldiers, leaves just so much less for white soldiers to do in saving the Union.[821]

As we have just seen, however, Lincoln's assumption that Southern blacks would pour northward and join his armies was an absurd fantasy. This was, in great part, because the president, who consistently and vehemently proclaimed that he was not an abolitionist,[822] did not promise citizenship to blacks—newly freed or already free (and indeed blacks would not become U.S. citizens until 1868, three years after Lincoln's death).[823]

Whatever the many reasons for the apathetic response by Southern blacks to his proclamation, between 1863 and 1865 only a small fraction, less than 90,000, of the South's 3.5 million servants ended up in Lincoln's military.[824] (Even then, as we will see, many of these so-called black "enrollments" were not voluntary; they were forced under threat of physical violence.)[825] As stated, this indicates that 80 percent more blacks fought for the Confederacy than for the Union, a fact one will never find in any pro-North history book on the "Civil War."

The fourth principal reason Lincoln had for issuing the Emancipation Proclamation again had nothing to do with African-American civil rights. The 1864 election was just around the corner and he was desperate to be reelected. But he faced a major problem: he had lost the eleven Confederate states and their eighty-eight electoral votes (obviously the Confederacy, now a separate nation, did not vote in the Union's 1860 election—and Lincoln had, strangely and illegally, banned them from doing so anyway), along with the support of both anti-war activists and abolitionists.[826] How to accrue additional votes, he asked himself?

Again the answer was the Emancipation Proclamation. He would free millions of Southern blacks in the expectation that most would enlist and, as soldiers, would gratefully cast their votes to reelect him for a second term (he never offered *non-military* blacks the franchise). As we have seen, however, the incumbent president's scheme in this regard was completely unsuccessful.

The fifth and final reason for signing an emancipation proclamation into law concerned Lincoln's lifelong goal, known today by educated blacks as "Abraham Lincoln's white dream": the deportation of all African-Americans out of the country. Lincoln could not even begin this process as long as the South's 3.5 million black servants were considered the "property" of their owners. Emancipation, however, would instantly transform them into "freemen," allowing their legal deportation; or so "Honest Abe" believed.

As we will see in the next chapter, this aspect of the Final Emancipation Proclamation also failed, for not only would it have been financially impossible for the U.S. government to pay for the emigration of millions of people, the idiotic bigoted plan had absolutely no support, except for a handful of Lincoln's fellow white supremacists and white separatists.[827]

All in all then, from Lincoln's perspective at least, the Emancipation Proclamation was a pathetic blunder. Little more than a transparent and cynical political move, his "war measure" and "military emancipation" did not help gain European support; it did not incite a single slave rebellion in the South; it did not motivate Southern blacks to enlist in his army; it did not inspire Southern blacks to vote for him; and finally, it did not allow him to launch his nationwide black deportation program.

The fact that it actually freed no slaves did not trouble Lincoln in the least, as this was never the intention of his proclamation to begin with.

**WHAT YOU WERE TAUGHT:** Lincoln issued the Emancipation Proclamation voluntarily.

**THE TRUTH:** From the first day of his presidency Lincoln had to be cajoled, pushed, and pressured, even threatened, to do something about abolishing slavery. Every step of the way he resisted.[828] It took him over two years—from November 6, 1860, the day he was elected president, to January 1, 1863, the day he issued the Final Emancipation Proclamation—to even begin taking abolition seriously. Even then he never became a full-blooded authentic abolitionist. He was always an emancipationist-colonizationist at heart (that is, a "free 'em up and ship 'em out" advocate), and nothing ever changed his mind on the subject.

It was just such bullheadedness and illogical stall tactics that prompted severe criticism from abolitionists in his party. Wendell Phillips, for instance, began calling him "a first-rate second-rate man,"[829] while famed antislavery advocate William Lloyd Garrison referred to Lincoln's policies as "stumbling, halting, prevaricating, irresolute, weak, besotted."[830]

On September 13, 1862, just prior to issuing the Preliminary Emancipation Proclamation (on the 22nd) Lincoln wavered, procrastinated, and resisted, seriously questioning whether it was the right thing to do—even when pressed by a group of angry clergymen.[831] At the same time he continued to refuse to enlist freedmen as combatants, or give blacks either citizenship or voting rights.[832]

In short, there was nothing voluntary about Lincoln's issuance of the proclamation. It would be more accurate to say that it was done with great reluctance, doubt, and misgiving.

Indeed, the president himself once intimated that he felt forced to free the slaves, and that he would not have done so had the South not "rebelled." In a rare conversation in the Oval Office with former Northern slave Sojourner Truth (for most of his administration Lincoln barred free blacks from entering the White House),[833] he noted that it was only because Southerners had not "behaved themselves" that he had been "compelled" to issue his abolitionary edict.[834] Otherwise, according to Lincoln himself, there would have been no Emancipation Proclamation, the institution of slavery would have remained untouched, and the South's 3.5 million slaves, along with and the 500,000 to 1 million black slaves in the North, would have continued in bondage indefinitely.[835]

**WHAT YOU WERE TAUGHT:** Lincoln issued the Emancipation Proclamation in a timely manner.

**THE TRUTH:** If Lincoln's goal was truly to "free the slaves" we must ask ourselves why he waited so long to issue his proclamation. From the first day of his inauguration, both white and black civil rights leaders, such as Horace Greeley and Frederick Douglass, put constant pressure on the president to abolish slavery. Yet time and time again he refused. First the year 1861 passed. Then 1862. Nearly two years into the War, Lincoln still would not be moved to emancipate America's slaves, earning him the well deserved nickname the "tortoise President."[836]

As discussed above, it was only the need to maintain European support, the manpower shortage crisis, his desire to start a slave insurrection in the South, his desperation to be reelected, and his black colonization goals that finally prompted Lincoln to issue the Final Emancipation Proclamation on January 1, 1863. This is why the topics of black suffrage and black citizenship—the ultimate dream of Victorian blacks and abolitionists—are never once mentioned in that document. For Lincoln it was merely a "war measure" and a "military emancipation" (that is, something utilized for the sole purpose of winning the conflict), which is exactly how he termed it.[837]

If some of Lincoln's Northern constituents did not notice the diabolical hypocrisy of the Emancipation Proclamation, Southerners and Europeans certainly did. Agreeing with President Jefferson Davis, the Richmond *Examiner* called it the most shocking crime perpetuated by a politician in U.S. history.[838] English newspapers, like the London *Times*, called it a tragic document, while the London *Spectator* termed it a deceitful fabrication.[839]

And what rank hypocrisy it was, for at the time not only was slavery still alive and well in the North,[840] but free Northern blacks were still not allowed to vote, sit on juries, attend white churches, be buried in white cemeteries, marry whites, or even become U.S. citizens.[841]

**WHAT YOU WERE TAUGHT:** Lincoln wanted to end slavery as quickly as possible.

**THE TRUTH:** Lincoln had no such definitive goal in mind and was actually quite malleable on the topic. In his Annual Message to Congress December 1, 1862, for example, he proposed three new amendments to the Constitution. In the first, Article One, he said:

> Every state wherein slavery now exists which shall abolish the same therein at any time or times before the first day of January in the year of our Lord one thousand and nine hundred, shall receive compensation from the United States . . .[842]

In other words, as a compromise with the South Lincoln was prepared to give any Southern state that wished to practice slavery another thirty-eight years, until January 1, 1900, to abolish it.

In the same speech Lincoln explained Article One so that there would be no misunderstanding:

> The plan leaves to each State choosing to act under it to abolish
> slavery now, or at the end of the century, or at any intermediate
> time, or by degrees extending over the whole or any part of the
> period . . .[843]

Clearly Lincoln was in no hurry to end slavery.

**WHAT YOU WERE TAUGHT:** Lincoln planned on making the abolition of slavery permanent.

**THE TRUTH:** Far from intending to destroy slavery forever, Lincoln acknowledged that his Emancipation Proclamation was neither permanent or unchangeable, and that he would consider allowing the Southern states to reinstate slavery and maintain it permanently if only they would rejoin the Union and pay their taxes.[844]

The only permanence Lincoln demanded pertained to slaves themselves: once a servant was set free he could never be re-enslaved, he declared,[845] a law in perfect keeping with his lifelong black colonizationist goal to free the slaves and, along with free blacks, ship as many out of the country as possible.[846]

As for the time of emancipation and the duration of emancipation laws in the South, however, he was entirely flexible. That Lincoln viewed his Emancipation Proclamation in this exact manner is supported by reams of evidence, though nearly all of it has been buried under a mountain of Yankee mythology. Let us uncover some of it here.

Lincoln was once severely criticized by Northern Democrats, for instance, because he had absent-mindedly called for *complete* and *permanent* emancipation in all the Southern states. Realizing his error, on July 18, 1864, he immediately sent out a notice humbly rescinding the demand. It read:

> Any proposition which embraces the restoration of peace, the
> integrity of the whole Union, and the abandonment of slavery . . .
> will be received and considered . . . and will be met by liberal
> terms on other substantial and collateral points . . .[847]

Yankee historians have long wondered what "substantial and collateral points" Lincoln was so willing to "receive and consider." But we Southern historians have been perfectly aware of them since the 1860s.

Lincoln himself spoke openly of at least one of these, one that included the possibility of ending the War without total and lasting abolition. On August 17, 1864, in a letter to the Honorable Charles R. Robinson, Lincoln responded to the many attacks on his emancipation plan with these startling words:

To me it seems plain that saying reunion and abandonment of slavery would be considered, if offered, is not saying that nothing *else* or *less* would be considered, if offered. . . . If [Confederate President] Jefferson Davis wishes, for himself, or for the benefit of his friends at the North, to know what I would do if he were to offer peace and reunion, saying nothing about slavery, let him try me.[848]

A half year later, on February 3, 1865, at the Hampton Roads Peace Conference (the one and only time imperious Lincoln agreed to meet with Confederate peace delegates), the U.S. president reiterated that his primary concern was "preserving the Union." And he would go to nearly any length to do so, he told the Rebel peace representatives, Vice President Alexander H. Stephens, Senator Robert M. T. Hunter, and Assistant Secretary of War John A. Campbell. These lengths included allowing the South to continue practicing slavery after it rejoined the U.S. According to those present, Lincoln's

. . . own opinion was, that as the Proclamation was a *war measure*, and would have effect only from its being an exercise of the war power, as soon as the war ceased, it would be inoperative for the future. It would be held to apply only to such slaves as had come under its operation while it was in active exercise. This was his individual opinion . . .[849]

In true Lincolnian fashion, the Yankee president preached against slavery in public, but behind closed doors he was busy thinking up loophole laws, like his proposed 1861 amendment to the U.S. Constitution that would have allowed slavery to continue in perpetuity without any interference from the national government. It was passed by the U.S. House of Representatives on February 28, 1861, and by the U.S. Senate on March 2, 1861, two days before his presidential inauguration[850]—during which Lincoln publicly mentioned the "proposed amendment" in his address on March 4. "I have no objection to its being made express and irrevocable," he stated emphatically before the nation that day.[851]

By this time three states had actually ratified the amendment, and certainly the rest would have as well, if given the chance. However, the act was dropped with the start of the Battle of Fort Sumter, on April 12, 1861. Had hostilities not exploded between the South and the North that spring day, what can only be called Lincoln's "proslavery amendment" would have been signed into law, and American slavery would have continued indefinitely.[852]

Further evidence that Lincoln did not set out to make abolition in the South permanent is his "Ten Percent Plan," issued in December 1863.[853] Here a Confederate state could be readmitted to the Union if just 10 percent of its citizens took an oath of allegiance to the U.S.[854] Afterward, that state, under its own new state government, could reestablish slavery if it so desired.[855]

The final death blow to this particular Yankee myth came in 1864, when, according to Confederate Secretary of State Judah Benjamin, far from demanding complete and immediate abolition, Lincoln let it be known that he was willing to let the issue be decided on by a general vote in both the South and the North.[856]

Despite overwhelming evidence to the contrary, much of it from Lincoln's own pen, pro-North writers continue to pretend that the Yankee president wanted to end slavery quickly and permanently, and that he issued the Emancipation Proclamation for the sole purpose of granting blacks full civil rights.

But all of the purposeful misrepresentation, obfuscation, and subterfuge in the world cannot hide the Truth.

# ★ 13 ★

# LINCOLN'S BLACK COLONIZATION PLAN

**WHAT YOU WERE TAUGHT:** After issuing the Emancipation Proclamation, Lincoln planned to fully incorporate blacks into American society.

**THE TRUTH:** Lincoln planned on doing nothing of the kind. Actually, after abolition the president's number one goal for freed blacks was to ship as many of them out of the country as possible, as quickly as possible.

So adamant was he about expatriating American blacks that he was willing to settle them almost anyplace—as long as it was, as he said, "without the United States."[857] This included Europe, Latin America, or the Caribbean, or anywhere else they would be accepted. As such, he funded experimental black colonies in what are now Panama and Belize, as well as in Haiti.[858] But he seemed to have a special interest in the African colony of Liberia. Indeed, Africa was always his first choice. He would even pay the resettlement costs of any and all African-Americans willing to volunteer to be shipped out of the U.S. The more the better, in his opinion.[859]

If his deportation plan turned out to be unworkable, he had another nearly as good, or so Old Abe believed: corral American blacks in their own all-black state, preferably one far from his own home state of Illinois. This idea, yet another one of his many harebrained racist notions, was presented by Lincoln to the public on September 15, 1858, at one of his famous debates with Senator Stephen A. Douglas.[860]

Lincoln's true feelings about blacks were never in doubt at the time. Just two months earlier, on July 17, 1858, for instance, our future sixteenth president told an audience at Springfield, Illinois:

> What I would most desire would be the separation of the white and black races.[861]

Why was Lincoln so anti-black? Being a Victorian Northerner, it all came down to white racism and money.

Like other white racist politicians before him, Lincoln was at first confused about how to deal with slavery: free them and they would compete with whites for jobs and land; keep them enslaved and, as he himself glibly put it, "the inferior race bears the superior down."[862]

In 1820 Thomas Jefferson phrased the seemingly insurmountable problem this way:

> We have the wolf by the ears, and we can neither hold him, nor safely let him go.[863]

If the brilliant, highly educated, Christian Southerner Thomas Jefferson was at a loss as to how to deal with slavery, the slow, self-taught, atheist Northerner Abraham Lincoln was not. Eventually he hit upon a simple solution, one that he described bluntly on October 16, 1854, in a speech at Peoria, Illinois:

> If all earthly power were given me, I should not know what to do as to the existing institution. My first impulse would be to free all the slaves, and send them to Liberia [Africa]—to their own native land.[864]

Seven years later, now in the White House, the new president's support for what was called "black colonization" was, if anything, even stronger, as is evidenced in his political documents. The most famous of these, of course, is the Emancipation Proclamation.

What historians call the Emancipation Proclamation was actually the final version of a document that underwent several minor and major revisions in draft form.[865] As such, it would be more accurate to call the last one, issued January 1, 1863, the Final Emancipation Proclamation.

The document that is of most interest to us in regards to this particular Yankee myth, however, is known as the Preliminary Emancipation Proclamation, and what an interesting article it is. If only it was studied as closely as the Final Emancipation Proclamation, our sixteenth president would never have been wrongly apotheosized as the "Great Emancipator."

The Preliminary Emancipation Proclamation, which Lincoln said he "fixed up a little" over the previous weekend,[866] then read to his cabinet on September 22, 1862—just four months before issuing the Final Emancipation

Proclamation—contained the following remarkable statement:

> it is my purpose . . . to again recommend . . . that the effort to colonize [that is, deport] persons of African descent with their consent upon this continent or elsewhere . . . will be continued.[867]

Why did this sensational clause, directed at the U.S. Congress, not make it into the Final Emancipation Proclamation? Against his wishes Lincoln's own cabinet members talked him out of including it because it might further alienate abolitionists, a group that was already bitterly disappointed with Lincoln's refusal to abolish slavery after being in the White House for over two years. Lincoln would need their votes in his upcoming bid for reelection in 1864. Promising to deport newly freed blacks out of the country was hardly the way to win the hearts, minds, and votes of abolitionists. And so the item on black colonization, one of Lincoln's most ardent lifelong aspirations, was struck from the Final Emancipation Proclamation.[868]

Thus this version, the only one known by the public today, is *not* the Emancipation Proclamation Lincoln wanted. It is the one forced on him by his cabinet and by political expediency.

Shortly thereafter, however, just one month before issuing the Final Emancipation Proclamation, he reemphasized his position on the issue, lest anyone should forget. In his Second Annual Message to Congress on December 1, 1862, Lincoln stated unambiguously:

> I cannot make it better known than it already is, that I strongly favor colonization.[869]

In this same speech he once again asks Congress to set aside funding for black deportation, and even suggests adding an amendment to the Constitution to expedite it.[870] According to Lincoln:

> Congress may appropriate money and otherwise provide for colonizing free colored persons, with their own consent, at any place or places without the United States.[871]

While Congress continued to allocate money for Lincoln's bizarre deportation scheme, by this time few politicians besides the president actually believed it was feasible.[872]

When it came to the Northern populace, however, Lincoln was far from being alone in his desire to rid America of blacks. At the time, all across the North, white racism was deeply entrenched, far more so than in the much more tolerant South.[873] For it was the common Yankee belief that people of African descent were inferior to those of European descent, inferior in intellect, morality, psychology, emotionality, creativity, and physicality. They were a kind of "bridge" between apes and man, many white Northerners staunchly maintained.

Respected Yankee historian James Ford Rhodes, for instance, described slaves as "indolent and filthy," "stupid" and "duplicitous," with "brute-like countenances."[874] Other Northerners were even less charitable. Famed Harvard scientist Louis Agassiz declared that "the negro race groped in barbarism and never originated a regular organization among themselves."[875] Agassiz, like his English associate, Charles Darwin (who originated the idea of natural selection, or "survival of the fittest"),[876] believed that blacks were so evolutionarily feeble that once freed from slavery they would eventually "die out" in the U.S.[877]

Thus no Northerners blinked, except a few authentic abolitionists,[878] when on September 16, 1858, Lincoln made the following remarks during a senatorial debate with rival Stephen A. Douglas at Columbus, Ohio:

> . . . this is the true complexion of all I have ever said in regard to the institution of slavery and the black race. This is the whole of it, and anything that argues me into his idea of perfect social and political equality with the negro is but a specious and fantastic arrangement of words, by which a man can prove a horse-chestnut to be a chestnut horse. I will say here, while upon this subject, that I have no purpose either directly or indirectly to interfere with the institution of slavery in the States where it exists. I believe I have no lawful right to do so, and I have no inclination to do so. I have no purpose to introduce political and social equality between the white and the black races. There is a physical difference between the two which, in my judgment, will probably forever forbid their living together upon the footing of perfect equality, and inasmuch as it becomes a necessity that there must be a difference, I, as well as Judge Douglas, am in favor of the race to which I belong having the superior position. I have never said anything to the contrary . . . I agree with Judge Douglas, he [the black man] is not my equal in many respects—certainly not in color, perhaps not in moral or intellectual endowments.[879]

Lincoln preferred the idea of living in a black-free America, and his own words prove it.

What then was the solution to "America's racial problem," as white Northerners referred to the presence of blacks in the U.S.? For Lincoln and many other Yankees there was only one: black colonization, resettling African-Americans in colonies outside the U.S. To this end Lincoln spent years developing his own deportation scheme, one he openly and enthusiastically promoted to both his cabinet members and to the public throughout his entire political career.

As he did whenever the opportunity arose, President Lincoln used his First Annual Message to Congress on December 3, 1861, to promote the idea of deporting blacks, in this case, free blacks:

> It might be well to consider, too, whether the free colored people already in the United States could not, so far as individuals may desire, be included in such colonization.[880]

As a result of this speech, in 1861 and 1862 the U.S. Congress had $600,000 (about $15 million in today's currency) set aside to aid in Lincoln's colonization plan to send as many free blacks as possible out of the country.[881]

None of this is surprising when we learn that Lincoln was a rank and file member of the American Colonization Society (ACS),[882] a popular Yankee organization founded in 1816 in Washington, D.C., by a Northerner, New Jerseyan Reverend Robert Finley.[883] The stated purpose of the ACS was to make America white from coast to coast.[884]

Besides Lincoln, other early leaders, officers, and supporters included such famed Yankees as New England statesman Daniel Webster (after whom the town of Webster, Massachusetts, was named), New Yorker William H. Seward (Lincoln's secretary of state and the man who coordinated the purchase of what is now the state of Alaska), and Marylander Francis Scott Key (author of the U.S. National Anthem, *The Star-Spangled Banner*).[885]

Other famous Yankee supporters (at some point in their lives) of deporting blacks were abolitionists William Lloyd Garrison (founder of the defamatory abolitionist paper *The Liberator*),[886] Horace Greeley (owner of the liberal New York *Tribune*), and Harriet Beecher Stowe (author of the worldwide bestselling antislavery fantasy *Uncle Tom's Cabin*).[887]

The nation's largest and most enthusiastic ACS chapter was in Boston, Massachusetts, the birthplace of American slavery, where both antislavery and anti-black sentiment (the two were not mutually exclusive in New England at the time) remained high well into the late 1800s.[888]

The ACS believed that in order to preserve white American culture, all American blacks, both free and emancipated ("freed"), would have to be evicted then resettled outside the U.S., a daft racist notion that enlightened modern blacks have appropriately labeled "Abraham Lincoln's white dream."[889] Though he would have loved to force the issue, the president finally agreed that only those who *volunteered* would be thrown out of the country, or "by the mutual consent of the people to be deported," as he so callously put it.[890]

So enamored was Lincoln with the ACS—at one time headed by his beloved political idol, slave owner Henry Clay[891]—that he eventually became a leader of the Illinois chapter,[892] a state whose legislature he personally convinced to finance the deportation of free blacks.[893]

During his famous February 27, 1860, Cooper Union speech in New York, the soon-to-be Republican presidential nominee brought up, as he so often did, the topic of colonization, hoping to make new converts. Quoting Thomas Jefferson's autobiography,[894] Lincoln said hopefully:

> In the language of Mr. Jefferson, uttered many years ago, "It is still in our power to direct the process of emancipation, and deportation, peaceably, and in such slow degrees, as that the evil will wear off insensibly; and their places be . . . filled up by free white laborers."[895]

We can see here that for Lincoln colonization served a dual purpose. Not only would it help protect whites from having to compete with freed blacks for jobs, it would also help prevent that most dreaded of all racists' nightmares: "amalgamation," that is, miscegenation, the mixing and interbreeding of the races.[896] It was thus that on June 26, 1857, at Springfield, Illinois, Lincoln lectured his Northern audience on the many benefits of "a separation of the races":

> Judge [Stephen] Douglas is especially horrified at the thought of the mixing of blood by the white and black races: agreed for once—a thousand times agreed. There are white men enough to marry all the white women, and black men enough to marry all the black women; and so let them be married. . . . A separation of the races is the only perfect preventive of amalgamation; but as an immediate separation is impossible the next best thing is to keep them apart where they are not already together. If white and black people never get together in Kansas, they will never mix blood in Kansas. That is at least one self-evident truth. A few free colored persons may get into the free States, in any event; but their number is too insignificant to amount to much in the way of mixing blood. . . . In 1850 there were in the United States 405,751 mulattoes. Very few of these are the offspring of whites and *free* blacks; nearly all have sprung from the black *slaves* and white masters. These statistics show that slavery is the greatest source of amalgamation.[897]

And here we find one of the real reasons Lincoln was both antislavery and pro-colonization. According to the Northern president, it was slavery that put whites and blacks in close proximity to one another, inevitably increasing the chances of interracial coupling, one of the greatest taboos to white separatists like Lincoln. Apparently he had spent some time researching the topic for, as he fearfully put it, "statistics show that slavery is the greatest source of amalgamation . . ."

Even in his July 6, 1852, eulogy to liberal Henry Clay, Lincoln managed to bring up the topic of colonization, no doubt something many in the audience found crass and improper. Besides preventing an increase in the population of mulattos, or "mongrels," as Lincoln called all mixed-racial, light brown-skinned people (such as Mexicans),[898] sending blacks back to Africa would have an added benefit, he insensitively noted that day at Springfield, Illinois: that of disseminating Christianity and civilization, with God's blessing, among a primitive and barbaric people. Quoting slave-owner Clay, Lincoln went on to say:

> "There is a moral fitness in the idea of returning Africa her children, whose ancestors have been torn from her by the ruthless hand of fraud and violence. Transplanted in a foreign land, they will carry back to their native soil the rich fruits of religion, civilization, law, and liberty. May it not be one of the great designs of the Ruler of the universe . . . thus to transform an original crime, into a signal blessing to that most unfortunate portion of the globe?"[899]

Lincoln, referring to himself not as one of the friends of the black man, but as one of the "friends of colonization,"[900] then called the possibility of successful black deportation a "glorious consummation,"[901] adding that Clay's

> suggestion of the possible ultimate redemption of the African race and African continent, was made twenty-five years ago. Every succeeding year has added strength to the hope of its realization.—May it indeed be realized![902]

Lincoln left no question as to why he was so passionate about colonization. It would, he said, not only restore "a captive people to their long-lost father-land," but at the same time it would free "our land from the dangerous presence of slavery . . ." And colonization was not just for black servants or newly freed blacks, he asserted. It would also help relieve white society "from the troublesome presence of the free negroes . . ." If Clay's dream of colonization could become a reality, he concluded, it would certainly be the most "valuable labor" the U.S. statesman had ever provided his country.[903]

Lincoln was talking here about a man who had not only been the U.S. secretary of state for four years under President John Quincy Adams, but who had also served as the speaker of the House of Representatives three times between 1811 and 1825. Still Lincoln felt that, if successful, the realization of black colonization would be Clay's greatest contribution to America!

Even Lincoln's District of Columbia Emancipation Act turned out to be for the benefit of, not blacks, but colonizationists like himself: the bill, issued on April 16, 1862—and then only after a year of intense pressure from abolitionists—finally ended slavery in Washington, D.C. Yet in it the Northern president included a colonization clause calling for the immediate deportation of all Negroes out of the city upon their liberation.[904] That same day Lincoln wrote a letter to the House and Senate applauding them for recognizing his call for the expatriation of the town's newly freed blacks and for setting aside funds for their colonization.[905]

Educated blacks were understandably furious. Black teacher and former Southern servant Booker T. Washington summed up the feelings of most African-Americans toward Lincoln's colonization plan this way:

> I was born in the South. I have lived and labored in the South. I wish to be buried in the South.[906]

Unfortunately for black civil rights, this simple and obvious concept completely escaped Lincoln, who wished for nothing less than American apartheid: the geographical separation of the races across the U.S.

What Lincoln never understood, and what is completely unknown to the average American today, is that the racial segregation he so desperately craved is merely another form of slavery—in this case one known as "collective slavery," which is exactly how apartheid is defined by Anti-Slavery International, the world's oldest international human rights organization.[907] Thus, it must go down as one of American history's greatest ironies that Lincoln is credited (wrongly) with ending chattel slavery, yet he actually spent his entire adult life promoting another form of the institution, collective slavery (that is, apartheid), one just as onerous, degrading, and exploitative.

Lincoln never abandoned his obsession with exiling all blacks from the U.S. In fact, he lobbied feverishly for colonization right up to the day he died, two years after issuing the Emancipation Proclamation, as Yankee General Benjamin "the Beast" Butler attests. According to Butler, in March 1865, just one month before Lincoln was assassinated by Northerner John Wilkes Booth, the president called the general to the White House to discuss the practicalities of black expatriation.[908]

Emancipation first. Colonization second. This was Lincoln's plan for blacks from the beginning to the very end of his life. Had he survived John Wilkes Booth's attack, there is no question that he would have done everything in his power to fulfill the second half of his plan. Thus it was, in great part, Booth who finally freed American blacks, not Abraham Lincoln. For the stark reality is that African-Americans, whether enslaved or free, would have never been completely liberated while Lincoln was alive—and indeed they were not.[909] Booth's bullet was the true "Great Emancipator."[910]

Lincoln's entire mad colonization scheme was eventually tossed out after his death, due mainly to the enormous costs and logistical complications that would have been involved. Nearly everyone seemed to be aware of these obstacles. Except our sixteenth president.

Just as bizarre, while he was alive, the man who longed so desperately for American apartheid, seemed completely oblivious of the bold fact that whites and blacks could indeed live together, peacefully, harmoniously, even affectionately. One hundred largely quiet years of Southern slavery, whatever one thought of it at the time, had proven this for all who had eyes to see.[911] But Lincoln did not view blacks and whites as equals, therefore he could not perceive what was plain to nearly everyone else, particularly Southerners.

**WHAT YOU WERE TAUGHT:** Lincoln's primary goal in life was to abolish slavery.

**THE TRUTH:** Lincoln always did what was most politically expedient at the moment, a trait for which he was roundly criticized,[912] even by members of his own party and constituency. However, there was one topic on which he never wavered: slavery. But contrary to Yankee myth, Lincoln's number one goal when it came to slavery was never to totally eliminate it. It was merely to *limit* it, as he himself said on countless occasions.

On December 22, 1860, in a letter to Southerner and soon-to-be Confederate Vice President Alexander H. Stephens, Lincoln wrote: "You think slavery . . . ought to be extended; while we think it . . . ought to be restricted." "Honest Abe," for once being completely honest, ended his letter to Stephens with this sensational statement: This is the "only substantial difference between us."[913]

Just a few months later, on March 4, 1861, he would repeat the same sentiment almost word for word in his First Inaugural Address:

> One section of our country believes slavery . . . ought to be extended, while the other believes it . . . ought not . . . be extended. This is the only substantial dispute.[914]

Thus, just prior to the War, Lincoln held that the only real difference between the South's view of slavery and the North's was that the former wanted to allow it to spread (mainly into the new Western Territories, eventually to become America's Western states), while the latter wanted to contain it where it already existed (that is, mainly in the South). No mention of emancipation or abolition. Just limitation.

Six years earlier, in his debate with Stephen A. Douglas on October 16, 1854, at Peoria, Illinois, Lincoln outlined his reasons for wanting to restrict, not end, slavery:

> Whether slavery shall go into Nebraska, or other new Territories, is not a matter of exclusive concern to the people who may go there. The whole nation is interested that the best use shall be made of these Territories. We want them for homes of free white people. This they cannot be, to any considerable extent, if slavery shall be planted within them. Slave States are places for poor white people to remove from, not to remove to. New free States are the places for poor people to go to, and better their condition. For this use the nation needs these Territories.[915]

Four years later, on October 15, 1858, at Alton, Illinois, in his seventh and final joint debate with Douglas, Lincoln reasserted his views on the matter, this time even more vigorously:

> Now, irrespective of the moral aspect of this question as to whether there is a right or wrong in enslaving a negro, I am still in favor of our new Territories being in such a condition that white men may find a home—may find some spot where they can better their condition—where they can settle upon new soil, and better their condition in life. I am in favor of this not merely (I must say it here as I have elsewhere) for our own people who are born amongst us, but as an outlet for free white people everywhere, the world over—in which Hans, and Baptiste, and Patrick, and all other men from all the world, may find new homes and better their condition in life.[916]

As he declared in a speech on June 26, 1857, the deportation of blacks is the only way to prevent whites from having to live in close association with them. But,

> as an immediate separation is impossible the next best thing is to keep them apart where they are not already together.[917]

Thus, even if his colonization plan did not work out, he knew of other ways of "keeping whites and blacks apart where they are not already together."

On September 15, 1858, at one of the Lincoln-Douglas Debates, Lincoln shared one of these with his audience. After reading a quote by newspaper editor Z. B. Mayo of DeKalb County, Illinois, he added his own comment at the end (in italics):

> [Quoting Mayo] "Our opinion is that it would be best for all concerned to have the colored population in a State by themselves." *In this I agree with him* [Lincoln's comment].[918]

This is the same Abraham Lincoln, the so-called "Great Emancipator," who said the following:

> [I give] the most solemn pledge that I will to the very last stand by the law of this State, which forbids the marrying of white people with negroes.[919]

> I do not perceive how I can express myself, more plainly, than I have done . . . I have expressly disclaimed all intention to bring about social and political equality between the white and black races . . . I say . . . that Congress, which lays the foundations of society, should . . . be strongly opposed to the incorporation of slavery among its elements. But it does not follow that social and political equality between whites and blacks, must be incorporated . . .[920]

> [Southerners, we] mean to marry your girls when we have a chance—the white ones, I mean . . .[921]

> If there was a necessary conflict between the white man and the negro, I should be for the white man . . .[922]

> In the course of his reply, Senator Douglas remarked, in substance, that he had always considered this government was made for the white people and not for the negroes. Why, in point of mere fact, I think so too.[923]

Reading such statements, is it surprising that Lincoln was so interested in apartheid, black deportation, and limiting instead of abolishing slavery? Not at all. As he himself states in his own words, he had good reason for his beliefs: jobs, housing, and racism.

# ★ 14 ★

# THE CONFEDERACY & BLACKS

**WHAT YOU WERE TAUGHT:** Southern blacks did not support the Confederacy. Why would they?

**THE TRUTH:** Almost all Victorian Southern blacks, in their millions, supported the Confederacy, and for a number of rational and practical reasons. And we will note here that enlightened modern day blacks continue to endorse and back the ideals of the Southern Confederacy, and even proudly display the Confederate Flag, the many reasons for which will be described in this chapter.[924]

**WHAT YOU WERE TAUGHT:** No black man ever fought for the Confederacy.

**THE TRUTH:** Unofficially an estimated 300,000 Southern black men armed themselves, enlisted, and served heroically under the Rebels' Stars and Bars, tens of thousands more *Southern* blacks than served under the Yanks' Stars and Stripes.[925] This number is even more impressive when we consider that Southern blacks were exempt from the Confederate draft: though many were impressed into service, the rest volunteered.[926]

Additionally, when raw percentages are taken into account, far more blacks fought for the Confederacy than for the Union. The Union possessed about 3 million soldiers. Of these about 200,000 were black, 6 percent of the total. The Confederacy had about 1 million soldiers.[927] Of these an estimated 300,000 were black,[928] 30 percent of the total—24 percent more than fought for Lincoln.

And these numbers are conservative if we use the definition of a "private soldier" as determined by German-American Union general, August Valentine Kautz, in 1864:

> In the fullest sense, any man in the military service who receives pay, whether sworn in or not, is a soldier, because he is subject to military law. Under this general head, laborers, teamsters, sutlers,

chaplains, etc., are soldiers.[929]

Using Kautz's definition of a "private soldier," some 2 million Southerners fought in the Confederacy: 1 million whites and perhaps as many as 1 million blacks. As most of the 4 million blacks (3.5 million servants, 500,000 free) living in the South at the time of Lincoln's War remained loyal to Confederacy, and as at least 500,000 to 1 million of these either worked in or fought in the Rebel army and navy in some capacity, Kautz' definition raises the percentage of Southern blacks who defended the Confederacy as real soldiers to as much as 50 percent of the total Confederate soldier population!

There were so many black Rebels on the battlefield that Northern soldiers, most who were overtly racist,[930] were completely dumbstruck at the sight. And their fear was justified: Confederate blacks were known to be ferocious fighters, fearless soldiers, and crack shots. Indeed, the first Northerner killed in the War, Major Theodore Winthrop of the 7th Regiment, New York State Militia, was brought down by a black Confederate sharpshooter at the Battle of Bethel Church, June 10, 1861.[931]

General Stonewall Jackson's army alone contained some 3,000 black soldiers. Clad "in all kinds of uniforms," and armed with "rifles, muskets, sabres, bowie-knives, dirks, etc.," to the shocked Yankee soldiers they were "manifestly an integral portion of the Southern Confederacy."[932] On March 1, 1865, Yankee Colonel John G. Parkhurst sent a battlefield dispatch to General William D. Whipple, reporting that: "The rebel authorities are enrolling negroes in Mississippi preparatory to putting them into service."[933]

If more proof of Southern black support for the Confederacy is needed we need look no further than a letter written by former Northern slave Frederick Douglass to Lincoln in 1862. In it the black civil rights leader uses the example of the overwhelming number of blacks in the Confederate army to urge the president to allow blacks to officially enlist in the Union army (Lincoln had steadfastly refused up until that time). Wrote Douglass to the president:

> There are at the present moment, many colored men in the Confederate Army doing duty not only as cooks, servants and laborers, but as real soldiers, having muskets on their shoulders and bullets in their pockets, ready to shoot down loyal [Yankee] troops, and do all that soldiers may do to destroy the Federal government and build up that of the traitors and rebels. There were such soldiers at Manassas, and they are probably there still. There is a negro in the [Confederate] army as well as in the fence, and our Government is likely to find it out before the war comes to an end. That the negroes are numerous in the rebel army, and do for that army it heaviest work, is beyond question.[934]

Unfortunately, the reality of the black Confederate soldier does not conform to
Northern and New South myths about Southern blacks and slavery, and so it has
been disregarded and suppressed.

**WHAT YOU WERE TAUGHT:** The South never officially enlisted blacks in
it military forces as soldiers.

**THE TRUTH:** While blacks fought *unofficially* for the South from day one, the
Confederacy began *official* black enlistment on March 13, 1865, with
congressional passage of the "Act to Increase the Military Force of the
Confederate States." The initial bill only allowed for the enrollment of blacks,
not their emancipation, an unfortunate oversight that President Jefferson Davis
quickly resolved.   A few days later, on March 23, through the War
Department, Davis issued General Order No. 14, which stated in part:

> . . . No slave will be accepted as a recruit unless with his own
> consent and with the approbation of his master by a written
> instrument conferring, as far as he may, the rights of a freedman .
> . .[935]

In other words, Southern slaves could now not only officially enlist, but they
were immediately emancipated and fought under the Confederate flag as free
men, on the same footing as Southern white soldiers.

**WHAT YOU WERE TAUGHT:** All Southern blacks fled North as soon as
Lincoln issued the Emancipation Proclamation.

**THE TRUTH:** Almost no Southern blacks went North when Lincoln issued his
famous edict on January 1, 1863, much to the relief of Northern whites,[936] most
who, like Lincoln himself, feared that a massive "flood" of freed slaves would
immediately head north and "run over the helpless Yankees like sheep," as the
president put it.[937]

Indeed, this is one of the many reasons Lincoln hesitated for so long to
issue the Emancipation Proclamation: he and his Northern constituents believed
that abolishing Southern slavery would push millions of African-Americans
northward to intermix with their children, dilute and corrupt the white race,
endanger racial purity, threaten prosperity, lower moral standards, scare off
visitors and tourists, discourage new business, spread diseases, drive down
property values, instigate a massive crime wave, thwart black colonization,
promote abolitionist doctrines, "Africanize" the white North, and worst of all,
take away jobs from whites.[938]

But "Honest Abe" and his Yankee neighbors need not have worried.
Southern historical studies reveal that only 5 percent or less left Dixie for the

North. A full 95 percent of the South's black servants remained right where they were after "emancipation,"[939] preferring to stay with their families and friends on the land of their birth, on the farms and plantations they loved, near the graves of their time-honored ancestors.[940]

**WHAT YOU WERE TAUGHT:** No black man or woman ever aided the Confederate Cause.

**THE TRUTH:** Postwar Southern whites credited Southern blacks with literally saving the Confederacy from complete and utter destruction. In fact, Southern blacks were more important to the Confederate Cause during Lincoln's War than they were before it. Their talents, intelligence, experience, and labor were absolutely vital to the South's survival, and Dixie would have lost the War much sooner without their assistance.

Distinguished African-American historian Benjamin Quarles maintains that the Southern black's contributions to the Confederate Cause were beyond counting,[941] and with good reason. The support of countless Southern slaves (and also free Southern blacks) who served in the Confederate Army as teamsters, construction workers, drivers, cooks, nurses, body servants, and orderlies,[942] not to mention the hundreds of thousands who served as soldiers,[943] helped prolong the South's military efforts against Lincoln and his Yankee invaders.[944]

Just as importantly, with the bulk of young and middle-aged white males away on the battlefield, it was primarily the bravery, strength, strong work ethic, and ingeniousness of Southern African-American servants—who remained at home and kept the farms going, provided food and supplies for the Confederate armies, and protected white females and their children against the ravages of Lincoln's violent blue-coated meddlers—that spared Dixie from utter annihilation.[945]

Yankee commanders on the battlefield frequently complained of this very reality, which is one of the reasons they suggested "emancipating" Southern black slaves. Not to give blacks freedom and equal rights with whites, but to eliminate the Confederacy's primary support system: millions of loyal Southern blacks who refused to leave their homes, farms, and plantations. For by remaining in the South they helped maintain Southern resolve, supported Confederate troops, and protected Southern families.

After the War, white Confederate soldier Luther W. Hopkins had this to say about Southern blacks and their relationship to white Southerners:

> Now I want to say that I shall ever have a tender spot in my breast
> for the colored people, owing to what I know of the race, judged
> from my association with them from early childhood up to and

including the years of the Civil War, and, indeed, some years after.

My home in Loudoun county [Virginia], on the border line between the North and South, gave me an unusual opportunity of judging how far the negro could be trusted in caring for and protecting the homes of the men who were in the Southern armies. Scattered all through the South, and especially in the border States, there were white men who were not in sympathy with the South, and some of them acted as spies and guides for the Northern troops as they marched and counter-marched through the land. But I never knew of negroes being guilty of like conduct. They not only watched over and protected the women and children in their homes, but were equally as faithful and careful to protect the Southern soldier from capture when he returned home to see his loved ones.

No soldier in Loudoun or Fauquier counties ever feared that his or his neighbor's servants would betray him to the enemy. The negro always said, in speaking of the Southern soldiers, "our soldiers," although he well knew that the success of the North meant his freedom, while the success of the South meant the [temporary] continuation of slavery.

Another remarkable thing. No one ever heard of a negro slave, or, so far as I know, a free negro of the South, offering an insult or an indignity to a white woman. They were frequently commissioned to escort the daughters of the family to church or to school, or on any expedition taking them from home. Sometimes the distance was long and across fields and through lonely woods, but the . . . colored man always delivered his charge safely, and would have died in his footsteps to do it if the occasion required. Freedom, education, or both, or something else, has developed in the negro a trait that no one ever dreamed he possessed until after the close of the Civil War. Hence, I have a great respect for the race.[946]

Many blacks, though they did not wear Confederate uniforms, served the Confederate armies in a myriad of clever and dangerous ways. This next account, of the Union's Kilpatrick-Dahlgren Raid (February 28–March 3, 1864), illustrates an example. Related by Confederate Brigadier Generals Armistead L. Long and Marcus J. Wright, it is the story of a Southern servant, Martin Robinson, who had been captured by Union soldiers. Known to Yankees by the derogatory term "contraband," the courageous African-American paid the ultimate price for remaining loyal to the Southland that he loved:

[Union General Hugh Judson] Kilpatrick, having failed to meet

[Union Colonel Ulric] Dahlgren at the appointed time before Richmond, determined not to wait, but to attack [the Rebels] at once. He crossed the outer line of defences without resistance, but on reaching the second line he was so warmly [that is, violently] received that he was obliged to retire, and with difficulty made good his retreat through the Confederate lines. This lack of co-operation in the Federal forces was due to the fact that Dahlgren put in the responsible position of guide a contraband [Robinson] who showed his fidelity to the Southern cause by misleading him from his proposed line of march, and thus created a delay which prevented his forming a junction with Kilpatrick. We are told that the negro was executed on the alleged charge of treachery [Dahlgren hanged Robinson on the spot, using the reins of his horse]. When Dahlgren approached the neighborhood of Richmond he was met by a Confederate force and signally defeated; he himself was killed, and only a remnant of his command escaped destruction.[947]

Truly, the citizens of Richmond, Virginia, should immortalize Robinson in marble for his devotion to the South!

Thousands of similar stories have come down to us from wartime eyewitnesses. Even Lincoln recognized the immense contribution of Southern black soldiers to the Confederacy, as he stated on March 17, 1865:

There is one thing about the negro's fighting for the rebels which we can know as well as they can, and that is that they cannot at the same time fight in their armies and stay at home and make bread for them.[948]

Yankee Quartermaster-General Montgomery C. Meigs had the same complaint, as he grumbled in an official report on November 18, 1862:

The labor of the colored man supports the rebel soldier, enables him to leave his plantation to meet our armies, builds his fortifications, cooks his food, and sometimes aids him on picket by rare skill with the rifle.[949]

Meigs then recommended liberating Southern blacks; again, not for the purpose of civil rights. He, like Lincoln, merely wanted to employ them in the Northern army, and then only if segregated and "put under strict military control." As the Union officer wrote:

In all these modes it [that is, the labor of Southern blacks] is

available to assist our Army, and it is probable that there will be
less outrage, less loss of life, by freeing these people, if put under
strict military control, than if left to learn slowly that war has
removed the white men who have heretofore held them in check,
and to yield at last to the temptation to insurrection and
massacre. [950]

Like Lincoln's, Meigs' wish for a Southern black "insurrection and
massacre" also failed to materialize, and millions of Dixie's African-Americans
remained at home where they continued to support the Confederate Cause in
whatever way they could. This is how the Southern tradition of sharecropping
began: after the War planters subdivided their land into small plots known as
"fragmented plantations," that were then tilled by millions of former black
servants. Pro-North historians, of course, never mention where these men and
women came from, but we will: they never left the South to begin with! When
Lincoln illegally invaded the Confederacy in 1861 they refused to forsake their
homeland, families, friends, farms, and businesses. [951]

Hopkins gives us the following wartime story, yet another example
showing the undying fidelity that Southern blacks had for both whites and for
their homeland Dixie:

. . . there was not a day that we [Confederate soldiers] were not in
danger of being surrounded and captured. The bluecoats were
scouting through the country almost continuously in search of
Mosby's "gang," as they called it. We had to keep on guard and
watch the roads and hilltops every hour of the day. We had the
advantage of knowing the country and the hiding places and the
short cuts, and then we had our loyal servants, always willing to aid
us to escape "them Yankees."

For instance, I made a visit to Sunny Bank, the home of
my brother-in-law, E. C. Broun. My horse was hitched to the
rack, and I was inside enjoying the hospitalities of an old Virginia
home, when one of the little darkies rushed in and said, "Yankees."
They were soon all around the house, but, before they got there,
one of the servants took the saddle and bridle off my steed, hid
them, and turned him loose in the garden, where he posed as the
old family driving nag, while I went to the back porch, climbed a
ladder, and lifting a trap-door, got in between the ceiling and the
roof. The trapdoor was so adjusted that it did not show an
opening. The ladder was taken away, and there I stayed until the
enemy departed. I got back home safely, eight miles off, and had
other close calls, but owing to the fidelity of the colored people,
who were always on the watch, and whose loyalty to the

Confederate soldiers, whether they belonged to the family in which they lived or not, was touching and beautiful beyond comprehension. They always called the Confederates "Our Soldiers," and the other side "Them Yankees."[952]

In May 1865, one month after War's end, South Carolina diarist Mary Chesnut remarked that in her region there was not a single case of a servant betraying their master or mistress, and that on most plantations "things looked unchanged." Blacks, now free laborers known as "plantation hands," were still working in the fields of their original white families, as if not one of them had ever seen a Yankee or even knew they existed.[953]

Thus it could truly be said that while white Southern soldiers lost on the battlefield, Southern black servants won the War on the home front by helping to preserve both white and black families and their agricultural holdings across Dixie. Except for the many Southern lives themselves that were expended in the fight against the North, no single greater contribution to the South's War effort can be named.

**WHAT YOU WERE TAUGHT:** During the Civil War the Southern armies were all white.
**THE TRUTH:** Actually, like Southern society itself at the time, as now, the Rebel military was a highly multiracial, multicultural group comprised of every race and dozens of different nationalities.

Though—thanks to the vicious Yankee custom of burning down Southern courthouses[954]—exact statistics are impossible to come by, Southern historians have determined that the following numbers are roughly accurate. In descending numerical order the Confederate army and navy was composed of about 1 million European-Americans,[955] 300,000 to 1 million African-Americans,[956] 70,000 Native-Americans, 60,000 Latin-Americans,[957] 50,000 foreigners,[958] 12,000 Jewish-Americans,[959] and 10,000 Asian-Americans.[960]

True Southerners, of all races, continue to be proud of our region's multiracial history, and of the many contributions made to Dixie by individuals of all colors, creeds, and nationalities. For it is my theory that what I call "racism-phobes"—that is, those who fear that they see racism in everything and who label everyone they dislike a "racist"—are actually themselves latent racists.[961]

**WHAT YOU WERE TAUGHT:** No Confederate officer or politician ever called for the enlistment and emancipation of blacks.
**THE TRUTH:** Numerous Southern militiamen and politicians had long sought enlistment and emancipation of blacks. One of these was Virginian General

Robert E. Lee, to this day still the most beloved and highly regarded Confederate officer across the South.

On December 27, 1856, five years before Lincoln's War, Lee, who unlike General Grant and many other Northern officers,[962] never owned slaves, and who had always been opposed to slavery, wrote a letter to his wife in which he stated that slavery is a "moral and political evil," worse even for the white race than for the black race.[963]

This view is not surprising coming from one who was born in Virginia, the state where the American abolition movement began,[964] and whose native sons, most notably U.S. Presidents George Washington[965] and Thomas Jefferson,[966] struggled for so long to rid America of this vile institution; and this while the North was sending hundreds of slave ships to Africa, and whose main port cities, like New York, Providence, Philadelphia, Baltimore, and Boston, functioned as the literal epicenters of slave trading in the Western hemisphere.[967]

Regarding the enlistment of Southern blacks, Lee made his views clear in a letter to Southern Congressman Ethelbert Barksdale on February 18, 1865:

> . . . in my opinion, the negroes, under proper circumstances, will make efficient soldiers. I think we could at least do as well with them as the enemy . . . Under good officers, and good instructions, I do not see why they should not become soldiers. . . . They furnish a more promising material than many armies of which we read in history . . . I think those who are employed should be freed. It would be neither just nor wise, in my opinion, to require them to serve as slaves. . . . I have no doubt that if Congress would authorize their reception into service, and empower the President [Jefferson Davis] to call upon individuals or States for such as they are willing to contribute, with the condition of emancipation to all enrolled, a sufficient number would be forthcoming to enable us to try the experiment. If it proved successful, most of the objections to the measure would disappear, and if individuals still remained unwilling to send their negroes to the army, the force of public opinion in the States would soon bring about such legislation as would remove all obstacles.[968]

General Lee mentions that "the force of public opinion" in the abolitionist South would push black enlistment through eventually, no matter what the military thought. However, as Representative Barksdale stated before the House in early 1865, *all* Confederate soldiers, whatever their rank, wanted black enlistment. This sentiment was backed up by such establishments as the renowned Virginia Military Institute, which agreed to train Southern blacks in the art of soldiering.[969]

But Lee was far from being the first prominent Confederate to advocate emancipation and enlistment of Southern blacks. On March 24, 1862, Louisiana governor and commander-in-chief, Thomas O. Moore, who had commissioned the first black militia in the Confederacy (the Native Guards of Louisiana), called on an organized militia of blacks, one that had already been protecting New Orleans for several months, to "maintain their organization, and . . . hold themselves prepared for such orders as may be transmitted to them." Their purpose? To guard homes, property, and Southern rights against "the pollution of a ruthless [Northern] invader."[970]

In the summer of 1863 both a number of Confederates and the Alabama legislature asked the Confederate government to enlist blacks,[971] and on November 11, 1863, in a letter to Confederate Secretary of War James A. Seddon, Confederate Major Samuel W. Melton suggested that conscription be extended to include "free negroes."[972]

Another noteworthy pro-black white Confederate officer was General Patrick R. Cleburne, known as the "Stonewall Jackson of the West" for his bold tactics on the battlefield.[973] A native of Ireland and a division commander in the Army of Tennessee, at an officers' meeting on January 2, 1864, the Irishman disclosed a written proposal that would soon become known as the "Cleburne Memorial." Calling for the immediate enlistment and training of black soldiers, it promised complete emancipation for *all* Southern slaves at the end of the War.[974]

Cleburne, who died eleven months later fighting Yankee interlopers at the Battle of Franklin II,[975] wrote:

> Adequately to meet the causes which are now threatening ruin to our country, we propose . . . that we retain in service for the war all troops now in service, and that we immediately commence training a largo reserve of the most courageous of our slaves, and further that we guarantee freedom within a reasonable time to every slave in the South who shall remain true to the Confederacy in this war. As between the loss of independence and the loss of slavery, we assume that every patriot will freely give up the latter—give up the negro slave rather than be a slave himself. If we are correct in this assumption it only remains to show how this great national sacrifice is, in all human probabilities, to change the current of success and sweep the [Yankee] invader from our country. . . . The immediate effect of the emancipation and enrollment of negroes on the military strength of the South would be: To enable us to have armies numerically superior to those of the North, and a reserve of any size we might think necessary; to

enable us to take the offensive, move forward, and forage on the enemy. It would open to us in prospective another and almost untouched source of supply, and furnish us with the means of preventing temporary disaster, and carrying on a protracted struggle. It would instantly remove all the vulnerability, embarrassment, and inherent weakness which result from slavery. . . .We can only get a sufficiency by making the negro share the danger and hardships of the war. If we arm and train him and make him fight for the country in her hour of dire distress, every consideration of principle and policy demand that we should set him and his whole race who side with us free. It is a first principle with mankind that he who offers his life in defense of the State should receive from her in return his freedom and his happiness, and we believe in acknowledgment of this principle. The Constitution of the Southern States has reserved to their respective governments the power to free slaves for meritorious services to the State. It is politic besides. For many years, ever since the agitation of the subject of slavery commenced, the negro has been dreaming of freedom, and his vivid imagination has surrounded that condition with so many gratifications that it has become the paradise of his hopes. To attain it he will tempt dangers and difficulties not exceeded by the bravest soldier in the field. The hope of freedom is perhaps the only moral incentive that can be applied to him in his present condition. It would be preposterous then to expect him to fight against it with any degree of enthusiasm, therefore we must bind him to our cause by no doubtful bonds; we must leave no possible loop-hole for treachery to creep in. The slaves are dangerous now, but armed, trained, and collected in an army they would be a thousand fold more dangerous: therefore when we make soldiers of them we must make free men of them beyond all question, and thus enlist their sympathies also. We can do this more effectually than the North can now do, for we can give the negro not only his own freedom, but that of his wife and child, and can secure it to him in his old home. . . . If, then, we touch the institution at all, we would do best to make the most of it, and by emancipating the whole race upon reasonable terms, and within such reasonable time as will prepare both races for the change, secure to ourselves all the advantages, and to our enemies all the disadvantages that can arise, both at home and abroad, from such a sacrifice. Satisfy the negro that if he faithfully adheres to our standard during the war he shall receive his freedom and that of his race. Give him as an earnest of our intentions such immediate immunities as will impress him with our sincerity and be in keeping with his new condition, enroll a portion of his class as soldiers of the Confederacy, and we change the race from a dreaded weakness to a position of strength. . . . It is said slavery is all we are fighting for, and if we give it up we give up all. Even if this were true, which we deny, slavery is not all our enemies are fighting for. It is merely the pretense to establish sectional superiority and a more centralized form of government, and to deprive us of our rights and liberties. We have now briefly proposed a plan which we believe will save our country. It may be imperfect, but in all human probability it would give us our independence.[976]

Cleburne's proposal was signed by over a dozen other Confederate officers. When it came to African-Americans, anti-abolitionist Lincoln never came close to espousing such humanitarian ideas.

**WHAT YOU WERE TAUGHT:** Southern slaves detested their white owners before, during, and after the War, particularly former Confederate soldiers. **THE TRUTH:** The opposite is true. Throughout the antebellum, bellum, and postbellum periods we have thousands of stories of warm relations between Southern whites and Southern blacks,[977] and of free blacks and slaves providing various forms of support for both the war effort[978] and for former white slave owners who had been made indigent by Lincoln's War. In 1901, celebrated former Virginia slave and black educator, Booker T. Washington, wrote:

As a rule, not only did the members of my race entertain no feelings of bitterness against . . . [Southern] whites before and during the war, but there are many instances of Negroes tenderly caring for their former masters and mistresses who for some reason have become poor and dependent since the war. I know of instances where the former masters of slaves have for years been supplied with money by their former slaves to keep them from suffering. I have known of still other cases in which the former slaves have assisted in the education of the descendants of their former owners. I know of a case on a large plantation in the South in which a young white man, the son of the former owner of the estate, has become so reduced in purse and self control by reason of drink that he is a pitiable creature; and yet, notwithstanding the poverty of the coloured people themselves on this plantation, they have for years supplied this young white man with the necessities of life. One sends him a little coffee or sugar, another a little meat, and so on. Nothing that the coloured people possess is too good for the son of "old Mars Tom," who will perhaps never be permitted to suffer while any remain on the place who knew directly or indirectly of "old Mars Tom."[979]

# ★ 15 ★

# THE UNION & BLACKS

**WHAT YOU WERE TAUGHT:** The North, under President Lincoln, enlisted blacks long before the South did under President Davis.

**THE TRUTH:** The opposite is true. Southern black enlistment came even before the War's first major conflict, the Battle of First Manassas (First Bull Run to Yanks) on July 18, 1861.[980] In June 1861, one year and three months before the Union officially sanctioned the recruitment of blacks in August 1862,[981] and almost two years before Lincoln began arming blacks in March 1863, the Tennessee legislature passed a statute allowing Governor Isham G. Harris to receive into military service "all male free persons of color, between the ages of 15 and 50 . . ."[982]

On February 4, 1862, the Virginia legislature passed a bill to enroll all of the state's free Negroes for service in the Confederate army. Earlier, on November 23, 1861, a seven-mile long line of Confederate soldiers was marched through the streets of New Orleans. Among them was a regiment of 1,400 free black volunteers.[983] Hundreds of other such examples could be given.[984] We have already seen that perhaps as many as 80 percent more blacks fought for the Confederacy than for the Union.

Anti-South proponents have carefully suppressed such facts, making our already Northern-slanted history books even more incomplete, inaccurate, and misleading than they should be.

**WHAT YOU WERE TAUGHT:** The Union formed all-black troops before the Confederacy did.

**THE TRUTH:** The South's first all-black militia was officially formed on April 23, 1861, only nine days after the first battle of the War at Fort Sumter, South Carolina. The unit, known as the "Native Guards (colored)," was "duly and legally enrolled as a part of the militia of the State, its officers being commissioned by Thomas O. Moore, Governor and Commander-in-Chief of the State of Louisiana . . ."[985]

In contrast, the North's first all-black militia, the First South Carolina Volunteers, was not commissioned until over a year and a half later (on November 7, 1862), under Yankee Colonel Thomas Wentworth Higginson.[986]

**WHAT YOU WERE TAUGHT:** The Confederacy was racist towards her black soldiers, and treated them unfairly and abused them. The Union was not racist toward hers, and treated them equally with white soldiers.

**THE TRUTH:** We have discussed the facts that Lincoln postponed both the emancipation of slaves and the enlistment of blacks into the Union army for as long as possible, and that Northern racism was at the root of these delay tactics. There was certainly white racism in Old Dixie, and her people have never tried to hide this fact as the North has tried to conceal its own wartime white racism. But because, as Tocqueville and others have pointed out, white racism was far less severe in the South,[987] the Confederacy treated its black soldiers far more equitably than the Union did its black soldiers. In fact, the Rebel military was ordered to do so by the Confederate government.

White Yankee soldiers were well-known for their racial bigotry and utter intolerance of blacks. This is just one of the many reasons Lincoln would not permit blacks to serve as active combatants in the U.S. military during the first half of his War.[988] As hesitant Lincoln put it to a group of abolitionist clergyman on September 13, 1862, a few days prior to issuing his Preliminary Emancipation Proclamation:

> . . . I am not so sure we could do much with the blacks. If we were to arm them, I fear that in a few weeks the arms would be in the hands of the rebels; and, indeed, thus far we have not had arms enough to equip our white troops.[989]

Lincoln's hesitation was warranted, but not for the reason he states: when he finally allowed full-fledged black recruitment, white soldiers hissed and booed, desertions increased, and a general "demoralization" set in across the entire Federal military.[990]

The mere mention of the idea of "black enlistment" brought many white regiments close to insurrection.[991] A Yankee soldier with the 90th Illinois reported on the general feeling among his fellow Union compatriots at the time: Not one of our boys wants to give guns to the Negroes. This is a white man's war and that's the way we want to keep it. Besides we have no desire to fight next to blacks on the battlefield, he asserted.[992]

Northern white outrage at the idea of enlisting blacks was somewhat mitigated when Lincoln ordered the army and navy to be racially segregated, but newly recruited blacks were not happy with the president's command that all colored troops were to be officered by whites.[993] Even pro-North historians have had to concede that white Northern soldiers were "bitterly hostile . . . to Negro troops."[994]

White Yankee racism continued well into the War. During inclement weather, for example, white Yankee soldiers were known to beat black Yankee soldiers, then push them out into the freezing night air in order to have the tents all to themselves.[995]

Most white Union officers never completely accepted commanding black troops, as there was "no prestige" in it. In fact so few white officers could be found who were willing to "lower" themselves to leading blacks that white privates, induced with the promise of promotion,[996] finally had to be virtually coerced into taking the positions.[997]

The situation got so out of hand that Federal officers had to be ordered to "treat black soldiers as soldiers," and the "n" word, along with degrading disciplinary action and routine offensive language aimed at blacks, had to be banned with harsh punishments.[998] Meanwhile white Union soldiers continued to put on minstrel shows that satirized and humiliated African-Americans, a not uncommon form of entertainment, particularly on Yankee warships.[999]

But Northern white racism in the U.S. army often manifested in far more serious and diabolical ways. Southern diaries, letters, and journals are replete with reports of incredible Yankee brutality against not only white Southern women they came across, but black Southern women as well, even against those that had at first cheered them on as liberators. Yankee soldiers' crimes against black females included robbery, pillage, beatings, torture, rape, and even murder.[1000]

Southern black males were often treated even worse by their Northern "emancipators." Those who survived such crimes were taken, against their will at gunpoint, from their relatively peaceful, healthy, and safe lives of service and domesticity on the plantation, to the filth, hardships, and dangers of life on the battlefield, where at least 50 percent of them died alone in muddy ditches fighting for the Yanks against their own native land: the South.[1001]

Those blacks who resisted "involuntary enlistment" into Lincoln's army were sometimes shot or bayoneted on the spot. When black soldiers rebelled against the abuse of white Yankee soldiers, they were whipped.[1002] Both white and black Union soldiers were known to abuse Southern slaves who remained loyal to Dixie, entering their homes, shooting bullets through the walls, overturning furniture, and stealing various personal items.[1003]

Is this shocking? Not when we realize that this was all merely a continuation of Lincoln's policy of coercion, the same one he had used to invade the South in an attempt to destroy states' rights to begin with.[1004]

Many newly "freed" black males were used as Yankee shock troops, sent first into battle in conflicts usually known beforehand to be hopeless, where they would take the brunt of the violence, sparing the lives of Northern whites.[1005] This is almost certainly what Lincoln was intimating in his letter to James C. Conkling on August 26, 1863, when he wrote:

> . . . whatever negroes can be got to do as soldiers, leaves just so much less for white soldiers to do in saving the Union.[1006]

This included, of course, receiving cold Confederate steel.

Blacks who were finally allowed to enlist in the Union army by their reluctant president, however, were in for a rude surprise if they expected to don a fancy new uniform and fight next to whites on the battlefield. For at the beginning of black enlistment, Lincoln turned nearly all freed black males into common workers who performed what can only be described as "forced labor";[1007] in other words, slavery. Their drudgery work, in fact, was identical to what they had experienced as slaves. Black military duties under Lincoln included construction, serving officers (known in the South as "body servants"), cooking, washing clothes and dishes, tending livestock, and cleaning stables.[1008]

Actually, the first black soldiers in the U.S. military were not allowed to serve as active combatants in any form; rather they were signed up specifically to work as ordinary grunts: teamsters, blacksmiths, carpenters, masons, scouts, longshoremen, pioneers, wheelwrights, medical assistants, orderlies, laundry workers, spies, and of course, "slaves,"[1009] almost anything but armed fighters.[1010] Most were to be used merely for monotonous guard duty, or as Lincoln put it in his Final Emancipation Proclamation,

> to garrison forts, positions, stations, and other places, and to man vessels of all sorts in said service.[1011]

This so-called "Freedmen's labor system," authorized by Lincoln and overseen by Yankee General Nathaniel Prentiss Banks, was so blatantly racist that Banks was even roundly criticized by other Northerners, who accused him of forcing blacks back into slavery. The brutal U.S. government program was also rife with corruption and fraud: freed blacks were regularly whipped while their already paltry wages were often "withheld" by unscrupulous and inhumane white Northerners who pocketed the money then disappeared.[1012]

The fact that one of Lincoln's top officers, the cross-eyed General Benjamin "the Beast" Butler, insisted on referring to freed Southern blacks as "contraband" (that is, illegal goods) certainly did not help the cause of black civil rights.[1013] Instead, it revealed that the North still regarded blacks as inferior to whites[1014] and as the legitimate property of whites—even after so-called "emancipation."[1015]

But Lincoln never objected to the dehumanizing title. In fact he approved it. The name stuck and continued to be widely used in the North, even after the War.[1016] This was only natural, as the North's commander-in-chief, Abraham Lincoln, who led the North by example, always referred to whites as the "superior race"[1017] and blacks (and all non-whites) as the "inferior race."[1018]

Southern blacks were far from being truly free after Lincoln's Emancipation Proclamation. Indeed, this is why Lincoln and the rest of the North referred to them as "freedmen" rather than as "freemen": they had been freed from the "shackles of slavery," but they were not yet free from the shackles of Northern racism.

Lincoln's own personal racism seemed boundless. Along with the bigoted policies already mentioned, he also refused to grant Northern black soldiers equal treatment in any way.[1019] For example, he gave his black soldiers half the pay of white soldiers:[1020] white U.S. privates were paid thirteen dollars per month, while black U.S. privates were paid just seven dollars per month.[1021] Contrast this with the Confederacy: in some Southern states blacks were actually paid up to three times the rate of whites for military service.[1022]

Three of the seven dollars of the black Union soldiers' monthly pay was a deduction for clothing, a deduction not imposed on white Union soldiers. Often even this small amount was withheld from black recruits by Yank officers, who sometimes simply "skimmed" the money for themselves, only one of dozens of ways the U.S. defrauded African-Americans during the War.[1023]

Lincoln also refused to give black soldiers bonuses, pensions, or support for dependents, all which were routinely accorded to white soldiers.[1024] He would not even allow black soldiers equal medical treatment. Medicines and emergency care were to go to whites first, blacks second.[1025]

To add to the insult, blacks in Lincoln's army could not officially be promoted beyond the level of noncommissioned officer.[1026] And in those rare cases when they were, black officers were paid the same as white privates. At least eighteen blacks who protested Lincoln's inequitable wages were charged with "mutiny" and executed by hanging or firing squad. These executions went on even after Lincoln's death and the War had ended. As late as December 1, 1865, six black Union privates accused of "mutiny" (that is, for protesting Lincoln's racist pay scale) were rounded up and killed by musketry at Fernandina, Florida. This was a full year-and-a-half after the U.S. Congress authorized retroactive equal pay for black soldiers in June 1864.[1027]

During his life, Lincoln, an avowed atheist and anti-Christian,[1028] had not been the forgiving type, and neither were many of those who followed in his footsteps. One Yankee newspaper journalist at the time wrote:

> Many, very many of the [Federal] soldiers and not a few of the officers have habitually treated the [Southern and Northern] negroes [who join their ranks] with the coarsest and most brutal insolence and inhumanity; never speaking to them but to curse and revile them.[1029]

An eyewitness living on Hilton Head Island, South Carolina, in 1862, reported that the occupying white Yankee soldiers there repeatedly talked down to blacks using the foulest and most disrespectful language imaginable, while in Norfolk, Virginia, a freed black woman wrote of seeing other blacks being continually abused psychologically, verbally, and physically by Union troops. These Yankee crimes included the destruction of property, pillage, assault and battery, and even rape, against innocent blacks who had fled to them, believing them to be emancipators. This same African-American woman forlornly penned: I'm nothing more than one of master Lincoln's slaves now.[1030]

It is obvious that even after reluctantly allowing blacks into the Union army and navy, Lincoln and his military men continued to see them as little more than servile laborers and cannon-fodder.[1031]

In comparison to the Yankees' grossly unjust treatment of her black soldiers, the Southern Confederacy's approach was the epitome of equality. Not only were blacks paid equal with whites and integrated into all military units under President Davis' General Order No. 14, issued March 23, 1865, but:

> All officers . . . are enjoined to a provident, considerate, and humane attention to whatever concerns the health, comfort, instruction, and discipline of those [black] troops, and to the uniform observance of kindness, forbearance, and indulgence in their treatment of them, and especially that they will protect them from injustice and oppression.[1032]

In sharp contrast to the equal rights accorded to African-American combatants in the Confederacy, Lincoln's prejudices against his own "sable soldiery" continued throughout the War. Black civil rights leaders, like Sojourner Truth, complained to the U.S. president about his pitiful treatment of black soldiers, but to no avail.[1033] Another, celebrated African-American orator Frederick Douglass, expressed his displeasure with Lincoln's long-time reluctance to allow blacks to enroll in the Union military. Mr. President, he asked, if blacks were good enough to serve under U.S. General George

Washington, why are they not now good enough to serve under U.S. General George B. McClellan?[1034]

Most black men who eventually joined Lincoln's army probably did not want to serve under McClellan anyway. Like so many other Northern officers, he spent much of his time enforcing the Fugitive Slave Law of 1850, which required runaway servants to be returned to their owners. This was the same law that Lincoln promised to strengthen in his First Inaugural Address,[1035] despite the fact that overturning it, or even ignoring it, would have helped bring slavery to an end much sooner.[1036]

Southern female servants and their children, meanwhile, could expect little better in the way of treatment from their "Northern liberators." Driven from their homes in cattle-like droves, they were set to work on "U.S. government plantations," so-called "abandoned" Southern farms.[1037] In reality these were Confederate plantations whose original owners had been chased off or killed, replaced by Yankee bosses who often withheld food, clothing, bedding, and medicine from their new black charges, resulting in an appalling death toll.[1038] Though their numbers were never recorded, eyewitnesses testify that the vast majority of blacks rounded up and put in Yankee "contraband camps" did indeed die, the U.S. government apparently placing little importance on their survival.[1039]

Southern blacks were so frightened of Lincoln's soldiers that they went to almost any length to avoid being taken away by them, for they knew that they would very likely be tortured, forced into labor camps, or even killed. Some simply wanted to avoid hearing the Yanks' horrible un-Christian language or having to gaze upon what they had heard were their "hideous looking" faces. One of the most ingenious methods Southern blacks came up with to escape being "freed" by Yankees was to feign illness. Many a Southern black, for instance, was spared "a fate worse than death" by faking a limp, wearing a perfectly good arm in a sling, or taking to bed with a host of alarming moaning sounds.[1040]

The dread of Northern racism was great enough in Dixie that during the War whites "refugeed" their servants by sending them further South for protection.[1041] But almost none had to be coerced, for no Southern black wanted to be "freed," then re-enslaved by the invading Union army, only to end up fighting against their own homeland and people. Thus most went further South voluntarily, requested to be moved, or simply moved "down yonder" on their own.[1042]

The reality of this fact was brought to life by Southern belle Mary Chesnut. In 1862 she noted in her journal that after Confederate General Richard Taylor's home had been attacked and (typically) looted by foraying

Yanks, his black servants then deliberately moved themselves southward to the city of Algiers, not far from New Orleans.  Apparently the white Yankee penchant for intimidating and abusing Southern blacks was contagious. According to Chesnut, black Union soldiers treated Southern blacks even worse than white Union soldiers did.[1043]

Yanks viewed Southern blacks no better after the War than they did during the conflict.  We have record of an incident in South Carolina, for instance, of a black man running up to thank a white Federal officer for Lincoln's emancipation.  The grateful former servant threw his arms around the Union general, embracing him affectionately.  But the Yank violently pulled himself away, quickly pulled a gun, and shot the innocent man dead.  I want nothing to do with such ridiculous falderal, he yelled sternly, and walked calmly away.[1044]

It was not just Southern blacks who feared white Yankees, of course. Tens of thousands of Northern blacks, as well, experienced the horrors of "Yankee rule" between 1641—the year slavery was first legalized in an American colony (Massachusetts),[1045] and 1862—the year the North officially, and finally, ceased trading in slaves.[1046]

As the innocent victims of the instigators of the American slave trade, Northern blacks certainly had much to fear from their Yankee masters.  This is why former Northern slave Sojourner Truth often referred to the U.S. flag, not as the "Stars and Stripes," but as the "Scars and Stripes."[1047]  Her attitude is not surprising considering the facts that: Lincoln used slave labor to build many of Washington D.C.'s most important Federal structures (including the White House and the U.S. Capitol);[1048] the District once possessed America's largest slave mart;[1049] and slavery continued to be practiced within sight of these same buildings well after Lincoln issued his Final Emancipation Proclamation.[1050]

The fears of Northern blacks were particularly understandable when we consider that it was Lincoln (the man leading the Northern government) who repeatedly referred to blacks using the "n" word[1051] and described them as a base and primitive type of human,[1052] while it was Grant (the man leading the Northern military) who disliked Jews[1053] and refused to fight for abolition.[1054] And let us not forget that it was William T. Sherman, to this day still one of the North's most idolized war heroes, who said:

> A ni**er as such is a most excellent fellow, but he is not fit to
> marry, associate, or vote with me or mine.[1055]

With such information at hand, can there be any doubt that white Southerners saved thousands of black lives during Lincoln's War by refugeeing them further South?[1056]

**WHAT YOU WERE TAUGHT:** All of the 180,000 blacks who fought for Lincoln and the Union were freed slaves from the South.

**THE TRUTH:** Just half, or 90,000, of the 180,000 blacks who eventually fought for Lincoln were "emancipated" Southern blacks. It is important to note, however, that a large percentage of these men did not enroll voluntarily. They were forced to join up at gunpoint—or risk physical assault, a whipping, or even being murdered.[1057]

The other 50 percent of Lincoln's African-American soldiers were "free" Northern blacks,[1058] many who were probably "emancipated" from the pool of 500,000 to 1 million black slaves who were still enslaved in the "abolitionist" North in 1860.[1059]

**WHAT YOU WERE TAUGHT:** Southern blacks could not wait for the arrival of the Northern armies and greeted them with open arms.

**THE TRUTH:** Those few Southern blacks who welcomed the sight of the invading Yankee troops only did so because their heads had been filled with anti-South, pro-North propaganda from Union sympathizers, or other equally misinformed African-Americans.

The reality is that most Southern blacks wanted nothing to do with Lincoln, the North, the U.S. government, or Federal soldiers. The more typical response to the arrival of the Union armies is illustrated in the following account. It was recorded shortly after the War by a white former Confederate soldier who witnessed the scene firsthand:

> In a raid by the Federals, on the Mississippi river, they took off [with] the son of [Jenkins,] a negro man belonging to Senator Henry. The boy was about ten years old; and when Jenkins ascertained that his son was on board the Yankee boat, he immediately repaired to the boat, foaming at the mouth, like an enraged tiger. He went on board, knife in hand, and demanded his boy. "Give me back my boy!" exclaimed he, in those terrible, fierce tones that electrify with fear all who hear them, "or I will make the deck of this boat slippery with your blood. You are nothing but a set of vile robbers and plunderers, and I will spill the last drop of my blood but I will have my child. Give him to me, or I will plunge my knife into the heart of the first man I reach." The captain of the boat seeing the desperate determination of Jenkins, told the soldiers they had better give him up, or some of them would be killed, and he was given up. Hurrah for Jenkins! He had previously resisted all appeals to him to desert his master, and he took his boy back to his contented home in triumph. He is one amongst a thousand [Southern blacks who would have done the

same].[1060]


Confederate General Robert E. Lee's son, Robert, Jr., wrote of the following story concerning a Yankee raid on their property in the Summer of 1863. One of the family's servants, captured by U.S. soldiers, hazarded life and limb to not only return to the home and people he loved, but to protect the Lees' horses:

> The next day I found out that all the horses but one had been saved by the faithfulness of our servants. The one lost, my brother's favourite and best horse, was [accidently] ridden straight into the [Union] column [of troops] by Scott, a negro servant, who had him out for exercise. Before he knew our enemies [were there], he and the horse were prisoners. Scott watched his opportunity, and, not being guarded, soon got away. By crawling through a culvert, under the road, while the cavalry was passing along, he made his way into a deep ditch in the adjoining field, thence succeeded in reaching the farm where the rest of the horses were, and hurried them off to a safe place in the woods, just as the Federal cavalry rode up to get them.[1061]

Countless such examples could be given.

If Southern slaves were treated so terribly, and if they detested their white owners and the South so vehemently—as anti-South writers enjoy repeatedly telling us, why did nearly all of Dixie's black servants resist Yankee capture? And why did those who were taken prisoner or "freed" always try to return home, at great risk, at the first opportunity? Why do we never read about any of these brave, intelligent, and faithful African-Americans in pro-North histories?

It is because their stories would expose the truth, revealing Lincoln's War for what it really was: not a battle to "preserve the Union" or "abolish slavery," but an unconstitutional and unnecessary assault on the South and states' rights.

# ★ 16 ★

# THE SOUTH'S

# PARTISAN RANGERS

**WHAT YOU WERE TAUGHT:** The South allowed illegal bands of outlaws and guerillas, the so-called "Partisan Rangers," to fight under the banner of the Confederate flag, committing numerous atrocities.

**THE TRUTH:** Our Partisan Rangers were not outlaws or guerillas, nor did they operate illegally. In April 1862 the Confederacy passed the Partisan Ranger Law that allowed and even encouraged the legal formation of small detached troops, whose main mission was to harass Lincoln's soldiers from behind enemy lines. In the opinion of the South these brave men committed few if any "atrocities," and words like "guerillas" and "outlaws" were merely used by the North for any Confederate cavalry they could not defeat.[1062]

Far from being underground irregulars or illicit insurgents, the Partisan Rangers wore army regulation uniforms (when possible), were officially received into military service, and were reimbursed for captured supplies turned over to the Confederate government.[1063]

Perhaps out of jealousy at the freedom the rangers enjoyed, some of the Rebel top brass began to complain about them, and the Confederate Congress revoked the Partisan Ranger Law in 1864. However, the secretary of war was permitted to continue to enlist whatever ranger groups he deemed necessary to the Southern Cause[1064] (most continued to operate in the field, ignoring all orders from their superiors anyway).[1065]

Overall the South's Partisan Rangers, led by such Southern heroes as John S. Mosby,[1066] John H. Morgan, Harry Gilmore, Elijah V. White, Bill Anderson, J. H. McNeill, George Todd, and William Clarke Quantrill,[1067] were of enormous value to the Rebel war effort. In particular, partisan leaders, like my cousins Jesse James, Morgan, and Mosby (the latter known as the "Gray

Ghost"),[1068] severely hampered the progress of the Northern invaders and delayed the close of the War for at least one year (Union soldiers never were able to disband Mosby's unit).[1069] Yankee war criminals Ulysses S. Grant and Philip H. Sheridan were just two of Lincoln' officers who complained bitterly about the rangers' effectiveness.[1070]

Lincoln himself found much to dislike about the Confederate partisans, finding them so efficient, competent, and successful that at one time he seems to have considered creating Yankee partisan rangers in an effort to combat the South's. On February 17, 1863, here is what the Union president said in a letter to one of his generals, William S. Rosecrans:

> In no other way does the enemy give us so much trouble at so little expense to himself as by the raids of rapidly moving small bodies of troops, largely if not wholly mounted, harassing and discouraging loyal residents, supplying themselves with provisions, clothing, horses, and the like, surprising and capturing small detachments of our forces, and breaking our communications. And this will increase just in proportion as his larger armies shall weaken and wane. Nor can these raids be successfully met by even larger forces of our own of the same kind acting merely on the defensive. I think we should organize proper forces and make counter raids. We should not capture so much of supplies from them as they have done from us, but it would trouble them more to repair railroads and bridges than it does us. What think you of trying to get up such a corps in your army? Could you do it without any or many additional troops (which we have not to give you), provided we furnish horses, suitable arms, and other appointments? Please consider this not as an order, but as a suggestion.[1071]

Our Partisan Rangers certainly got under Lincoln's skin. This alone makes them heroes in the eyes of the South.

# ★ 17 ★

# YANKEE WAR CRIMES

**WHAT YOU WERE TAUGHT:** With God on their side the Northern military was an ethical army that did not hurt, or even intend to harm, the Southern people or their land. Only preserve the Union.

**THE TRUTH:** While many Northerners and New South Southerners find consolation in this self-serving image, traditional Southerners know the Truth, for it was their very ancestors who were the victims of Yankee treachery and violence. There are some even alive today—like Nelson W. Winbush, who wrote the foreword to this book—who remember the tales of horror told them by Southern grandparents who managed to survive the "Civil War."[1072]

We have already studied some of Lincoln's war crimes (Chapter 10). What about the crimes of his military men?

While the anti-South movement will not admit it, volumes have been written on the execrations and barbarities of Yankee soldiers, most of which was taken from firsthand accounts found in the journals, letters, diaries, and even official war reports of Confederate troops and Southern civilians.[1073] Probably no one better articulated the foul deeds perpetuated on the South by the North than Southern writer and historian Edward A. Pollard, who left us a detailed record in his splendid history of the "Civil War," *The Lost Cause.*

After Yankee General Benjamin "the Beast" Butler subdued New Orleans in April 1862, he issued his infamous "woman order." According to the arrogant decree, Southern females who showed the slightest hint of "contempt" toward Yankee soldiers (including even disrespectful facial expressions) were to be treated as "whores," subject to arrest and imprisonment. This was, writes Pollard,

> the prelude to a rule in New Orleans that excited the horrour and
> disgust of the civilized world. The newspapers which declined to
> publish an edict so disreputable were threatened with suppression;
> and Mayor [John T.] Monroe and some of the city authorities who
> ventured to protest against it, were arrested, shipped down to Fort

Jackson [near Triumph, Louisiana], and for many months kept in confinement there. Then followed a series of acts of cruelty, despotism and indecency. Citizens accused of contumacious disloyalty, were confined at hard labour, with balls and chains attached to their limbs. Men, whose only offence was selling medicines to sick Confederate soldiers, were arrested and imprisoned. A physician who, as a joke, exhibited a skeleton in his window as that of a Yankee soldier, was sentenced to be confined at Ship Island for two years, at hard labour. A lady, the wife of a former member of Congress of the United States, who happened to laugh as the funeral train of a Yankee officer passed her door, received this sentence: "It is, therefore, ordered that she be not 'regarded and treated as a common woman,' of whom no officer or soldier is bound to take notice, but as an uncommon, bad, and dangerous woman, stirring up strife, and inciting to riot, and that, therefore, she be confined at Ship Island, in the State of Mississippi, within proper limits there, till further orders." The distinction of sex seems only to have been recognized by Butler as a cowardly opportunity for advantage. In his office, in the St. Charles Hotel, the inscription was placed in plain sight: "There is no difference between a he and a she adder in their venom." His officers were allowed to indulge their rapacity and lust at will; they seized houses of respectable citizens, and made them the shops of infamous female characters; they appropriated the contents of wine-rooms; they plundered the wardrobes of ladies and gentlemen; they sent away from the city the clothing of whole families; they "confiscated" pianos, libraries, and whatever articles of luxury and ornament pleased their fancy, and sent them as presents and souvenirs to their friends at home. It was the era of plunder and ill-gotten gains. Fines were collected at pleasure. Recusants were threatened with ball and chain. A trade was opened in provisions for cotton, and Butler's own brother was made banker and broker of the corrupt operations, buying confiscated property, trading provisions and even military stores for cotton, and amassing out of the distress of an almost starving people fortunes of princely amount and villainous history. . . .

A shocking incident of Butler's despotism in New Orleans was the execution of William B. Mumford, a citizen of the Confederate States, charged with the singular crime of having taken the Federal flag from the United States Mint, which was done before the city had surrendered, and was, in any circumstances, but an act of war. He was condemned to death for an insult to the enemy's ensign. It was scarcely to be believed that on such a charge a human life would be taken, deliberately and in cold blood. Butler was inexorable. The wife and children of the condemned man piteously plead for his life. Butler's answer was cruel and taunting. A number of citizens joined in a petition for mercy. Butler answered that some vicious men in New Orleans had sent him defiant letters about Mumford's fate; that an issue had been raised, that it was "to be decided whether he was to govern in New Orleans or not"—and he decided it by keeping the word he had first pronounced, and sending Mumford to the gallows.

The condemned man was one of humble station in life, and was said to have been of dissipated habits. But he was faultlessly brave. On the gallows the suggestion was made to him that he might yet save his life by a humiliating and piteous confession. He replied to the officer who thus tempted him: "Go away." He turned to the crowd, and said, with a distinct and steady voice: "I consider that the manner of my death will be no disgrace to my wife and children; my country will honour them." More than a thousand spectators stood around the gallows; they could not believe that the last act of the tragedy was really to be performed; they looked on in astonished and profound silence.

Before the era of Butler in New Orleans, the Confederates had had a large and instructive experience of the ferocity of their enemies, and their disregard of all the rules of war and customs of civilization. At Manassas [Virginia] and Pensacola [Florida] the Federals had repeatedly and deliberately fired upon hospitals. In the naval battle in Hampton Roads [Virginia], they had hung out a white flag, and then opened a perfidious fire upon our [Southern] seamen. At Newbern [North Carolina] they had attempted to shell a town containing several thousand women and children, before either demanding a surrender, or giving the citizens notice of their intentions. They had broken faith on every occasion of expediency; they had disregarded flags of truces; they had stolen private property; they had burned houses, and desecrated churches; they had stripped widows and orphans of death's legacies by a barbarous law of confiscation; they had overthrown municipalities and State Governments; they had imprisoned citizens, without warrant and regardless of age or sex; and they had set at defiance the plainest laws of civilized warfare.

Butler's government in New Orleans, and his "ingenious" war upon the helplessness of men and virtue of women was another step in atrocity. The Louisiana soldiers in Virginia went into battle, shouting: "Remember Butler!" It was declared that the display of Federal authority in the conquered city of New Orleans was sufficient to make the soldiers of the South devote anew whatever they had of life and labour and blood to the cause of the safety and honour of their country. And yet it was but the opening chapter of cruelty and horrors, exaggerated at each step of the war, until

Humanity was to stand aghast at the black volume of misery and ruin.[1074]

We in the South take Pollard at his word: he was a traditional conservative Southerner, an editor of the Richmond *Examiner*, and a highly perceptive writer who lived through the "Civil War," saw Union atrocities with his own eyes, and even spent time in a Yankee prison.

Though thousands of similar Yankee war criminals could be cited besides Butler, we only have room for a few more examples. One who must be named is Union Colonel Fielding Hurst, who made it a habit of extorting, robbing, torturing, mutilating, and shooting unarmed Confederate soldiers as well as Southern civilians—including "helpless" physically handicapped children.[1075] Understandably, my cousin Confederate General Nathan Bedford Forrest promised to kill Hurst and his men on the spot if he ever caught up with them.[1076]

Unbelievably, there were even more terrible Yankee war criminals than Hurst and Butler. Among the worst of the worst was William T. Sherman, whose name is still cursed here in Dixie. On October 29, 1864, at Rome, Georgia, "Uncle Billy," as Sherman was affectionately known by his troops, sent out an order to a subordinate officer that read:

> Cannot you send over about Fairmount and Adairsville, burn ten or twelve houses of known secessionists, kill a few at random, and let them know that it will be repeated every time a train is fired on from Resaca to Kingston?[1077]

All three of the commands in this order were illegal and against the Geneva Conventions. Amazingly, it is just for such ruthlessness and lawlessness that Sherman is still worshiped in the North.

Eyewitness testimony of Sherman's crimes exist to this day, such as the following detailed description by Reverend Dr. John Bachman of Charleston, South Carolina:

> When Sherman's army came sweeping through Carolina, leaving a broad track of desolation for hundreds of miles, whose steps were accompanied with fire, and sword, and blood . . . I happened to be at Cash's Depot, six miles from Cheraw. The owner was a widow, Mrs. Ellerbe, seventy-one years of age. Her son, Colonel Cash, was absent. I witnessed the barbarities inflicted on the aged, the widow, and young and delicate females. [Yankee] [o]fficers, high in command, were engaged tearing from the ladies their watches, their ear and wedding rings, the daguerreotypes [a type of early

photograph] of those they loved and cherished. A lady of delicacy and refinement, a personal friend, was compelled to strip before them, that they might find concealed watches and other valuables under her dress. A system of torture was practiced toward the weak, unarmed, and defenseless, which as far as I know and believe, was universal throughout the whole course of that invading army. Before they arrived at a plantation, they inquired the names of the most faithful and trustworthy family servants; these were immediately seized, pistols were presented at their heads; with the most terrific curses, they were threatened to be shot if they did not assist them in finding buried treasures.[1078] If this did not succeed, they were tied up and cruelly beaten. Several poor creatures [that is, black Southern slaves] died under the infliction. The last resort was that of hanging, and the officers and men of the triumphant army of General Sherman were engaged in erecting gallows and hanging up these faithful and devoted servants. They were strung up until life was nearly extinct, when they were let down, suffered to rest awhile, then threatened and hung up again. It is not surprising that some should have been left hanging so long that they were taken down dead. Coolly and deliberately these hardened men proceeded on their way, as if they had perpetrated no crime, and as if the God of heaven would not pursue them with his vengeance. But it was not alone the poor blacks to whom they professed to come as liberators that were thus subjected to torture and death. Gentlemen of high character, pure and honorable and gray-headed, unconnected with the military, were dragged from their fields or their beds, and subjected to this process of threats, beating, and hanging. Along the whole track of Sherman's army, traces remain of the cruelty and inhumanity practiced on the aged and the defenseless. Some of those who were hung up died under the rope, while their cruel murderers have not only been left unreproached and unhung, but have been hailed as heroes and patriots. The list of those martyrs whom the cupidity of the officers and men of Sherman's army sacrificed to their thirst for gold and silver, is large and most revolting.[1079]

On March 5, 1865, Mary Chesnut recorded the following in her diary:

Sherman's men had burned the convent. . . . Men were rolling tar barrels and lighting torches to fling on the house when the nuns came. Columbia is but dust and ashes, burned to the ground. Men, women, and children are left there, houseless, homeless, without a particle of food—reduced to picking up corn that was left by Sherman's horses on picket grounds and parching it to stay their hunger.[1080]

Yankee war criminal General Philip H. Sheridan was no less barbaric and unfeeling.[1081] During the Union's Shenandoah Valley Campaign, he personally approved the torching of barns and crops,[1082] after which he and his men left the region a blackened wasteland, pillaging, burning, and murdering as they went. Sheridan then joked that "a crow could not fly over it without carrying his rations with him."[1083] Civilians who opposed him were hanged on the spot.[1084] In October 1864 Sheridan boasted to Grant:

> I have destroyed over 2,000 barns, filled with wheat, hay, and farming implements; over 70 mills, filled with flour and wheat; have driven in front of the army over 4,000 head of stock, and have killed and issued to the troops not less than 3,000 sheep. . . . all the houses within an area of five miles were burned.[1085]

Sheridan's soldiers bragged that "we stripped the Valley to the bare earth; when we got through there weren't enough crumbs left to feed a pigeon." Sheridan himself—a man who, for "some light entertainment," would often burn every fifth house[1086]—pronounced his "scorched earth" approach to warfare a "humanitarian" policy, since he believed that Southerners would give in rather than die of starvation.[1087] (He was wrong!)

Lincoln knew about all this, *and* approved it.[1088] Why else would he repeatedly thank, reward, and promote men like Sherman?[1089] After all, "Honest Abe's" Yankee officers took their orders directly from him.[1090]

# ★ 18 ★

# PRISONS

**WHAT YOU WERE TAUGHT:** The Confederacy was needlessly cruel to Union prisoners, particularly at places like Georgia's Andersonville Prison, where some 12,000 Federal inmates died unnecessarily.

**THE TRUTH:** Wartime prisons are places of filth, pain, anguish, sorrow, and even death. That is a reality. Those in charge of Confederate prisons were not sadistic psychopaths. They did their best under horrible conditions. What Yankee myth does not teach you is the fact that these conditions were made worse by the North during a war that the North herself started!

On July 22, 1862, a cartel was ratified by both sides for the mutual exchange of all prisoners.[1091] Had this agreement been honored throughout the conflict, horrors like the Confederacy's Andersonville Prison would not have occurred. Unfortunately for the 12,912 Union prisoners who perished at Andersonville, along with thousands in other Confederate prisons, the Yankees broke the cartel on April 17, 1863.[1092]

It was on this date that Secretary of War Edwin M. Stanton and General Ulysses S. Grant, foolishly believing that the Union-Confederate prisoner exchange was benefitting the South and hurting the North, ordered a halt to the program. The results of this unethical action were inevitable. Southern prisons quickly became overcrowded, with all of the attendant ills of any overpopulated city: dirt, infections, illness and disease, lack of food and clothing, scarcity of medicines, increased violence and death.

Stanton and Grant were only partially responsible for this nightmare, however. Lincoln must also be held accountable, for it was he who, as commander-in-chief, sanctioned their order to break the prison exchange cartel. Lincoln was responsible in other ways as well. His heartless and illegal blockade of Southern ports, for example, virtually stopped the import of medical supplies, such as life saving medicines, bandages, pain killers, and surgical equipment.

Yankee inmates at places like Andersonville themselves caused a host of problems, such as those Union soldiers from New York who formed gangs in order to harass, bully, rob, and even kill their fellow prisoners.[1093] A number of these individuals, known as "raiders," were so violent that they had to be removed from Andersonville by the U.S. government itself. Six eventually swung on the gallows.[1094]

The situation both North and South became so awful that even soulless Lincoln and stone-hearted Grant were forced to recognize the cruelty and stupidity of their actions. While Lincoln refused to end his unlawful blockade, in February 1865 he did terminate Grant's order to halt the exchange of prisoners, at which time he began allowing the transfer of sick inmates. Lamentably, this came too late in the conflict: thousands were already dead or permanently disabled.

For Southerners one of the most heartrending consequences of Andersonville was the Yankee court-martial, shameful trial (in which Northern "eyewitnesses" lied openly in court), and illegal execution of the prison camp's commandant, Confederate Major Henry Wirz. Anti-South crusaders, who refer to him as "the fiend," will never acknowledge what all true Southerners know: under the worst circumstances imaginable the Swiss-American Wirz had not only not committed any crimes,[1095] he had done an amazing job (prison rations were the same, for example, as Rebel soldiers in the field) under horrendous circumstances.[1096]

The real problem was that he, like all other Confederate prison commandants, had been severely handicapped by the imprudent, self-serving, immoral actions of Lincoln, Grant, and others.[1097] Why exchange a Confederate who was willing to fight to the death for a Yankee who only wanted to go home?, Federal officials reasoned.[1098] Wirz was up against a truly implacable and malevolent force.

Despite the North's dastardly attempt to tarnish his name, Wirz is still considered a hero in Dixie, where he is seen as a victim of Yankee incompetence and ruthlessness, a whipping boy for the Yank's lust for retribution.[1099]

The South has repeatedly apologized for Andersonville. The North, however, has yet to apologize for its own horrid Yankee prisons, such as Chicago's Camp Douglas (see next entry).

**WHAT YOU WERE TAUGHT:** Yankee prisons were not anywhere near as bad as Rebel prisons.

**THE TRUTH:** This statement would have been deeply disturbing to most traditional 19th-Century Southerners, particularly the nearly 6,000 Confederate prisoners who were tortured then purposefully starved to death by Yankee

Colonel Benjamin J. Sweet at Chicago's notorious Camp Douglas—a Yankee prison rightly referred to by all who witnessed it as "Eighty Acres of Hell."

Numerous other such places could be named, such as the Yankees' Johnson's Island Prison, known as the "Northern Andersonville";[1100] Lincoln's gulag, the barbaric and horribly overcrowded Fort Lafayette in New York Harbor;[1101] and the New York Federal garrison called Elmira Prison (or "Hellmira," as inmates referred to it), where nearly 3,000 Confederates died unnecessarily.[1102] Is it any wonder that Rebel prisoners believed they had a better chance of surviving on the battlefield?[1103]

The truth of the matter, as Lincoln's own Secretary of War Stanton noted, is that a higher percentage of Southern POWs perished in Yankee prisons than Northern POWs in Confederate prisons.[1104] Some estimate the Rebel prisoner loss to be as high as 200,000,[1105] while the Yankee prisoner loss was closer to between 23,000[1106] and 30,000.[1107]

As hard as anti-South, pro-North historians try, no amount of whitewashing American history or brainwashing the American public can change these facts.

# ★ 19 ★

# EUROPE

**WHAT YOU WERE TAUGHT:** The main reason Europe would not give the Confederacy diplomatic recognition was because it knew the North was in the right and the South was in the wrong.

**THE TRUTH:** The real reason Europe hesitated to give the South diplomatic recognition was because it feared offending and possibly provoking the U.S. into war, a frightening scenario that at one point almost became a reality.

Through Lincoln's secretary of state, William H. Seward, Lincoln privately threatened war on any nation that interfered with his invasion of the South,[1108] in particular England and France,[1109] where sympathy for the Confederacy was the strongest.[1110] Lincoln's fears were warranted: England's and France's ruling classes were always highly interested in and supportive of the Confederate Cause,[1111] while the English population as a whole expressed "widespread sentiment" in favor of recognizing the Confederacy as a sovereign nation.[1112]

It was Lincoln's menacing warning, in place throughout the duration of the conflict, that prevented neutral Europe from publicly supporting "belligerent" Dixie, and which in turn prolonged the War, caused thousands of unnecessary deaths, and aided in the South's eventual downfall.[1113]

As usual Lincoln was a hypocrite and his threat of violence was an outrageous political fraud, for the U.S. herself had long insisted on the right to assist "belligerent" nations, for example, in 1793, 1841, and 1855. As recently as the 1860s, Lincoln's Secretary of State Seward had declared that the U.S. be allowed to sell arms to Mexico, which was then at war with France. Such facts, however, did not suit Lincoln's purposes, so he chose not to remind the world of them.[1114]

In short, Europe's decision to withhold recognition had nothing to do with the Confederacy or her cause (self-determination). It was fear of war with the U.S.[1115]

**WHAT YOU WERE TAUGHT:** Europe wholly sided with and supported the North throughout the War.

**THE TRUTH:** Europe—which in regards to the Confederacy was basically England and France—never fully stood behind Lincoln and the U.S. Union. For one thing, England, still smarting from losing the American colonies, was no friend of the U.S., and the recent search-and-seizure debacle known as the "Trent Affair," had not helped matters.

On November 8, 1861, as two Confederate commissioners, James M. Mason (representative to St. James' Court in England) and John Slidell (representative to the French Court), sailed out of Havana, Cuba, for Europe aboard the British mail packet *Trent*, they were unlawfully seized by Yankee Captain Charles Wilkes and the U.S. sloop of war *San Jacinto*.[1116]

While Wilkes achieved instant hero status in the North, the two Southern commissioners' arrest and their forced journey to Boston, Massachusetts (where they were illegally imprisoned at cold and dingy Fort Warren), caused an international uproar, with Confederate demands for their immediate release and British calls for war against the U.S.[1117] The French joined in by sending a letter to Lincoln supporting England's war-like stance. Seeing the U.S. seizure of the British *Trent* as an act of aggression, Britain even sent 8,000 soldiers to Canada to construct new forts and reenforce the Canadian-U.S. border.[1118]

Though the U.S. had clearly been in the wrong (by violating international law concerning search and seizure on the high seas), arrogant Northerner Lincoln refused to apologize.[1119] However, finally realizing the seriousness of America's mistake, in early January 1862 he "cheerfully surrendered" Mason and Slidell and the incident eventually blew over. Still, war between England and the U.S. had only narrowly been averted.

The Trent Affair was just one more reminder that the U.S. was not the true friend of either England or France, and as such could not be trusted. In fact, the incident only provoked more intense European sympathy for the Confederacy, particularly among the English.[1120]

Not surprisingly, both England and France saw advantages of a permanent division between the Union and the Confederacy (in particular European nationalists), which is one reason the two nations decided to form an alliance and act in harmony together regarding America's "Civil War."

In essence England would have much rather seen the U.S.A. lose than the C.S.A. So she decided to remain neutral rather than side with the South and get dragged into her own war with Lincoln and the North, one that would have exhausted Britain's already thin resources. France, who had fought on three continents over the preceding decade, was of a similar mind: militarily spent and financially drained, if she had thrown her support behind the Confederacy she too would have risked being pulled into a conflict with the U.S., one she could ill afford.

In the end, since both Britain and France knew that the South would not go to war with them either way (unlike the meddlesome and imperialistic Yanks, the Confederates had no desire to conquer foreign nations and only wanted to be "left alone"),[1121] the two nations voted for neutrality.[1122]

**WHAT YOU WERE TAUGHT:** Europe never recognized the Southern Confederacy.

**THE TRUTH:** Though, as part of its neutral position toward both the South and the North, it never went through with official formal recognition of the Confederacy, Europe did recognize the "belligerency" of the Rebels.[1123] The Confederacy actually gained its most vital diplomatic victories in this respect. For example, at the very start of the War, when England's Queen Victoria recognized the belligerency status of the South on May 13, 1861, France's leader, Emperor Napoleon III, followed up shortly thereafter, granting the rights of a belligerent to the Confederacy.[1124]

Britain even went so far as to "hope" for the success of the South, especially in light of recent wins against Lincoln and the North. On September 29, 1862, in a letter to England's Lord John Russell, Second Earl of Granville, George Gower, wrote:

> It would not be a good moment to recognize the South just before a great Federal Success. If on the other hand, the Confederates continue victorious, *as is to be hoped*, we should stand better than now in recognizing them.[1125]

It is noteworthy that while Europe proper ultimately let the Confederacy go unrecognized out of fear of warmongerer Lincoln, the Vatican at Rome did not.[1126] On December 8, 1863, Pope Pius IX sent the South's highest official a warm letter, addressing him as the "Illustrious and Honorable Jefferson Davis, President of the Confederate States of America."[1127] In his missive to Davis the Pope wrote:

> [I am doing all that I can] to put an early end to the fatal civil war prevailing in that country, and to re-establish among the American people peace and concord, as well as feelings of mutual charity and love. It was also peculiarly gratifying to Us to hear that You, Illustrious and Honorable Sir, as well as the people whom you govern, are animated by the same desire for peace and tranquillity which We so earnestly . . . [seek]. Would to God that the other

inhabitants of those regions (the Northern people), and their rulers, seriously reflecting upon the fearful and mournful nature of intestine warfare, might, in a dispassionate mood, hearken to and adopt the counsels of peace.[1128]

When Lincoln's emissaries at Rome complained to Cardinal Giacomo Antonelli that the Pope was giving aid and comfort to Southern Rebels traveling through the region, the clergyman replied that

> he intended to take all such 'rebels' under his special protection, because it would be making exactions upon humanity which it was incapable of consistently complying with to expect them to take an oath of allegiance to a country which they bitterly detested. Frequently the Cardinal would take . . . [the hand of Confederate Commissioner Ambrose Dudley Mann] between his and exclaim: 'Mon cher Monsieur, your Government has accomplished prodigies, alike in the Cabinet and in the field.'[1129]

We Southerners salute the Catholic Church and thank her for her support and recognition during Lincoln's heinous, bloody, and illegal war upon the Confederacy.

**WHAT YOU WERE TAUGHT:** Europe refused to support the South because of slavery; because it was still being legally practiced throughout the Confederacy.

**THE TRUTH:** To begin with, this cannot have been the reason, for slavery, although by then banned by most of the Northern states, was still being practiced by many Yankees at the time. Slavery was legal in Washington, D.C., for example, until April 16, 1862, the day Lincoln reluctantly passed the District of Columbia Emancipation Act.[1130]

Most slave owning Yanks, like General (and later U.S. President) Ulysses S. Grant, held onto their slaves until the passage of the Thirteenth Amendment on December 6, 1865, eight months after Lincoln's War ended.[1131] Estimates of the number of Northern slaves in the 1860s range from 500,000 to 1 million,[1132] figures you will find in few pro-North history books.

Second, there is also the bold fact that Europe herself made it clear that slavery had nothing to do with why she would not support Dixie. In early 1865 Confederate President Jefferson Davis sent Louisiana Congressman Duncan F. Kenner on a secret mission to Britain with a proposal: the South would immediately emancipate her slaves in exchange for Britain's recognition. Prime Minister Henry John Temple, better known as Lord Palmerston, responded with an unwavering but friendly "no." Slavery was in no way preventing

England from recognizing the legitimacy of the Confederacy.[1133] Due to Lincoln's aggressive military threats there were no circumstances, the English statesman asserted, that could convince the British government to recognize the C.S.A. as an autonomous nation.[1134]

In France Napoleon III stuck by Britain, stating that the issue of slavery had never once been taken into consideration concerning its decisions and reactions regarding the Confederacy.[1135] Some French regions, Paris, for instance, where there were no active antislavery organizations, evinced little or no concern about slavery at all.[1136]

Clearly, Lincoln was barking up the wrong tree by thinking that he could "obtain the favor of Europe" while preventing her from supporting the Confederacy over the issue of slavery.[1137] As was so often the case, he was his own worst enemy in this regard: beginning with his First Inaugural Address on March 4, 1861, Lincoln had repeatedly promised not to interfere with Southern slavery,[1138] while at the same time he continually assured the world that his one and only goal in invading Dixie was to "preserve the Union."[1139]

Plainly, the War was not over slavery. Lincoln and the Northern people knew it, Davis and the Southern people knew it, and Queen Victoria, Napoleon, and the European people knew it.

# ★ 20 ★

# THE KU KLUX KLAN

**WHAT YOU WERE TAUGHT:** The original Southern KKK was a racist, anti-black organization.

**THE TRUTH:** Actually it was an *anti-Yankee* organization, one that quite correctly described itself as an institution of "chivalry, humanity, mercy, and patriotism."[1140] In fact, during the first two years of its existence this social aid organization[1141] was comprised of thousands of white *and* black members,[1142] for its sole mission was to protect and care for the weak, the disenfranchised, and the innocent, whatever their race. This explains why there was an all-black Ku Klux Klan that operated for several years in the Nashville area.[1143]

The KKK's other primary goal was to help maintain law and order across the South. Though Lincoln's Reconstruction program had called for military rule, its implementation had the opposite effect. Lawlessness and vicious criminal behavior became commonplace, problems exacerbated by the appearance of thick-skinned, greedy carpetbaggers (Northerners) and treasonous, unscrupulous scallywags (Northernized Southerners), both groups which sought to prey on and exploit the long-suffering Southern survivors of Lincoln's War.[1144]

In 1869 the social atmosphere in the South changed dramatically. By this time the government-sponsored black Loyal Leagues and the Freedmen's Bureau had been formed, organizations meant to aid Southern blacks dispossessed by Lincoln's cruel, illegal, and unplanned emancipation (note that no U.S. government leagues were ever formed to aid dispossessed Southern whites specifically). Instead, carpetbaggers and scallywags used the Leagues to inculcate freed slaves in pro-North, anti-South propaganda,[1145] training them to use weapons and military tactics to taunt, punish, and even murder their former employers ("owners").[1146]

As part of their counter-Reconstruction efforts, KKK members responded by carrying coffins through the streets with the names of prominent Bureau leaders on them. Underneath their names were the words: "Dead,

Damned, and Delivered!"[1147]  The Bureau, as it turned out, was not only unnecessary, as Southerners had long maintained, but it was an absolute hindrance to any kind of racial harmony in the South—one of the reasons Yankees created it to begin with. This is why former Confederates saw it as nothing less than the imposition of an alien government, reinforced by an occupying army.[1148]

The Bureau's overt political efforts to create racial warfare in Dixie (by attempting to make former black servants hate their former white owners) were intended to further divide the Southern people by breaking down their morale. Ultimately, to the great remorse of Northern Radicals (Yankee abolitionists), it did not work. But various white elements in the KKK began to understandably turn their attention, some of it violent, toward African-Americans, particularly those who were committing hate crimes against white families under the directives of the U.S. government's Black Leagues. Again, these particular white groups were acting out of self-preservation, not racism.[1149]

Proof of this is that when carpetbag rule ended that year, in 1869, this, the original KKK, immediately came to an end as well all across the "Invisible Empire" (that is, the Southern states). For when Southerners were allowed to begin to take back political control of their own states, there was no longer any need for a self-protective social welfare organization like the KKK. This is why former Confederate officer and Southern hero General Nathan Bedford Forrest, the Klan's most famous and influential supporter, called in its members and shut the entire fraternity down in March of that year.[1150]  By the end of 1871 the KKK had disappeared from most areas of the South.[1151]

Still, now inaccurately associated with bigotry, the damage had been done, and to this day the original Reconstruction KKK has been branded, unfairly and unhistorically, with the racist label.

We will note here for the record that the KKK of today, which emerged in the 1920s, is in no way similar or even connected to the original KKK of the Southern postbellum period, which lasted a mere three years and four months: December 1865 to March 1869. Indeed, there are indications that the modern KKK is far more popular in the North than in the South, with flourishing clans in Indiana, New York, California, Oregon, and Connecticut, just to name a few.[1152]  Illinois, Lincoln's adopted home state, has also seen a recent resurgence of Klan activity.[1153]

**WHAT YOU WERE TAUGHT:** Confederate General Nathan Bedford Forrest founded the KKK and was its first grand wizard.

**THE TRUTH:**  The names of the six men who founded the KKK on

Christmas Eve 1865 in a haunted house in Pulaski, Tennessee, are well-known.[1154] They are: J. Calvin Jones, Captain John C. Lester, Richard R. Reed, Captain James R. Crowe, Frank O. McCord, and Captain John B. Kennedy.[1155] Forrest did not begin to associate with the organization until two years later, in 1867.[1156] Obviously then he could not have been either the founder or the first grand wizard.

The members of the original "Civil War" KKK never wrote anything down, so there is no hard physical evidence stating who the first grand wizard was. Where then did South-haters come up with the name Forrest? They fabricated it. The mysterious man's true identity was eventually revealed by Ora Susan Paine, the widow of my cousin George W. Gordon.[1157] According to Ora's sworn testimony, Gordon served as the organization's first grand wizard from 1865 to 1869.[1158]

**WHAT YOU WERE TAUGHT:** The KKK was a purely Southern invention. **THE TRUTH:** While the founding of the original KKK in 1865 did indeed occur in the South (as mentioned, at Pulaski, Tennessee),[1159] it was not a purely Southern entity. This is because it borrowed heavily from numerous similar secret *Northern* organizations that long preceded it.

One of these was the anti-Catholic, anti-immigrant group known as The Order of the Star Spangled Banner, founded in Boston, Massachusetts, in 1849. The original Southern KKK adopted many of the Order's traditions, such as its esoteric signals, handclasps, rituals, and codes, and later, it seems, even some of it strong arm tactics, including nighttime terrorist attacks, and general deception, fraud, and hocus-pocus antics (known as "dark lantern tactics").[1160]

In 1854 The Order of the Star Spangled Banner evolved into the Know-Nothing or American Party, a rabid anti-immigration, anti-Catholic, anti-foreigner movement that got its start in New York.[1161] When this too dissolved in 1856, the organization's racially intolerant members cast about for a political group to join. By 1860 there was only one logical choice: the party of white supremacy, white racism, and white separatism. The party of Abraham Lincoln.[1162]

# THE CONFEDERATE FLAG

**WHAT YOU WERE TAUGHT:** The Confederate flag is a symbol of racism and should be banned from all public use and display.

**THE TRUTH:** Like all symbols the Confederate flag means something different to different people. Consequently it has picked up erroneous meanings over the years. The question is which is the right meaning and which is the wrong meaning?

The view that it is a symbol of racism or hate in any way, shape, or form is ridiculous, outrageous, false, and historically inaccurate, as we will now prove.

There were (and still are) three national Confederate flags: the First National, the Second National, and the Third National. These three flags are proudly displayed all over the U.S., and even in some foreign countries, without a whimper of protest. Why? Because they have never been used by any hate groups.

It is the Confederate Battle Flag (a distinctive military flag designed for specific use on the battlefield), with its striking blue cross, thirteen white stars, and bright red field, that has caused all the uproar. Why? Because it *has* been used by hate groups.

The reason such groups use this particular flag comes from a lack of knowledge of *authentic* Southern history. For as has been made plain throughout this very book, the goals and dreams of the Confederacy were never about race, nor were they based on racism, or even slavery. The "Southern Cause," as it is called, was always about upholding the original Constitution of the Founding Fathers and this document's sacred Jeffersonian promise of states' rights, a small weak central government, self-determination, and personal freedom, all which liberal Lincoln and most Northerners detested, and fought against every step of the way (liberals today are still fighting Lincoln's war on individual liberty).

Despite this fact, the misuse of the Confederate Battle Flag, as well as the ignorance surrounding it, continues unabated. The situation is now so serious that some pro-South organizations are actually suing hate groups who use and display the flag in an attempt to get the practice prohibited.

The question we must ask ourselves is this: if a symbol is used by a racist hate group does this automatically make that symbol one of racism and hate? We traditional Southerners rightly say, absolutely not.

Anti-South partisans say yes, which, of course, presents them with a dilemma: if they are correct, then the United States flag must also be considered a symbol of hatred and bigotry, because not only is this the flag that flew on the masts of *all* American slave ships, it is the flag most often seen at modern white racist rallies and on white racist Websites. In fact, the U.S. flag seems to be the actual official symbol of some hate groups.[1163]

Rational people understand, however, that the U.S. flag is not a symbol of intolerance, and that its use by bigoted groups does not make it a symbol of bigotry. They also understand that this same reasoning applies to the Confederate Battle Flag: *it is not, and never was, a symbol of racism, and its use by racist groups does not make it one.* Tragically, this fact is habitually ignored by enemies of the South.

What then is the correct meaning of the "Starry Cross," as our fetching flag is proudly called?

Designed by my cousin Confederate General P. G. T. Beauregard,[1164] it is a symbol of Southern heritage, a heritage that includes *all* races. For not only did *all* races help settle and build the South, *all* races also fought against the Yankees under the Confederate Battle Flag. We will recall that the Confederate military was comprised of 1 million European-Americans,[1165] 300,000 to as many as 1 million African-Americans,[1166] 70,000 Native-Americans, 60,000 Latin-Americans,[1167] 50,000 foreigners,[1168] 12,000 Jewish-Americans,[1169] and 10,000 Asian-Americans.[1170]

These statistics prove to the world like nothing else can, that from the beginning the Confederacy was a multiracial, multicultural society, one that fought, not to oppress the black race or any other race, but for the constitutional rights and personal freedom of all her people. Those who say anything different are either lying or are ignorant of genuine Southern history, plain and simple.

Some from the anti-flag movement, like the intolerant Northern-based NAACP, know full well the true meaning of what we in Dixie also call the "Southern Cross." Unfortunately, such groups (which even other blacks, like Reverend Jesse Lee Peterson, have labeled "hate groups")[1171] have a vested interest in fanning the flames of racism, for without racial divisiveness they would go out of business.[1172]

Our most racist liberal president, Abraham Lincoln, thought along similar lines. He, along with the Radicals (that is, abolitionists) in his party, believed that by pitting whites and blacks against each other, the resulting tension, emotion, and fear would divide and weaken the South, allowing him to manipulate and overcome her people easier. Happily, Lincoln's attempt to poison Southern race relations failed, for the majority of whites and blacks saw through the ruse and remained loyal to one another both during and after his War.[1173]

The South did not immediately become a multiracial, multicultural society in 1861 with the start of Lincoln's War, of course. The South has always been a racially inclusive region. Native-Americans were inhabiting the South for tens of thousands of years prior to European settlement, and blacks were in the area now known as Virginia as early as 1526,[1174] long before the European ancestors of most of today's white Southerners arrived. It is for this very reason that by 1860, 99 percent of all blacks were native born Americans, a larger percentage than for whites.[1175]

Hispanics too had a hand in the development of the Southern states. Spanish explorer Juan Ponce de León was in Florida in 1513, and in 1565 Spaniards founded St. Augustine, the oldest continually occupied city in the U.S. It is true, as has been said, that the American South once spoke Spanish.[1176]

Contrary to popular thought, the South is not a "white region," and never was. Indeed, Dixie is the unique and special place it is today because of the culinary, architectural, sartorial, political, social, artistic, musical, and literary contributions made by all the races.[1177] If one section of the U.S. had to be called a melting pot of multiracial influences, it would be the South, not the North.

The Confederate Battle Flag then turns out to be anything but a symbol of white racism or white supremacy. Those who created it never intended it to have this meaning, and those who fought under it never thought of it as having this meaning. The descendants of those soldiers today have also never perceived it in this way, as both myself and my foreword writer, Nelson W. Winbush, can testify.

If anything it would be more accurate to call our flag a symbol of racial inclusiveness and multiculturalism, one founded on the Christian principles extolled by Jesus, whose main tenants were love and universal brotherhood.[1178] The Confederate Battle Flag itself was designed around the Christian crosses of Great Britain's flag (Saint George's Cross), Scotland's flag (Saint Andrew's Cross), and Ireland's flag (Saint Patrick's Cross).[1179]

In summary, our Battle Flag, the beautiful Southern Cross, is an emblem of American patriotism, strict constitutionalism, Christian love, and Southern heritage. As such, it is a flag that all Southerners, and all lovers of liberty, should display with pride and honor whenever and wherever possible. Conservative Southern Founder, Thomas Jefferson, the "Father of the Declaration of Independence," would heartily approve.

# RECONSTRUCTION

**WHAT YOU WERE TAUGHT:** Reconstruction was a successful and necessary program to help rebuild the belligerent South and reestablish peaceful relations between the two regions.

**THE TRUTH:** Like the term the "Civil War," the term "Reconstruction" is one of the greatest misnomers of all time, for no true rebuilding of the Southern states was intended, and indeed none ever took place during the Reconstruction years, 1865 to 1877.

What *did* take place was an attempt at the deconstruction of the Old South and its replacement by the "New South," for one of Lincoln's stated goals was always to Northernize the South and recreate it in the image of the North. This was to occur primarily through massive industrialization and the wholesale takeover of homes, plantations, towns, and businesses by Yankee investors, and more perniciously, the takeover of Southern schools by Yankee teachers.[1180]

Since, naturally, the agrarian South would not go down this road willingly, she had to be coerced, which is exactly what the North proceeded to do the very day Lee laid down his weapons at Appomattox.

But turning the South into a military state under the rule of despotic and often corrupt, arrogant, and violent Yankee officers, did nothing to engender warm feelings toward the North.[1181] At the same time, in an attempt to thoroughly "Unionize" Southerners,[1182] Confederate flags and uniforms were banned,[1183] former Confederate officers were required to pay exorbitant taxes and barred from holding political office,[1184] and former white Confederates were prohibited from voting while illiterate blacks were given the franchise.[1185]

Worse, the North's Reconstruction soldiers often harassed Dixie's citizens, ousted her families from their farms, pillaged their homes, robbed their men, and raped their women.[1186] Sadistically, many Southerners were even put on racks and tortured with thumbscrews.[1187] Why? What could possibly justify such acts? Only the Yankees who committed these crimes know the answer.

Southerners responded to the violent insanity of carpetbag-scallywag rule just as they did to the North's first illegal invasion of their homeland in 1861: they "rebelled" a second time, and with the help of a new and more enlightened president, Rutherford B. Hayes, by 1877 they were able to drive the last hated Yankee soldiers out of the South.

Free at last from the iron fist of Yankee dictatorship, Southern families returned to their homes and reopened their shops and schools (what was left of them). Former Confederate officers were quickly voted into office and the Confederate Flag was proudly flown once again outside every house, farm, and storefront. With Dixie now in tatters, Southerners did their level best to pick up where they had left off before Lincoln's illegal invasion twelve years earlier.

In the end, like the "Civil War" itself, Reconstruction was an utter failure, doomed by the impossibility of its very mission: to make the leisurely, religious, agricultural South into an exact duplicate of the fast-paced, atheistic, industrialized North. Victorian traditional Southerners were not about to let this happen. Even many carpet-baggers themselves realized the futility of trying to Northernize Dixie, correctly calling it "a fool's errand." One of these, Ohio carpetbagger Albion W. Tourgee, put it this way:

> The North and the South are simply convenient names for two distinct, hostile, and irreconcilable ideas,—two civilizations they are sometimes called, especially at the South. At the North there is somewhat more of intellectual arrogance; and we are apt to speak of the one as civilization, and of the other as a species of barbarism. These two must always be in conflict until the one prevails, and the other falls. To uproot the one, and plant the other in its stead, is not the work of a moment or a day. That was our mistake. We [Yankees] tried to superimpose the civilization, the idea of the North, upon the South at a moment's warning. We presumed, that, by the suppression of rebellion, the Southern white man had become identical with the Caucasian of the North in thought and sentiment; and that the slave, by emancipation, had become a saint and a Solomon at once. So we tried to build up communities there which should be identical in thought, sentiment, growth, and development, with those of the North. It was a fool's errand.[1188]

Unfortunately, Lincoln's left wing liberal dream (to Northernize the South) is still very much alive. Now aided by thousands of disloyal "New South" scallywags, the sinister process to eliminate all Southernness from Dixie continues, stronger now than ever before. At every opportunity true Southerners continue to resist the trend to exterminate Southern society. To those who are committed to Northernizing us, we say: heed the words of Mr. Tourgee!

**WHAT YOU WERE TAUGHT:** The Civil War taught Southerners a valuable lesson: to respect the Northern states and their people.

**THE TRUTH:** The War for Southern Independence left the South with an overriding feeling of loathing for Yankees specifically and Northern society in general. Few children of Dixie epitomized the Southern revulsion toward Yankeedom more than Edmund Ruffin, Virginian, farmer, agricultural reformer, and worshiper of the Old South and her traditions.

After being conquered and humiliated for four years during Lincoln's War, he loaded up his shotgun and made one last entry in his diary. The date was June 17, 1865. "Reconstruction" had already begun:

> I here declare my unmitigated hatred to Yankee rule—to all political, social and business connections with the Yankees and to the Yankee race. Would that I could impress these sentiments, in their full force, on every living Southerner and bequeath them to every one yet to be born! May such sentiments be held universally in the outraged and down-trodden South, though in silence and stillness, until the now far-distant day shall arrive for just retribution for Yankee usurpation, oppression and atrocious outrages, and for deliverance and vengeance for the now ruined, subjugated and enslaved Southern States! . . . And now with my latest writing and utterance, and with what will be near my latest breath, I here repeat and would willingly proclaim my unmitigated hatred to Yankee rule—to all political, social and business connections with Yankees, and the perfidious, malignant and vile Yankee race.[1189]

After setting down his pen, Ruffin put the gun barrel in his mouth and pulled the trigger. For the Virginia farmer, like hundreds of thousands of other loyal Southerners who fought against Lincoln, death was preferable to living under the imperialistic thumb of Yankee rule.

The love Ruffin had for the South and the bitterness he felt toward the North has not yet abated in Dixie a century and a half later. The severity, the insanity, the illegality, and the brutality of Lincoln's War against the South insures that these feelings among Southerners will never completely disappear. Confederate flags still wave proudly from thousands of homes, barns, flag poles, and pickup trucks, while anti-North bumper stickers are still big-sellers across the South, some of the more popular being "Yankee go home!" and "We don't care how you do it up North!" And such sentiments are only increasing, not decreasing, with time.

In most cases, traditional Southerners—still a genteel people raised in the art of Old European manners and proper etiquette—do not proclaim their abhorrence for the North outwardly. In fact, we actually welcome outsiders, even Yanks: *as long as they respect our history and heritage.* But when we are disrespected, we are most likely to express our displeasure in subtle ways all but unperceivable to Northerners. It's just a Southern thang y'all.

In the November 28, 1977, edition of *Newsweek*, for instance, Georgia's best known peanut farmer, President Jimmy Carter,[1190] told the magazine that his favorite movie was *Gone With the Wind* and that his favorite scene was "the burning of Schenectady, New York, and President Grant surrendering to Robert E. Lee."[1191] A year later, in 1978, Carter went one step further in gently disesteeming the North when he officially restored U.S. citizenship to President Jefferson Davis,[1192] a status that had been illegally stripped from the Confederate leader over 100 years earlier by Lincoln.[1193]

**WHAT YOU WERE TAUGHT:** Southerners were happy to return to the Union during Reconstruction, and nearly all of them did.

**THE TRUTH:** Countless numbers of Southerners actually moved out of the country rather than live under Yankee dictatorship. Many went to the Caribbean or Mexico, while several thousand emigrated to South America, and more specifically to Brazil.

There were eventually so many Confederates living in one area of the state of São Paulo that it was named "Americana," a town that thrives to this day. The nearby city of Santa Barbara d'Oeste still hosts a joyous Confederate festival four times each year (*Festa Confederada*), sponsored by the *Fraternidade Descendencia Americana*, made up of the modern day descendants of Confederate soldiers and officers. The area, which also boasts a Confederate cemetery (Protestant Rebels were not allowed to be buried in Catholic graveyards), proudly calls itself the southernmost and last true unreconstructed part of Dixie still in existence.[1194]

Many thousands of former Confederates also moved to Europe, one of the better known being Judah Benjamin, President Davis' right hand man. Benjamin fled to England where he established a successful legal practice and became Queen Victoria's counsel before passing away in 1884.[1195]

Another was Rebel diplomat Ambrose Dudley Mann. Sailing from Virginia in 1861, he vowed to return only after the Southern states had won the War. Mann remained in Europe and eventually died in Paris, France.[1196]

**WHAT YOU WERE TAUGHT:** The Reconstruction ratification of the Fourteenth Amendment, on July 9, 1868, was an important step in the late President Lincoln's plan to give citizenship to all American blacks.

**THE TRUTH:** Both assertions in this sentence are false.

The Fourteenth Amendment is rightly known in the South as the Anti-South Amendment. Not because it made African-Americans citizens, as Yankee myth asserts, but because it was written, issued, and used by the North to try and destroy the idea of states' rights (including secession) across Dixie. It was, in short, a rejection of both the Constitution and the very "cornerstone of the Confederacy": not slavery, but *state sovereignty.*[1197]   Little wonder that Southerners were outraged and fought mightily against its passage.

What many people do not realize is that the Fourteenth Amendment, one of the three postwar "Reconstruction" amendments (the other two are the Thirteenth and Fifteenth Amendments), is concerned with far more than just black citizenship.  In fact, it consists of five sections:

1) Section One makes all former slaves citizens and adds additional protections to their rights.
2) Section Two stipulates that 100 percent of all males over age twenty-one, regardless of color, are to be counted as part of the population (prior to this only three-fifths of blacks had been included, a *Yankee* idea).
3) Section Three prohibits all former Confederate leaders from holding public office.
4) Section Four prohibits both the national government and the state governments from paying any debts that were incurred as a result of supporting the Confederacy.
5) Section Five empowers the U.S. Congress to enforce "the provisions of this article."

Obviously, the entire amendment was anti-South in wording, tone, and character. But it was Section Three that was most upsetting to Southerners, for it denied Dixie the use of her most qualified leaders at a time when they were most needed: during so-called "Reconstruction," an eight-year period of postbellum punishment inflicted on the South for daring to go her own way.[1198]

The irony of all this of course is that the North had illegally invaded the South and killed 2 million of her citizens in order to "preserve the Union." Yet not only was it now denying the South congressional representation, which in effect prevented her from rejoining the Union, but Lincoln never admitted that the South had ever legally separated from the Union to begin with.[1199]

There was pure villainy behind the Fourteenth Amendment: it was a small piece of the North's ultimate anti-South plan to fully transform Thomas Jefferson's Constitutional Confederacy (powerful independent states, weak central government) into a strongly centralized Federation (weak dependent states, powerful central government), something the traditional South had always been strongly against. The amendment's many references to Dixie's "insurrection" and "rebellion," its granting citizenship to Southern blacks, its implied declaration that state efforts to regulate business and economic activities were now unconstitutional, and its promise to penalize Southern states who did not allow blacks to vote (most who were not able to read or write), reveal the true motivation behind this pro-North act.[1200] It was an undisguised "Reconstruction" attempt to squash states' rights and humiliate, steal away power from, and punish the South.

We will note here that as Mary Chesnut and other Confederates often mention in their writings, most white Southerners were more than happy to give blacks their due civil rights. What they were unhappy about was that the North was constantly telling them how and when to do it. Not only was this just plain nosey, bossy, and meddlesome, it was an overt infringement of states' rights. The Southern people wanted to be able to discuss the issue and vote on it in their own time and in their own way—just as they had wanted to do with slavery. (Tragically for all concerned, the U.S. government denied the South this opportunity on both occasions, and instead prematurely forced the issues at the tip of a Yankee gun barrel.)

Understandably Southerners were infuriated with the pushy Yankee government, and expressed their anger in the only way left open to them: they rejected the detested Fourteenth Amendment.

Traditional Constitutionalists in Tennessee were particularly incensed when the anti-South, Southern-born governor at the time, William Gannaway Brownlow, convened a special session of the Tennessee Legislature to try and push the amendment through against popular sentiment. Fifty-six members were needed for the necessary quorum, but only fifty-four attended, and of these only three-fourths voted to ratify. Despite this, Brownlow declared the act "Tennessee law" even though it was not, and subsequently never has been, legally ratified in the Volunteer State.[1201]

Nine other Southern states also tried to block passage of the Fourteenth Amendment by refusing to officially approve it. But it was forced through anyway by South-hating Northerners. So, not only is it still not legal in Tennessee, it is not legal in any other U.S. state, and to this day it remains technically unratified.[1202]

As for the second part of this Yankee myth, that the Fourteenth Amendment was an important part of Lincoln's plan to give citizenship to blacks, we will let "Honest Abe" speak for himself.

Throughout his political career the Illinoisan was repeatedly challenged as to whether he was in favor of "negro citizenship," and he repeatedly gave the same answer, as he did at Charleston, Illinois, on September 18, 1858.[1203] "Very frankly," Lincoln asserted,

> I am not in favor of Negro citizenship. . . . Now, my opinion is that the different States have the power to make a negro a citizen, under the constitution of the United States, if they choose. . . . If the State of Illinois had that power, I should be against the exercise of it. That is all I have to say about it.[1204]

This is the same man who uttered the following on October 16, 1854, proving once again that Lincoln was not against slavery, but merely its growth and expansion outside the South:

> Whether slavery shall go into Nebraska, or other new [Western] Territories, is not a matter of exclusive concern to the people who may go there. The whole nation is interested that the best use shall be made of the Territories. We want them for homes of free white people.[1205]

It was just such racist and ignorant comments that would later prompt regret among many Confederates for "surrendering" to Lincoln and his Northern henchmen. One of the foremost of these was non-slave owner and abolitionist General Robert E. Lee, who always referred to Yankees using the impersonal phrase "those people."[1206] In 1870, shortly before his death, at the peak of Reconstruction, Lee told Fletcher Stockdale, the former Confederate governor of Texas:

> Governor, if I had foreseen the use those people designed to make of their victory, there would have been no surrender at Appomattox Courthouse; no, sir, not by me. Had I foreseen these results of subjugation, I would have preferred to die at Appomattox with my brave men, my sword in this right hand.[1207]

# NOTES

**1.** See e.g., Seabrook, TQNBF, pp. 91, 116, 118.

**2.** See e.g., R. Taylor, pp. vii, 1, 2, 15, 46, 125, 296, 308, 362.

**3.** See e.g., Seabrook, TQNBF, p. 6.

**4.** See e.g., A. H. Stephens, RAHS, p. 56.

**5.** See e.g., Seabrook, TQJD, pp. 30, 38, 76.

**6.** See e.g., J. Davis, RFCG, Vol. 2, pp. 4, 161, 454, 610.

**7.** Grissom, p. 513.

**8.** For some odd reason that has never been made clear, most liberals expect to be treated tolerantly by traditional Southerners while refusing to grant this same courtesy in return. Many progressives also seem to have a strong predilection for censorship, supporting freedom of speech only for themselves. These traits are in stark contrast to most conservatives, who enjoy open dialogue, even with those they do not agree with it, and who maintain that the First Amendment applies to *all* people—no matter what their beliefs. This is, after all, one of the rights that makes the U.S. great, strong, and unique. If liberals want to live in a country where freedom of speech is curtailed and where only their views are taught, we suggest they emigrate. There are plenty of nations in the world where First Amendments rights do not exist.

**9.** There *are* some Yanks who respect, understand, and love the South. God bless 'em.

**10.** The teens who shot Westerman happened to be black. But their skin color is irrelevant. Thousands of white Southern children too have been brainwashed to despise their own heritage, symbols, heroes, and history.

**11.** Kettell, p. 84.

**12.** Mitgang, pp. 8-12, 205.

**13.** Nicolay and Hay, ALCW, Vol. 1, p. 298.

**14.** Kennedy and Kennedy, SWR, p. 276.

**15.** For more on the constitutionality and legality of secession, see Seabrook, AL, pp. 81-102. See also Bledsoe, DT, passim; Graham, CHS, passim; Howe, passim; Perkins, passim; Powell, passim; Samuel, passim.

**16.** ORA, Ser. 1, Vol. 52, Pt. 2, p. 587.

**17.** Lincoln once told an interior department official, T. J. Barnett, that as part of his "Reconstruction" plans, the entire South would have to be obliterated and replaced with new businessmen and new ideas; *Northern* ones, that is. Catton, Vol. 2, p. 443.

**18.** McGuire and Christian, pp. viii-ix.

**19.** Denney, p. 25.

**20.** Nicolay and Hay, ALCW, Vol. 2, p. 70.

**21.** Nicolay and Hay, ALCW, Vol. 2, p. 239.

**22.** Nicolay and Hay, ALCW, Vol. 2, p. 94.

**23.** Nicolay and Hay, ALCW, Vol. 2, p. 103.

**24.** Nicolay and Hay, ALCW, Vol. 1, p. 65.

**25.** See e.g., Nicolay and Hay, ALCW, Vol. 2, pp. 243, 310, 420, 439, 595.

**26.** Pollard, SHW, Vol. 2, pp. 550. See also Jensen, NN, passim.

**27.** Mish, s.v. "civil war."

**28.** See Kettell, p. 84.

**29.** For more on the South's agrarian movement and its proponents, see Simpson, passim.

**30.** Gragg, pp. 90-93, 175-192.

**31.** See e.g., J. Davis, RFCG, Vol. 2, pp. 632-633; C. Johnson, p. 157; Lott, pp. 158-159; L. Johnson, p. 188; Grissom, pp. 115-116; Christian, p. 15.

**32.** S. Andrews, p. 35; C. Johnson, p. 157.

**33.** Hopkins, p. 186.

**34.** R. E. Lee, Jr., p. 234.

**35.** Hurmence, pp. 99-102; J. Davis, RFCG, Vol. 2, p. 716; Gragg, pp. 182-183, 188.

**36.** Sandburg, SOL, p. 415.

**37.** Chesnut, DD, p. 238.

**38.** Blakeman, p. 173. This figure has been calculated in today's currency.

**39.** Lang, p. 4.

**40.** Katcher, CWSB, p. 46.

**41.** Timothy D. Manning, Sr., personal correspondence.

**42.** J. Davis, RFCG, Vol. 1, p. 439; F. Moore, Vol. 4, pp. 201; Tocqueville, Vol. 2, p. 426.

**43.** R. S. Phillips, s.v. "Emancipation Proclamation."

**44.** See Nicolay and Hay, ALCW, Vol. 2, p. 1; Beard and Beard, Vol. 2, pp. 39-40.

**45.** In other words, it cost Americans ten times more to fight and kill each other for four years than if they would have simply ended slavery (more proof that Lincoln's War was not over slavery). Rutland, p. 226. See also C. Johnson, p. 200.

**46.** The phrase "the irrepressible conflict" was coined by Lincoln's future secretary of state Seward in a speech he gave at Rochester, New York, on October 25, 1858. For the full speech, see Baker, Vol. 4, pp. 289-302.

**47.** Pollard, LC, p. 93; W. B. Garrison, CWTFB, p. 109.

**48.** Nicolay and Hay, ALCW, Vol. 11, pp. 97-98. For a modern, and factual, appraisal of Lincoln's true agenda, see DiLorenzo, RL, pp. 54-55.

**49.** Lang, p. 215.

**50.** Chesnut, DD, p. 38.

**51.** For more on the constitutionality and legality of secession, see Bledsoe, DT, passim; Graham, CHS, passim; Howe, passim; Perkins, passim; Powell, passim; Samuel, passim.

**52.** Neely, pp. 109-112; Simmons, s.v. "Civil rights in the Confederacy."

**53.** Timothy D. Manning, Sr., personal correspondence. Some Southern historians, like Manning, estimate that Lincoln's War took the lives of as many as 1 million Northerners and 2 million Southerners. These figures include all races and both noncombatants and black slaves, men, women, and children. Additionally, it is important to note that nearly *all* civilian deaths occurred in the South. While the exact Southern death toll is not known, and will never be known, Jefferson Davis estimated that Lincoln killed at least half of the South's Negro population, or about 1,750,000 black men, women, and children, free and bonded. See F. Moore, pp. 278-279.

**54.** See Bergh, Vol. 1, pp. 167-168.

**55.** See e.g., E. McPherson, PHUSADGR, p. 106.

**56.** For a somewhat biased look at the Battle of Fort Sumter from the point of view of a Northern eyewitness, see Crawford, passim.

**57.** Fort Sumter is now a national monument and is once again—to the discontentment of pro-South sympathizers everywhere—flying the U.S. flag. For more information on modern Fort Sumter, visit the following Website: www.nps.gov/fosu.

**58.** LeVert, s.v. "Fort Sumter."

**59.** Like many in Lincoln's army, Kentucky-born Anderson was pro-slavery. Faust, s.v. "Anderson, Robert."

**60.** Meriwether, p. 263.

**61.** Tilley, FHLO, pp. 38-47; Meriwether, p. 263.

**62.** Henry, SC, p. 30; J. M. McPherson, ACW, p. 21; W.B. Garrison, LNOK, p. 81.

**63.** Rhodes, HUS, Vol. 3, p. 333.

**64.** ORA, Ser. 1, Vol. 1, pp. 200-201; D. H. Donald, L., pp. 287, 288.

**65.** ORA, Ser. 1, Vol. 1, pp. 196, 197.

**66.** C. Adams, p. 20.

**67.** J. M. McPherson, BCF, p. 271.

**68.** Harwell, p. 344.

**69.** Grissom, p. 108.

**70.** Scharf, pp. 129-130; Tilley, FHLO, p. 50.

**71.** ORA, Ser. 1, Vol. 4, pp. 224-225.

**72.** Tilley, FHLO, pp. 50-51.

**73.** Tilley, FHLO, p. 51.

**74.** Thompson and Wainwright, Vol. 1, p. 44.

**75.** Ashe, p. 56.

**76.** Nicolay and Hay, ALCW, Vol. 2, p. 346.

**77.** DiLorenzo, RL, pp. 119-121.

**78.** Foote, Vol. 1, p. 47.

**79.** J. Davis, RFCG, Vol. 1, pp. 323-324.

**80.** Pollard, LC, p. 108.

**81.** LeVert, s.v. "Fort Sumter."

**82.** C. Johnson, p. 151.

**83.** Bowman, s.v. "Fort Sumter, Capture of."

**84.** Faust, s.v. "Anderson, Robert."

**85.** Nicolay and Hay, ALCW, Vol. 2, p. 34.

**86.** Seabrook, L, p. 955.

**87.** Conquest, passim.

**88.** Driscoll and Breshears, p. 210.

**89.** Nicolay and Hay, ALCW, Vol. 2, p. 657; W. Wilson, HAP, Vol. 9, p. 137.

**90.** See e.g., Nicolay and Hay, ALCW, Vol. 2, pp. 50, 75, 94, 99, 103, 124, 239, 261.

**91.** Durden, p. 191.
**92.** J. Davis, RFCG, Vol. 1, p. 292.
**93.** Pollard, LC, pp. 111-112.
**94.** *Southern Historical Society Papers*, Vol. 1, January to June, 1876, p. 455.
**95.** Lester, p. 359.
**96.** Nicolay and Hay, ALCW, Vol. 2, p. 1.
**97.** Nicolay and Hay, ALCW, Vol. 2, pp. 3-4.
**98.** Seabrook, AL, pp. 303-304.
**99.** Lester, pp. 359-360.
**100.** Nicolay and Hay, ALCW, Vol. 2, pp. 227-228.
**101.** F. Moore, Vol. 4, pp. 201.
**102.** Nicolay and Hay, ALCW, Vol. 2, p. 674; See also Owsley, KCD, pp. 65-66.
**103.** J. Davis, RFCG, Vol. 2, p. 764.
**104.** DeGregorio, s.v. "Thomas Jefferson."
**105.** Kennedy, p. 91.
**106.** Foley, p. 813.
**107.** Tocqueville, Vol. 1, pp. 383-385.
**108.** Litwack, pp. 4, 6.
**109.** For the typical Yankee soldier's feelings concerning abolition, see e.g., Henderson, Vol. 2, p. 411; Murphy, p. 86; Page Smith, pp. 308-309; Barrow, Segars, and Rosenburg, BC, p. 45; Jordan, p. 141; Wiley, LBY, p. 281; D. H. Donald, L, p. 385; B. Thornton, p. 176; Foote, Vol. 1, p. 538.
**110.** M. M. Smith, pp. 4-5.
**111.** Stampp, pp. 425-426.
**112.** Garraty, p. 302; Simpson, pp. 80-81.
**113.** T. N. Page, p. 57; R. H. McKim, p. 31.
**114.** Rutherford, FA, p. 38; Wallechinsky, Wallace, and Wallace, p. 11; Woods, p. 67.
**115.** Meriwether, p. 219.
**116.** Stiles, pp. 49-50.
**117.** McKim, pp. 31-33.
**118.** See e.g., Munford, pp. 52-53.
**119.** Mitgang, p. 264.
**120.** Nicolay and Hay, ALCW, Vol. 2, p. 674.
**121.** For more on the constitutionality and legality of secession, see Bledsoe, DT, passim; Graham, CHS, passim; Howe, passim; Perkins, passim; Powell, passim; Samuel, passim.
**122.** Seabrook, L, pp. 242-243.
**123.** Seabrook, L, pp. 244-245.
**124.** Nicolay and Hay, ALCW, Vol. 1, p. 468.
**125.** Nicolay and Hay, ALCW, Vol. 1, pp. 433, 451.
**126.** See Merrill Jensen, NN, passim; and also AC, passim.
**127.** Collier and Collier, p. 4.
**128.** Stephens, CV, Vol. 1, pp. 281-282.
**129.** J. Davis, RFCG, Vol. 1, p. 80.
**130.** For more on the original U.S. Confederacy, see Jensen, NN, passim; AC, passim.
**131.** Simpson, p. 72.
**132.** Rozwenc, pp. 10-11.
**133.** McWhiney and Jamieson, pp. 171-172.
**134.** *The American Annual Cyclopedia (of 1861)*, Vol. 1, p. 648.
**135.** Bode and Cowley, pp. xx-xxix.
**136.** E. M. Thomas, p. 8.
**137.** Lang, pp. 215, 216.
**138.** Horwitz, pp. 68-69.
**139.** Cannon, pp. 18, 25, 60.
**140.** McWhiney and Jamieson, pp. 170-191.
**141.** Seabrook, TMCP, pp. 233-236.
**142.** Bultman, pp. 23-24, passim.
**143.** E. M. Thomas, pp. 3-5.
**144.** Rosenbaum and Brinkley, s.v. "Jefferson Republican Party."
**145.** Weintraub, p. 55.
**146.** Thornton and Ekelund, pp. xiv, 16; Weintraub, p. 58.

**147.** Woods, p. 53.

**148.** Fogel, p. 296.

**149.** Bowman, CWDD, p. 11.

**150.** C. Eaton, HSC, p. 50.

**151.** Seabrook, TQREL, p. 213.

**152.** Harrison, p. 158.

**153.** "The Confederate Pledge of Allegiance" copyright © 2010, by Lochlainn Seabrook.

**154.** It is no small irony to traditional Southerners, the very people who tried to preserve Thomas Jefferson's Confederate Republic in 1861 (see Stephens, CV, Vol. 1, pp. 504-505), that they are today forced to recite the North's socialistic, anti-South Pledge of Allegiance. It is hoped that when the Southern states secede a second time, the new Confederacy will adopt my South positive pledge—or something close to it.

**155.** Foley, pp. 969, 971.

**156.** F. Moore, p. 204.

**157.** See Stephens, CV, Vol. 1, pp. 504-505. As a political entity the original American Confederacy lasted a mere eight years, from 1781 to 1789. However, because the new U.S. government contained various important aspects carried over from the Confederacy, Americans would continue to refer to the U.S. as "the Confederacy" for many generations to come. See Seabrook, AL, pp. 42-43; Jensen, NN, pp. 348, 421, passim; Collier and Collier, passim.

**158.** See Rutland, passim.

**159.** Napolitano, pp. 25, 63.

**160.** F. Moore, Vol. 7, p. 377.

**161.** E. McPherson, PHUSADGR, p. 95.

**162.** Findlay and Findlay, pp. 168-169.

**163.** Rives, p. 347.

**164.** Samuel, Vol. 1, p. 290.

**165.** McHenry, pp. xliii-xliv.

**166.** Tenney, p. 17.

**167.** F. Moore, Vol. 2, p. 327.

**168.** Gordon, p. 111.

**169.** Spaeth and Smith, p. 12.

**170.** Rayner, p. 259.

**171.** Randolph, Vol. 3, p. 284.

**172.** See e.g., Nicolay and Hay, ALCW, Vol. 2, pp. 70, 261, 327, 606.

**173.** Bergh, Vol. 5, p. 65.

**174.** J. Davis, RFCG, Vol. 2, p. 764.

**175.** See Cooper, JDA, p. 672.

**176.** For more on the constitutionality and legality of secession, see Bledsoe, DT, passim; Graham, CHS, passim; Howe, passim; Perkins, passim; Powell, passim; Samuel, passim.

**177.** C. Johnson, pp. 101-109.

**178.** Bergh, Vol. 1, p. 48.

**179.** Cannon, pp. 7, 11, 14.

**180.** C. Adams, p. 89.

**181.** Hacker, p. 580.

**182.** C. Johnson, pp. 115-117.

**183.** For plotting with Alexander Hamilton against administration policy, Pickering was dismissed by Adams, the first and only secretary of state to be terminated in this manner. DeGregorio, s.v. "John Adams."

**184.** DeGregorio, s.v. "James Monroe."

**185.** C. King, Vol. 4, pp. 364-366.

**186.** C. Adams, p. 15.

**187.** DeGregorio, s.v. "James Madison."

**188.** Smelser, DR, p. 78.

**189.** H. Adams, p. 351.

**190.** H. Adams, p. 338.

**191.** See Website: www.nps.gov/jela/the-treaty-of-ghent.htm.

**192.** For more on early American secession attempts, see Powell, passim.

**193.** Dilorenzo, RL, pp. 93-101.

**194.** Pollard, LC, p. 85.

**195.** Tocqueville, Vol. 1, pp. 383-385.

**196.** Buckingham, Vol. 2, p. 112.

**197.** Hawthorne, Vol. 2, pp. 109-110.

**198.** Peterson, JM, p. 377.

**199.** Sturge, p. 40.

**200.** Dicey, Vol. 1, pp. 70-72.

**201.** Olmsted, an author of numerous anti-South books, including, *A Journey in the Seaboard Slave States* (1856), is best known for being the designer of New York City's Central Park.

**202.** Stampp, p. 164.

**203.** See Fogel and Engerman, pp. 179-180.

**204.** Olmsted, CK, Vol. 1, p. 39.

**205.** Crandall's Connecticut school for colored girls was eventually torched by the townspeople, but not before Yankees harassed, arrested, and imprisoned her. Eventually, under continuing threats of violence, she was driven from the state. C. Adams, pp. 130-131; Nye, p. 63; Buckley, p. 62; G. W. Williams, HNRA, Vol. 2, p. 151; Garrison and Garrison, Vol. 1, p. 323.

**206.** U. B. Phillips, pp. 439-440.

**207.** *The Liberator*, August 15, 1862. For more on the thoughts and writings of 18th- and 19th-Century Northern blacks, see Sterling, passim.

**208.** Douglass, LTFD, p.186.

**209.** Website: www.nps.gov/archive/frdo/fdlife.htm.

**210.** Douglass, NLFD, p. xiv; K. C. Davis, p. 439.

**211.** Douglass, NLFD, p. 116.

**212.** See Nicolay and Hay, CWAL, Vol. 11, pp. 105-106; Nicolay and Hay, ALCW, Vol. 1, p. 483; Holzer, pp. 22-23, 67, 318, 361.

**213.** Litwack, p. 226.

**214.** Garrison and Garrison, Vol. 1, p. 327.

**215.** Litwack, pp. 205-208.

**216.** Litwack, p. 227.

**217.** *The Congressional Globe*, Vol. 13, p. 239.

**218.** See J. M. McPherson, NCW, pp. 245-270; Litwack, pp. 104-112.

**219.** Greenberg and Waugh, p. 152.

**220.** Wiley, SN, pp. 64-66.

**221.** Barrow, Segars, and Rosenburg, BC, p. 4.

**222.** Wiley, LJR, p. 328.

**223.** Barrow, Segars, and Rosenburg, BC, pp. 155-156.

**224.** Stampp, pp. 147, 279, 406-407; Fogel, p. 191.

**225.** Gates, p. 375.

**226.** Meltzer, Vol. 1, pp. 1-35.

**227.** As in most other modern countries, slavery is still alive and well in 21st-Century America: according to a recent CIA study, 50,000 people (mostly women and children) of all colors and races are enslaved in the U.S. each year. Website: www.pbs.org/newshour/bb/law/jan-june01/slavery_3-8.html.

**228.** Note: Today, even the most objective discussion of slavery brings automatic charges of "racism" from the unenlightened. In this atmosphere of political correctness gone mad it is therefore necessary to offer the following statement. Nothing in Chapter 7 should be construed in any way as a defense of slavery, for not only do I believe that slavery is one of the most abominable institutions ever developed by humanity, but I maintain, along with abolitionist William Lloyd Garrison, that "prejudice against color is rebellion against God." (Garrison and Garrison, Vol.2, p. 292.) What the reader will find in this particular chapter is a description of what slavery was actually like in the Victorian South (as opposed to what Yankee myth has taught us it was like), and how both white and black Southerners viewed and experienced it.

**229.** Davidson, pp. 30, 32.

**230.** See Meltzer, passim.

**231.** R. S. Phillips, s.v. "Slavery."

**232.** For a discussion of the authentic history of prostitution, see my book *Aphrodite's Trade*.

**233.** Meltzer, Vol. 1, p. 2.

**234.** R. S. Phillips, s.v. "Slavery."

**235.** Meltzer, Vol. 2, pp. 61-73.

**236.** R. S. Phillips, s.v. "Slavery."

**237.** Cartmell, p. 26; Norwood, p. 31; Meltzer, Vol. 2, p. 139.

**238.** G. H. Moore, p. 5; R. S. Phillips, s.v. "Slavery."

**239.** Meltzer, Vol. 1, pp. 1-6.

**240.** Davidson, p. 30.

**241.** Davidson, pp. 120-121, 123-124, 229, 242, 251.

**242.** McKissack and McKissack, p. 119.

**243.** Furnas, p. 115.

**244.** Blassingame, p.14.
**245.** Garraty, p. 77.
**246.** J. Thornton, p. 307.
**247.** Nicolay and Hay, ALCW, Vol. 1, p. 197.
**248.** Stonebraker, pp. 50-51.
**249.** Hacker, p. 18.
**250.** Shillington, pp. 174, 175.
**251.** Drescher and Engerman, p. 34.
**252.** Blassingame, p. 3.
**253.** Website: www.infoplease.com/spot/slavery1.html. For more information on modern day slavery, see Website: www.antislavery.org/english/slavery_today/default.aspx.
**254.** Ransom, p. 41.
**255.** Drescher and Engerman, p. 239.
**256.** Stampp, p. 16; R. S. Phillips, s.v. "Slavery."
**257.** Garraty and McCaughey, p. 26.
**258.** Wilson and Ferris, s.v. "Plantations." Many Northern whites, like Yankee judge Samuel Sewell, disliked blacks so much that they advocated using white slaves instead. Adams and Sanders, p. 23. For more on white slavery in the early Americas, see Baepler, passim; Ballagh, passim; Galenson, passim; Hildreth, passim; Hoffman, passim; Jordan and Walsh, passim.
**259.** Smelser, ACRH, p. 58.
**260.** Shenkman and Reiger, p. 96; DeGregorio, s.v. "Millard Fillmore"; DeGregorio, s.v. "Andrew Johnson."
**261.** DeGregorio, s.v. "Martin Van Buren."
**262.** DeGregorio, s.v. "Ulysses S. Grant."
**263.** Furnas, p. 108. For more on white slavery in early America, see Baepler, passim; Ballagh, passim; Galenson, passim; Hildreth, passim; Hoffman, passim; Jordan and Walsh, passim.
**264.** Garraty and McCaughey, p. 214.
**265.** Mish, s.v. "slave."
**266.** Rosenbaum, s.v. "Slavs"; "Slavonic Languages."
**267.** Gwatkin and Whitney, Vol. 2, pp. 421, 430.
**268.** Meltzer, Vol. 1, p. 3.
**269.** Montefiore, p. 643.
**270.** The American South had a population of 3.5 million black servants in 1860.
**271.** Meltzer, Vol. 2, pp. 270-277.
**272.** Drescher and Engerman, p. 289.
**273.** Lott, pp. 35-60.
**274.** Ashe, p. 10.
**275.** Stonebraker, p. 46.
**276.** Foote, Vol. 1, p. 537. For Lincoln's letter to Captain Gordon confirming his sentence to be hanged, see Nicolay and Hay, ALCW, Vol. 2, pp. 121-122. Lincoln refers to Captain Gordon, along with several other seized Yankee slave ships, in his First Annual Message to Congress. See Nicolay and Hay, ALCW, Vol. 2, p. 101.
**277.** Farrow, Lang, and Frank, pp. 131-132.
**278.** Kennedy, pp. 104-105.
**279.** R. S. Phillips, s.v. "Slavery."
**280.** Meltzer, Vol. 2, p. 139. Also see Cartmell, p. 26. The 120-ton *Desire* was built at Marblehead, Massachusetts, in 1636. Norwood, p. 31.
**281.** McManus, BBN, pp. 9, 10, 11.
**282.** Bowen, p. 217.
**283.** See B. Steiner, passim.
**284.** For more on the history of the New England slavery system, see Greene, passim.
**285.** McManus, BBN, pp. 6-7.
**286.** K. C. Davis, pp. 20, 23.
**287.** Website: www.tracesofthetrade.org/guides-and-materials/historical/the-dewolf-family/.
**288.** Meltzer, Vol. 2, pp. 145, 148; C. Johnson, pp. 125-126.
**289.** The Royall's original home and slave quarters have been turned into a museum located in Medford, MA. See Website: www.royallhouse.org.
**290.** Francie Latour, "New England's Hidden History," *The Boston Globe*, September 26, 2010.
**291.** See Lemire, passim.
**292.** K. C. Davis, p. 7.
**293.** M. M. Smith, p. 25.
**294.** For more on Bristol, Rhode Island, and the African slave trade, see M. A. D. Howe, passim.

**295.** Garraty, p. 77.

**296.** C. Johnson, p. 125.

**297.** Hacker, pp. 19, 25.

**298.** For more on Rhode Island and the African slave trade, see Coughtry, passim.

**299.** October 25, 2010,"America Live," FOX News. For early evidence of Rhode Island's official full name, "Rhode Island and Providence Plantations," see Article 1 of *The Treaty With Great Britain*, the famous secession contract between England's King George III and America's original thirteen colonies, signed at Paris, France, November 30, 1782. J. Williams, p. 365; Rouse, pp. 78-79. Rhode Island's true official name was also mentioned in the first draft of the Preamble to the U.S. Constitution, written about August 1787. J. B. Scott, pp. 84-85. See also pp. 86-87.

**300.** Rosenbaum and Brinkley, s.v. "Slavery."

**301.** Spooner, NT, No. 6, p. 54. See also Graham, BM, passim; Melish, passim.

**302.** See Adams and Sanders, pp. 144, 272, 281; Nye, p. 54; Buckley, p. 61; De Angelis, pp. 12-18, 49; W. Wilson, DR, p. 125; Green, W, pp. 180-181; Lott, pp. 61, 64, 65; Leech, pp. 291-292.

**303.** For more on the history of slavery in Pennsylvania, see Turner, passim.

**304.** Lott, pp. 6-7.

**305.** Nye, p. 27.

**306.** Farrow, Lang, and Frank, pp. xxvii, 4-5, 82-90; Hacker, p. 525; Ellis, FB, p. 103.

**307.** McKissack and McKissack, p. 3. Strangely, while Sewell had understandable sympathy for enslaved blacks, he had absolutely none for the free whites who were hanged (or crushed under rock) for witchcraft, due, in great part, to his judicial support of the accusations. To his credit Sewell later expressed remorse over his actions, even asking his church congregation for forgiveness.

**308.** McManus, BBN, pp. 16, 17.

**309.** Farrow, Lang, and Frank, pp. 82-90.

**310.** Farrow, Lang, and Frank, pp. 4-5.

**311.** Hacker, p. 525.

**312.** Ellis, FB, p. 103.

**313.** Farrow, Lang, and Frank, p. xxvii.

**314.** Buckley, p. 103.

**315.** Stonebraker, p. 81.

**316.** Nicolay and Hay, ALCW, Vol. 2, p. 1.

**317.** See Spooner, NT, No. 6, p. 54; Pollard, LC, p. 154; Graham, BM, passim.

**318.** G. H. Moore, p. 5; R. S. Phillips, s.v. "Slavery." Massachusetts was also the first state to ban interracial marriage. Wilson and Ferris, s.v. "Miscegenation"; K. C. Davis, p. 9.

**319.** McKissack and McKissack, p. 3.

**320.** For the history of slavery in Delaware, see W. H. Williams, passim.

**321.** Simpson, p. 78.

**322.** P. M. Roberts, p. 198; Garraty and McCaughey, p. 81; Rosenbaum and Brinkley, s.v. "Slavery"; "Slave States."

**323.** Meltzer, Vol. 2, pp. 141-142.

**324.** Litwack, pp. 4, 6.

**325.** Nicolay and Hay, ALCW, Vol. 1, pp. 231-232.

**326.** J. Williams, pp. 27-50.

**327.** C. Adams, pp. 4, 58.

**328.** Burns, Peltason, Cronin, Magleby, and O'Brien, p. 151.

**329.** Curti, Thorpe, and Baker, p. 572; Rosenbaum and Brinkley, s.v. "Slavery."

**330.** Zinn, p. 185.

**331.** Nicolay and Hay, ALCW, Vol. 2, p. 1.

**332.** Findlay and Findlay, p. 227; Fogel, p. 207.

**333.** For more on New England's so-called "abolition" of slavery, see Melish, passim.

**334.** Pollard, SHW, Vol. 2, pp. 202, 296-297, 562.

**335.** Ransom, p. 41.

**336.** Cooper, JDA, p. 666. For an example of Davis using the word servitude, see Richardson, Vol. 1, p. 494.

**337.** Grissom, p. 128.

**338.** Stampp, p. 192.

**339.** Fogel and Engerman, pp. 151-152, 241; M. M. Smith, pp. 184-185.

**340.** Fogel, p. 194.

**341.** Nye, pp. 146-147.

**342.** Garraty and McCaughey, p. 159; Rosenbaum, s.v. "Vesey, Denmark"; Bowman, CWDD, s.v. "May 1822." Modern day American blacks who, like Vesey, are enamored with Africa, would do well to read Ken Hamblin's book *Pick a Better Country*. See the Bibliography.

**343.** K. C. Davis, p. 23.

344. C. Johnson, pp. 131, 188-189; Quarles, p. 128.
345. Fogel, p. 194.
346. Traupman, s.v. "slave."
347. M. M. Smith, pp. 4-5.
348. R. S. Phillips, s.v. "Slavery"; Fogel, pp. 187-193; M. M. Smith, pp. 175-182, 184-185, 188-197; Wiley, SN, pp. 137-138; Fogel and Engerman, pp. 56, 151-152, 241; Stampp, pp. 58-59, 72.
349. H. A. White, p. 63.
350. For more on white slavery in early America, see Baepler, passim; Ballagh, passim; Galenson, passim; Hildreth, passim; Hoffman, passim; Jordan and Walsh, passim.
351. C. Johnson, pp. 81-84.
352. Greenberg and Waugh, p. 376.
353. See Foner, FSFLFM, pp. 87-88. See also Hacker, p. 581; Quarles, p. xiii; Weintraub, p. 70; Cooper, JDA, p. 378; Rosenbaum and Brinkley, s.v. "Civil War"; C. Eaton, HSC, p. 93; Hinkle, p. 125.
354. See Website: www.nps.gov/timu/historyculture/kp.htm.
355. Greenberg and Waugh, pp. 392-393.
356. M. M. Smith, p. 205.
357. In the 1850s prime field slaves cost as much as $1,800, about $51,000 apiece in today's money. Garraty and McCaughey, p. 214.
358. Greenberg and Waugh, p. 393.
359. Grissom, pp. 131, 182; Stonebraker, p. 46; J. C. Perry, pp. 96, 99, 101, 174; Rosenbaum and Brinkley, s.v. "Five Civilized Tribes"; M. Perry, p. 183; Simmons, s.v. "Stand Watie"; "Indians, in the War"; Jahoda, pp. 85, 148, 154, 225, 241, 246, 247, 249.
360. C. Eaton, HSC, p. 49.
361. Gragg, p. 84; DiLorenzo, LU, p. 174.
362. J. C. Perry, p. 101.
363. For more on black slave owners, see Johnson and Roark, passim; Koger, passim.
364. F. Moore, Vol. 1, p. 45.
365. Nicolay and Hay, ALCW, Vol. 1, p. 272.
366. Nicolay and Hay, ALCW, Vol. 1, p. 539.
367. See e.g., Nicolay and Hay, ALCW, Vol. 1, pp. 257, 259, 449, 469.
368. Kennedy, pp. 191, 233.
369. Nicolay and Hay, ALCW, Vol. 1, p. 231.
370. Nicolay and Hay, ALCW, Vol. 2, p. 1.
371. C. Adams, p. 4.
372. Parker, p. 343.
373. To his great credit, Virginian John Tyler (1790-1862), America's tenth president, was the only man of that office, former or future, to either join the Confederacy or serve in the Confederate government. Though he did not fight in Lincoln's "Civil War" (being too old at the time), he served as a member of the Provisional Congress of the Confederacy. He was later elected to the Confederate House of Representatives, but passed away before taking his seat. Tyler was an example of the overt anti-South bias that has long permeated the U.S. government: because of his devotion to the Confederate Cause, Northerners in his day regarded him as a traitor, his death in 1862 was ignored in Washington, and an official U.S. memorial was not placed over his grave until 1915, fifty-three years after he died. DeGregorio, s.v. "John Tyler." In total, six men who would become U.S. presidents fought in the War for Southern Independence; unfortunately for history, all got it wrong by siding with Lincoln and the North: Benjamin Harrison, James A. Garfield, Ulysses S. Grant, Rutherford B. Hayes, Chester A. Arthur, and William McKinley.
374. Tyler, LTT, Vol. 2, p. 567.
375. McManus, BBN, pp. 6-7.
376. C. Adams, pp. 4, 58.
377. Nicolay and Hay, ALCW, Vol. 2, p. 1.
378. See Spooner, NT, No. 6, p. 54; Graham, BM, passim.
379. H. A. White, p. 63.
380. See e.g., Seabrook, TMCP, pp. 145-146.
381. Lincoln called his "Emancipation Proclamation" exactly what it was: not a civil rights emancipation, but a "military emancipation." In other words, its true purpose was to "liberate" black servants, not so they could be free, but so the liberal Yankee president could use them in his armies. See e.g., Seabrook, L, p. 647.
382. H. A. White, pp. 63-64.
383. Long and Long, p. 702.
384. E. M. Thomas, p. 6.
385. Gragg, p. 84; DiLorenzo, LU, p. 174; Wilkens, p. 153.
386. Wilson and Ferris, s.v. "Plantations."

387. E. M. Thomas, p. 6.
388. Channing, p. 8.
389. M. M. Smith, pp. 4-5.
390. Gragg, p. 84; DiLorenzo, LU, p. 174.
391. Parker, p. 343. Important note: in an attempt to tarnish the South, anti-South proponents like to artificially inflate the numbers of white Southern slave owners (they completely ignore black and red slave owners) by calculating using the number of *households* ("families") instead of the *total number of white Southerners*. Using the lower number of households as opposed to the higher number of total whites, of course, gives a higher number of slave owners, which is why they use this method: it makes the South look as bad as possible, and gives further justification for Lincoln's unjustifiable War. Be aware of this cowardly and treacherous pro-North trick, one found in nearly every anti-South book.
392. E. M. Thomas, p. 6.
393. White, Foscue, and McKnight, p. 209.
394. Kennedy and Kennedy, SWR, p. 83.
395. Ransom, p. 174.
396. Grant, Vol. 1, p. 223.
397. Nicolay and Hay, ALCW, Vol. 1, p. 581.
398. Foote, Vol. 3, p. 755.
399. Wilson and Ferris, s.v. "Plantations."
400. Munford, p. 156.
401. Seabrook, TQREL, pp. 110-111.
402. Meltzer, Vol. 2, p. 139.
403. G. H. Moore, p. 5; R. S. Phillips, s.v. "Slavery."
404. Litwack, pp. 3-4. Northern plantations date back to at least the Pilgrims, who were establishing them as early as the 1600s, long before they were found in the South. October 25, 2010, "America Live," FOX News.
405. Fogel, pp. 203-204.
406. McManus, BBN, p. 5.
407. Meltzer, Vol. 2, p. 127.
408. R. S. Phillips, s.v. "Emancipation Proclamation."
409. U. B. Phillips, pp. 119-120.
410. P. M. Roberts, p. 198; Garraty and McCaughey, p. 81.
411. Eaton, HSC, p. 93.
412. Hinkle, p. 125.
413. For the Northern white population in 1860, see Current, CWSB, p. 46.
414. Rutherford, FA, p. 38; Wallechinsky, Wallace, and Wallace, p. 11; Woods, p. 67.
415. McElroy, p. 357.
416. Recently I had occasion to travel to Massachusetts on business, where I found myself, as I often do, exploring a cemetery, this one named Woodlawn, in the town of Acton. It was here that I experienced the most interesting part of my journey: the discovery of a small gray headstone that read simply, "Peter, slave." Revealingly, Peter's grave was completely isolated, situated by a road many yards from the surrounding graves of white Yankees. This is quite unlike what one finds in the South. Here, where relations between Victorian whites and blacks were far warmer and more intimate than in the North, the graves of both races are often located right next to one another. For more on the subject of white-black relationships in the Old South, see my books *A Rebel Born: A Defense of Nathan Bedford Forrest* (pp. 151-155), and *The McGavocks of Carnton Plantation: A Southern History*.
417. Many of these individuals were slaves in more than one Northern state.
418. Nicolay and Hay, ALCW, Vol. 1, p. 176.
419. Website: www.factasy.com/civil_war/2008/03/02/slave_owners_slaves_and_life_plantation.
420. Website: www.factasy.com/civil_war/2008/03/02/slave_owners_slaves_and_life_plantation.
421. Manegold, pp. 132-134.
422. Rosenbaum and Brinkley, s.v. "Underground Railroad."
423. Gragg, pp. 191-192.
424. DiLorenzo, RL, pp. 26-27. See also Kennedy, p. 219.
425. See e.g., Tocqueville, Vol. 1, pp. 383-385; Buckingham, Vol. 2, p. 112; Hawthorne, Vol. 2, pp. 109-110; Peterson, JM, p. 377; Sturge, p. 40; Dicey, Vol. 1, pp. 70-72.
426. Stampp, pp. 408-418; E. M. Thomas, pp. 14-15.
427. Fogel, pp. 73-76. See also Fogel and Engerman, pp. 158-257. This explains other studies which show that after emancipation blacks produced 50 percent less than when they were slaves. Garraty and McCaughey, p. 268.
428. See Fogel and Engerman, pp. 38-106.
429. Strangely, most black Southerners today do not express shame for their involvement in black slavery, nor have they ever apologized for it. As far as I am aware, neither have Native-Americans or Latin-Americans.

**430.** Meltzer, Vol. 2, p. 139. Also see Cartmell, p. 26; Norwood, p. 31.
**431.** Lott, pp. 35-60.
**432.** G. H. Moore, pp. 5, 11, 17-19.
**433.** Rosenbaum and Brinkley, s.v. "Slavery"; Melish, passim.
**434.** Seabrook, AL, pp. 163-165.
**435.** Fogel and Engerman, pp. 232, 238-239, 240.
**436.** Fogel and Engerman, p. 146.
**437.** *Appendix to the Congressional Globe*, 31ˢᵗ Congress, 1ˢᵗ Session, 1850, Vol. 23, Part 1, p. 150.
**438.** Stampp, pp. 178, 179.
**439.** *De Bow's Review*, Vol. 22, Third Series, Vol. 2, New Orleans, LA, 1857, p. 379.
**440.** Fox-Genovese, p. 360.
**441.** Stampp, pp. 219-222.
**442.** Fogel and Engerman, p. 146.
**443.** Ashe, p. 64.
**444.** Coit, pp. 37, 48.
**445.** Collier and Collier, p. 51.
**446.** Jensen, NN, p. 33.
**447.** Channing, p. 29; Wiley, SN, p. 45.
**448.** Harwell, p. 339.
**449.** Wiley, SN, pp. 213, 244, 245.
**450.** See Quarles, pp. 208-209; Wiley, SN, pp. 316-317.
**451.** Henry, ASTF, p. 246.
**452.** Blassingame, p. 15.
**453.** See e.g., Wiley, SN, pp. 213, 214, 244, 245.
**454.** ORA, Ser. 1, Vol. 6, p. 204.
**455.** See e.g., J. Davis, RFCG, Vol. 2, p. 626.
**456.** Grissom, p. 183.
**457.** McManus, BBN, p. 183.
**458.** See Fogel, p. 26; Genovese, pp. 356, 368, 371, 374, 378-380, 385, 386, 542.
**459.** Fogel and Engerman, pp. 210-215.
**460.** See e.g., J. C. Perry, p. 174; Grissom, p. 131; Stonebraker, p. 46; C. Johnson, pp. 81-84; Greenberg and Waugh, p. 376.
**461.** Drescher and Engerman, pp. 214, 215.
**462.** See Genovese, pp. 470, 482, 504, 508-511.
**463.** DeGregorio, s.v. "Jimmy Carter" (p. 619).
**464.** Nicolay and Hay, ALCW, Vol. 1, p. 89.
**465.** See Fogel and Engerman, pp. 232, 238-239.
**466.** Drescher and Engerman, p. 207.
**467.** See Seabrook, AL, pp. 137-162.
**468.** H. A. White, p. 63.
**469.** Hopkins, pp. 14-17.
**470.** Fogel, p. 207.
**471.** G. H. Moore, pp. 5, 11, 17-19.
**472.** R. S. Phillips, s.v. "Slavery."
**473.** Greenberg and Waugh, p. 376; Grissom, pp. 131, 182; Stonebraker, p. 46; J. C. Perry, pp. 96, 99, 101, 174.
**474.** Kennedy and Kennedy, SWR, p. 83; M. M. Smith, pp. 4-5.
**475.** Meltzer, Vol. 2, p. 4.
**476.** M. Perry, p. 49.
**477.** Lott, p. 18; Furnas, p. 27; Garraty and McCaughey, p. 25; Garraty, p. 77.
**478.** Furnas, p. 108.
**479.** Seabrook, TQJD, p. 68.
**480.** Beard and Beard, Vol. 1, pp. 652-653.
**481.** Garraty and McCaughey, p. 81.
**482.** Adams and Sanders, p. 118.
**483.** W. Wilson, DR, pp. 113-114.
**484.** Nicolay and Hay, ALCW, Vol. 2, p. 6.
**485.** Faust, s.v. "slavery"; Stampp, p. 271; Meltzer, Vol. 2, pp. 247-248; C. Johnson, pp. 126-128; Rosenbaum and Brinkley, s.v. "Slave Trade"; Durden, p. 288.
**486.** Ellis, FB, p. 105.

**487.** McCullough, p. 221.
**488.** Eaton, HSC, pp. 237-238.
**489.** U. B. Phillips, p. 493.
**490.** Chesnut, MCCW, p. 357.
**491.** Warner, GG, s.v. "James Johnston Pettigrew."
**492.** Cash, p. 63.
**493.** H. C. Bailey, p. 197.
**494.** Oates, AF, p. 29; M. Perry, passim.
**495.** Peterson, JM, p. 371; Ellis, AS, pp. 102, 173.
**496.** N. Adams, p. 77.
**497.** Seabrook, TQREL, p. 106.
**498.** E. M. Thomas, p. 242.
**499.** Seabrook, TQREL, p. 106.
**500.** Kennedy and Kennedy, SWR, p. 73.
**501.** Weintraub, p. 54.
**502.** Chesnut, DD, pp. 114, 163.
**503.** Chesnut, MCCW, pp. 729, 245, 246.
**504.** Simpson, pp. 77-78, 85.
**505.** Coit, p. 166. Randolph, my cousin, was known to attend senate meetings carrying a whip and wearing spurs and multiple overcoats, some that dragged along the ground, as he strode imperiously up and down the aisles in his buckskin breeches and leather boots. Coit, p. 162.
**506.** Woods, p. 33. John Taylor "of Caroline," a die-hard Jeffersonian and vehement anti-Federalist, would later inspire the supporters of states' rights (like John C. Calhoun), as well as members of the libertarian and Tea Party movements, with his strict constructionist views of the Constitution.
**507.** H. A. White, p. 65.
**508.** W. Wilson, DR, pp. 110-111.
**509.** Long and Long, pp. 593-594.
**510.** C. Johnson, pp. 187-188.
**511.** Richardson, Vol. 1, p. 494.
**512.** E. McPherson, PHUSADGR, pp. 151, 152.
**513.** R. S. Phillips, s.v. "Emancipation Proclamation."
**514.** P. M. Roberts, p. 198; Garraty and McCaughey, p. 81; Rosenbaum and Brinkley, s.v. "Slavery"; "Slave States."
**515.** Hopkins, pp. 17-18.
**516.** Melish, passim.
**517.** Seabrook, ARB, pp. 220-221.
**518.** Seabrook, TQREL, pp. 110-111.
**519.** McKim, p. 31.
**520.** Seabrook, L, p. 44.
**521.** Simpson, pp. 79-80.
**522.** Ironically, though he was partly responsible for inflaming already existing sectional animosities, Garrison himself believed that allowing the South to secede peacefully was preferable to war between the two regions. W. B. Garrison, LNOK, p. 144.
**523.** For the complete *true* story of the Nat Turner Rebellion, see T. R. Gray, passim.
**524.** Stampp, pp. 132-134; Blassingame, pp. 129-131.
**525.** Bowman, CWDD, s.v. "August 1831."
**526.** Rosenbaum and Brinkley, s.v. "Slave Revolts."
**527.** Simpson, p. 85.
**528.** Stonebraker, p. 250.
**529.** Garraty, p. 302.
**530.** Simpson, pp. 80-81.
**531.** Nicolay and Hay, ALCW, Vol. 1, p. 495.
**532.** White, Foscue, and McKnight, p. 211; Coit, pp. 298-299.
**533.** Coit, p. 306.
**534.** Mitgang, p. 413; Simpson, pp. 73-74; C. Adams, pp. 93-94; L. Johnson, p. 133; Crocker, p. 59.
**535.** Eaton, HSC, p. 28.
**536.** M. M. Smith, pp. 4-5.
**537.** Chesnut, DD, p. 20.
**538.** Lang, p. 233.
**539.** See e.g., Boatner, s.v. "Davis, Jefferson"; Simmons, s.v. "Davis, Jefferson Finis"; Bowman, ECW, s.v. "Davis, Jefferson"; Bradford, pp. 89-90.

**540.** September, 17, 2009 (Constitution Day, 222nd anniversary), "Glenn Beck," FOX News.

**541.** Coffin, p. 235.

**542.** Findlay and Findlay, pp. 84-85; Napolitano, pp. 14-15.

**543.** J. Davis, RFCG, Vol. 2, pp. 621, 622. Only a dictator can issue laws overturning constitutional rights. See Crocker, p. 59.

**544.** Mitgang, pp. 403, 404; L. Johnson, pp. 123-124; Meriwether, p. 157; Horn, IE, p. 217.

**545.** Neely, pp. 109-112.

**546.** See e.g., J. Davis, RFCG, Vol. 2, pp. 632-633; C. Johnson, p. 157; Lott, pp. 158-159; L. Johnson, p. 188; Grissom, pp. 115-116; Christian, p. 15; Cisco, passim; Grimsley, passim.

**547.** C. Adams, pp. 117-118.

**548.** "My policy is to have no policy," our crafty sixteenth president once said. Nicolay and Hay, ALAH, Vol. 4, p. 76.

**549.** D. H. Donald, WNWCW, pp. 84-88; Simmons, s.v. "Civil rights in the Confederacy"; L. Johnson, p. 176; Current, TC, s.v. "Davis, Jefferson."

**550.** Hacker, p. 580; Rosenbaum and Brinkley, s.v. "Lincoln and Douglas"; L. Johnson, p. 54; DeGregorio, s.v. "Abraham Lincoln"; C. Adams, p. 159; Litwack, p. 276; Wade, p. 39. See Bennett, passim. See also Nicolay and Hay, ALCW, Vol. 1, p. 284; Basler, ALSW, pp. 400, 402, 403-404; Stern, pp. 492-493; Holzer, pp. 189, 251.

**551.** Garraty and McCaughey, p. 253; Hacker, p. 584; Grissom, p. 127.

**552.** Findlay and Findlay, p. 227; Fogel, p. 207.

**553.** Long and Long, pp. 593-594.

**554.** Richardson, Vol. 1, p. 494.

**555.** Faust, s.v. "Davis, Jefferson Finis."

**556.** Nicolay and Hay, ALCW, Vol. 1, p. 533.

**557.** Villard, Vol. 1, p. 96.

**558.** V. Davis, Vol. 1, pp. 574-575.

**559.** Faust, s.v. "Davis, Jefferson Finis."

**560.** Current, TC, s.v. "Davis, Jefferson."

**561.** See Peter and Hull, passim.

**562.** Bowman, ECW, s.v. "Davis, Jefferson." For more on Forrest from the Southern point of view, see my books *A Rebel Born: A Defense of the Nathan Bedford Forrest* and *Nathan Bedford Forrest: Southern Hero, American Patriot*.

**563.** Hattaway and Jones, p. 277.

**564.** George Washington and Ulysses S. Grant are two exceptions that could be named.

**565.** Though Lincoln claimed to be a "combat veteran" of the Black Hawk War, the truth is that he never saw a single day of combat, or even a single Indian, during his entire tour of duty. Woodworth, p. xi; Zinn, p. 129; C. Johnson, pp. 119-120.

**566.** Ver Steeg and Hofstadter, p. 331.

**567.** See C. Johnson, pp. 187-188.

**568.** J. Davis, RFCG, Vol. 2, p. 701.

**569.** Hinkle, p. 108.

**570.** J. Davis, RFCG, Vol. 2, p. 701.

**571.** Shenkman and Reiger, p. 124.

**572.** J. Davis, RFCG, Vol. 1, p. 518.

**573.** See Nicolay and Hay, ALCW, Vol. 2, p. 614.

**574.** Seabrook, ARB, p. 317.

**575.** Wyeth, LGNBF, p. 641.

**576.** Sheppard, pp. 306-307.

**577.** Grant, Vol. 2, p. 345.

**578.** Grant, Vol. 2, p. 167.

**579.** Seabrook, ARB, pp. 299-300.

**580.** As the following note reveals, it was Davis' illegal imprisonment that later caused him to become unhealthy.

**581.** C. Adams, p. 186. After his capture on May 10, 1865, near Irwinville, Georgia, Davis was imprisoned at Fort Monroe, Virginia, for "treason" where, for two long years he was chained, treated inhumanely, and suffered numerous indignities in a cold, dark, damp cell. He became ill on several occasions and nearly lost his life. To the great relief of his family and supporters, President Davis survived the ordeal, and on May 14, 1867, he was "released on bond." This was an intelligent move on the part of the U.S. government, as a trial would have certainly uncovered the unlawfulness of both the North's war on the South and Davis' imprisonment. Sobel, s.v. "Davis, Jefferson." Also hoping to prove that secession was legal, numerous other Confederates demanded that they be tried for "treason" by the U.S. government. All were turned down—for obvious reasons. C. Johnson, p. 201.

**582.** Stonebraker, p. 75.

**583.** Sandburg, SOL, pp. 412-414.

**584.** Current, TC, s.v. "Davis, Jefferson."

585. Faust, s.v. "Davis, Jefferson Finis."
586. J. W. Daniel, p. 32.
587. J. W. Daniel, pp. 32-33.
588. J. W. Daniel, p. 33.
589. Simmons, s.v. "Davis, Jefferson Finis."
590. Current, TC, s.v. "Davis, Jefferson."
591. Eaton, HSC, p. 57.
592. Faust, s.v. "Davis, Jefferson Finis."
593. For more on this topic, see Craven, passim.
594. See e.g., Meriwether, p. 47.
595. Crocker, p. 59.
596. Scruggs, p. 24; Napolitano, p. 69.
597. Neely, pp. 172-175.
598. Tatalovich and Daynes, p. 322.
599. L. Johnson, p. 125.
600. DiLorenzo, LU, p. 52.
601. Neely, pp. 109-112.
602. Burns and Peltason, p. 192.
603. Leech, p. 151; Black, p. 165. Lincoln later stripped Frémont of his command for freeing slaves in his assigned military area. K. C. Davis, p. 439.
604. Black, p. 165; Wiley, SN, pp. 296-298; Leech, pp. 305-306.
605. Quarles, pp. 115-116.
606. Quarles, pp. 113-114.
607. D. H. Donald, L, p. 363; Leech, p. 155.
608. Lincoln admitted that he nullified the emancipation proclamations of his officers because, as he put it, there was no "indispensable necessity." Nicolay and Hay, ALCW, Vol. 2, p. 508. The nation's 4 million slaves (North and South) must have wondered what he meant by this.
609. W. B. Garrison, CWC, p. 13; Findlay and Findlay, pp. 84-85; C. Adams, p. 39; Owsley, pp. 79-80, 229-267; K. L. Hall, s.v. "Lincoln, Abraham"; "Civil War."
610. Tyler, PH, pp. 13-14; Bailyn, Dallek, Davis, Donald, Thomas, and Wood, p. 5; Grissom, pp. 126-127; C. Adams, p. 57.
611. Gragg, p. 73; Tyler, PH, pp. 13-14.
612. Mish, s.v. "privateer."
613. J. Davis, RFCG, Vol. 2, pp. 460-468.
614. Tatalovich and Daynes, p. 322.
615. W. B. Garrison, LNOK, p. 281.
616. C. Adams, p. 57, pp. 208-209; Grissom, pp. 126-127.
617. Burns and Peltason, p. 437.
618. D. H. Donald, L, pp. 429, 450, 489, 510, 539.
619. See e.g., Nicolay and Hay, Vol. 2, p. 131.
620. J. Davis, RFCG, Vol. 2, pp. 460-468. For more on Lincoln's illegal subjugation of Maryland, see Pollard, LC, pp. 123-125.
621. DiLorenzo, LU, p. 137.
622. Lott, p. 158.
623. Neely, pp. 113-114.
624. Stephens, RAHS, pp. 356-357, passim.
625. Hacker, p. 584; Napolitano, p. 74.
626. Christian, p. 14; Hacker, p. 581.
627. Nicolay and Hay, ALCW, Vol. 2, p. 267; D. H. Donald, L, 392-395; W. B. Garrison, CWTFB, p. 62; C. Adams, p. 210.
628. DiLorenzo, LU, pp. 75, 89, 90.
629. E. M. Thomas, p. 152.
630. C. Adams, p. 58; W. B. Garrison, LNOK, pp. 193-197; D. H. Donald, L, pp. 300-301, 405; DiLorenzo, RL, pp. 148-149; G. C. Walker, p. 184.
631. L. Johnson, pp. 123-124; Horn, IE, p. 217; DiLorenzo, LU, p. 52; Simpson, p. 62.
632. Confederate Veteran, Vol. 28, January 1920, No. 1, p. 157.
633. W. B. Garrison, ACW, pp. 194-195; DeGregorio, s.v. "Abraham Lincoln"; D. H. Donald, L, p. 249.
634. K. L. Hall, s.v. "Civil War"; Christian, pp. 4-5; C. Adams, pp. 48-49; Rosenbaum and Brinkley, s.v. "Merryman, Ex Parte"; DiLorenzo, LU, pp. 92-96.
635. Ingersoll, p. 22.

**636.** Neely, p. 53.

**637.** See Remsburg, passim. See also Christian, p. 7; Meriwether, pp. 54-55; Oates, AL, p. 58; Current, LNK, pp. 58, 60-61; Kane, p. 163; *Southern Review*, January 1873, Vol. 12, No. 25, p. 364; Lamon, LAL, pp. 488, 489, 493; W. B. Garrison, LNOK, p. 265; Barton, p. 146; DeGregorio, s.v. "Abraham Lincoln."

**638.** Woods, p. 47.

**639.** See James Garfield Randall's book, *Lincoln: The Liberal Statesman*.

**640.** See e.g., Pollard, LC, p. 178; J. H. Franklin, pp. 101, 111, 130, 149. Lincoln himself acknowledged this. See e.g., Nicolay and Hay, ALCW, Vol. 1, p. 627.

**641.** For more on Lincoln's similarities to liberal socialistic FDR, see Napolitano, pp. 131-138; DiLorenzo, LU, p. 106. We will note that FDR's term the "New Deal" was taken from 1865, when it was coined to describe Lincoln's socialistic domestic policies. Thornton and Ekelund, p. 99.

**642.** Nicolay and Hay, ALCW, Vol. 1, p. 458.

**643.** U.S. gov. Website: www.nps.gov/gett/forteachers/upload/7%20Lincoln%20on%20Race.pdf.

**644.** Foley, p. 327.

**645.** For more on the tyranny of liberalism, see Levin, pp. 2-6, passim.

**646.** See Seabrook, AL, pp. 31-51.

**647.** See Hitler, Vol. 2, pp. 830-831.

**648.** See DiLorenzo, LU, pp. 81-84.

**649.** See e.g., Dilorenzo, LU, pp. 151-153.

**650.** Benson and Kennedy, passim.

**651.** Socialists have long been attracted to Lincoln and enjoy writing about him. See e.g., Schlüter, passim.

**652.** For Marx's letter, and the White House's reply, see Schlüter, pp. 188-193.

**653.** Nicolay and Hay, ALCW, Vol. 11, pp. 97-98. See DiLorenzo, RL, pp. 54-84.

**654.** Hacker, p. 584; Napolitano, p. 74.

**655.** For more on these topics, see DiLorenzo, LU, pp. 66, 171-179; DiLorenzo, RL, pp. 54, 59, 68.

**656.** Quarles, p. 68.

**657.** Hacker, p. 580.

**658.** That Lincoln did not consider himself an abolitionist, that he in fact intentionally separated himself from them, is clearly evidenced by a statement he made during a speech at Chicago, Illinois, on July 10, 1858: "I have always hated slavery, I think, as much as any Abolitionist." Nicolay and Hay, ALCW, Vol. 3, p. 33.

**659.** W. B. Garrison, CWC, p. 97; DiLorenzo, LU, pp. 52-61.

**660.** C. Adams, p. 135; DiLorenzo, GC, p. 255; Johannsen, p. 55.

**661.** Nicolay and Hay, CWAL, Vol. 1, p. 15.

**662.** Stephenson, p. 69.

**663.** Nicolay and Hay, ALCW, Vol. 1, p. 174.

**664.** McKissack and McKissack, pp. 134, 135.

**665.** W. Phillips, p. 456.

**666.** Stephenson, p. 70.

**667.** Lincoln and Douglas, p. 187.

**668.** Sandburg, SOL, p. 418.

**669.** Faust, s.v. "slavery." For examples of the many black contributions to American culture, see Wilson and Ferris, s.v. "Black life." See also M. M. Smith, p. 30; Rogers, AGA, passim.

**670.** W. B. Garrison, CWC, p. 220.

**671.** Faust, s.v. "Lincoln, Abraham"; Page Smith, p. 576; Grissom, p. 72.

**672.** Meriwether, p. 162.

**673.** Gragg, p. 211.

**674.** Lamon, LAL, p. 481.

**675.** M. Davis, p. 68.

**676.** Pollard, LC, p. 102.

**677.** M. Davis, p. 67.

**678.** Lamon, LAL, pp. 482, 483; Slotkin, p. 107; J. M. McPherson, BCF, p. 790.

**679.** Christian, pp. 4, 9, 10; Lamon, LAL, pp. 482, 483, 493; Current, LNK, p. 62; W. B. Garrison, LNOK, p. 265; Meriwether, p. 19.

**680.** D. H. Donald, LH, p. 158.

**681.** Christian, p. 9.

**682.** Tyler, PH, p. 11. For more on Lincoln's faults as viewed by Southerners, see Seabrook, AL, pp. 470-476; Meriwether, pp. 42-43.

**683.** *The Congressional Globe*, 37th Congress, 3rd Session, pp. 549, 550.

**684.** Guelzo, p. 90; Nye, p. 169.

685. DeGregorio, s.v. "Abraham Lincoln"; Beschloss, p. 113; K. C. Davis, p. 219; Flood, p. 37; D. H. Donald, L, p. 319.
686. Fite, p. 210.
687. Christian, p. 11.
688. Lincoln's "friends" made him so miserable that he once told his associate Ward Hill Lamon: "I wish I had never been born! I would rather be dead than as President thus abused in the house of my friends." Meriwether, p. 9.
689. Meriwether, p. 9.
690. Rosen, p. 161.
691. Hinkle, p. 108.
692. C. Johnson, p. 5.
693. Current, TC, s.v. "Benjamin, Judah P."
694. Faust, s.v. "Judah Philip Benjamin."
695. E. N. Evans, p. 483.
696. For more on the history of Jews and the South, see Ferris and Greenberg, passim.
697. Neely, p. 108.
698. ORA, Ser. 1, Vol. 17, Pt. 2, p. 424.
699. Simmons, s.v. "General Order, Number Eleven;" Shenkman and Reiger, p. 84.
700. Neely, p. 107.
701. In 1861, for example, the 5th Pennsylvania Cavalry appointed a rabbi to be its chaplain. When Lincoln found out about it, the Jewish clergyman was forced to resign. At the time, under Lincoln's orders, only ordained Christian ministers were allowed to serve as chaplains. Katcher, CWSB, pp. 176-177.
702. K. C. Davis, p. 273; Neely, p. 109.
703. Horwitz, p. 204.
704. Bowman, CWDD, s.v. "21 January 1863."
705. ORA, Ser. 1, Vol. 24, Pt. 1, p. 9.
706. Neely, pp. 108-109.
707. See Napolitano, p. 8.
708. Thornton and Ekelund, pp. 98-99.
709. C. Adams, pp. 198-199; Woods, p. 75.
710. A. Cooke, ACA, p. 214.
711. One writer has gone so far as to name his book, Lincoln's Gettysburg Address: Echoes of the Bible and Book of Common Prayer; this despite the fact that Lincoln was a proven lifelong, unwavering, anti-Christian and a devout atheist who despised the Bible and never prayed.
712. Seabrook, L, p. 712.
713. Mullen, p. 33; Rosenbaum and Brinkley, s.v. "Forty Acres and a Mule."
714. J. H. Franklin, p. 37.
715. Grissom, p. 162.
716. Foner, R, pp. 70-71.
717. Thornton and Ekelund, p. 96.
718. K. C. Davis, p. 427. For more on Lincoln's broken promises to "emancipated slaves," see McFeely, passim.
719. See Nicolay and Hay, ALCW, Vol. 2, pp. 287-288.
720. Seabrook, L, p. 647.
721. Rosenbaum and Brinkley, s.v. "Lincoln and Douglas."
722. Thornton and Ekelund, p. 96.
723. Stephens, RAHS, pp. 83, 137; Stephens, CV, Vol. 2, p. 615.
724. Bailyn, Dallek, Davis, Donald, Thomas, and Wood, p. 16.
725. K. C. Davis, p. 426.
726. Buckley, p. 116.
727. Website: www.archives.gov/nae/news/featured-programs/lincoln/080920Lincoln02Transcript.pdf.
728. A. Cooke, ACA, p. 216.
729. U.S. Grant: Warrior, PBS, January 10, 2011.
730. See e.g., Oates, AL, p. 17.
731. See e.g., Tagg, passim.
732. Hacker, p. 580.
733. Garraty and McCaughey, p. 241.
734. W. B. Garrison, CWTFB, p. 145.
735. E. M. Thomas, p. 49.
736. Christian, p. 25.
737. DiLorenzo, LU, p. 52.
738. See e.g., J. Davis, RFCG, Vol. 2, pp. 465-468, 476, 492; L. Johnson, p. 126.

739. See e.g., Napolitano, p. 69.
740. L. Johnson, p. 125; D. H. Donald, WNWCW, p. 87.
741. See Seabrook, AL, pp. 270-274.
742. W. B. Garrison, p. LNOK, p. 75.
743. Current, LNK, p. 200.
744. L. Johnson, p. 127.
745. D. H. Donald, LR, p. 65.
746. See e.g., Nicolay and Hay, CWAL, Vol. 11, pp. 105-106; Nicolay and Hay, ALCW, Vol. 1, p. 483; Nicolay and Hay, ALCW, Vol. 2, p. 237; Holzer, pp. 22-23, 67, 318, 361.
747. Douglass' Monthly, September 1862, Vol. 5, pp. 707-708.
748. Schwartz, p. 86.
749. Douglass, LTFD, p. 872.
750. C. Adams, p. 135; DiLorenzo, GC, p. 255; Johannsen, p. 55.
751. Nicolay and Hay, ALCW, Vol. 3, p. 33.
752. Nicolay and Hay, CWAL, Vol. 1, p. 15.
753. McKissack and McKissack, pp. 134, 135.
754. Seabrook, L, p. 647.
755. W. B. Garrison, LNOK, p. 186; DiLorenzo, LU, p. 28.
756. De Angelis, pp. 12-18; Lott, p. 65; J. J. Holland, passim.
757. Garrison, LNOK, p. 176; J. M. McPherson, BCF, pp. 788-789.
758. See Spooner, NT, No. 6, p. 54; Pollard, LC, p. 154; Graham, BM, passim.
759. See Nicolay and Hay, CWAL, Vol. 11, pp. 105-106; Nicolay and Hay, ALCW, Vol. 1, p. 483; Holzer, pp. 22-23, 67, 318, 361.
760. Current, LNK, pp. 242-246; W. C. Davis, AHD, p. 164; Garrison, LNOK, p. 181; Weintraub, p. 73.
761. B. F. Butler, p. 903. See also W. P. Pickett, pp. 326-327.
762. Current, LNK, p. 218-219; W. B. Garrison, LNOK, pp. 35-37; Greenberg and Waugh, p. 355.
763. Nicolay and Hay, ALCW, Vol. 2, p. 6; Beard and Beard, Vol. 2, p. 65; DiLorenzo, LU, pp. 24, 25.
764. M. Davis, p. 83. See also Seabrook, AL, passim.
765. E. M. Thomas, p. 175.
766. Katcher, CWSB, p. 42.
767. Faust, s.v. "blockade."
768. Eaton, HSC, p. 71.
769. Bowman, ECW, s.v. "Blockade."
770. Faust, s.v. "blockade runners"; Lang, pp. 189, 190.
771. R. S. Phillips, s.v. "Declaration of Paris."
772. Owsley, KCD, pp. 224, 428, 432, 286.
773. Nicolay and Hay, ALCW, Vol. 2, p. 674.
774. K. L. Hall, s.v. "Civil War."
775. Eaton, HSC, p. 71.
776. Owsley, KCD, pp. 286, 262, 229-267.
777. Boatner, s.v. "Blockade Running"; Katcher, CWSB, p. 44.
778. Thornton and Ekelund, pp. 36, 37.
779. Faust, s.v. "blockade runners."
780. Owsley, KCD, pp. 516-517.
781. Lang, pp. 189, 190.
782. Lang, pp. 199, 200.
783. Thornton and Ekelund, p. 30.
784. LeVert, s.v. "Blockade"; Faust, s.v. "blockade"; Bowman, CWDD, "19 April 1861."
785. Eaton, HSC, p. 81.
786. ORN, Ser. 2, Vol. 3, p. 393.
787. Owsley, KCD, pp. 275, 302, 152.
788. Owsley, KCD, pp. 152-153.
789. Nicolay and Hay, ALCW, Vol. 2, p. 302.
790. For more on the Anglo-American cotton trade, and Lincoln's role in interrupting it, see McHenry, passim.
791. Long and Long, s.v. "February 25, 1862."
792. R. S. Phillips, s.v. "Emancipation Proclamation."
793. Woods, p. 67; Rutherford, FA, p. 38; Wallechinsky, Wallace, and Wallace, p. 11. Grant did not free his slaves until he was forced to by the passage of the Thirteenth Amendment on December 6, 1865, eight months after Lincoln's War ended.

**794.** Nicolay and Hay, ALCW, Vol. 2, pp. 287-288.

**795.** Nicolay and Hay, ALCW, Vol. 2, pp. 287-288.

**796.** Sandburg, SOL, p. 152.

**797.** In reality, Lincoln waged war on the South neither to preserve the Union *or* end slavery. It was solely to install Henry Clay's big government "American System" in Washington. Rosenbaum and Brinkley, s.v. "American System"; DeGregorio, s.v. "John Quincy Adams"; Simpson, p. 75; Weintraub, pp. 48-49.

**798.** Nicolay and Hay, ALCW, Vol. 2, p. 302.

**799.** Owsley, pp. 65-66, 187-190; E. M. Thomas, pp. 293-294; Richardson, Vol. 2, pp. 709, 713; Owsley, pp. 538-541; Durden, pp. 149-150; Cooper, JDA, pp. 552-553; Eaton, HSC, p. 81.

**800.** Ashe, p. 35.

**801.** Nicolay and Hay, ALCW, Vol. 2, p. 237.

**802.** Sandburg, SOL, p. 154.

**803.** Eaton, HSC, pp. 74-75.

**804.** C. Johnson, p. 239.

**805.** Nicolay and Hay, ALCW, Vol. 2, p. 454.

**806.** Cooper, JDA, p. 378; Quarles, p. xiii.

**807.** Current, LNK, p. 228. See also Barney, p. 141.

**808.** Gragg, p. 88.

**809.** Current, LNK, p. 228.

**810.** L. Johnson, p. 180.

**811.** Quarles, p. 37; Greenberg and Waugh, pp. 372-373.

**812.** Barrow, Segars, and Rosenburg, BC, pp. 8, 25.

**813.** E. M. Thomas, p. 236; Fleming, p. 208; Quarles, pp. xiii, 48.

**814.** There were some 182,000 free blacks in the eleven states of the Confederacy (Quarles, p. 35), nearly all who sided with Dixie. In addition, most traditional Southern historians believe that between 100,000 and 300,000 Southern slaves fought for Dixie. See Barrow, Segars, and Rosenburg, BC, p. 97; *The United Daughters of the Confederacy Magazine*, Vols. 54-55, 1991, p. 32; Hinkle, p. 106; R. M. Brown, p. xiv; Shenkman and Reiger, p. 106.

**815.** See e.g., Barrow, Segars, and Rosenburg, BC, p. 19; Greenberg and Waugh, p. 385.

**816.** See Kautz, p. 11.

**817.** These numbers do not include the other three "races," yellow, brown, and red, that sided with and fought for the Confederacy. See C. Johnson, pp. 169-197.

**818.** Using Kautz' definition and these numbers, 200,000 blacks fought for the Union, 1 million blacks for the Confederacy. Thus, 80 percent more blacks wore Rebel gray than wore Yankee blue.

**819.** Seabrook, L, p. 647.

**820.** Nicolay and Hay, ALCW, Vol. 2, p. 318.

**821.** Nicolay and Hay, ALCW, Vol. 2, p. 398.

**822.** See e.g., C. Adams, p. 135; DiLorenzo, GC, p. 255; Johannsen, p. 55.

**823.** Kinder and Hilgemann, Vol. 2, p. 117.

**824.** C. Johnson, p. 170; Eaton, HSC, p. 93; Hinkle, p. 125.

**825.** Wiley, SN, pp. 241, 309-310, 317.

**826.** Simmons, s.v. "Lincoln, Abraham."

**827.** See Seabrook, L, pp. 584-633.

**828.** R. S. Phillips, s.v. "Emancipation Proclamation."

**829.** W. Phillips, p. 457.

**830.** Wilbur, p. 70.

**831.** Nicolay and Hay, ALCW, Vol. 2, p. 234.

**832.** See e.g., Nicolay and Hay, ALCW, Vol. 2, p. 674.

**833.** Buckley, p. 65. See also Greenberg and Waugh, pp. 351-358.

**834.** Greenberg and Waugh, p. 353; Coffin, p. 457; Current, LNK, p. 225.

**835.** For estimates on the number of Northern slaves in the early 1860s, see Eaton, HSC, p. 93; Hinkle, p. 125.

**836.** W. Phillips, p. 456.

**837.** Nicolay and Hay, ALCW, Vol. 2, pp. 287-288, 508.

**838.** Current, TC, p. 189.

**839.** Garrison, CWTFB, p. 93.

**840.** Hinkle, p. 125; Eaton, HSC, p. 93.

**841.** See J. M. McPherson, NCW, pp. 245-270; Litwack, pp. 104-112; Greenberg and Waugh, p. 152.

**842.** Nicolay and Hay, ALCW, Vol. 2, p. 270.

**843.** Nicolay and Hay, ALCW, Vol. 2, p. 272.

**844.** Current, LNK, pp. 242-246; W. C. Davis, AHD, p. 164; Garrison, LNOK, p. 181; Weintraub, p. 73.

**845.** Nicolay and Hay, ALCW, Vol. 2, pp. 237, 615.

846. See e.g., Lincoln's Preliminary Emancipation Proclamation, Nicolay and Hay, ALCW, Vol. 2, p. 237.
847. Nicolay and Hay, ALCW, Vol. 2, p. 550; E. McPherson, PHUSADGR, p. 301.
848. Nicolay and Hay, ALH, Vol. 9, pp. 215, 217.
849. Nicolay and Hay, ALH, Vol. 10, p. 123.
850. DiLorenzo, LU, pp. 24, 25.
851. Nicolay and Hay, ALCW, Vol. 2, p. 6.
852. Beard and Beard, Vol. 2, p. 65.
853. W. S. Powell, p. 144.
854. Simmons, s.v. "One-Tenth Plan, Lincoln's."
855. Current, LNK, pp. 223, 239, 240, 241. For Lincoln's actual wording, see Nicolay and Hay, ALCW, Vol. 2, pp. 443-444.
856. Harwell, p. 307.
857. Nicolay and Hay, ALCW, Vol. 2, p. 271.
858. Lincoln's colonization experiments in Panama, Belize, and Haiti all failed miserably, with death rates of over 50 percent in some cases. C. Johnson, p. 182.
859. Nicolay and Hay, ALCW, Vol. 2, p. 274-275.
860. Seabrook, TUAL, p. 81.
861. Seabrook, TUAL, p. 91.
862. Nicolay and Hay, ALCW, Vol. 1, p. 257.
863. Foley, pp. 811-812.
864. Nicolay and Hay, ALCW, Vol. 1, p. 288.
865. The issuance of Lincoln's several emancipations proceeded this way: the first, a draft submitted privately to his cabinet on July 22, 1862; the second, the Preliminary one released publicly on September 22, 1862; the third, a draft of the Final proclamation submitted to his cabinet on December 30, 1862; and the fourth, the Final version issued on January 1, 1863. See Nicolay and Hay, ALCW, Vol. 2, p. 213; Nicolay and Hay, ALCW, Vol. 2, pp. 237-238; Nicolay and Hay, ALCW, Vol. 2, p. 285; Nicolay and Hay, ALCW, Vol. 2, pp. 287-288.
866. D. H. Donald, L, p. 374.
867. Nicolay and Hay, ALCW, Vol. 2, p. 237.
868. Seabrook, L, p. 642.
869. Nicolay and Hay, ALCW, Vol. 2, p. 274.
870. Cornish, p. 95.
871. Nicolay and Hay, ALCW, Vol. 2, p. 271.
872. D. H. Donald, L, p. 355.
873. See e.g., Tocqueville, Vol. 1, pp. 383-385.
874. Rhodes, Vol. 1, pp. 307, 309.
875. Seligmann, p. 9.
876. See Darwin, p. 91.
877. Bailyn, Dallek, Davis, Donald, Thomas, and Wood, p. 29.
878. By "authentic abolitionists" I mean antislavery advocates who were both for abolition and for welcoming blacks into American society as full-fledged citizens with complete equal rights. Very few individuals, even the so-called most vociferous abolitionists, fell into this category. In fact, authentic abolitionists were so rare at the time that they could almost be counted on one hand. Even William Lloyd Garrison (the founder of the Northern abolition movement), Horace Greeley (abolitionist founder of the New York Tribune), and Harriet Beecher Stowe (abolitionist author of Uncle Tom's Cabin), at one time supported black colonization: the deportation of all free African-Americans. Fogel, p. 254; Burlingame, p. 50.
879. Nicolay and Hay, ALCW, Vol. 1, p. 539.
880. E. McPherson, PHUSADGR, 134.
881. Nicolay and Hay, ALAH, Vol. 6, p. 356. See also pp. 357-358.
882. For more on the history of the black colonization movement, see Staudenraus, passim.
883. Fogel, p. 252.
884. Nye, pp. 30, 49.
885. Website: www.slavenorth.com/colonize.htm.
886. For more on Garrison's views on black colonization, see W. L. Garrison, passim.
887. Fogel, p. 254; Burlingame, p. 50.
888. Nye, p. 20.
889. See Bennett, passim.
890. Nicolay and Hay, ALCW, Vol. 2, p. 274.
891. Nicolay and Hay, ALCW, Vol. 1, p. 299.
892. W. B. Garrison, LNOK, p. 186.
893. DiLorenzo, LU, p. 28. For more on the history of Illinois' massive slavery system, see N. D. Harris, passim.

**894.** See Foley, p. 816.

**895.** Nicolay and Hay, ALCW, Vol. 1, p. 608.

**896.** We will note here that like racism itself those who are against interracial relationships can be found among all races, creeds, and colors.

**897.** Nicolay and Hay, ALCW, Vol. 1, p. 234. Actually, Lincoln was wrong: later scientific studies, such as those done by Edward Byron Reuter, revealed that the percentage of mulattos went up only *after* slavery ended. Reuter, pp. 120-122. Thus there was almost no connection between slavery and "amalgamation" (race mixing), as Lincoln derogatorily referred to it. See Fogel and Engerman, pp. 130-136.

**898.** See e.g., Nicolay and Hay, ALCW, Vol. 1, p. 449; Lincoln and Douglas, p. 221.

**899.** Nicolay and Hay, ALCW, Vol. 1, p. 175.

**900.** Nicolay and Hay, ALCW, Vol. 1, p. 176.

**901.** Nicolay and Hay, ALCW, Vol. 1, p. 176.

**902.** Nicolay and Hay, ALCW, Vol. 1, pp. 175-176.

**903.** Nicolay and Hay, ALCW, Vol. 1, pp. 175-176.

**904.** *The National Almanac* (1863), p. 250.

**905.** See Nicolay and Hay, ALCW, Vol. 2, p. 144.

**906.** Scott and Stowe, p. 321. Dr. Washington's expectation was fulfilled. He was buried in Tuskegee, Alabama, on November 17, 1915.

**907.** Drescher and Engerman, p. 165.

**908.** B. F. Butler, p. 903. See also W. P. Pickett, p. 326; M. Davis, pp. 147-148; Adams and Sanders, p. 192.

**909.** W. P. Pickett, pp. 328, 330.

**910.** Lincoln's death in April 1865, at Booth's hands, allowed the Radicals (abolitionists) in his party to take over the government, after which they pushed through the Thirteenth Amendment in December 1865. It was this bill, not Lincoln's Emancipation Proclamation, that finally ended slavery across the entire U.S. In this sense then Booth was the "Great Emancipator," not Lincoln.

**911.** M. Perry, p. 49.

**912.** See Nicolay and Hay, ALCW, Vol. 1, pp. 433, 451, 468.

**913.** Nicolay and Hay, ALCW, Vol. 1, p. 659.

**914.** Nicolay and Hay, ALCW, Vol. 2, p. 268.

**915.** Nicolay and Hay, ALCW, Vol. 1, p. 197.

**916.** Nicolay and Hay, ALCW, Vol. 1, p. 508.

**917.** Nicolay and Hay, ALCW, Vol. 1, p. 234.

**918.** Seabrook, TUAL, p. 81.

**919.** Seabrook, TUAL, p. 80.

**920.** Seabrook, TUAL, p. 80.

**921.** Seabrook, TUAL, p. 81.

**922.** Seabrook, TUAL, p. 80.

**923.** Seabrook, TUAL, pp. 77-78.

**924.** For more on contemporary black support of the Confederacy, see Hervey, passim. Especially see H. K. Edgerton's Website: www.southernheritage411.com.

**925.** Barrow, Segars, and Rosenburg, BC, p. 97; *The United Daughters of the Confederacy Magazine*, Vols. 54-55, 1991, p. 32. Though the exact number is not known, estimates of the number of Southern blacks who fought for the Confederacy range from 30,000 to 93,000, from 100,000 to 300,000. See e.g., Hinkle, p. 106; R. M. Brown, p. xiv; Shenkman and Reiger, p. 106. I have chosen to go with the largest figure for reasons that will be discussed shortly. Skewing the already confusing figures were the thousands of blacks who posed as whites (presumably the lighter skinned blacks), eager to join the Confederate army or navy. See e.g., Jordan, p. 217. Since these particular men were never counted, the number 300,000 is almost certainly quite conservative.

**926.** E. M. Thomas, p. 236. As Yankees cruelly and unnecessarily bombed Southern courthouses where records were stored (see e.g., Henry, ATSF, p. 188), there is no documentation of the exact number of blacks that served on the Confederate side. But reliable estimates are still possible.

**927.** The exact number of Yanks and Rebels, by some estimates, was 2,898,304 of the former, 1,234,000 of the latter. Livermore, pp. 1, 22, 63. These are *Yankee* estimates, however, and as such hold little value for Southern historians.

**928.** Barrow, Segars, and Rosenburg, BC, p. 97; *The United Daughters of the Confederacy Magazine*, Vols. 54-55, 1991, p. 32. See also Hinkle, p. 106.

**929.** Kautz, p. 11.

**930.** For a European's view of the severity of Northern white racism (as compared to Southern white racism) in the early 1800s, see Tocqueville, Vol. 1, pp. 383-385. See also Seabrook, AL, pp. 187-239.

**931.** Greenberg and Waugh, p. 385.

**932.** L. H. Steiner, pp. 19-20.

**933.** ORA, Ser. 2, Vol. 8, p. 324.

**934.** *Douglass' Monthly*, September, 1861, Vol. 4, p. 516.
**935.** ORA, Ser. 4, Vol. 3, p. 1161.
**936.** L. Johnson, p. 135.
**937.** Nicolay and Hay, ALCW, Vol. 1, p. 556.
**938.** Litwack, pp. 113-152; Quarles, pp. 235-238; Garraty and McCaughey, p. 254.
**939.** Gragg, p. 88.
**940.** Current, LNK, p. 228.
**941.** Quarles, p. 273.
**942.** E. M. Thomas, p. 236.
**943.** See Barrow, Segars, and Rosenburg, BC and FC, passim; also see Segars and Barrow, BSCA, passim.
**944.** Kennedy and Kennedy, SWR, p. 89.
**945.** Gragg, pp. 191-192.
**946.** Hopkins, pp. 203-205.
**947.** Long and Wright, pp. 319-320.
**948.** Nicolay and Hay, ALCW, Vol. 2, p. 662.
**949.** ORA, Ser. 3, Vol. 2, p. 809.
**950.** ORA, Ser. 3, Vol. 2, p. 809.
**951.** White, Foscue, and McKnight, p. 212. It should be pointed out that there were also white sharecroppers. See Wilson and Ferris, s.v. "Plantations."
**952.** Hopkins, pp. 136-137.
**953.** Chesnut, DD, p. 403.
**954.** Seabrook, ARB, p. 259.
**955.** Eaton, HSC, p. 93.
**956.** Barrow, Segars, and Rosenburg, BC, p. 97; Hinkle, p. 106; *The United Daughters of the Confederacy Magazine*, Vols. 54-55, 1991, p. 32. If we utilize Yankee General August Valentine Kautz's definition of a "soldier," then as many as 1 million Southern blacks served in one capacity or another in the Confederate military. See Kautz, p. 11.
**957.** Hinkle, p. 108. See also Quintero, Gonzales, and Velazquez, passim.
**958.** Lonn, p. 218.
**959.** Rosen, p. 161.
**960.** Hinkle, p. 108; Blackerby, passim.
**961.** The real reason racism-phobes engage in this behavior is to shut down dialog, and also to distract others from seeing their own bigotry and intolerance. Actually they only end up drawing more attention to it. For more on American racism, among all races, see Min, passim.
**962.** See Rutherford, FA, p. 38; Wallechinsky, Wallace, and Wallace, p. 11; Woods, p. 67.
**963.** Seabrook, TQREL, p. 106.
**964.** Kennedy, p. 91.
**965.** Smelser, DR, p. 42; Buckley, p. 37.
**966.** Foley, p. 970.
**967.** Farrow, Lang, and Frank, pp. 82-90, 179-191; Meltzer, Vol. 2, p. 139, 145, 148; McManus, BBN, pp. 6-7, 9, 10, 11; Bowen, p. 217; C. Johnson, pp. 125-126.
**968.** Seabrook, TQREL, pp. 113-114.
**969.** Durden, pp. 245, 215.
**970.** ORA, Ser. 4, Vol. 1, p. 1020.
**971.** ORA, Ser. 4, Vol. 2, p. 767.
**972.** ORA, Ser. 4, Vol. 2, pp. 947-948.
**973.** McDonough and Connelly, pp. 137-138.
**974.** Warner, GG, s.v. "Patrick Ronayne Cleburne."
**975.** Seabrook, EBF, s.v. "Cleburne, Patrick Ronayne"; Seabrook, CPGS, pp. 55-57.
**976.** See ORA, Ser. 1, Vol. 52, Pt. 2, pp. 586-592.
**977.** Kennedy and Kennedy, p. 112.
**978.** Barrow, Segars, and Rosenburg, BC, pp. 12-13, 94.
**979.** B. T. Washington, pp. 13-14.
**980.** Cornish, p. 15.
**981.** Jordan, pp. 218, 266.
**982.** ORA, Ser. 4, Vol. 1, p. 409.
**983.** Greeley, AC, Vol. 2, p. 522.
**984.** See e.g., Seabrook, AL, pp. 333-341.
**985.** ORA, Ser. 1, Vol. 15, pp. 556-557.
**986.** J. M. McPherson, NCW, p. 165.
**987.** Tocqueville, Vol. 1, pp. 383-385.

**988.** At first Lincoln also refused to allow Native-Americans to serve in the Union army. Secretary of War Cameron was speaking for Lincoln when he said that the conflict "forbids the use of savages." ORA, Ser. 3, Vol. 1, p. 184.

**989.** Nicolay and Hay, ALCW, Vol. 2, p. 235.

**990.** Page Smith, p. 308.

**991.** Henderson, Vol. 2, p. 411; C. Adams, p. 134.

**992.** Page Smith, p. 308.

**993.** Foote, Vol. 2, p. 393; Katcher, CWSB, p. 159.

**994.** Eaton, HSC, p. 263.

**995.** Catton, Vol. 3, p. 24.

**996.** Garrison, CWC, p. 105.

**997.** Simmons, s.v. "Negro Troops."

**998.** Page Smith, p. 309.

**999.** ORA, Ser. 3, Vol. 4, p. 1029; Katcher, CWSB, pp. 128, 158-159.

**1000.** Gragg, p. 192.

**1001.** Pollard, SHW, Vol. 2, pp. 196-198.

**1002.** Wiley, SN, pp. 241, 309-310, 317.

**1003.** Henry, ATSF, p. 248.

**1004.** Eaton, HSC, p. 30.

**1005.** Cornish, pp. 87, 269.

**1006.** Nicolay and Hay, ALCW, Vol. 2, p. 398.

**1007.** Furnas, p. 750.

**1008.** Simmons, s.v. "Negro Troops."

**1009.** Wiley, SN, p. 321.

**1010.** Buckley, p. 82.

**1011.** Nicolay and Hay, ALCW, Vol. 2, p. 288.

**1012.** Wiley, SN, pp. 201-202, 212-213.

**1013.** Leech, p. 293.

**1014.** Quarles, p. 60.

**1015.** Wiley, SN, p. 175.

**1016.** Rhodes, Vol. 3, p. 466.

**1017.** See e.g., Nicolay and Hay, ALCW, Vol. 1, p. 539; Nicolay and Hay, ALCW, Vol. 2, pp. 257, 289, 369-370, 433.

**1018.** See e.g., Nicolay and Hay, ALCW, Vol. 2, pp. 257, 449, 469.

**1019.** Garrison, LNOK, p. 176.

**1020.** J. M. McPherson, BCF, pp. 788-789.

**1021.** Mullen, p. 25.

**1022.** Channing, p. 23.

**1023.** Wiley, SN, pp. 322-323.

**1024.** Current, TC, s.v. "African-Americans in the Confederacy."

**1025.** Cartmell, pp. 144, 145.

**1026.** Wiley, SN, pp. 323-324.

**1027.** Alotta, pp. 26-28.

**1028.** Seabrook, L, pp. 918-938; Christian, p. 7; Meriwether, pp. 54-55; Oates, AL, pp. 5, 40, 53; Current, LNK, pp. 58, 60-61; Kane, p. 163; *Southern Review*, January 1873, Vol. 12, No. 25, p. 364; Lamon, LAL, pp. 488, 489, 493; W. B. Garrison, LNOK, p. 265; Barton, p. 146; DeGregorio, s.v. "Abraham Lincoln."

**1029.** Channing, p. 129.

**1030.** Jimerson, p. 81; Swint, p. 61; Jaquette, p. 37.

**1031.** Simmons, s.v. "Negro Troops."

**1032.** Durden, p. 269.

**1033.** McKissack and McKissack, pp. 138-139.

**1034.** N. A. Hamilton, p. 120; Förster and Nagler, p. 207; Masur, p. 110; J. M. McPherson, NCW, p. 163.

**1035.** Nicolay and Hay, ALCW, Vol. 2, p. 1.

**1036.** DiLorenzo, RL, p. 21.

**1037.** L. Johnson, p. 135.

**1038.** Pollard, SHW, Vol. 2, p. 198.

**1039.** Wiley, SN, p. 202.

**1040.** Page Smith, pp. 362-363.

**1041.** Quarles, pp. 46-47.

**1042.** Seabrook, TMCP, pp. 289, 300.

**1043.** Chesnut, DD, p. 227.

**1044.** Chesnut, MCCW, p. 798.

**1045.** G. H. Moore, pp. 5, 11, 17-19.

**1046.** Foote, Vol. 1, p. 537.

**1047.** Truth, p. 254.

**1048.** De Angelis, pp. 12-18; Lott, p. 65.

**1049.** De Angelis, p. 49.

**1050.** McKissack and McKissack, pp. 142, 143, 144.

**1051.** See Nicolay and Hay, CWAL, Vol. 11, pp. 105-106; Nicolay and Hay, ALCW, Vol. 1, p. 483; Holzer, pp. 22-23, 67, 318, 361.

**1052.** See e.g., Nicolay and Hay, ALCW, Vol. 1, pp. 257, 259, 449, 469.

**1053.** Horwitz, p. 204.

**1054.** Meriwether, p. 219.

**1055.** C. Johnson, p. 167.

**1056.** Tragically, refugeeing slaves sometimes meant the breakup of black families as well as plantation communities themselves, a rich social network of white and black relationships, many of them tender, loving, and lifelong. E. M. Thomas, p. 240. In this way, among many others, Lincoln actually damaged race relations in the South, one of his goals to begin with.

**1057.** See e.g., Wiley, SN, pp. 241, 309-310, 317.

**1058.** C. Johnson, p. 170.

**1059.** Eaton, HSC, p. 93; Hinkle, p. 125.

**1060.** Confederate, p. 83.

**1061.** R. E. Lee, Jr., p. 100.

**1062.** Pollard, LC, pp. 221-222.

**1063.** Katcher, CWSB, p. 228.

**1064.** LeVert, s.v. "Partisans."

**1065.** Katcher, CWSB, p. 229.

**1066.** See Siepel, passim.

**1067.** Like Nathan Bedford Forrest and so many other of the South's "Civil War" heroes, Quantrill too has been excoriated by Northern and New South authors and historians over the years. But as this book makes clear, little of what such individuals publish is accurate or historical. It is all just another excuse to bash the South. True Southerners know the facts and come to Quantrill's defense, as Paul R. Peterson does in his South-positive work, *Quantrill of Missouri* (see, passim). If Quantrill ever truly committed any misdeeds, they could never come close to matching the atrocities of the real criminals of the War. We are speaking here of course of Yankees like Ulysses S. Grant, William T. Sherman, Benjamin F. Butler, and Philip H. Sheridan (not to mention Lincoln), under whose watch, and often direct orders, untold hundreds of thousands of Southerners died, including innocent women and children. If Yanks want to deify men like Grant, we have no problem with that. In fact, if the Confederacy had won we would have done precisely what the North did: put Quantrill on our fifty-dollar bill.

**1068.** I am a direct descendant of the Mosby family: my fifth great-grandmother is Elizabeth Bacon Mosby (b. 1739, Henrico Co., VA), wife of John Canute Cornett. Elizabeth is the second cousin of Colonel John Singleton Mosby, making him my fifth cousin.

**1069.** Bowman, ECW, s.v. "Partisan Rangers."

**1070.** Faust, s.v. "Partisan Rangers."

**1071.** Nicolay and Hay, ALCW, Vol. 2, pp. 310-311. For more on the South's Partisan Rangers, see A. R. Johnson, passim.

**1072.** My own family was impacted by Yankee war crimes. In 1864 my third great-grandfather, Confederate cavalryman Elias Jent, Sr., who served in the 1st Regiment of the 13th Kentucky Cavalry (known as "Caudill's Army"), was unlawfully executed by Yankee soldiers while at home in Kentucky on furlough. Elias thus became one of the conservatively estimated 329,000 Confederate soldiers who died needlessly due to Lincoln's illegitimate warmongering. Tragically, Elias' wife, Rachel Cornett, my third great-grandmother, was also murdered. The unarmed, gentle farming couple had been visiting relatives in Perry County, Kentucky, when they were discovered by marauding Union soldiers. Ignoring the heart-rending screams and futile entreaties of kin, the pitiless Yankee wretches dragged Elias and Rachel unceremoniously into the yard and, at gunpoint, hanged them side-by-side from a large tree in front of family, friends, and neighbors. No reason was given and no punishment was ever meted out. This was typical Lincolnian military procedure, and our family still holds "Honest Abe" directly responsible for Elias and Rachel's deaths.

**1073.** For a detailed examination of Lincoln's crimes against the Southern people, see Cisco, passim; Grimsley, passim.

**1074.** Pollard, LC, pp. 257-260.

**1075.** See ORA, Ser. 1, Vol. 32, Pt. 3, pp. 664-665; ORA, Ser. 1, Vol. 32, Pt. 1, pp. 118-119.

**1076.** ORA, Ser. 1, Vol. 32, Pt. 1, p. 119.

**1077.** ORA, Ser. 1, Vol. 39, Pt. 3, p. 494.

**1078.** Southerners usually hid their valuables to prevent them from being stolen by Yankee soldiers. Burial, often below a walkway, was the traditional method.

**1079.** Letter dated September 14, 1865. J. Davis, RFCG, Vol. 2, pp. 710-711.

**1080.** Chesnut, DD, p. 358.

**1081.** Sheridan's restrictive, cruel, and overly severe policies continued even after the War. Finally, during "Reconstruction," President Andrew Johnson was forced to remove him from his post as commander of the Fifth Military District after only six months. Warner, GB, s.v. "Philip Henry Sheridan."

**1082.** J. C. Bradford, p. 90.

**1083.** C. T. Brady, p. 408.

**1084.** E. M. Thomas, p. 284.

**1085.** ORA, Ser. 1, Vol. 43, Pt. 2, p. 308.

**1086.** Grissom, p. 116.

**1087.** W. B. Garrison, CWTFB, p. 211.

**1088.** Oates, AL, p. 136; Civil War Society, CWB, s.v. "Sherman's March to the Sea."

**1089.** See e.g., Denney, p. 551.

**1090.** Christian, p. 18.

**1091.** Katcher, CWSB, p. 120.

**1092.** Eaton, HSC, pp. 108-109.

**1093.** Katcher, CWSB, p. 115.

**1094.** Eaton, HSC, p. 109.

**1095.** Kennedy and Kennedy, SWR, pp. 46-47.

**1096.** Boatner, s.v. "Andersonville Prison." In 1909 the Daughters of the Confederacy (forerunner of today's United Daughters of the Confederacy) erected a monument to Wirz, rightly asserting that he was innocent and thus had been "judicially murdered" by the North. K. C. Davis, p. 354.

**1097.** Livermore, p. 4.

**1098.** W. B. Garrison, CWT, p. 153. Also see p. 244.

**1099.** Faust, s.v. "Wirz, Heinrich Hartmann." War criminal Lincoln tried one last time to humiliate Wirz and hurt the South just before the prison official was sent to the gallows on November 10, 1865. Lincoln had a secret emissary from the War Department offer Wirz his freedom if he would agree to testify against President Jefferson Davis "for conspiracy to murder prisoners." To his lasting credit Wirz replied: "Jefferson Davis had no connection with me as to what was done at Andersonville, and if I knew anything about him I would not become a traitor to save my life." Rutherford, TH, p. 49.

**1100.** Current, TC, s.v. "Prisons."

**1101.** DiLorenzo, RL, pp. 140-141.

**1102.** W. B. Garrison, CWT, p. 160.

**1103.** Hopkins, p. 172.

**1104.** Seabrook, TQJD, p. 94.

**1105.** Livermore, pp. 4, 7.

**1106.** W. B. Garrison, CWT, p. 153.

**1107.** Katcher, CWSB, p. 120. Also see *The Civil War Book of Lists*, p. 95.

**1108.** P. J. Buchanan, p. 131.

**1109.** L. Johnson, p. 150.

**1110.** D. H. Donald, WNWCW, pp. 59-62.

**1111.** *Encyclopedia Britannica.*, s.v. "Lincoln, Abraham"; Owsley, pp. 63-64; Hacker, p. 582.

**1112.** DeGregorio, s.v. "John Quincy Adams." See also Vanauken, passim.

**1113.** For examples of Lincoln's various dire warnings, threats, and promises to wage war on any European nation that impeded his illegal assault on the South, see Owsley, pp. 309, 315, 331, 350, 359, 399, 401, 402, 408, 411, 423, 425, 436, 440, 446, 453, 464, 507, 510, 516-517, 524, 539-540, 544.

**1114.** Owsley, p. 405. See also, pp. 401-412.

**1115.** For a fuller treatment of the relationship between England, the CSA, and the USA during Lincoln's War, see Sargent, passim; Vanauken, passim.

**1116.** Current, TC, s.v. "Trent Affair."

**1117.** J. M. McPherson, BCF, p. 390.

**1118.** Lang, pp. 251, 252; Eaton, HSC, pp. 70-71.

**1119.** D. H. Donald, L, p. 322.

**1120.** Boatner, s.v. "Trent Affair."

**1121.** Kettell, p. 84.

**1122.** E. M. Thomas, p. 170.

**1123.** Owsley, p. 58.

**1124.** Eaton, HSC, p. 70.

1125. Littell, p. 200.
1126. Lang, pp. 249, 250.
1127. Owsley, pp. 502-503.
1128. Mode, pp. 470-471.
1129. "The Pope and Jefferson Davis—Revelations of an Ex-Rebel—Did the Vatican Once Recognize the Southern Confederacy?" Chicago *Tribune*, August 23, 1884.
1130. Logan, pp. 392-393.
1131. Rutherford, FA, p. 38; Wallechinsky, Wallace, and Wallace, p. 11; Woods, p. 67.
1132. Eaton, HSC, p. 93; Hinkle, p. 125.
1133. Owsley, pp. 65-66, 187-190.
1134. E. M. Thomas, pp. 293-294.
1135. Richardson, Vol. 2, pp. 709, 713; Owsley, pp. 538-541; Durden, pp. 149-150; Cooper, JDA, pp. 552-553.
1136. Eaton, HSC, p. 81.
1137. Nicolay and Hay, ALCW, Vol. 2, p. 302.
1138. Nicolay and Hay, ALCW, Vol. 2, p. 1.
1139. See e.g., Nicolay and Hay, ALCW, Vol. 2, pp. 227-228.
1140. Fleming, p. 665.
1141. Seabrook, NBF, p. 56.
1142. Hurst, p. 305; Lester and Wilson, p. 26; Rogers, KKS, p. 34.
1143. Horn, IE, pp. 362-363. We will note that at one time (1920s-1930s) even the modern KKK—though it has no connection with the original KKK of the Reconstruction period—possessed African-American members, and treated both whites and blacks the same. Terkel, p. 239. In Indiana, for example, white Klansmen decided to broaden their racial base by organizing a "colored division" whose uniform was comprised of white capes, blue masks, and red robes. Blee, p. 169.
1144. Few things were worse to traditional Southerners than the scallywag. Known widely across the South as "vile, vindictive, unprincipled," and "scaly, scabby runts in a herd of cattle" (J. H. Franklin, pp. 98, 101), Wade Hampton referred to them as "the mean, lousy and filthy kind that are not fit for butchers or dogs." Harrell, Gaustad, Boles, Griffith, Miller, and Woods, p. 525. Known by Southern conservatives as "the lepers of the community," scallywags were hated even more than carpetbaggers. A former governor of North Carolina said: We have no problem with Northerners per se, even those who fought against us in Lincoln's War. What we can't and won't abide is one of our own here in the South turning against us. Such a man will never get respect and will never be trusted. Foner, R, p. 297. To this day, revulsion toward the scallywag is a sentiment still very much alive across the South.
1145. Horn, IE, pp. 124, 169, 264-265; Simpson, p. 62.
1146. C. Adams, p. 153; Weintraub, p. 75.
1147. *Index to Reports of the Committees of the House of Representatives for the Second Session of the Forty-Third Congress, 1874-1875*, p. 344.
1148. See J. H. Franklin, pp. 38-39.
1149. C. Adams, pp. 153-155.
1150. Seabrook, ARB, p. 443; Lytle, p. 385; Morton, p. 345; Hurst, p. 327.
1151. Butler and Watson, p. 293.
1152. See Wade, passim.
1153. December 17, 2000, "Sunday Morning News," CNN.
1154. Henry, FWMF, p. 443.
1155. Seabrook, ARB, pp. 446-447; Lester and Wilson, pp. 19-21.
1156. For more on the facts about Forrest and his life, see my books *Nathan Bedford Forrest: Southern Hero, American Patriot*, and *A Rebel Born: A Defense of Nathan Bedford Forrest*.
1157. Wills, p. 336.
1158. Seabrook, ARB, p. 448. Gordon was one of the unlucky 702 Rebels captured at the Battle of Franklin II, November 30, 1864.
1159. C. Adams, p. 151.
1160. Wade, p. 39.
1161. Weintraub, p. 89.
1162. Wade, p. 39. As noted earlier, Lincoln's Republican party was what we would now call the Democratic party (i.e., liberals), while the Democratic party of the mid 1800s was what we would now refer to as the Republican party (i.e., conservatives). Thus, though Lincoln was a Republican, today he would be considered a Democrat.
1163. See e.g., Website: http://kukluxklan.bz/.
1164. J. McPherson, BCF, p. 342.
1165. Eaton, HSC, p. 93.
1166. Barrow, Segars, and Rosenburg, BC, p. 97; Hinkle, p. 106; *The United Daughters of the Confederacy Magazine*, Vols. 54-55, 1991, p. 32.

**1167.** Hinkle, p. 108. See also Quintero, Gonzales, and Velazquez, passim.
**1168.** Lonn, p. 218.
**1169.** Rosen, p. 161.
**1170.** Hinkle, 108; Blackerby, passim.
**1171.** See Peterson's Brotherhood Organization of a New Destiny (BOND) Website: www.bondinfo.org.
**1172.** Hinkle, pp. 132-133.
**1173.** Seabrook, AL, pp. 226-234. See also Bultman, p. 285; C. Johnson, pp. 37-38.
**1174.** Meltzer, Vol. 2, p. 127.
**1175.** Fogel and Engerman, pp. 23-24.
**1176.** C. Johnson, pp. 78-79.
**1177.** For examples of black contributions to American culture, see Wilson and Ferris, s.v. "Black life." See also M. M. Smith, p. 30.
**1178.** Matthew 22:36-40; John 13:34; 15:17; 1 John 4:8, 16.
**1179.** For more on the topic of the development of the Confederate Battle Flag, as well as the Confederacy's many other flags, see Cannon, passim.
**1180.** For a full discussion of Lincoln's plans to Northernize the South, see Seabrook, AL, pp. 501-546.
**1181.** J. H. Franklin, p. 40.
**1182.** Simpson, pp. 62-63.
**1183.** Grissom, p. 180.
**1184.** Simpson, p. 62; J. H. Franklin, p. 144.
**1185.** A. Cooke, ACA, p. 219.
**1186.** Horn, IE, pp. 287-288.
**1187.** Horn, IE, pp. 258-260.
**1188.** Tourgee, p. 300.
**1189.** *Tyler's Quarterly Historical and Genealogical Magazine*, 1924, Vol. 5, pp. 193-195.
**1190.** Historical note: President Carter's great-grandfather, Littleberry Walker Carter, proudly fought for the Confederacy in the War for Southern Independence.
**1191.** E. M. Thomas, p. 306.
**1192.** K. C. Davis, p. 438.
**1193.** DeGregorio, s.v. "Abraham Lincoln."
**1194.** See Website: http://fdasbo.org.br/fdasbo/. There are Sons of Confederate Veterans camps in Brazil as well. See e.g., Website: http://www.confederados.com.br/.
**1195.** Neilson, s.v. "Benjamin, Judah Philip."
**1196.** Lang, pp. 273, 274.
**1197.** Spaeth and Smith, p. 16.
**1198.** Findlay and Findlay, p. 233.
**1199.** DiLorenzo, RL, pp. 207-208.
**1200.** Spaeth and Smith, p. 27; Findlay and Findlay, pp. 228-235.
**1201.** Page Smith, p. 710.
**1202.** Kennedy and Kennedy, SWR, pp. 170-171. We will note here that Ohio and New Jersey later revoked their states' ratification of the Fourteenth Amendment. This, along with the Southern states, meant that Congress never came close to achieving the voluntary three-fourths majority required for passage. Instead, Congress simply declared the amendment valid and rammed it through. Thus the Fourteenth Amendment was never properly formalized into law. DiLorenzo, RL, p. 211.
**1203.** Seabrook, AL, p. 34.
**1204.** Seabrook, TUAL, pp. 86-87.
**1205.** Seabrook, TUAL, p. 62.
**1206.** E. M. Thomas, p. 161.
**1207.** Seabrook, TQREL, p. 213.

# BIBLIOGRAPHY

Abbott, John Stevens Cabot. *The Life of General Ulysses S. Grant*. Boston, MA: B. B. Russell, 1868.

Adams, Charles. *When in the Course of Human Events: Arguing the Case for Southern Secession*. Lanham, MD: Rowman and Littlefield, 2000.

Adams, Francis D., and Barry Sanders. *Alienable Rights: The Exclusion of African Americans in a White Man's Land, 1619-2000*. 2003. New York, NY: Perennial, 2004 ed.

Adams, Henry (ed.). *Documents Relating to New-England Federalism, 1800-1815*. Boston, MA: Little, Brown, and Co., 1877.

Adams, Nehemiah, Rev. *A South-side View of Slavery: Three Months at the South in 1854*. Boston, MA: T. R. Marvin, 1855.

Alotta, Robert I. *Civil War Justice: Union Army Executions Under Lincoln*. Shippensburg, PA: White Mane, 1989.

*An Appeal From the Colored Men of Philadelphia to the President of the United States*. Philadelphia, PA, 1862.

Anderson, John Q. (ed.). *Brokenburn: The Journal of Kate Stone, 1861-1868*. 1955. Baton Rouge, LA: Louisiana State University Press, 1995 ed.

Andrews, Sidney. *The South Since the War: As Shown by Fourteen Weeks of Travel and Observation*. Boston, MA: Ticknor and Fields, 1866.

Angle, Paul M. (ed.). *The Complete Lincoln-Douglas Debates of 1858*. Chicago, IL: University of Chicago Press, 1991.

Annunzio, Frank (chairman). *The Capitol: A Pictorial History of the Capitol and of the Congress*. Washington, D.C.: U.S. Joint Committee on Printing, 1983.

Anonymous. *Life of John C. Calhoun: Presenting a Condensed History of Political Events, From 1811 to 1843*. New York, NY: Harper and Brothers, 1843.

Appleman, Roy Edgar (ed.). *Abraham Lincoln: From His Own Words and Contemporary Accounts*. Washington, D.C.: U.S. Department of the Interior, National Park Service, 1942.

Arnold, Isaac Newton. *The History of Abraham Lincoln, and the Overthrow of Slavery*. Chicago, IL: Clarke and Co., 1866.

Ashdown Paul, and Edward Caudill. *The Myth of Nathan Bedford Forrest*. 2005. Lanham, MD: Rowman and Littlefield, 2006 ed.

Ashe, Captain Samuel A'Court. *A Southern View of the Invasion of the Southern States and War of 1861-1865*. 1935. Crawfordville, GA: Ruffin Flag Co., 1938 ed.

Ashworth, John. *Slavery, Capitalism, and Politics in the Antebellum Republic*. 2 vols. New York, NY: Cambridge University Press, 2007.

Astor, Gerald. *The Right to Fight: A History of African Americans in the Military*. Cambridge, MA: Da Capo, 2001.

Baepler, Paul (ed.). *White Slaves, African Masters: An Anthology of American Barbary Captivity Narratives*. Chicago, IL: University of Chicago Press, 1999.

Bailey, Anne C. *African Voices of the Atlantic Slave Trade: Beyond the Silence and the Shame*. Boston, MA: Beacon Press, 2005.

Bailey, Hugh C. *Hinton Rowan Helper: Abolitionist-Racist*. Tuscaloosa, AL: University of Alabama Press, 1965.

Bailyn, Bernard, Robert Dallek, David Brion Davis, David Herbert Donald, John L. Thomas, and Gordon S. Wood. *The Great Republic: A History of the American People*. 1977. Lexington, MA: D. C. Heath and Co., 1992 ed.

Baker, George E. (ed.). *The Works of William H. Seward*. 5 vols. 1861. Boston, MA: Houghton, Mifflin and Co., 1888 ed.

Ballagh, James Curtis. *White Servitude in the Colony of Virginia: A Study of the System of Indentured Servitude in the American Colonies*. Whitefish, MT: Kessinger Publishing, 2004.

Bancroft, Frederic. *The Life of William H. Seward*. 2 vols. New York, NY: Harper and Brothers, 1900.

———. *Slave-Trading in the Old South*. Baltimore, MD: J. H. Furst, 1931.

Bancroft, Frederic, and William A. Dunning (eds.). *The Reminiscences of Carl Schurz*. 3 vols. New York, NY: McClure Co., 1909.

Barnes, Gilbert H., and Dwight L. Dumond (eds.). *Letters of Theodore Dwight Weld, Angelina Grimké Weld and Sarah Grimké, 1822-1844*. 2 vols. New York, NY: D. Appleton-Century Co., 1934.

Barney, William L. *Flawed Victory: A New Perspective on the Civil War*. New York, NY: Praeger Publishers, 1975.

Barrow, Charles Kelly, J. H. Segars, and R. B. Rosenburg (eds.). *Black Confederates*. 1995. Gretna, LA: Pelican Publishing Co., 2001 ed.

———. *Forgotten Confederates: An Anthology About Black Southerners*. Saint Petersburg, FL: Southern Heritage Press, 1997.

Bartlett, Irving H. *John C. Calhoun: A Biography*. New York, NY: W. W. Norton, 1994.

———. *Wendell Phillips: Brahmin Radical*. Boston, MA: Beacon Press, 1961.

Barton, William E. *The Soul of Abraham Lincoln*. New York, NY: George H. Doran, 1920.

Basler, Roy Prentice (ed.). *Abraham Lincoln: His Speeches and Writings*. 1946. New York, NY: Da Capo Press, 2001 ed.

——— (ed.). *The Collected Works of Abraham Lincoln*. 9 vols. New Brunswick, NJ: Rutgers University Press, 1953.

Bateman, William O. *Political and Constitutional Law of the United States of America*. St. Louis, MO: G. I. Jones and Co., 1876.

Baxter, Maurice G. *Henry Clay and the American System*. Lexington, KY: University Press of Kentucky, 2004.

Beard, Charles A., and Birl E. Schultz. *Documents on the State-Wide Initiative, Referendum and Recall*. New York, NY: Macmillan, 1912.

Beard, Charles A., and Mary R. Beard. *The Rise of American Civilization*. 1927. New York, NY: MacMillan, 1930 ed.

Beck, Glenn. *Glenn Beck's Common Sense: The Case Against an Out-of-Control Government, Inspired by Thomas Paine*. New York, NY: Threshold, 2009.

Bennett, Lerone. *Forced into Glory: Abraham Lincoln's White Dream*. Chicago, IL: Johnson Publishing Co., 2000.

Benson, Al, Jr., and Walter Donald Kennedy. *Lincoln's Marxists*. Gretna, LA: Pelican Publishing, 2011.

Benton, Thomas Hart. *Thirty Years View; or A History of the Working of the American Government for Thirty Years, From 1820 to 1850*. 2 vols. New York, NY: D. Appleton and Co., 1854.

Bergh, Albert Ellery (ed.). *The Writings of Thomas Jefferson*. 20 vols. Washington, D.C.: Thomas Jefferson Memorial Association of the U.S., 1905.

Bernhard, Winfred E. A. (ed.). *Political Parties in American History* (Vol. 1, 1789-1828). New York, NY: G. P. Putnams' Sons, 1973.

Berry, Wendell. *The Unsettling of America: Culture and Agriculture*. San Francisco, CA: Sierra Club Books, 1996.

Berwanger, Eugene H. *The Frontier Against Slavery: Western Anti-Negro Prejudice and the Slavery Extension Controversy*. 1967. Urbana, IL: University of Illinois Press, 1971 ed.

Beschloss, Michael R. *Presidential Courage: Brave Leaders and How They Changed America, 1789-1989*. New York, NY: Simon and Schuster, 2007.

Black, Chauncey F. *Essays and Speeches of Jeremiah S. Black*. New York, NY: D. Appleton and Co., 1886.

Black, Robert W., Col. *Cavalry Raids of the Civil War*. Mechanicsburg, PA: Stackpole, 2004.

Blackerby, Hubert R. *Blacks in Blue and Gray*. New Orleans, LA: Portals Press, 1979.

Blakeman, A. Noel. *Personal Recollections of the War of Rebellion*. New York, NY: G. P. Putnam's Son, 1912.

Blassingame, John W. *The Slave Community: Plantation Life in the Antebellum South*. 1972. New York, NY: Oxford University Press, 1974 ed.

Bledsoe, Albert Taylor. *An Essay on Liberty and Slavery*. Philadelphia, PA: J. B. Lippincott and Co., 1856.

———. *A Theodicy; or a Vindication of the Divine Glory, as Manifested in the Constitution and Government of the Moral World*. New York, NY: Carlton and Porter, 1856.

———. *Is Davis a Traitor; or Was Secession a Constitutional Right Previous to the War of 1861?* Richmond, VA: Hermitage Press, 1907.

Blee, Kathleen M. *Women of the Klan: Racism and Gender in the 1920s*. 1991. Berkeley, CA: University of California Press, 1992 ed.

Blight, David W. *Frederick Douglass' Civil War: Keeping Faith in Jubilee*. 1989. Baton Rouge, LA: Louisiana State University Press, 1991 ed.

Bliss, William Dwight Porter (ed.). *The Encyclopedia of Social Reform*. New York, NY: Funk and Wagnalls, 1897.

Boatner, Mark Mayo. *The Civil War Dictionary*. 1959. New York, NY: David McKay Co., 1988 ed.

Bode, Carl, and Malcolm Cowley (eds.). *The Portable Emerson*. 1941. Harmondsworth, UK: Penguin, 1981 ed.

Bowen, Catherine Drinker. *John Adams and the American Revolution*. 1949. New York, NY: Grosset and Dunlap, 1977 ed.

Bowers, John. *Chickamauga and Chattanooga: The Battles that Doomed the Confederacy*. New York, NY: HarperCollins, 1994.

Bowman, John S. (ed.). *The Civil War Day by Day: An Illustrated Almanac of America's Bloodiest War*. 1989. New York, NY: Dorset Press, 1990 ed.

———. *Encyclopedia of the Civil War* (ed.). 1992. North Dighton, MA: JG Press, 2001 ed.

Bradford, James C. (ed.). *Atlas of American Military History*. New York, NY: Oxford University Press, 2003.

Bradford, Ned (ed.). *Battles and Leaders of the Civil War*. 1-vol. ed. New York, NY: Appleton-Century-Crofts, 1956.

Bradley, Michael R. *Nathan Bedford Forrest's Escort and Staff*. Gretna, LA: Pelican Publishing Co., 2006.

Brady, Cyrus Townsend. *Three Daughters of the Confederacy*. New York, NY: G. W. Dillingham, 1905.

Brady, James S. (ed.). *Ronald Reagan: A Man True to His Word - A Portrait of the 40th President of the United States In His Own Words*. Washington D.C.: National Federation of Republican Women, 1984.

Brinkley, Alan. *The Unfinished Nation: A Concise History of the American People*. 1993. Boston, MA: McGraw-Hill, 2000 ed.

Brockett, Linus Pierpont. *The Life and Times of Abraham Lincoln, Sixteenth President of the United States*. Philadelphia, PA: Bradley and Co., 1865.

Brooks, Gertrude Zeth. *First Ladies of the White House*. Chicago, IL: Charles Hallberg and Co., 1969.

Brooksher, William R., and David K. Snider. *Glory at a Gallop: Tales of the Confederate Cavalry*. 1993. Gretna, LA: Pelican Publishing Co., 2002 ed.

Brown, Dee. *Bury My Heart at Wounded Knee: An Indian History of the American West*. 1970. New York, NY: Owl Books, 1991 ed.

Brown, Rita Mae. *High Hearts*. New York, NY: Bantam, 1987.

Brown, William Wells. *The Black Man: His Antecedents, His Genius, and His Achievements*. New York, NY: Thomas Hamilton, 1863.

Browne, Ray B., and Lawrence A. Kreiser, Jr. *The Civil War and Reconstruction*. Westport, CT: Greenwood Publishing, 2003.

Bruce, Philip Alexander. *The Plantation Negro As a Freeman*. New York, NY: G. P. Putnam's Sons, 1889.

Brunner, Borgna (ed.). *The Time Almanac* (1999 ed.). Boston, MA: Information Please, 1998.

Bryan, William Jennings. *The Commoner Condensed*. New York, NY: Abbey Press, 1902.

Buchanan, James. *The Works of James Buchanan*. 12 vols. Philadelphia, PA: J. B. Lippincott Co., 1911.

Buchanan, Patrick J. *A Republic, Not an Empire: Reclaiming America's Destiny*. Washington, D.C.: Regenry, 1999.

Buckingham, James Silk. *The Slave States of America*. 2 vols. London, UK: Fisher, Son, and Co., 1842.

Buckley, Gail. *American Patriots: The Story of Blacks in the Military from the Revolution to Desert Storm*. New York, NY: Random House, 2001.

Bultman, Bethany. *Redneck Heaven: Portrait of a Vanishing Culture*. New York, NY: Bantam, 1996.

Burlingame, Michael. *The Inner World of Abraham Lincoln*. Champaign, IL: University of Illinois Press, 1997.

Burns, James MacGregor, and Jack Walter Peltason. *Government by the People: The Dynamics of American National, State, and Local Government*. 1952. Englewood Cliffs, NJ: Prentice-Hall, 1964 ed.

Burns, James MacGregor, Jack Walter Peltason, Thomas E. Cronin, David B. Magleby, and David M. O'Brien. *Government by the People* (National Version). 1952. Upper Saddle River, NJ: Prentice Hall, 2001-2002 ed.

Burton, Robert. *The Anatomy of Melancholy*. 3 vols. 1621. London, UK: George Bell and Sons, 1896 ed.

Bushnell, Horace. *The Census and Slavery, Thanksgiving Discourse, Delivered in the Chapel at Clifton Springs, New York, November 29, 1860*. Hartford, CT: L. E. Hunt, 1860.

Butler, Benjamin Franklin. *Butler's Book (Autobiography and Personal Reminiscences of Major-General Benjamin F. Butler: A Review of His Legal, Political, and Military Career)*. Boston, MA: A. M. Thayer and Co., 1892.

Butler, Lindley S., and Alan D. Watson (eds.). *The North Carolina Experience: An Interpretive and Documentary History*. Chapel Hill, NC: University of North Carolina Press, 1984.

Calvert, Thomas H. *The Federal Statutes Annotated*. 10 vols. Northport, NY: Edward Thompson, 1905.

Crallé, Richard Kenner. (ed.). *The Works of John C. Calhoun*. 6 vols. New York: NY: D. Appleton and Co., 1853-1888.

Cannon, Devereaux D., Jr. *The Flags of the Confederacy: An Illustrated History*. Memphis, TN: St. Lukes Press, 1988.

Carey, Matthew, Jr. (ed.). *The Democratic Speaker's Hand-Book*. Cincinnati, OH: Miami Print and Publishing Co., 1868.

Carlton, Frank Tracy. *Organized Labor in America*. New York, NY: D. Appleton and Co., 1920.

Carpenter, Stephen D. *Logic of History: Five Hundred Political Texts, Being Concentrated Extracts of Abolitionism*. Madison, WI: published by author, 1864.

Cartmell, Donald. *Civil War 101*. New York, NY: Gramercy, 2001.

Cash, W. J. *The Mind of the South*. 1941. New York, NY: Vintage, 1969 ed.

Catton, Bruce. *The Coming Fury* (Vol. 1). 1961. New York, NY: Washington Square Press, 1967 ed.

———. *Terrible Swift Sword* (Vol. 2). 1963. New York, NY: Pocket Books, 1967 ed.

———. *A Stillness at Appomattox* (Vol. 3). 1953. New York, NY: Pocket Books, 1966 ed.

Celeste, Sister Mary. *The Old World's Gifts to the New*. 1932. Long Prairie, MN: Neumann Press, 1999 ed.

Chambers, Robert (ed.). *The Book of Days: A Miscellany of Popular Antiquities in Connection with the Calender*. 2 vols. London, UK: W. & R. Chambers, 1883.

Channing, Steven A. *Confederate Ordeal: The Southern Home Front*. 1984. Morristown, NJ: Time-Life Books, 1989 ed.

Chesnut, Mary. *A Diary From Dixie: As Written by Mary Boykin Chesnut, Wife of James Chesnut, Jr., United States Senator from South Carolina, 1859-1861, and afterward an Aide to Jefferson Davis and a Brigadier-General in the Confederate Army*. (Isabella D. Martin and Myrta Lockett Avary, eds.). New York, NY: D. Appleton and Co., 1905 ed.

———. *Mary Chesnut's Civil War*. 1860-1865 (Woodward, Comer Vann, ed.). New Haven, CT: Yale University Press, 1981 ed.

Chodes, John. *Destroying the Republic: Jabez Curry and the Re-Education of the Old South*. New York, NY: Algora, 2005.

Christian, George L. *Abraham Lincoln: An Address Delivered Before R. E. Lee Camp, No. 1 Confederate Veterans at Richmond, VA, October 29, 1909*. Richmond, VA: L. H. Jenkins, 1909.

Cimprich, John. *Fort Pillow, a Civil War Massacre, and Public Memory*. Baton Rouge, LA: Louisiana State University Press, 2005.

Cisco, Walter Brian. *War Crimes Against Southern Civilians*. Gretna, LA: Pelican Publishing Co., 2007.

*Civil War Book of Lists*. 1993. Edison, NJ: Castle Books, 2004 ed.

Civil War Society, The. *Civil War Battles: An Illustrated Encyclopedia*. 1997. New York, NY: Gramercy, 1999 ed.

———. *The Civil War Society's Encyclopedia of the Civil War*. New York, NY: Wings Books, 1997.

Clarke, James W. *The Lineaments of Wrath: Race, Violent Crime, and American Culture*. 1998. New Brunswick, NJ: Transaction, 2001 ed.

Cmiel, Kenneth. *Democratic Eloquence: The Fight Over Popular Speech in Nineteenth-Century America*. Berkeley, CA: University of California Press, 1990.

Coe, Joseph. *The True American*. Concord, NH: I. S. Boyd, 1840.

Coffin, Charles Carleton. *Abraham Lincoln*. New York, NY: Harper and Brothers, 1893.

Coit, Margaret L. *John C. Calhoun: American Portrait*. Boston, MA: Sentry, 1950.

Collier, Christopher, and James Lincoln Collier. *Decision in Philadelphia: The Constitutional Convention of 1787*. 1986. New York, NY: Ballantine, 1987 ed.

Collins, Elizabeth. *Memories of the Southern States*. Taunton, UK: J. Barnicott, 1865.

Collins, John A. (ed.). *The Anti-Slavery Picknick: A Collection of Speeches, Poems, Dialogues and Songs Intended for Use in Schools and Anti-Slavery Meetings*. Boston, MA: H. W. Williams, 1842.

Commager, Henry Steele, and Erik Bruun (eds.). *The Civil War Archive: The History of the Civil War in Documents*. 1950. New York, NY: Black Dog and Leventhal, 1973 ed.

Confederate [no name]. *The Grayjackets and How They Lived, Fought, and Died For Dixie*. Richmond, VA: Jones Brothers and Co., 1867.

Conner, Frank. *The South Under Siege, 1830-2000: A History of the Relations Between the North and the South*. Newnan, GA: Collards Publishing Co., 2002.

Conquest, Robert. *The Great Terror: Stalin's Purge of the Thirties*. 1968. New York, NY: Macmillan, 1973 ed.

Conway, Moncure Daniel. *Testimonies Concerning Slavery*. London, UK: Chapman and Hall, 1865.

Cooke, Alistair. *Alistair Cooke's America*. 1973. New York, NY: Alfred A. Knopf, 1984 ed.

Cooke, John Esten. *A Life of General Robert E. Lee*. New York, NY: D. Appleton and Co., 1871.

Cooley, Henry S. *A Study of Slavery in New Jersey*. Baltimore, MD: Johns Hopkins University Press, 1896.

Cooper, William J., Jr. *Jefferson Davis, American*. New York, NY: Vintage, 2000.

——. (ed.). *Jefferson Davis: The Essential Writings*. New York, NY: Random House, 2003.

Cornish, Dudley Taylor. *The Sable Arm: Black Troops in the Union Army, 1861-1865*. 1956. Lawrence, KS: University Press of Kansas, 1987 ed.

Coughtry, Jay. *The Notorious Triangle: Rhode Island and the African Slave Trade, 1700-1807*. Philadelphia, PA: Temple Press, 1981.

Coulter, Ann. *Guilty: Liberal "Victims" and Their Assault on America*. New York, NY: Three Rivers Press, 2009.

Craven, John J. *Prison Life of Jefferson Davis*. New York: NY: Carelton, 1866.

Crawford, Samuel Wylie. *The Genesis of the Civil War: The Story of Sumter, 1860-1861*. New York, NY: Charles L. Webster and Co., 1887.

Crocker, H. W., III. *The Politically Incorrect Guide to the Civil War*. Washington, D.C.: Regnery, 2008.

Cromie, Alice Hamilton. *A Tour Guide to the Civil War: The Complete State-by-State Guide to Battlegrounds, Landmarks, Museums, Relics, and Sites*. 1964. Nashville, TN: Rutledge Hill Press, 1990 ed.

Cromwell, John Wesley. *The Negro in American History: Men and Women Eminent in the Evolution of the American of African Descent*. Washington, D.C.: American Negro Academy, 1914.

Cross, F. L., and F. A. Livingston (eds.). *The Oxford Dictionary of the Christian Church*. 1957. London, UK: Oxford University Press, 1974 ed.

Crutchfield, James A. *Franklin: A Photographic Recollection*. 2 vols. Franklin, TN: Canaday Enterprises, 1996.

Crutchfield, James A., and Robert Holladay. *Franklin: Tennessee's Handsomest Town*. Franklin, TN: Hillsboro Press, 1999.

Cummins, Joseph. *Anything For a Vote: Dirty Tricks, Cheap Shots, and October Surprises in U.S. Presidential Campaigns*. Philadelphia, PA: Quirk, 2007.

Current, Richard N. *The Lincoln Nobody Knows*. 1958. New York, NY: Hill and Wang, 1963 ed.

——. (ed.) *The Confederacy (Information Now Encyclopedia)*. 1993. New York, NY: Macmillan, 1998 ed.

Curry, Leonard P. *Blueprint for Modern America: Nonmilitary Legislation of the First Civil War Congress*. Nashville, TN: Vanderbilt University Press, 1968.

Curti, Merle, Willard Thorpe, and Carlos Baker (eds.). *American Issues: The Social Record*. 1941. Chicago, IL: J. B. Lippincott, 1960 ed.

Curtin, Philip D. *The Atlantic Slave Trade: A Census*. Madison, WI: The University of Wisconsin Press, 1969.

——. *The Rise and Fall of the Plantation Complex: Essays in Atlantic History*. 1990. Cambridge, UK: Cambridge University Press, 1999 ed.

Curtis, George Ticknor. *Life of James Buchanan: Fifteenth President of the United States*. 2 vols. New York, NY: Harper and Brothers, 1883.

Curtis, William Eleroy. *Abraham Lincoln*. Philadelphia, PA: J. B. Lippincott Co., 1902.

Cushman, Horatio Bardwell. *History of the Choctaw, Chickasaw and Natchez Indians*. Greenville, TX: Headlight Printing House, 1899.

Custer, George Armstrong. *Wild Life on the Plains and Horrors of Indian Warfare*. St. Louis, MO: Excelsior Publishing, 1891.

Dabney, Robert Lewis. *A Defense of Virginia and the South*. Dahlonega, GA: Confederate Reprint Co., 1999.

Daniel, John M. *The Richmond Examiner During the War*. New York, NY: John M. Daniel, 1868.

Daniel, John W. *Life and Reminiscences of Jefferson Davis by Distinguished Men of His Time*. Baltimore, MD: R. H. Woodward, and Co., 1890.

Darwin, Charles. *On the Origin of Species By Means of Natural Selection*. London, UK: John Murray, 1866.

Daugherty, James. *Abraham Lincoln*. 1943. New York, NY: Scholastic Book Services, 1966 ed.

Davidson, Basil. *The African Slave Trade*. 1961. Boston, MA: Back Bay Books, 1980 ed.

Davis, Jefferson. *The Rise and Fall of the Confederate Government*. 2 vols. New York, NY: D. Appleton and Co., 1881.

——. *A Short History of the Confederate States of America*. New York, NY: Belford, 1890.

Davis, Kenneth C. *Don't Know Much About the Civil War: Everything You Need to Know About America's Greatest Conflict But Never Learned.* 1996. New York, NY: HarperCollins, 1997 ed.

Davis, Michael. *The Image of Lincoln in the South.* Knoxville, TN: University of Tennessee Press, 1971.

Davis, Varina. *Jefferson Davis: Ex-President of the Confederate States of America - A Memoir by His Wife.* 2 vols. New York, NY: Belford Co., 1890.

Davis, William C. *Jefferson Davis: The Man and His Hour.* New York, NY: HarperCollins, 1991.

——. *An Honorable Defeat: The Last Days of the Confederate Government.* New York, NY: Harcourt, 2001.

——. *Look Away: A History of the Confederate States of America.* 2002. New York, NY: Free Press, 2003 ed.

Davenport, Robert R. *Roots of the Rich and Famous: Real Cases of Unlikely Lineage.* Dallas, TX: Taylor Publishing Co., 1998.

Dawson, Sarah Morgan. *A Confederate Girl's Diary.* London, UK: William Heinemann, 1913.

Dean, Henry Clay. *Crimes of the Civil War, and Curse of the Funding System.* Baltimore, MD: William T. Smithson, 1869.

De Angelis, Gina. *It Happened in Washington, D.C.* Guilford, CT: Globe Pequot Press, 2004.

DeCaro, Louis A., Jr. *Fire From the Midst of You: A Religious Life of John Brown.* New York, NY: New York University Press, 2002.

Deems, Edward Mark. *Holy-Days and Holidays: A Treasury of Historical Material, Sermons in Full and Brief, Suggestive Thoughts, and Poetry.* New York, NY: Funk and Wagnalls, 1902.

De Forest, John William. *A Volunteer's Adventures: A Union Captain's Record of the Civil War.* 1946. North Haven, CT: Archon, 1970 ed.

DeGregorio, William A. *The Complete Book of U.S. Presidents.* 1984. New York, NY: Barricade, 1993 ed.

Delbanco, Andrew. *The Portable Abraham Lincoln.* New York, NY: Penguin, 1992.

Deloria, Vine, Jr. *Custer Died for Your Sins: An Indian Manifesto.* 1969. New York, NY: Avon, 1973 ed.

Denney, Robert E. *The Civil War Years: A Day-by-Day Chronicle of the Life of a Nation.* 1992. New York, NY: Sterling Publishing, 1994 ed.

Denson, John V. (ed.). *Reassessing the Presidency: The Rise of the Executive System and the Decline of Freedom.* Auburn, AL: Mises Institute, 2001.

Derosa, Marshall L. *The Confederate Constitution of 1861: An Inquiry into American Constitutionalism.* Columbia, MO: University of Missouri Press, 1991.

Diamond, Jared. *Guns, Germs, and Steel: The Fate of Human Societies.* 1997. New York, NY: W. W. Norton, 1999 ed.

Dicey, Edward. *Six Months in the Federal States.* 2 vols. London, UK: Macmillan and Co., 1863.

DiLorenzo, Thomas J. "The Great Centralizer: Abraham Lincoln and the War Between the States." *The Independent Review,* Vol. 3, No. 2, Fall 1998, pp. 243-271.

——. *The Real Lincoln: A New Look at Abraham Lincoln, His Agenda, and an Unnecessary War.* Three Rivers, MI: Three Rivers Press, 2003.

——. *Lincoln Unmasked: What You're Not Supposed to Know About Dishonest Abe.* New York, NY: Crown Forum, 2006.

——. *Hamilton's Curse: How Jefferson's Archenemy Betrayed the American Revolution—and What It Means for America Today.* New York, NY: Crown Forum, 2008.

Dinkins, James. *1861 to 1865: Personal Recollections and Experiences in the Confederate Army, by an "Old Johnnie".* Cincinnati, OH: Robert Clarke, 1897.

Doddridge, Joseph. *Notes on the Settlement and Indian Wars of the Western Parts of Virginia and Pennsylvania, From 1763 to 1783, Inclusive.* Albany, NY: Joel Munsell, 1876.

Donald, David Herbert. *Lincoln Reconsidered: Essays on the Civil War Era.* 1947. New York, NY: Vintage Press, 1989 ed.

——. (ed.). *Why the North Won the Civil War.* 1960. New York, NY: Collier, 1962 ed.

——. *Lincoln's Herndon.* New York, NY: Alfred A. Knopf, 1989.

——. *Lincoln.* New York, NY: Simon and Schuster, 1995.

Douglas, Henry Kyd. *I Rode With Stonewall: The War Experiences of the Youngest Member of Jackson's Staff.* 1940. Chapel Hill, NC: University of North Carolina Press, 1968 ed.

Douglass, Frederick. *Narrative of the Life of Frederick Douglass: An American Slave.* 1845. New York, NY: Signet, 1997 ed.

——. *The Life and Times of Frederick Douglass, From 1817 to 1882.* London, UK: Christian Age Office, 1882.

Drescher, Seymour, and Stanley L. Engerman (eds.). *A Historical Guide to World Slavery.* New York, NY: Oxford University Press, 1998.

Driscoll, Mark, and Gerry Breshears. *Vintage Jesus: Timeless Answers to Timely Questions.* Wheaton, IL: Crossway, 2007.

Du Bois, William Edward Burghardt. *Darkwater: Voices From Within the Veil.* New York, NY: Harcourt, Brace and Howe, 1920.

DuBose, John Witherspoon. *General Joseph Wheeler and the Army of Tennessee.* New York, NY: Neale Publishing Co., 1912.

Duff, Mountstuart E. Grant. *Notes From a Diary, 1851-1872.* 2 vols. London, UK: John Murray, 1897.

Duke, Basil W. *Reminiscences of General Basil W. Duke, C.S.A.* New York, NY: Doubleday, Page and Co., 1911.

Durden, Robert F. *The Gray and the Black: The Confederate Debate on Emancipation.* Baton Rouge, LA: Louisiana State University Press, 1972.

Early, Jubal A. *A Memoir of the Last Year of the War for Independence in the Confederate States of America.* Lynchburg, VA: Charles W. Button, 1867.

Eaton, Clement. *A History of the Southern Confederacy*. 1945. New York, NY: Free Press, 1966 ed.

———. *Jefferson Davis*. New York, NY: Free Press, 1977.

Eaton, John, and Ethel Osgood Mason. *Grant, Lincoln and the Freedmen: Reminiscences of the Civil War, With Special Reference to the Work of the Contrabands and Freedmen of the Mississippi Valley*. New York, NY: Longmans, Green, and Co., 1907.

Edmonds, Franklin Spencer. *Ulysses S. Grant*. Philadelphia, PA: George W. Jacobs and Co., 1915.

Elliot, Jonathan. *The Debates in the Several State Conventions on the Adoption of the Federal Constitution, As Recommended by the General Convention at Philadelphia in 1787*. 5 vols. Philadelphia, PA: J. B. Lippincott, 1891.

Elliott, E. N. *Cotton is King, and Pro-Slavery Arguments: Comprising the Writings of Hammond, Harper, Christy, Stringfellow, Hodge, Bledsoe, and Cartwright, on this Important Subject*. Augusta, GA: Pritchard, Abbott and Loomis, 1860.

Ellis, Joseph J. *American Sphinx: The Character of Thomas Jefferson*. 1996. New York, NY: Vintage, 1998 ed.

———. *Founding Brothers: The Revolutionary Generation*. 2000. New York, NY: Vintage, 2002 ed.

Eltis, David. *The Rise of African Slavery in the Americas*. Cambridge, UK: Cambridge University Press, 2000.

Emerson, Bettie Alder Calhoun. *Historic Southern Monuments: Representative Memorials of the Heroic Dead of the Southern Confederacy*. New York, NY: Neale Publishing Co., 1911.

Emerson, Ralph Waldo. *The Complete Works of Ralph Waldo Emerson*. 12 vols. 1878. Boston, MA: Houghton, Mifflin and Co., 1904 ed.

———. *Journals of Ralph Waldo Emerson*. 10 vols. Edward Waldo Emerson and Waldo Emerson Forbes, eds. Boston, MA: Houghton, Mifflin and Co., 1910.

———. *The Journals and Miscellaneous Notebooks of Ralph Waldo Emerson*. 16 vols. Cambridge, MA: Belknap Press, 1975.

Emison, John Avery. *Lincoln Über Alles: Dictatorship Comes to America*. Gretna, LA: Pelican Publishing Co., 2009.

*Encyclopedia Britannica*. 1768. New York, NY: Encyclopedia Britannica Co., 1911 ed.

Escott, Paul D. (ed.). *North Carolinians in the Era of the Civil War and Reconstruction*. Chapel Hill, NC: University of North Carolina Press, 2008.

Essah, Patience. *A House Divided: Slavery and Emancipation in Delaware, 1638-1865*. Charlottesville, VA: University Press of Virginia, 1996.

Evans, Clement Anselm (ed.). *Confederate Military History: A Library of Confederate States History, in Twelve Volumes, Written By Distinguished Men of the South*. 12 vols. Atlanta, GA: Confederate Publishing Co., 1899.

Evans, Eli N. *Judah P. Benjamin: The Jewish Confederate*. 1988. New York, NY: Free Press, 1989 ed.

Evans, Lawrence B. (ed.). *Writings of George Washington*. New York, NY: G. P. Putnam's Sons, 1908.

Faragher, John Mack. *Sugar Creek: Life on the Illinois Prairie*. New Haven, CT: Yale University Press, 1986.

Farrar, Victor John. *The Annexation of Russian America to the United States*. Washington D.C.: W. F. Roberts, 1937.

Farrow, Anne, Joel Lang, and Jennifer Frank. *Complicity: How the North Promoted, Prolonged, and Profited From Slavery*. New York, NY: Ballantine, 2005.

Faulkner, William. *The Unvanquished*. 1934. New York, NY: Vintage, 1966 ed.

Faust, Patricia L. (ed.). *Historical Times Illustrated Encyclopedia of the Civil War*. New York, NY: Harper and Row, 1986.

Fay, Edwin Hedge. *This Infernal War: The Confederate Letters of Edwin H. Fay*. Austin, TX: University of Texas Press, 1958.

Fehrenbacher, Don E. (ed.). *Abraham Lincoln: A Documentary Portrait Through His Speeches and Writings*. New York, NY: Signet, 1964.

———. *Lincoln in Text and Context: Collected Essays*. Stanford, CA: Stanford University press, 1987.

———. (ed.) *Abraham Lincoln: Speeches and Writings, 1859-1865*. New York, NY: Library of America, 1989.

———. *The Slaveholding Republic: An Account of the United States Government's Relations to Slavery*. New York, NY: Oxford University Press, 2002.

Ferris, Marcie Cohen, and Mark I. Greenberg (eds.). *Jewish Roots in Southern Soil: A New History*. Waltham, MA: Brandeis University Press, 2006.

Fields, Annie (ed.) *Life and Letters of Harriet Beecher Stowe*. Cambridge, MA: Riverside Press, 1897.

Findlay, Bruce, and Esther Findlay. *Your Rugged Constitution: How America's House of Freedom is Planned and Built*. 1950. Stanford, CA: Stanford University Press, 1951 ed.

Fite, Emerson David. *The Presidential Election of 1860*. New York, NY: MacMillan, 1911.

Fleming, Walter Lynwood. *Civil War and Reconstruction in Alabama*. New York, NY: Macmillan, 1905.

Flood, Charles Bracelen. *1864: Lincoln At the Gates of History*. New York, NY: Simon and Schuster, 2009.

Fogel, Robert William. *Without Consent or Contract: The Rise and Fall of American Slavery*. New York, NY: W. W. Norton, 1989.

Fogel, Robert William, and Stanley L. Engerman. *Time On the Cross: The Economics of American Negro Slavery*. Boston, MA: Little, Brown, and Co., 1974.

Foley, John P. (ed.). *The Jeffersonian Cyclopedia*. New York, NY: Funk and Wagnalls, 1900.

Foner, Eric. *Free Soil, Free Labor, Free Men: The Ideology of the Republican Party Before the Civil War*. New York, NY: Oxford University Press, 1970.

———. *Reconstruction: America's Unfinished Revolution, 1863-1877*. 1988. New York, NY: Harper and Row, 1989 ed.

Foote, Shelby. *The Civil War: A Narrative, Fort Sumter to Perryville, Vol. 1*. 1958. New York, NY: Vintage, 1986 ed.

———. *The Civil War: A Narrative, Fredericksburg to Meridian, Vol. 2*. 1963. New York, NY: Vintage, 1986 ed.

——. *The Civil War: A Narrative, Red River to Appomattox, Vol. 3.* 1974. New York, NY: Vintage, 1986 ed.

Ford, Paul Leicester (ed.). *The Works of Thomas Jefferson.* 12 vols. New York, NY: G. P. Putnam's Sons, 1904.

Ford, Worthington Chauncey (ed.). *A Cycle of Adams Letters.* 2 vols. Boston, MA: Houghton Mifflin, 1920.

Forman, S. E. *The Life and Writings of Thomas Jefferson.* Indianapolis, IN: Bowen-Merrill, 1900.

Förster, Stig, and Jörg Nagler (eds.). *On the Road to Total War: The American Civil War and the German Wars of Unification, 1861-1871.* 1997. Cambridge, UK: Cambridge University Press, 2002 ed.

Foster, John W. *A Century of American Diplomacy.* Boston, MA: Houghton, Mifflin and Co., 1901.

Fowler, John D. *The Confederate Experience Reader: Selected Documents and Essays.* New York, NY: Routledge, 2007.

Fowler, William Chauncey. *The Sectional Controversy; or Passages in the Political History of the United States, Including the Causes of the War Between the Sections.* New York, NY: Charles Scribner, 1864.

Fox-Genovese, Elizabeth. *Within the Plantation Household: Black and White Women of the Old South (Gender and American Culture).* Chapel Hill, NC: University of North Carolina Press, 1988.

Franklin, Benjamin. *The Complete Works of Benjamin Franklin.* 10 vols. New York, NY: G. P. Putnam's Sons, 1887.

Franklin, John Hope. *Reconstruction After the Civil War.* Chicago, IL: University of Chicago Press, 1961.

Fredrickson, George M. *The Black Image in the White Mind: The Debate on Afro-American Character and Destiny, 1817-1914.* New York, NY: Harper and Row, 1971.

Fremantle, Arthur James. *Three Months in the Southern States, April-June, 1863.* New York, NY: John Bradburn, 1864.

Furguson, Ernest B. *Freedom Rising: Washington in the Civil War.* 2004. New York, NY: Vintage, 2005 ed.

Furnas, J. C. *The Americans: A Social History of the United States, 1587-1914.* New York, NY: G. P. Putnam's Sons, 1969.

Galenson, David W. *White Servitude in Colonial America.* New York, NY: Cambridge University Press, 1981.

Garland, Hugh A. *The Life of John Randolph of Roanoke.* New York, NY: D. Appleton and Co., 1874.

Garraty, John A. (ed.). *Historical Viewpoints: Notable Articles From American Heritage, Vol. One to 1877.* 1970. New York, NY: Harper and Row, 1979 ed.

Garraty, John A., and Robert A. McCaughey. *A Short History of the American Nation.* 1966. New York, NY: HarperCollins, 1989 ed.

Garrison, Webb B. *Civil War Trivia and Fact Book.* Nashville, TN: Rutledge Hill Press, 1992.

——. *The Lincoln No One Knows: The Mysterious Man Who Ran the Civil War.* Nashville, TN: Rutledge Hill Press, 1993.

——. *Civil War Curiosities: Strange Stories, Oddities, Events, and Coincidences.* Nashville, TN: Rutledge Hill Press, 1994.

——. *The Amazing Civil War.* Nashville, TN: Rutledge Hill Press, 1998.

Garrison, Wendell Phillips, and Francis Jackson Garrison. *William Lloyd Garrison, 1805-1879.* 4 vols. New York, NY: Century Co., 1889.

Garrison, William Lloyd. *Thoughts on African Colonization.* Boston, MA: Garrison and Knapp, 1832.

Gates, Henry Louis, Jr. (ed.) *The Classic Slave Narratives.* New York, NY: Mentor, 1987.

Genovese, Eugene D. *Roll, Jordan, Roll: The World the Slaves Made.* New York, NY: Pantheon, 1974.

Gerster, Patrick, and Nicholas Cords (eds.). *Myth and Southern History.* 2 vols. 1974. Champaign, IL: University of Illinois Press, 1989 ed.

Golay, Michael. *A Ruined Land: The End of the Civil War.* New York, NY: John Wiley and Sons, 1999.

Gordon, Armistead Churchill. *Figures From American History: Jefferson Davis.* New York, NY: Charles Scribner's Sons, 1918.

Gower, Herschel, and Jack Allen (eds.). *Pen and Sword: The Life and Journals of Randal W. McGavock.* Nashville, TN: Tennessee Historical Commission, 1959.

Gragg, Rod. *The Illustrated Confederate Reader: Extraordinary Eyewitness Accounts by the Civil War's Southern Soldiers and Civilians.* New York, NY: Gramercy Books, 1989.

Graham, John Remington. *A Constitutional History of Secession.* Gretna, LA: Pelican Publishing Co., 2003.

——. *Blood Money: The Civil War and the Federal Reserve.* Gretna, LA: Pelican Publishing Co., 2006.

Grant, Ulysses Simpson. *Personal Memoirs of U. S. Grant.* 2 vols. 1885-1886. New York, NY: Charles L. Webster and Co., 1886.

Gray, Robert, Rev. (compiler). *The McGavock Family: A Genealogical History of James McGavock and His Descendants, from 1760 to 1903.* Richmond, VA: W. E. Jones, 1903.

Gray, Thomas R. *The Confessions of Nat Turner: The Leader of the Late Insurrection in Southampton, Virginia.* Richmond, VA: Thomas R. Gray, 1831.

Greeley, Horace (ed.). *The Writings of Cassius Marcellus Clay.* New York, NY: Harper and Brothers, 1848.

——. *A History of the Struggle for Slavery Extension or Restriction in the United States From the Declaration of Independence to the Present Day.* New York, NY: Dix, Edwards and Co., 1856.

——. *The American Conflict: A History of the Great Rebellion in the United States, 1861-1865.* 2 vols. Hartford, CT: O. D. Case and Co., 1867.

Green, Constance McLaughlin. *Eli Whitney and the Birth of American Technology.* Boston, MA: Little, Brown, and Co., 1956.

——. *Washington: A History of the Capital, 1800-1950.* 1962. Princeton, NJ: Princeton University Press, 1976 ed.

Greenberg, Martin H., and Charles G. Waugh (eds.). *The Price of Freedom: Slavery and the Civil War—Vol. 1, The Demise of Slavery.* Nashville, TN: Cumberland House, 2000.

Greene, Lorenzo Johnston. *The Negro in Colonial New England, 1620-1776*. New York, NY: Columbia University Press, 1942.

Grimsley, Mark. *The Hard Hand of War: Union Military Policy Toward Southern Civilians, 1861-1865*. 1995. Cambridge, UK: Cambridge University Press, 1997 ed.

Grissom, Michael Andrew. *Southern By the Grace of God*. 1988. Gretna, LA: Pelican Publishing Co., 1995 ed.

Groom, Winston. *Shrouds of Glory - From Atlanta to Nashville: The Last Great Campaign of the Civil War*. New York, NY: Grove Press, 1995.

Guelzo, Allen C. *Abraham Lincoln As a Man of Ideas*. Carbondale, IL: Southern Illinois University Press, 2009.

Gwatkin, H. M., and J. P. Whitney (eds.). *The Cambridge Medieval History, Vol. 2: The Rise of the Saracens and the Foundation of the Western Empire*. New York, NY: Macmillan, 1913.

Hacker, Louis Morton. *The Shaping of the American Tradition*. New York, NY: Columbia University Press, 1947.

Hall, B. C., and C. T. Wood. *The South: A Two-step Odyssey on the Backroads of the Enchanted Land*. New York, NY: Touchstone, 1996.

Hall, Kermit L. (ed). *The Oxford Companion to the Supreme Court of the United States*. New York, NY: Oxford University Press, 1992.

Hamblin, Ken. *Pick a Better Country: An Unassuming Colored Guy Speaks His Mind About America*. New York, NY: Touchstone, 1997.

Hamilton, Alexander, James Madison, and John Jay. *The Federalist Papers*. New York, NY: Signet Classics, 2003.

Hamilton, Neil A. *Rebels and Renegades: A Chronology of Social and Political Dissent in the United States*. New York, NY: Routledge, 2002.

Hannity, Sean. *Let Freedom Ring: Winning the War of Liberty Over Liberalism*. New York, NY: HarperCollins, 2002.

Hansen, Harry. *The Civil War: A History*. 1961. Harmondsworth, UK: Mentor, 1991 ed.

Harding, Samuel Bannister. *The Contest Over the Ratification of the Federal Constitution in the State of Massachusetts*. New York, NY: Longmans, Green, and Co., 1896.

Harper, William, James Henry Hammond, William Gilmore Simms, and Thomas Roderick Dew. *The Pro-Slavery Argument, As Maintained by the Most Distinguished Writers of the Southern States*. Charleston, SC: Walker, Richards and Co., 1852.

Harrell, David Edwin, Jr., Edwin S. Gaustad, John B. Boles, Sally Foreman Griffith, Randall M. Miller, and Randall B. Woods. *Unto a Good Land: A History of the American People*. Grand Rapids, MI: William B. Eerdmans, 2005.

Harris, Joel Chandler. *Stories of Georgia*. New York, NY: American Book Co., 1896.

Harris, Norman Dwight. *The History of Negro Servitude in Illinois*. Chicago, IL: A. C. McClurg and Co., 1904.

Harrison, Peleg D. *The Stars and Stripes and Other American Flags*. 1906. Boston, MA: Little, Brown, and Co., 1908 ed.

Hartzell, Josiah. *The Genesis of the Republican Party*. Canton, OH: n.p., 1890.

Harwell, Richard B. (ed.). *The Confederate Reader: How the South Saw the War*. 1957. Mineola, NY: Dover, 1989 ed.

Hattaway, Herman, and Archer Jones. *How the North Won: A Military History of the Civil War*. 1983. Champaign, IL: University of Illinois Press, 1991 ed.

Hawthorne, Julian (ed.). *Orations of American Orators*. 2 vols. New York, NY: Colonial Press, 1900.

Hawthorne, Julian, James Schouler, and Elisha Benjamin Andrews. *United States, From the Discovery of the North American Continent Up to the Present Time*. 9 vols. New York, NY: Co-operative Publication Society, 1894.

Haygood, Atticus G. *Our Brother in Black: His Freedom and His Future*. Nashville, TN: M. E. Church, 1896.

Hedrick, Joan D. (ed.). *The Oxford Harriet Beecher Stowe Reader*. New York, NY: Oxford University Press, 1999.

Helper, Hinton Rowan. *The Impending Crisis of the South: How to Meet It*. New York, NY: A. B. Burdick, 1860.

——. *Compendium of the Impending Crisis of the South*. New York, NY: A. B. Burdick, 1860.

——. *Nojoque: A Question for a Continent*. New York, NY: George W. Carleton, 1867.

——. *The Negroes in Negroland: The Negroes in America; and Negroes Generally*. New York, NY: George W. Carlton, 1868.

——. *Oddments of Andean Diplomacy and Other Oddments*. St. Louis, MO: W. S. Bryan, 1879.

Henderson, George Francis Robert. *Stonewall Jackson and the American Civil War*. 2 vols. London, UK: Longmans, Green, and Co., 1919.

Henry, Robert Selph (ed.). *The Story of the Confederacy*. 1931. New York, NY: Konecky and Konecky, 1999 ed.

——. *As They Saw Forrest: Some Recollections and Comments of Contemporaries*. 1956. Wilmington, NC: Broadfoot Publishing Co., 1991 ed.

——. *First with the Most: Forrest*. New York, NY: Konecky and Konecky, 1992.

Henson, Josiah. *Father Henson's Story of His Own Life*. Boston, MA: John P. Jewett and Co., 1858.

Herndon, William H., and Jesse W. Weik. *Abraham Lincoln: The True Story of a Great Life*. New York, NY: D. Appleton and Co., 1909.

Hertz, Emanuel. *The Hidden Lincoln*. New York, NY: Blue Ribbon Works, 1940.

Hervey, Anthony. *Why I Wave the Confederate Flag, Written By a Black Man: The End of Niggerism and the Welfare State*. Oxford, UK: Trafford Publishing, 2006.

Hey, David. *The Oxford Guide to Family History*. Oxford, UK: Oxford University Press, 1993.

Hickey, William. *The Constitution of the United States*. Philadelphia, PA: T. K. and P. G. Collins, 1853.

Highsmith, Carol M. and Ted Landphair. *Civil War Battlefields and Landmarks: A Photographic Tour*. New York, NY: Random House, 2003.

Hildreth, Richard. *The White Slave: Another Picture of Slave Life in America*. Boston, MA: Adamant Media Corp., 2001.

Hinkle, Don. *Embattled Banner: A Reasonable Defense of the Confederate Battle Flag*. Paducah, KY: Turner Publishing Co., 1997.

Hitler, Adolf. *Mein Kampf*. 2 vols. 1925, 1926. New York: NY: Reynal and Hitchcock, 1941 English translation ed.

Hoffman, Michael A., II. *They Were White and They Were Slaves: The Untold History of the Enslavement of Whites in Early America*. Dresden, NY: Wiswell Ruffin House, 1993.

Hofstadter, Richard. *The American Political Tradition, and the Men Who Made It*. New York, NY: Alfred A. Knopf, 1948.

Holland, Jesse J. *Black Men Built the Capitol: Discovering African-American History in and Around Washington, D.C.* Guilford, CT: The Globe Pequot Press, 2007.

Holland, Rupert Sargent (ed.). *Letters and Diary of Laura M. Towne: Written From the Sea Islands of South Carolina, 1862-1884*. Cambridge, MA: Riverside Press, 1912.

Holzer, Harold (ed.). *The Lincoln-Douglas Debates: The First Complete, Unexpurgated Text*. 1993. Bronx, NY: Fordham University Press, 2004 ed.

Hood, John Bell. *Advance and Retreat: Personal Experiences in the United States and Confederate States Armies*. New Orleans, LA: G. T. Beauregard, 1880.

Hopkins, Luther W. *From Bull Run to Appomattox: A Boy's View*. Baltimore, MD: Fleet-McGinley Co., 1908.

Horn, Stanley F. *Invisible Empire: The Story of the Ku Klux Klan, 1866-1871*. 1939. Montclair, NJ: Patterson Smith, 1969 ed.

——. *The Decisive Battle of Nashville*. 1956. Baton Rouge, LA: Louisiana State University Press, 1991 ed.

Horwitz, Tony. *Confederates in the Attic: Dispatches From the Unfinished Civil War*. 1998. New York, NY: Vintage, 1999 ed.

Howe, Daniel Wait. *Political History of Secession*. New York, NY: G. P. Putnam's Sons, 1914.

Howe, George L. *Mount Hope: A New England Chronicle*. New York, NY: Viking Press, 1959.

Howe, Henry. *Historical Collections of Virginia*. Charleston, SC: William R. Babcock, 1852.

Howe, M. A. DeWolfe (ed.). *Home Letters of General Sherman*. New York, NY: Charles Scribner's Sons, 1909.

——. *Bristol, Rhode Island: A Town Biography*. Cambridge, MA: Harvard University Press, 1930.

Hubbard, John Milton. *Notes of a Private*. St. Louis, MO: Nixon-Jones, 1911.

Hunt, John Gabriel (ed.). *The Essential Abraham Lincoln*. Avenel, NJ: Portland House, 1993.

Hurmence, Belinda (ed.). *Before Freedom, When I Can Just Remember: Twenty-seven Oral Histories of Former South Carolina Slaves*. 1989. Winston-Salem, NC: John F. Blair, 2002 ed.

Hurst, Jack. *Nathan Bedford Forrest: A Biography*. 1993. New York, NY: Vintage, 1994 ed.

Ingersoll, Thomas G., and Robert E. O'Connor. *Politics and Structure: Essential of American national Government*. North Scituate, MA: Duxbury Press, 1979.

Jaquette, Henrietta Stratton (ed.). *South After Gettysburg: Letters of Cornelia Hancock, 1863-1868*. Philadelphia, PA: University of Pennsylvania Press, 1937.

Jahoda, Gloria. *The Trail of Tears: The Story of the American Indian Removals, 1813-1855*. 1975. New York, NY: Wings Book, 1995 ed.

Jefferson, Thomas. *Notes on the State of Virginia*. Boston, MA: H. Sprague, 1802.

——. *Thomas Jefferson's Farm Book*. (Edwin Morris Betts, ed.). Charlottesville, VA: Thomas Jefferson Memorial Foundation, 1999.

Jensen, Merrill. *The New Nation: A History of the United States During the Confederation, 1781-1789*. New York, NY: Vintage, 1950.

——. *The Articles of Confederation: An Interpretation of the Social-Constitutional History of the American Revolution, 1774-1781*. Madison, WI: University of Wisconsin Press, 1959.

Jimerson, Randall C. *The Private Civil War: Popular Thought During the Sectional Conflict*. Baton Rouge, LA: Louisiana State University Press, 1988.

Johannsen, Robert Walter. *Lincoln, the South, and Slavery: The Political Dimension*. Baton Rouge, LA: Louisiana State University Press, 1991.

Johnson, Adam Rankin. *The Partisan Rangers of the Confederate States Army*. Louisville, KY: George G. Fetter, 1904.

Johnson, Benjamin Heber. *Making of the American West: People and Perspectives*. Santa Barbara, CA: ABC-Clio, 2007.

Johnson, Clint. *The Politically Incorrect Guide to the South (and Why It Will Rise Again)*. Washington, D.C.: Regnery, 2006.

Johnson, Ludwell H. *North Against South: The American Iliad, 1848-1877*. 1978. Columbia, SC: Foundation for American Education, 1993 ed.

Johnson, Michael, and James L. Roark. *Black Masters: A Free Family of Color in the Old South*. New York, NY: W.W. Norton, 1984.

Johnson, Oliver. *William Lloyd Garrison and His Times*. 1879. Boston, MA: Houghton Mifflin and Co., 1881 ed.

Johnson, Robert Underwood (ed.). *Battles and Leaders of the Civil War*. 4 vols. New York, NY: The Century Co., 1884-1888.

Johnson, Thomas Cary. *The Life and Letters of Robert Lewis Dabney*. Richmond, VA: Presbyterian Committee of Publication, 1903.

Jones, John Beauchamp. *A Rebel War Clerk's Diary at the Confederate States Capital*. 2 vols. in 1. Philadelphia, PA: J. B. Lippincott and Co., 1866.

Jones, John William. *Personal Reminiscences, Anecdotes, and Letters of Gen. Robert E. Lee.* New York, NY: D. Appleton and Co., 1874.

Jones, Wilmer L. *Generals in Blue and Gray.* 2 vols. Westport, CT: Praeger, 2004.

Jordan, Don, and Michael Walsh. *White Cargo: The Forgotten History of Britain's White Slaves in America.* New York, NY: New York University Press, 2008.

Jordan, Ervin L. *Black Confederates and Afro-Yankees in Civil War Virginia.* Charlottesville, VA: University Press of Virginia, 1995.

Jordan, Thomas, and John P. Pryor. *The Campaigns of General Nathan Bedford Forrest and of Forrest's Cavalry.* New Orleans, LA: Blelock and Co., 1868.

Julian, George Washington. *Speeches on Political Questions.* New York, NY: Hurd and Houghton, 1872.

Kane, Joseph Nathan. *Facts About the Presidents: A Compilation of Biographical and Historical Data.* 1959. New York, NY: Ace, 1976 ed.

Katcher, Philip. *The Civil War Source Book.* 1992. New York, NY: Facts on File, 1995 ed.

———. *Brassey's Almanac: The American Civil War.* London, UK: Brassey's, 2003.

Kautz, August Valentine. *Customs of Service for Non-Commissioned Officers and Soldiers (as Derived from Law and Regulations and Practised in the Army of the United States).* Philadelphia, PA: J. B. Lippincott and Co., 1864.

Keckley, Elizabeth. *Behind the Scenes, or Thirty Years a Slave, and Four Years in the White House.* New York, NY: G. W. Carlton and Co., 1868.

Kelly, Alfred H., Winfred A. Harbison, and Herman Belz. *The American Constitution: Its Origins and Development* (Vol. 2). 1965. New York, NY: W.W. Norton, 1991 ed.

Kennedy, James Ronald, and Walter Donald Kennedy. *The South Was Right!* Gretna, LA: Pelican Publishing Co., 1994.

———. *Why Not Freedom!: America's Revolt Against Big Government.* Gretna, LA: Pelican Publishing Co., 2005.

———. *Nullifying Tyranny: Creating Moral Communities in an Immoral Society.* Gretna, LA: Pelican Publishing Co., 2010.

Kennedy, Walter Donald. *Myths of American Slavery.* Gretna, LA: Pelican Publishing Co., 2003.

Kennett, Lee B. *Sherman: A Soldier's Life.* 2001. New York, NY: HarperCollins, 2002 ed.

Kettell, Thomas Prentice. *History of the Great Rebellion.* Hartford, CT: L. Stebbins, 1865.

Kinder, Hermann, and Werner Hilgemann. *The Anchor Atlas of World History: From the French Revolution to the American Bicentennial.* 2 vols. Garden City, NY: Anchor, 1978.

King, Charles R. (ed.). *The Life and Correspondence of Rufus King.* 6 vols. New York, NY: G. P. Putnam's Sons, 1897.

King, Edward. *The Great South: A Record of Journeys.* Hartford, CT: American Publishing Co., 1875.

Kinshasa, Kwando Mbiassi. *Black Resistance to the Ku Klux Klan in the Wake of the Civil War.* Jefferson, NC: McFarland and Co., 2006.

Kirkland, Edward Chase. *The Peacemakers of 1864.* New York, NY: Macmillan, 1927.

Klingaman, William K. *Abraham Lincoln and the Road to Emancipation, 1861-1865.* 2001. New York, NY: Penguin, 2002 ed.

Knox, Thomas Wallace. *Camp-Fire and Cotton-Field: Southern Adventure in Time of War - Life With the Union Armies, and Residence on a Louisiana Plantation.* New York, NY: Blelock and Co., 1865.

Koger, Larry. *Black Slaveowners: Free Black Slave Masters in South Carolina, 1790-1860.* Columbia, SC: University of South Carolina Press, 1995.

Lamon, Ward Hill. *The Life of Abraham Lincoln: From His Birth to His Inauguration as President.* Boston, MA: James R. Osgood and Co., 1872.

———. *Recollections of Abraham Lincoln: 1847-1865.* Chicago, IL: A. C. McClurg and Co., 1895.

Lang, J. Stephen. *The Complete Book of Confederate Trivia.* Shippensburg, PA: Burd Street Press, 1996.

Lanning, Michael Lee. *The African-American Soldier: From Crispus Attucks to Colin Powell.* 1997. New York, NY: Citadel Press, 2004 ed.

Lawrence, William. *Life of Amos A. Lawrence.* Boston, MA: Houghton, Mifflin, and Co., 1899.

Leech, Margaret. *Reveille in Washington, 1860-1865.* 1941. Alexandria, VA: Time-Life Books, 1980 ed.

Lee, Robert E., Jr. *Recollections and Letters of General Robert E. Lee.* New York, NY: Doubleday, Page and Co., 1904.

Lemay, J. A. Leo, and P. M. Zall (eds.). *Benjamin Franklin's Autobiography: An Authoritative Text, Backgrounds, Criticism.* 1791. New York, NY: W. W. Norton and Co., 1986 ed.

Lemire, Elise. *Black Walden: Slavery and Its Aftermath in Concord, Massachusetts.* Philadelphia, PA: University of Pennsylvania Press, 2009.

Lester, Charles Edwards. *Life and Public Services of Charles Sumner.* New York, NY: U.S. Publishing Co., 1874.

Lester, John C., and D. L. Wilson. *Ku Klux Klan: Its Origin, Growth, and Disbandment.* 1884. New York, NY: Neale Publishing, 1905 ed.

Lewis, Lloyd. *Myths After Lincoln.* 1929. New York, NY: The Press of the Reader's Club, 1941 ed.

LeVert, Suzanne (ed.). *The Civil War Society's Encyclopedia of the Civil War.* New York, NY: Wings Books, 1997.

Levin, Mark R. *Liberty and Tyranny: A Conservative Manifesto.* New York, NY: Threshold, 2009.

Lincoln, Abraham. *The Autobiography of Abraham Lincoln* (selected from the *Complete Works of Abraham Lincoln*, 1894, by John G. Nicolay and John Hay). New York, NY: Francis D. Tandy Co., 1905.

Lincoln, Abraham, and Stephen A. Douglas. *Political Debates Between Abraham Lincoln and Stephen A. Douglas.* Cleveland, OH: Burrows Brothers Co., 1894.

Littell, Eliakim (ed.). *The Living Age*. Seventh Series, Vol. 30. Boston, MA: The Living Age Co., 1906.

Litwack, Leon F. *North of Slavery: The Negro in the Free States, 1790-1860*. Chicago, IL: University of Chicago Press, 1961.

Livermore, Thomas L. *Numbers and Losses in the Civil War in America, 1861-65*. 1900. Carlisle, PA: John Kallmann, 1996 ed.

Livingstone, William. *Livingstone's History of the Republican Party*. 2 vols. Detroit, MI: William Livingstone, 1900.

Locke, John. *Two Treatises of Government* (Mark Goldie, ed.). 1924. London, UK: Everyman, 1998 ed.

Lodge, Henry Cabot (ed.). *The Works of Alexander Hamilton*. 12 vols. New York, NY: G. P. Putnam's Sons, 1904.

Logan, John Alexander. *The Great Conspiracy: Its Origin and History*. New York, NY: A. R. Hart, 1886.

Logsdon, David R. (ed.). *Eyewitnesses at the Battle of Franklin*. 1988. Nashville, TN: Kettle Mills Press, 2000 ed.

———. *Tennessee Antebellum Trail Guidebook*. Nashville, TN: Kettle Mills Press, 1995.

Long, Armistead Lindsay, and Marcus J. Wright. *Memoirs of Robert E. Lee: His Military and Personal History*. New York, NY: J. M. Stoddart and Co., 1887.

Long, Everette Beach, and Barbara Long. *The Civil War Day by Day: An Almanac, 1861-1865*. 1971. New York, NY: Da Capo Press, 1985 ed.

Lonn, Ella. *Foreigners in the Confederacy*. 1940. Chapel Hill, NC: University of North Carolina Press, 2002 ed.

Lott, Stanley K. *The Truth About American Slavery*. 2004. Clearwater, SC: Eastern Digital Resources, 2005 ed.

Lubbock, Francis Richard. *Six Decades in Texas, or Memoirs of Francis Richard Lubbock, Governor of Texas in War-Time, 1861-1863*. 1899. Austin, TX: Ben C. Jones, 1900 ed.

Ludlow, Daniel H. (ed.). *Encyclopedia of Mormonism: The History, Scripture, Doctrine, and Procedure of the Church of Jesus Christ of Latter-Day Saints*. New York, NY: Macmillan, 1992.

Lytle, Andrew Nelson. *Bedford Forrest and His Critter Company*. New York, NY: G. P. Putnam's Sons, 1931.

MacDonald, William. *Select Documents Illustrative of the History of the United States 1776-1861*. New York, NY: Macmillan, 1897.

Mackay, Charles. *Life and Liberty in America, or Sketches of a Tour in the United States and Canada in 1857-58*. New York, NY: Harper and Brothers, 1859.

Madison, James. *Letters and Other Writings of James Madison, Fourth President of the United States*. 4 vols. Philadelphia, PA: J. B. Lippincott and Co., 1865.

Maihafer, Harry J. *War of Words: Abraham Lincoln and the Civil War Press*. Dulles, VA: Brassey's, 2001.

Main, Jackson Turner. *The Anti-Federalists: Critics of the Constitution, 1781-1788*. 1961. New York, NY: W. W. Norton and Co., 1974 ed.

Mandel, Bernard. *Labor, Free and Slave: Workingmen and the Anti-Slavery Movement in the United States*. New York, NY: Associated Authors, 1955.

Manegold, C. S. *Ten Hills Farm: The Forgotten History of Slavery in the North*. Princeton, NJ: Princeton University Press, 2010.

Manning, Timothy D., Sr. (ed.) *Lincoln Reconsidered: Conference Reader*. High Point, NC: Heritage Foundation Press, 2006.

Marten, James. *The Children's Civil War*. Chapel Hill, NC: University of North Carolina Press, 1998.

Martin, Iain C. *The Quotable American Civil War*. Guilford, CT: Lyons Press, 2008.

Martinez, James Michael. *Carpetbaggers, Cavalry, and the Ku Klux Klan: Exposing the Invisible Empire During Reconstruction*. Lanham, MD: Rowman and Littlefield, 2007.

Masur, Louis P. *The Real War Will Never Get In the Books: Selections From Writers During the Civil War*. New York, NY: Oxford University Press, 1993.

Mathes, Capt. J. Harvey. *General Forrest*. New York, NY: D. Appleton and Co., 1902.

Maury, Dabney Herndon. *Recollections of a Virginian in the Mexican, Indian, and Civil Wars*. New York, NY: Charles Scribner's Sons, 1894.

Mayer, David N. *The Constitutional Thought of Thomas Jefferson*. Charlottesville, VA: University of Virginia Press, 1995.

Mayer, Henry. *All on Fire: William Lloyd Garrison and the Abolition of Slavery*. New York, NY: St. Martin's Press, 1998.

McAfee, Ward M. *Citizen Lincoln*. Hauppauge, NY: Nova History Publications, 2004.

McCabe, James Dabney. *Our Martyred President: The Life and Public Services of Gen. James A. Garfield, Twentieth President of the United States*. Philadelphia, PA: National Publishing Co., 1881.

McClure, Alexander Kelly. *Abraham Lincoln and Men of War-Times: Some Personal Recollections of War and Politics During the Lincoln Administration*. Philadelphia, PA: Times Publishing Co., 1892.

———. *Our Presidents and How We Make Them*. New York, NY: Harper and Brothers, 1900.

McCullough, David. *John Adams*. New York, NY: Touchstone, 2001.

McDonald, Forrest. *States' Rights and the Union: Imperium in Imperio, 1776-1876*. Lawrence, KS: University Press of Kansas, 2000.

McDonough, James Lee, and Thomas L. Connelly. *Five Tragic Hours: The Battle of Franklin*. 1983. Knoxville, TN: University of Tennessee Press, 2001 ed.

McElroy, Robert. *Jefferson Davis: The Unreal and the Real*. 1937. New York, NY: Smithmark, 1995 ed.

McFeely, William S. *Yankee Stepfather: General O. O. Howard and the Freedmen - The Story of a Civil War Promise to Former Slaves Made—and Broken*. 1968. New York, NY: W. W. Norton, 1994.

McGehee, Jacob Owen. *Causes That Led to the War Between the States.* Atlanta, GA: A. B. Caldwell, 1915.
McGuire, Hunter, and George L. Christian. *The Confederate Cause and Conduct in the War Between the States.* Richmond, VA: L. H. Jenkins, 1907.
McHenry, George. *The Cotton Trade: Its Bearing Upon the Prosperity of Great Britain and Commerce of the American Republics, Considered in Connection with the System of Negro Slavery in the Confederate States.* London, UK: Saunders, Otley, and Co., 1863.
McIlwaine, Shields. *Memphis Down in Dixie.* New York, NY: E. P. Dutton, 1848.
McKim, Randolph H. *The Soul of Lee.* New York, NY: Longmans, Green and Co., 1918.
McKissack, Patricia C., and Frederick McKissack. *Sojourner Truth: Ain't I a Woman?* New York: NY: Scholastic, 1992.
McManus, Edgar J. *A History of Negro Slavery in New York.* Syracuse, NY: Syracuse University Press, 1966.
———. *Black Bondage in the North.* Syracuse, NY: Syracuse University Press, 1973.
McMaster, John Bach. *Our House Divided: A History of the People of the United States During Lincoln's Administration.* 1927. New York, NY: Premier, 1961 ed.
McPherson, Edward. *The Political History of the United States of America, During the Great Rebellion (from November 6, 1860, to July 4, 1864).* Washington, D.C.: Philp and Solomons, 1864.
———. *The Political History of the United States of America, During the Period of Reconstruction, (from April 15, 1865, to July 15, 1870,) Including a Classified Summary of the Legislation of the Thirty-ninth, Fortieth, and Forty-first Congresses.* Washington, D.C.: Solomons and Chapman, 1875.
McPherson, James M. *The Struggle for Equality: Abolitionists and the Negro in the Civil War and Reconstruction.* 1964. Princeton, NJ: Princeton University Press, 1992 ed.
———. *The Negro's Civil War: How American Negroes Felt and Acted During the War for the Union.* 1965. Chicago, IL: University of Illinois Press, 1982 ed.
———. *Battle Cry of Freedom: The Civil War Era.* Oxford, UK: Oxford University Press, 2003.
———. *The Atlas of the Civil War.* Philadelphia, PA: Courage Books, 2005.
McPherson, James M., and the staff of the *New York Times. The Most Fearful Ordeal: Original Coverage of the Civil War by Writers and Reporters of the New York Times.* New York, NY: St. Martin's Press, 2004.
McWhiney, Grady, and Judith Lee Hallock. *Braxton Bragg and Confederate Defeat.* 2 vols. Tuscaloosa, AL: University of Alabama Press, 1991.
McWhiney, Grady, and Perry D. Jamieson. *Attack and Die: Civil War Military Tactics and the Southern Heritage.* Tuscaloosa, AL: University of Alabama Press, 1982.
Melish, Joanne Pope. *Disowning Slavery: Gradual Emancipation and 'Race' in New England 1780-1860.* Ithaca, NY: Cornell University Press, 1998.
Meltzer, Milton. *Slavery: A World History.* 2 vols. in 1. 1971. New York, NY: Da Capo Press, 1993 ed.
Meriwether, Elizabeth Avery. *Facts and Falsehoods Concerning the War on the South, 1861-1865.* (Originally written under the pseudonym "George Edmonds.") Memphis, TN: A. R. Taylor, 1904.
*Message of the President of the United States and Accompanying Documents to the Two Houses of Congress at the Commencement of the Third Session of the 40th Congress.* Washington, D.C.: Government Printing Office, 1868.
Metzger, Bruce M., and Michael D. Coogan (eds.). *The Oxford Companion to the Bible.* New York, NY: Oxford University Press, 1993.
Miller, Francis Trevelyan. *Portrait Life of Lincoln.* Springfield, MA: Patriot Publishing Co., 1910.
Miller, John Chester. *The Wolf By the Ears: Thomas Jefferson and Slavery.* 1977. Charlottesville, VA: University Press of Virginia, 1994 ed.
Miller, Marion Mills (ed.). *Great Debates in American History.* 14 vols. New York, NY: Current Literature, 1913.
Miller, Nathan. *Star-Spangled Men: America's Ten Worst Presidents.* New York, NY: Touchstone, 1998.
Min, Pyong Gap (ed.). *Encyclopedia of Racism in the United States.* 3 vols. Westport, CT: Greenwood Press, 2005.
Minor, Charles Landon Carter. *The Real Lincoln: From the Testimony of His Contemporaries.* Richmond, VA: Everett Waddey Co., 1904.
Mirabello, Mark. *Handbook for Rebels and Outlaws.* Oxford, UK: Mandrake of Oxford, 2009.
Mish, Frederick C. (ed.). *Webster's Ninth New Collegiate Dictionary.* 1984. Springfield, MA: Merriam-Webster.
Mitchell, Margaret. *Gone With the Wind.* 1936. New York, NY: Avon, 1973 ed.
Mitgang, Herbert (ed.). *Lincoln As They Saw Him.* 1956. New York, NY: Collier, 1962 ed.
Mode, Peter George. *Source Book and Bibliographical Guide for American Church History.* Menasha, WI: Collegiate Press, 1921.
Montefiore, Simon Sebag. *Stalin: The Court of the Red Star.* 2003. New York, NY: Vintage, 2004 ed.
Montgomery, David Henry. *The Student's American History.* 1897. Boston, MA: Ginn and Co., 1905 ed.
Moore, Frank (ed.). *The Rebellion Record: A Diary of American Events.* 12 vols. New York, NY: G. P. Putnam, 1861.
Moore, George Henry. *Notes on the History of Slavery in Massachusetts.* New York, NY: D. Appleton and Co., 1866.
Moorhead, James H. *American Apocalypse: Yankee Protestants and the Civil War, 1860-1869.* New Haven, CT: Yale University Press, 1971.
Morris, Benjamin Franklin (ed.). *The Life of Thomas Morris: Pioneer and Long a Legislator of Ohio, and U.S. Senator from 1833 to 1839.* Cincinnati, OH: Moore, Wilstach, Keys and Overend, 1856.

Morris, Thomas D. *Free Men All: The Personal Liberty Laws of the North, 1780-1861*. Baltimore, MD: John Hopkins University Press, 1974.

Morton, John Watson. *The Artillery of Nathan Bedford Forrest's Cavalry*. Nashville, TN: The M. E. Church, 1909.

Moses, John. *Illinois: Historical and Statistical, Comprising the Essential Facts of Its Planting and Growth as a Province, County, Territory, and State* (Vol. 2). Chicago, IL: Fergus Printing Co., 1892.

Mullen, Robert W. *Blacks in America's Wars: The Shift in Attitudes From the Revolutionary War to Vietnam*. 1973. New York, NY: Pathfinder, 1991 ed.

Munford, Beverly Bland. *Virginia's Attitude Toward Slavery and Secession*. 1909. Richmond, VA: L. H. Jenkins, 1914 ed.

Murphy, Jim. *A Savage Thunder: Antietam and the Bloody Road to Freedom*. New York, NY: Margaret K. McElderry, 2009.

Napolitano, Andrew P. *The Constitution in Exile: How the Federal Government has Seized Power by Rewriting the Supreme Law of the Land*. Nashville, TN: Nelson Current, 2006.

Neely, Mark E., Jr. *The Fate of Liberty: Abraham Lincoln and Civil Liberties*. New York, NY: Oxford University Press, 1991.

Neilson, William Allan (ed.). *Webster's Biographical Dictionary*. Springfield, MA: G. and C. Merriam Co., 1943.

Neufeldt, Victoria (ed.). *Webster's New World Dictionary of American English* (3rd college ed.). 1970. New York, NY: Prentice Hall, 1994 ed.

Nevins, Allan. *The Evening Post: A Century of Journalism*. New York, NY: Boni and Liveright, 1922.

Nicolay, John G., and John Hay (eds.). *Abraham Lincoln: A History*. 10 vols. New York, NY: The Century Co., 1890.

———. *Complete Works of Abraham Lincoln*. 12 vols. 1894. New York, NY: Francis D. Tandy Co., 1905 ed.

———. *Abraham Lincoln: Complete Works*. 12 vols. 1894. New York, NY: The Century Co., 1907 ed.

Nivola, Pietro S., and David H. Rosenbloom (eds.). *Classic Readings in American Politics*. New York, NY: St. Martin's Press, 1986.

Norwood, Thomas Manson. *A True Vindication of the South*. Savannah, GA: Citizens and Southern Bank, 1917.

Nye, Russel B. *William Lloyd Garrison and the Humanitarian Reformers*. Boston, MA: Little, Brown and Co., 1955.

Oates, Stephen B. *Abraham Lincoln: The Man Behind the Myths*. New York, NY: Meridian, 1984.

———. *The Approaching Fury: Voices of the Storm, 1820-1861*. New York, NY: Harper Perennial, 1998.

O'Brien, Cormac. *Secret Lives of the U.S. Presidents: What Your Teachers Never Told You About the Men of the White House*. Philadelphia, PA: Quirk, 2004.

———. *Secret Lives of the Civil War: What Your teachers Never Told You About the War Between the States*. Philadelphia, PA: Quirk, 2007.

Oglesby, Thaddeus K. *Some Truths of History: A Vindication of the South Against the Encyclopedia Britannica and Other Maligners*. Atlanta, GA: Byrd Printing, 1903.

Olmsted, Frederick Law. *A Journey in the Seaboard Slave States, With Remarks on Their Economy*. New York, NY: Dix and Edwards, 1856.

———. *A Journey Through Texas; or a Saddle-Trip on the Western Frontier*. New York, NY: Dix and Edwards, 1857.

———. *A Journey in the Back Country*. New York, NY: Mason Brothers, 1860.

———. *The Cotton Kingdom: A Traveler's Observations on Cotton and Slavery in the American Slave States*. 2 vols. London, UK: Sampson Low, Son, and Co., 1862.

Olson, Ted (ed.). *CrossRoads: A Southern Culture Annual*. Macon, GA: Mercer University Press, 2004.

ORA (full title: *The War of the Rebellion: A Compilation of the Official Records of the Union and Confederate Armies*. (Multiple volumes.) Washington, D.C.: Government Printing Office, 1880.

ORN (full title: *Official Records of the Union and Confederate Navies in the War of the Rebellion*). (Multiple volumes.) Washington, D.C.: Government Printing Office, 1894.

Owsley, Frank Lawrence. *King Cotton Diplomacy: Foreign Relations of the Confederate States of America*. 1931. Chicago, IL: University of Chicago Press, 1959 ed.

Page, Thomas Nelson. *Robert E. Lee: Man and Soldier*. New York, NY: Charles Scribner's Sons, 1911.

Palin, Sarah. *Going Rogue: An American Life*. New York, NY: HarperCollins, 2009.

Parker, Bowdoin S. (ed.). *What One Grand Army Post Has Accomplished: History of Edward W. Kinsley Post, No. 113*. Norwood, MA: Norwood Press, 1913.

Parry, Melanie (ed.). *Chambers Biographical Dictionary*. 1897. Edinburgh, Scotland: Chambers Harrap, 1998 ed.

Patrick, Rembert W. *Jefferson Davis and His Cabinet*. Baton Rouge, LA: Louisiana State University Press, 1944.

Paul, Ron. *The Revolution: A Manifesto*. New York, NY: Grand Central Publishing, 2008.

Pearson, Henry Greenleaf. *The Life of John A. Andrew, Governor of Massachusetts, 1861-1865*. 2 vols. Boston, MA: Houghton, Mifflin and Co., 1904.

Perkins, Henry C. *Northern Editorials on Secession*. 2 vols. D. Appleton and Co., 1942.

Perry, James M. *Touched With Fire: Five Presidents and the Civil War Battles That Made Them*. New York, NY: Public Affairs, 2003.

Perry, John C. *Myths and Realities of American Slavery: The True History of Slavery in America*. Shippenburg, PA: Burd Street Press, 2002.

Perry, Mark. *Lift Up Thy Voice: The Grimké Family's Journey From Slaveholders to Civil Rights Leaders*. New York, NY: Penguin, 2001.

Peter, Laurence J., and Raymond Hull  *The Peter Principle: Why Things Always Go Wrong.* New York, NY: William Morrow and Co., 1969.

Peterson, Merrill D. (ed.). *James Madison, A Biography in His Own Words.* (First published posthumously in 1840.) New York, NY: Harper and Row, 1974 ed.

——. (ed.). *Thomas Jefferson: Writings, Autobiography, A Summary View of the Rights of British America, Notes on the State of Virginia, Public Papers, Addresses, Messages and Replies, Miscellany, Letters.* New York, NY: Literary Classics, 1984.

Peterson, Paul R. *Quantrill of Missouri: The Making of a Guerilla Warrior, The Man, the Myth, the Soldier.* Nashville, TN: Cumberland House, 2003.

Phillips, Michael. *White Metropolis: Race, Ethnicity, and Religion in Dallas, 1841-2001.* Austin, TX: University of Texas Press, 2006.

Phillips, Robert S. (ed.). *Funk and Wagnalls New Encyclopedia.* 1971. New York, NY: Funk and Wagnalls, 1979 ed.

Phillips, Ulrich Bonnell. *American Negro Slavery: A Survey of the Supply, Employment and Control of Negro Labor as Determined by the Plantation Régime.* New York, NY: D. Appleton and Co., 1929.

Phillips, Wendell. *Speeches, Letters, and Lectures.* Boston, MA: Lee and Shepard, 1894.

Piatt, Donn. *Memories of the Men Who Saved the Union.* New York, NY: Belford, Clarke, and Co., 1887.

Piatt, Donn, and Henry V. Boynton. *General George H. Thomas: A Critical Biography.* Cincinnati, OH: Robert Clarke and Co., 1893.

Pickett, George E. *The Heart of a Soldier: As Revealed in the Intimate Letters of General George E. Pickett, CSA.* 1908. New York, NY: Seth Moyle, 1913 ed.

Pickett, William Passmore. *The Negro Problem: Abraham Lincoln's Solution.* New York, NY: G. P. Putnam's Sons, 1909.

Pike, James Shepherd. *The Prostrate State: South Carolina Under Negro Government.* New York, NY: D. Appleton and Co., 1874.

Pollard, Edward A. *Southern History of the War.* 2 vols. in 1. New York, NY: Charles B. Richardson, 1866.

——. *The Lost Cause.* 1867. Chicago, IL: E. B. Treat, 1890 ed.

——. *The Lost Cause Regained.* New York, NY: G. W. Carlton and Co., 1868.

——. *Life of Jefferson Davis, With a Secret History of the Southern Confederacy, Gathered "Behind the Scenes in Richmond."* Philadelphia, PA: National Publishing Co., 1869.

Post, Lydia Minturn (ed.). *Soldiers' Letters, From Camp, Battlefield and Prison.* New York, NY: Bunce and Huntington, 1865.

Potter, David M. *The Impending Crisis: 1848-1861.* New York, NY: Harper and Row, 1976.

Powell, Edward Payson. *Nullification and Secession in the United States: A History of the Six Attempts During the First Century of the Republic.* New York, NY: G. P. Putnam's Sons, 1897.

Powell, William S. *North Carolina: A History.* 1977. Chapel Hill, NC: University of North Carolina Press, 1988 ed.

Pritchard, Russ A., Jr. *Civil War Weapons and Equipment.* Guilford, CT: Lyons Press, 2003.

Putnam, Samuel Porter. *400 Years of Free Thought.* New York, NY: Truth Seeker Co., 1894.

Quarles, Benjamin. *The Negro in the Civil War.* 1953. Cambridge, MA: Da Capo Press, 1988 ed.

Quintero, José Agustín, Ambrosio José Gonzales, and Loreta Janeta Velazquez (Phillip Thomas Tucker, ed.). *Cubans in the Confederacy.* Jefferson, NC: McFarland and Co., 2002.

Rable, George C. *The Confederate Republic: A Revolution Against Politics.* Chapel Hill, NC: University of North Carolina Press, 1994.

Ramage, James A. *Rebel Raider: The Life of General John Hunt Morgan.* Lexington, KY: University Press of Kentucky, 1986.

Randall, James Garfield. *Lincoln: The Liberal Statesman.* New York, NY: Dodd, Mead and Co., 1947.

Randall, James Garfield, and Richard N. Current. *Lincoln the President: Last Full Measure.* 1955. Urbana, IL: University of Illinois Press, 2000 ed.

Randolph, Thomas Jefferson (ed.). *Memoir, Correspondence, and Miscellanies, from the Papers of Thomas Jefferson.* 4 vols. Charlottesville, VA: F. Carr and Co., 1829.

Ransom, Roger L. *Conflict and Compromise: The Political Economy of Slavery, Emancipation, and the American Civil War.* Cambridge, UK: Cambridge University Press, 1989.

Rawle, William. *A View of the Constitution of the United States of America.* Philadelphia, PA: Philip H. Nicklin, 1829.

Rayner, B. L. *Sketches of the Life, Writings, and Opinions of Thomas Jefferson.* New York, NY: Alfred Francis and William Boardman, 1832.

Reid, Richard M. *Freedom for Themselves: North Carolina's Black Soldiers in the Era of the Civil War.* Chapel Hill, NC: University of North Carolina Press, 2008.

Remsburg, John B. *Abraham Lincoln: Was He a Christian?* New York, NY: The Truth Seeker Co., 1893.

*Reports of Committees of the Senate of the United States (for the Thirty-eighth Congress).* Washington, D.C.: Government Printing Office, 1864.

*Report of the Joint Committee on Reconstruction (at the First Session, Thirty-ninth Congress).* Washington, D.C.: Government Printing Office, 1866.

*Reports of Committees of the Senate of the United States (for the Second Session of the Forty-second Congress).* Washington, D.C.: Government Printing Office, 1872.

*Report of the Joint Select Committee to Inquire into the Condition of Affairs in the Late Insurrectionary States.* Washington, D.C.: Government Printing Office, 1872.

Reuter, Edward Byron. *The Mulatto in the United States.* Boston, MA: Gorham Press, 1918.

Rhodes, James Ford. *History of the United States from the Compromise of 1850 to the Final Restoration of Home Rule at the South in 1877.* 7 vols. 1895. New York, NY: Macmillan Co., 1907 ed.

Rice, Allen Thorndike. *Reminiscences of Abraham Lincoln, by Distinguished Men of His Time.* 1888. New York, NY: North American Review, 1909 ed.

Richardson, James Daniel (ed.). *A Compilation of the Messages and Papers of the Confederacy.* 2 vols. Nashville, TN: United States Publishing Co., 1905.

Riley, Franklin Lafayette (ed.). *Publications of the Mississippi Historical Society.* Oxford, MS: The Mississippi Historical Society, 1902.

———. *General Robert E. Lee After Appomattox.* New York, NY: MacMillan Co., 1922.

Riley, Russell Lowell. *The Presidency and the Politics of Racial Inequality.* New York, NY: Columbia University Press, 1999.

Rives, John (ed.). *Abridgement of the Debates of Congress: From 1789 to 1856* (Vol. 13). New York, NY: D. Appleton and Co., 1860.

Roberts, Paul M. *United States History: Review Text.* 1966. New York, NY: Amsco School Publications, Inc., 1970 ed.

Roberts, R. Philip. *Mormonism Unmasked: Confronting the Contradictions Between Mormon Beliefs and True Christianity.* Nashville, TN: Broadman and Holman, 1998.

Robertson, James I., Jr. *Soldiers Blue and Gray.* 1988. Columbia, SC: University of South Carolina Press, 1998 ed.

Rockwell, Llewellyn H., Jr. "Genesis of the Civil War." Website: www.lewrockwell.com/rockwell/civilwar.html.

Rogers, Joel Augustus. *The Ku Klux Spirit.* 1923. Baltimore, MD: Black Classic Press, 1980 ed.

———. *Africa's Gift to America: The Afro-American in the Making and Saving of the United States.* St. Petersburg, FL: Helga M. Rogers, 1961.

Rosen, Robert N. *The Jewish Confederates.* Columbia, SC: University of South Carolina Press, 2000.

Rosenbaum, Robert A. (ed). *The New American Desk Encyclopedia.* 1977. New York, NY: Signet, 1989 ed.

Rosenbaum, Robert A., and Douglas Brinkley (eds.). *The Penguin Encyclopedia of American History.* New York, NY: Viking, 2003.

Rothschild, Alonzo. *"Honest Abe": A Study in Integrity Based on the Early Life of Abraham Lincoln.* Boston, MA: Houghton Mifflin Co., 1917.

Rouse, Adelaide Louise (ed.). *National Documents: State Papers So Arranged as to Illustrate the Growth of Our Country From 1606 to the Present Day.* New York, NY: Unit Book Publishing Co., 1906.

Rowland, Dunbar (ed.). *Jefferson Davis, Constitutionalist: His Letters, Papers, and Speeches.* 10 vols. Jackson, MS: Mississippi Department of Archives and History, 1923.

Rozwenc, Edwin Charles (ed.). *The Causes of the American Civil War.* 1961. Lexington, MA: D. C. Heath and Co., 1972 ed.

Rubenzer, Steven J., and Thomas R. Faschingbauer. *Personality, Character, and Leadership in the White House: Psychologists Assess the Presidents.* Dulles, VA: Brassey's, 2004.

Ruffin, Edmund. *The Diary of Edmund Ruffin: Toward Independence: October 1856-April 1861.* Baton Rouge, LA: Louisiana State University Press, 1972.

Rutherford, Mildred Lewis. *Four Addresses.* Birmingham, AL: The Mildred Rutherford Historical Circle, 1916.

———. *A True Estimate of Abraham Lincoln and Vindication of the South.* N.p., n.d.

———. *Truths of History: A Historical Perspective of the Civil War From the Southern Viewpoint.* Confederate Reprint Co., 1920.

———. *The South Must Have Her Rightful Place In History.* Athens, GA, 1923.

Rutland, Robert Allen. *The Birth of the Bill of Rights, 1776-1791.* 1955. Boston, MA: Northeastern University Press, 1991 ed.

Sachsman, David B., S. Kittrell Rushing, and Roy Morris, Jr. (eds.). *Words at War: The Civil War and American Journalism.* West Lafayette, IN: Purdue University Press, 2008.

Salley, Alexander Samuel, Jr. *South Carolina Troops in Confederate Service.* 2 vols. Columbia, SC: R. L. Bryan, 1913 and 1914.

Salzberger, Ronald P., and Mary C. Turck (eds.). *Reparations For Slavery: A Reader.* Lanham, MD: Rowman and Littlefield, 2004.

Samuel, Bunford. *Secession and Constitutional Liberty.* 2 vols. New York, NY: Neale Publishing, 1920.

Sancho, Ignatius. *Letters of the Late Ignatius Sancho, an African.* 1782. New York, NY: Cosimo Classics, 2005 ed.

Sandburg, Carl. *Abraham Lincoln: The War Years.* 4 vols. New York, NY: Harcourt, Brace and World, 1939.

———. *Storm Over the Land: A Profile of the Civil War.* 1939. Old Saybrook, CT: Konecky and Konecky, 1942 ed.

Sargent, F. W. *England, the United States, and the Southern Confederacy.* London, UK: Sampson Low, Son, and Co., 1863.

Scharf, John Thomas. *History of the Confederate Navy, From Its Organization to the Surrender of Its Last Vessel.* Albany, NY: Joseph McDonough, 1894.

Schauffler, Robert Haven. *Our American Holidays: Lincoln's Birthday - A Comprehensive View of Lincoln as Given in the Most Noteworthy Essays, Orations and Poems, in Fiction and in Lincoln's Own Writings.* 1909. New York, NY: Moffat, Yard and Co., 1916 ed.

Schlüter, Herman. *Lincoln, Labor and Slavery: A Chapter from the Social History of America.* New York, NY: Socialist Literature Co., 1913.
Schurz, Carl. *Life of Henry Clay.* 2 vols. 1887. Boston, MA: Houghton, Mifflin and Co., 1899 ed.
Schwartz, Barry. *Abraham Lincoln and the Forge of National Memory.* Chicago, IL: University of Chicago Press, 2000.
Scott, Emmett J., and Lyman Beecher Stowe. *Booker T. Washington: Builder of a Civilization.* Garden City, NY: Doubleday, Page, and Co., 1916.
Scott, James Brown. *James Madison's Notes of Debates in the Federal Convention of 1787, and Their Relation to a More Perfect Society of Nations.* New York, NY: Oxford University Press, 1918.
Scruggs, *The Un-Civil War: Truths Your Teacher Never Told You.* Hendersonville, NC: Tribune Papers, 2007.
Seabrook, Lochlainn. *Britannia Rules: Goddess-Worship in Ancient Anglo-Celtic Society - An Academic Look at the United Kingdom's Matricentric Spiritual Past.* 1999. Franklin, TN: Sea Raven Press, 2007 ed.
——. *The Caudills: An Etymological, Ethnological, and Genealogical Study - Exploring the Name and National Origins of a European-American Family.* 2003. Franklin, TN: Sea Raven Press, 2010 ed.
——. *Carnton Plantation Ghost Stories: True Tales of the Unexplained From Tennessee's Most Haunted Civil War House!* 2005. Franklin, TN: Sea Raven Press, 2010 ed.
——. *Nathan Bedford Forrest: Southern Hero, American Patriot: Honoring a Confederate Hero and the Old South.* 2007. Franklin, TN: Sea Raven Press, 2010 ed.
——. *The McGavocks of Carnton Plantation: A Southern History - Celebrating One of Dixie's Most Noble Confederate Families and Their Tennessee Home.* 2008. Franklin, TN: Sea Raven Press, 2011 ed.
——. *Abraham Lincoln: The Southern View - Demythologizing America's Sixteenth President.* Franklin, TN: Sea Raven Press, 2009.
——. *A Rebel Born: A Defense of Nathan Bedford Forrest, Confederate General, American Legend.* Franklin, TN: Sea Raven Press, 2011 ed.
——. *Lincolnology: The Real Abraham Lincoln Revealed In His Own Words.* Franklin, TN: Sea Raven Press, 2011.
——. *The Quotable Jefferson Davis: Selections From the Writings and Speeches of the Confederacy's First President.* Franklin, TN: Sea Raven Press, 2011.
——. *The Quotable Robert E. Lee: Selections From the Writings and Speeches of the Confederacy's Most Beloved Civil War General.* Franklin, TN: Sea Raven Press, 2011.
——. *The Unquotable Abraham Lincoln: The President's Quotes They Don't Want You To Know!* Franklin, TN: Sea Raven Press, 2011.
——. *The Quotable Nathan Bedford Forrest: Selections From the Writings and Speeches of the Confederacy's Most Brilliant Cavalryman.* Franklin, TN: Sea Raven Press, 2011.
——. *The Old Rebel: Robert E. Lee As He Was Seen By His Contemporaries.* Franklin, TN: Sea Raven Press, 2012.
——. *Give 'Em Hell Boys! The Complete Military Correspondence of Nathan Bedford Forrest.* Franklin, TN: Sea Raven Press, 2012.
——. *The Constitution of the Confederate States of America: Explained.* Franklin, TN: Sea Raven Press, 2012.
——. *Encyclopedia of the Battle of Franklin: A Comprehensive Guide to the Conflict That Changed the Civil War.* Franklin, TN: Sea Raven Press, 2012.
Segal, Charles M. (ed.). *Conversations with Lincoln.* 1961. New Brunswick, NJ: Transaction, 2002 ed.
Segars, J. H., and Charles Kelly Barrow. *Black Southerners in Confederate Armies: A Collection of Historical Accounts.* Atlanta, GA: Southern Lion Books, 2001.
Seligmann, Herbert J. *The Negro Faces America.* New York, NY: Harper and Brothers, 1920.
Semmes, Admiral Ralph. *Service Afloat, or the Remarkable Career of the Confederate Cruisers Sumter and Alabama During the War Between the States.* London, UK: Sampson Low, Marston, Searle, and Rivington, 1887.
Sewell, Richard H. *John P. Hale and the Politics of Abolition.* Cambridge, MA: Harvard University Press, 1965.
Shenkman, Richard, and Kurt Edward Reiger. *One-Night Stands with American History: Odd, Amusing, and Little-Known Incidents.* 1980. New York, NY: Perennial, 2003 ed.
Sherman, William Tecumseh. *Memoirs of General William T. Sherman.* 2 vols. 1875. New York, NY: D. Appleton and Co., 1891 ed.
Shillington, Kevin. *History of Africa.* 1989. New York, NY: St. Martin's Press, 1994 ed.
Shorto, Russell. *Thomas Jefferson and the American Ideal.* Hauppauge, NY: Barron's, 1987.
Shotwell, Walter G. *Life of Charles Sumner.* New York, NY: Thomas Y. Crowell and Co., 1910.
Siepel, Kevin H. *Rebel: The Life and Times of John Singleton Mosby.* New York, NY: St. Martin's Press, 1983.
Simmons, Henry E. *A Concise Encyclopedia of the Civil War.* New York, NY: Bonanza Books, 1965.
Simpson, Lewis P. (ed.). *I'll Take My Stand: The South and the Agrarian Tradition.* 1930. Baton Rouge, LA: University of Louisiana Press, 1977 ed.
Slotkin, Richard. *No Quarter: The Battle of the Crater, 1864.* New York, NY: Random House, 2009.
Smelser, Marshall. *American Colonial and Revolutionary History.* 1950. New York, NY: Barnes and Noble, 1966 ed.
——. *The Democratic Republic, 1801-1815.* New York, NY: Harper and Row, 1968.
Smith, Hedrick. *Reagan: The Man, The President.* Oxford, UK: Pergamon Press, 1980.
Smith, John David (ed.). *Black Soldiers in Blue: African American Troops in the Civil War Era.* Chapel Hill, NC: University of North Carolina Press, 2002.

Smith, Joseph. *The Pearl of Great Price*. Salt Lake City, UT: George Q. Cannon and Sons, 1891.

Smith, Mark M. (ed.). *The Old South*. Oxford, UK: Blackwell Publishers, 2001.

Smith, Page. *Trial by Fire: A People's History of the Civil War and Reconstruction*. New York, NY: McGraw-Hill, 1982.

Smith, Philip D., Jr. *Tartan for Me!: Suggested Tartan for 13,695 Scottish, Scotch-Irish, Irish and North American Names with Lists of Clan, Family, and District Tartans*. Bruceton, WV: Scotpress, 1990.

Smucker, Samuel M. *The Life and Times of Thomas Jefferson*. Philadelphia, PA: J. W. Bradley, 1859.

Sobel, Robert (ed.). *Biographical Directory of the United States Executive Branch, 1774-1898*. Westport, CT: Greenwood Press, 1990.

Spaeth, Harold J., and Edward Conrad Smith. *The Constitution of the United States*. 1936. New York, NY: HarperCollins, 1991 ed.

Spence, James. *On the Recognition of the Southern Confederation*. Ithaca, NY: Cornell University Library, 1862.

Spooner, Lysander. *No Treason* (only Numbers 1, 2, and 6 were published). Boston, MA: Lysander Spooner, 1867-1870.

Stampp, Kenneth M. *The Peculiar Institution: Slavery in the Antebellum South*. New York, NY: Vintage, 1956.

Stanford, Peter Thomas. *The Tragedy of the Negro in America*. Boston, MA: published by author, 1898.

Staudenraus, P. J. *The African Colonization Movement, 1816-1865*. New York, NY: Columbia University Press, 1961.

Stebbins, Rufus Phineas. *An Historical Address Delivered At the Centennial Celebration of the Incorporation of the Town of Wilbraham, June 15, 1863*. Boston, MA: George C. Rand and Avery, 1864.

Stedman, Edmund Clarence, and Ellen Mackay Hutchinson (eds.). *A Library of American Literature From the Earliest Settlement to the Present Time*. 10 vols. New York, NY: Charles L. Webster and Co., 1888.

Steele, Shelby. *White Guilt: How Blacks and Whites Together Destroyed the Promise of the Civil Rights Era*. New York, NY: Harper Perennial, 2007.

Stein, Ben, and Phil DeMuth. *How To Ruin the United States of America*. Carlsbad, CA: New Beginnings Press, 2008.

Steiner, Bernard. *The History of Slavery in Connecticut*. Baltimore, MD: Johns Hopkins University Press, 1893.

Steiner, Lewis Henry. *Report of Lewis H. Steiner: Inspector of the Sanitary Commission, Containing a Diary Kept During the Rebel Occupation of Frederick, MD, September, 1862*. New York, NY: Anson D. F. Randolph, 1862.

Stephens, Alexander H. *A Constitutional View of the Late War Between the States; Its Causes, Character, Conduct and Results*. 2 vols. Philadelphia, PA: National Publishing, Co., 1870.

——. *Recollections of Alexander H. Stephens: His Diary Kept When a Prisoner at Fort Warren, Boston Harbour, 1865*. New York, NY: Doubleday, Page, and Co., 1910.

Stephenson, Nathaniel Wright. *Lincoln: An Account of His Personal Life, Especially of Its Springs of Action as Revealed and Deepened by the Ordeal of War*. Indianapolis, IN: Bobbs-Merrill, 1922.

Sterling, Dorothy (ed.). *Speak Out in Thunder Tones: Letters and Other Writings by Black Northerners, 1787-1865*. 1973. Cambridge, MA: Da Capo, 1998 ed.

Stern, Philip Van Doren (ed.). *The Life and Writings of Abraham Lincoln*. 1940. New York, NY: Modern Library, 2000 ed.

Stiles, Robert. *Four Years Under Marse Robert*. New York, NY: Neal Publishing Co., 1910.

Stonebraker, J. Clarence. *The Unwritten South: Cause, Progress and Results of the Civil War - Relics of Hidden Truth After Forty Years*. Seventh ed., n.p., 1908.

Stovall, Pleasant A. *Robert Toombs: Statesman, Speaker, Soldier, Sage*. New York, NY: Cassell Publishing, 1892.

Strain, John Paul. *Witness to the Civil War: The Art of John Paul Strain*. Philadelphia, PA: Courage, 2002.

Strode, Hudson. *Jefferson Davis: American Patriot*. 3 vols. New York, NY: Harcourt, Brace and World, 1955, 1959, 1964.

Sturge, Joseph. *A Visit to the United States in 1841*. London, UK: Hamilton, Adams, and Co., 1842.

Sumner, Charles. *The Crime Against Kansas: The Apologies for the Crime - The True Remedy*. Boston, MA: John P. Jewett, 1856.

Swint, Henry L. (ed.) *Dear Ones at Home: Letters From Contraband Camps*. Nashville, TN: Vanderbilt University Press, 1966.

Sword, Wiley. *The Confederacy's Last Hurrah: Spring Hill, Franklin, and Nashville*. New York, NY: HarperCollins, 1992.

——. *Southern Invincibility: A History of the Confederate Heart*. New York, NY: St. Martin's Press, 1999.

Tarbell, Ida Minerva. *The Life of Abraham Lincoln*. 4 vols. New York, NY: Lincoln History Society, 1895-1900.

Tatalovich, Raymond, and Byron W. Daynes. *Presidential Power in the United States*. Monterey, CA: Brooks/Cole, 1984.

Taylor, Richard. *Destruction and Reconstruction: Personal Experiences of the Late War in the United States*. New York, NY: D. Appleton, 1879.

Taylor, Susie King. *Reminiscences of My Life in Camp With the 33rd United States Colored Troops Late 1st S. C. Volunteers*. Boston, MA: Susie King Taylor, 1902.

Taylor, Walter Herron. *General Lee: His Campaigns in Virginia, 1861-1865, With Personal Reminiscences*. Norfolk, VA: Nusbaum Book and News Co., 1906.

Tenney, William Jewett. *The Military and Naval History of the Rebellion in the United States*. New York, NY: D. Appleton and Co., 1865.

Terkel, Studs. *Hard Times: An Oral History of the Great Depression*. New York, NY: Avon, 1970.

*Testimony Taken By the Joint Select Committee to Inquire Into the Condition of Affairs in the Late Insurrectionary States*. 13 vols. Washington, D.C.: Government Printing Office, 1872.

Thackeray, William Makepeace. *Roundabout Papers*. Boston, MA: Estes and Lauriat, 1883.

*The American Annual Cyclopedia and Register of Important Events of the Year 1861*. New York, NY: D. Appleton and Co., 1868.

*The American Annual Cyclopedia and Register of Important Events of the Year 1862*. New York, NY: D. Appleton and Co., 1869.

*The Congressional Globe, Containing Sketches of the Debates and Proceedings of the First Session of the Twenty-Eighth Congress* (Vol. 13). Washington, D.C.: The Globe, 1844.

*The Great Issue to be Decided in November Next: Shall the Constitution and the Union Stand or Fall, Shall Sectionalism Triumph?* Washington, D.C.: National Democratic Executive Committee, 1860.

*The Oxford English Dictionary*. Compact edition, 2 vols. 1928. Oxford, UK: Oxford University Press, 1979 ed.

*The Quarterly Review* (Vol. 111). London, UK: John Murray, 1862.

Thomas, Emory M. *The Confederate Nation: 1861-1865*. New York, NY: Harper and Row, 1979.

Thomas, Gabriel. *An Account of Pennsylvania and West New Jersey*. 1698. Cleveland, OH: Burrows Brothers Co., 1903 ed.

Thompson, Frank Charles (ed.). *The Thompson Chain Reference Bible* (King James Version). 1908. Indianapolis, IN: B. B. Kirkbride Bible Co., 1964 ed.

Thompson, Neal. *Driving With the Devil: Southern Moonshine, Detroit Wheels, and the Birth of NASCAR*. Three Rivers, MI: Three Rivers Press, 2006.

Thompson, Robert Means, and Richard Wainwright (eds.). *Confidential Correspondence of Gustavus Vasa Fox, Assistant Secretary of the Navy, 1861-1865*. 2 vols. 1918. New York, NY: Naval History Society, 1920 ed.

Thorndike, Rachel Sherman (ed.). *The Sherman Letters*. New York, NY: Charles Scribner's Sons, 1894.

Thornton, Brian. *101 Things You Didn't Know About Lincoln: Loves and Losses, Political Power Plays, White House Hauntings*. Avon, MA: Adams Media, 2006.

Thornton, Gordon. *The Southern Nation: The New Rise of the Old South*. Gretna, LA: Pelican Publishing Co., 2000.

Thornton, John. *Africa and Africans in the Making of the Atlantic World, 1400-1800*. 1992. Cambridge, UK: Cambridge University Press, 1999 ed.

Thornton, Mark, and Robert B. Ekelund, Jr. *Tariffs, Blockades, and Inflation: The Economics of the Civil War*. Wilmington, DE: Scholarly Resources, 2004.

Tilley, John Shipley. *Lincoln Takes Command*. 1941. Nashville, TN: Bill Coats Limited, 1991 ed.

——. *Facts the Historians Leave Out: A Confederate Primer*. 1951. Nashville, TN: Bill Coats Limited, 1999 ed.

Tocqueville, Alexis de. *Democracy in America*. 2 vols. 1836. New York, NY: D. Appleton and Co., 1904 ed.

Tourgee, Albion W. *A Fool's Errand By One of the Fools*. London, UK: George Routledge and Sons, 1883.

Traupman, John C. *The New College Latin and English Dictionary*. 1966. New York, NY: Bantam, 1988 ed.

Trumbull, Lyman. *Speech of Honorable Lyman Trumbull, of Illinois, at a Mass Meeting in Chicago, August 7, 1858*. Washington, D.C.: Buell and Blanchard, 1858.

Truth, Sojourner. *Sojourner Truth's Narrative and Book of Life*. 1850. Battle Creek, MI: Sojourner Truth, 1881 ed.

Tucker, St. George. *On the State of Slavery in Virginia, in View of the Constitution of the United States, With Selected Writings*. Indianapolis, IN: Liberty Fund, 1999.

Turner, Edward Raymond. *The Negro in Pennsylvania, Slavery, Servitude, Freedom, 1639-1861*. Washington, D.C.: American Historical Association, 1911.

Tyler, Lyon Gardiner. *The Letters and Times of the Tylers*. 3 vols. Williamsburg, VA: N.P., 1896.

——. *Propaganda in History*. Richmond, VA: Richmond Press, 1920.

——. *The Gray Book: A Confederate Catechism*. Columbia, TN: Gray Book Committee, SCV, 1935.

Upshur, Abel Parker. *A Brief Enquiry Into the True Nature and Character of Our Federal Government*. Philadelphia, PA: John Campbell, 1863.

Vallandigham, Clement Laird. *Speeches, Arguments, Addresses, and Letters of Clement L. Vallandigham*. New York, NY: J. Walter and Co., 1864.

Vanauken, Sheldon. *The Glittering Illusion: English Sympathy for the Southern Confederacy*. Washington, D.C.: Regnery, 1989.

Ver Steeg, Clarence Lester, and Richard Hofstadter. *A People and a Nation*. New York, NY: Harper and Row, 1977.

Villard, Henry. *Memoirs of Henry Villard, Journalist and Financier, 1835-1900*. 2 vols. Boston, MA: Houghton, Mifflin and Co., 1904.

Voegeli, Victor Jacque. *Free But Not Equal: The Midwest and the Negro During the Civil War*. Chicago, IL: University of Chicago Press, 1967.

Wade, Wyn Craig. *The Fiery Cross: The Ku Klux Klan in America*. 1987. New York, NY: Touchstone, 1988 ed.

Walker, Barbara G. *The Woman's Encyclopedia of Myths and Secrets*. New York, NY: Harper and Row, 1983.

Walker, Gary C. *A General History of the Civil War: The Southern Point of View*. 2004. Gretna, LA: Pelican Publishing, 2008 ed.

Wallcut, R. F. (pub.). *Southern Hatred of the American Government, the People of the North, and Free Institutions*. Boston, MA: R. F. Wallcut, 1862.

Wallechinsky, David, Irving Wallace, and Amy Wallace. *The People's Almanac Presents The Book of Lists*. New York, NY: Morrow, 1977.

Walsh, George. *"Those Damn Horse Soldiers": True Tales of the Civil War Cavalry*. New York, NY: Forge, 2006.

Ward, John William. *Andrew Jackson: Symbol for an Age*. 1953. Oxford, UK: Oxford University Press, 1973 ed.

Waring, George Edward, Jr. *Whip and Spur*. New York, NY: Doubleday and McClure, 1897.

Warner, Ezra J. *Generals in Gray: Lives of the Confederate Commanders*. 1959. Baton Rouge, LA: Louisiana State University Press, 1989 ed.

——. *Generals in Blue: Lives of the Union Commanders*. 1964. Baton Rouge, LA: Louisiana State University Press, 2006 ed.

Warren, Robert Penn. *Who Speaks for the Negro?* New York, NY: Random House, 1965.

Washington, Booker T. *Up From Slavery: An Autobiography*. 1901. Garden City, NY: Doubleday, Page and Co., 1919 ed.

Washington, Henry Augustine. *The Writings of Thomas Jefferson*. 9 vols. New York, NY: H. W. Derby, 1861.

Watkins, Samuel Rush. *"Company Aytch," Maury Grays, First Tennessee Regiment; or, A Side Show of the Big Show*. 1882. Chattanooga, TN: Times Printing Co., 1900 ed.

Watson, Harry L. *Andrew Jackson vs. Henry Clay: Democracy and Development in Antebellum America*. New York, NY: St. Martin's Press, 1998.

Watts, Peter. *A Dictionary of the Old West*. 1977. New York, NY: Promontory Press, 1987 ed.

Waugh, John C. *Surviving the Confederacy: Rebellion, Ruin, and Recovery - Roger and Sara Pryor During the Civil War*. New York, NY: Harcourt, 2002.

Weintraub, Max. *The Blue Book of American History*. New York, NY: Regents Publishing Co., 1960.

Welles, Gideon. *Diary of Gideon Welles, Secretary of the Navy Under Lincoln and Johnson* (Vol. 1). Boston, MA: Houghton Mifflin, 1911.

White, Charles Langdon, Edwin Jay Foscue, and Tom Lee McKnight. *Regional Geography of Anglo-America*. 1943. Englewood Cliffs, NJ: Prentice-Hall, 1985 ed.

White, Henry Alexander. *Robert E. Lee and the Southern Confederacy, 1807-1870*. 1897. New York, NY: G. P. Putnam's Sons, 1900 ed.

White, Reginald Cedric. *A. Lincoln: A Biography*. New York, NY: Random House, 2009.

Whitman, Walt. *Leaves of Grass*. 1855. New York, NY: Modern Library, 1921 ed.

——. *Complete Prose Works*. Boston, MA: Small, Maynard, and Co., 1901.

Wilbur, Henry Watson. *President Lincoln's Attitude Towards Slavery and Emancipation: With a Review of Events Before and Since the Civil War*. Philadelphia, PA: W. H. Jenkins, 1914.

Wilder, Craig Steven. *A Covenant With Color: Race and Social Power in Brooklyn*. New York, NY: Columbia University Press, 2000.

Wiley, Bell Irvin. *Southern Negroes: 1861-1865*. 1938. New Haven, CT: Yale University Press, 1969 ed.

——. *The Life of Johnny Reb: The Common Soldier of the Confederacy*. 1943. Baton Rouge, LA: Louisiana State University Press, 1978 ed.

——. *The Life of Billy Yank: The Common Soldier of the Union*. 1952. Baton Rouge, LA: Louisiana State University Press, 2001 ed.

Wilkens, J. Steven. *America: The First 350 Years*. Monroe, LA: Covenant Publications, 1998.

Williams, Charles Richard. *The Life of Rutherford Birchard Hayes, Nineteenth President of the United States*. 2 vols. Boston, MA: Houghton Mifflin Co., 1914.

Williams, George Washington. *History of the Negro Race in America: From 1619 to 1880, Negroes as Slaves, as Soldiers, and as Citizens*. New York, NY: G. P. Putnam's Sons, 1885.

——. *A History of the Negro Troops in the War of the Rebellion 1861-1865*. New York, NY: Harper and Brothers, 1888.

Williams, James. *The South Vindicated*. London, UK: Longman, Green, Longman, Roberts, and Green, 1862.

Williams, William H. *Slavery and Freedom in Delaware, 1639-1865*. Wilmington, DE: Scholarly Resources, 1996.

Wills, Brian Steel. *The Confederacy's Greatest Cavalryman: Nathan Bedford Forrest*. Lawrence, KS: University Press of Kansas, 1992.

Wilson, Charles Reagan, and William Ferris. *Encyclopedia of Southern Culture* (Vol. 1). New York, NY: Anchor, 1989.

Wilson, Clyde N. *Why the South Will Survive: Fifteen Southerners Look at Their Region a Half Century After I'll Take My Stand*. Athens, GA: University of Georgia Press, 1981.

——. *A Defender of Southern Conservatism: M.E. Bradford and His Achievements*. Columbia, MO: University of Missouri Press, 1999.

——. *From Union to Empire: Essays in the Jeffersonian Tradition*. Columbia, SC: The Foundation for American Education, 2003.

——. *Defending Dixie: Essays in Southern History and Culture*. Columbia, SC: The Foundation for American Education, 2005.

Wilson, Henry. *History of the Rise and Fall of the Slave Power in America*. 3 vols. Boston, MA: James R. Osgood and Co., 1877.

Wilson, Joseph Thomas. *The Black Phalanx: A History of the Negro Soldiers of the United States in the Wars of 1775-1812, 1861-'65*. Hartford, CT: American Publishing Co., 1890.

Wilson, Woodrow. *Division and Reunion: 1829-1889*. 1893. New York, NY: Longmans, Green, and Co., 1908 ed.

——. *A History of the American People*. 5 vols. 1902. New York, NY: Harper and Brothers, 1918 ed.

Wood, W. J. *Civil War Generalship: The Art of Command*. 1997. New York, NY: Da Capo Press, 2000 ed.

Woodard, Komozi. *A Nation Within a Nation: Amiri Baraka (LeRoi Jones) and Black Power Politics*. Chapel Hill, NC: University of North Carolina Press, 1999.

Woods, Thomas E., Jr. *The Politically Incorrect Guide to American History*. Washington, D.C.: Regnery, 2004.

Woodson, Carter G. (ed.). *The Journal of Negro History* (Vol. 4). Lancaster, PA: Association for the Study of Negro Life and History, 1919.

Woodward, William E. *Meet General Grant*. 1928. New York, NY: Liveright Publishing, 1946 ed.

Woodworth, Steven E. *Jefferson Davis and His Generals: The Failure of Confederate Command in the West*. Lawrence, KS: University Press of Kansas, 1990.

Wright, John D. *The Language of the Civil War*. Westport, CT: Oryx, 2001.

Wyeth, John Allan. *Life of General Nathan Bedford Forrest*. 1899. New York, NY: Harper and Brothers, 1908 ed.

Zaehner, R. C. (ed.) *Encyclopedia of the World's Religions*. 1959. New York, NY: Barnes and Noble, 1997 ed.

Zinn, Howard. *A People's History of the United States: 1492-Present*. 1980. New York, NY: HarperCollins, 1995.

# INDEX

# MEET THE AUTHOR

L OCHLAINN SEABROOK, winner of the Jefferson Davis Historical Gold Medal for his "masterpiece," *A Rebel Born: A Defense of Nathan Bedford Forrest,* is an unreconstructed Southern historian, award-winning author, Forrest scholar, and traditional Southern Agrarian of Scottish, English, Irish, Welsh, German, and Italian extraction. An encyclopedist, lexicographer, musician, artist, graphic designer, genealogist, and photographer, as well as an award-winning poet, songwriter, and screenwriter, he has a thirty year background in historical nonfiction writing and is a member of the Sons of Confederate Veterans, the Civil War Trust, and the Grange.

(Illustration © Tracy Latham)

Due to similarities in their writing styles, ideas, and literary works, Seabrook is referred to as the "American ROBERT GRAVES," after his cousin, the prolific English writer, historian, mythographer, poet, and author of the classic tomes *The White Goddess* and *The Greek Myths.*

The grandson of an Appalachian coal-mining family, Seabrook is a seventh-generation Kentuckian, co-chair of the Jent/Gent Family Committee (Kentucky), founder and director of the Blakeney Family Tree Project, and a board member of the Friends of Colonel Benjamin E. Caudill. Seabrook's literary works have been endorsed by leading authorities, museum curators, award-winning historians, bestselling authors, celebrities, noted scientists, well respected educators, renown military artists, esteemed Southern organizations, and distinguished academicians from around the world.

As a professional writer Seabrook has authored some thirty popular adult books specializing in the following topics: the American Civil War, pro-South studies, Confederate biography and history, the anthropology of religion, genealogical monographs, Goddess-worship (thealogy), ghost stories, the paranormal, family histories, military encyclopedias, etymological dictionaries, ufology, social issues, comparative analysis of the origins of Christmas, and cross-cultural studies of the family and marriage.

Seabrook's seven children's books include a dictionary of religion and myth, a rewriting of the King Arthur legend (which reinstates the original pre-Christian motifs), two bedtime stories for preschoolers, a naturalist's guidebook to owls, a worldwide look at the family, and an examination of the Near-Death Experience.

Of blue-blooded Southern stock through his Kentucky, Tennessee, Virginia, West Virginia, and North Carolina ancestors, he is a direct descendant of European royalty via his 6th great-grandfather, the EARL OF OXFORD, after which London's famous Harley Street is named. Among his celebrated male Celtic ancestors is ROBERT THE BRUCE, King of Scotland, Seabrook's 22nd great-grandfather. The 21st great-grandson of EDWARD I "LONGSHANKS" PLANTAGENET), King of England, Seabrook is a thirteenth-generation Southerner through his descent from the colonists of Jamestown, Virginia (1607).

The 2nd, 3rd, and 4th great-grandson of dozens of Confederate soldiers, one of his closest connections to the War for Southern Independence is through his 3rd great-grandfather, ELIAS JENT, SR., who fought for the Confederacy in the Thirteenth Cavalry Kentucky under Seabrook's 2nd cousin, Colonel BENJAMIN E. CAUDILL. The Thirteenth, also known as "Caudill's Army," fought in numerous conflicts, including the Battles of Saltville, Gladsville, Mill Cliff, Poor Fork, Whitesburg, and Leatherwood.

Seabrook is also related to the following Confederates and other 19th-Century luminaries: ROBERT E. LEE, STEPHEN DILL LEE, JOHN SINGLETON MOSBY, STONEWALL JACKSON, NATHAN BEDFORD FORREST, JAMES LONGSTREET, JOHN HUNT MORGAN, JEB STUART, P. G. T. BEAUREGARD (designed the Confederate Battle Flag), JOHN BELL HOOD, ALEXANDER PETER STEWART, ARTHUR M. MANIGAULT, JOSEPH MANIGAULT, CHARLES SCOTT VENABLE, THORNTON A. WASHINGTON, JOHN A. WASHINGTON, ABRAHAM BUFORD, EDMUND W. PETTUS, THEODRICK "TOD" CARTER, JOHN B. WOMACK, JOHN H. WINDER, GIDEON J. PILLOW, STATES RIGHTS GIST, EDMUND WINCHESTER RUCKER, HENRY R. JACKSON, JOHN C. BRECKINRIDGE, LEONIDAS POLK, ZACHARY

(Photo © Lochlainn Seabrook)

TAYLOR, SARAH KNOX TAYLOR (the first wife of JEFFERSON DAVIS), RICHARD TAYLOR, DAVY CROCKETT, DANIEL BOONE, MERIWETHER LEWIS (of the Lewis and Clark Expedition) ANDREW JACKSON, JAMES K. POLK, ABRAM POINDEXTER MAURY (founder of Franklin, TN), WILLIAM GILES HARDING, ZEBULON VANCE,

THOMAS JEFFERSON, GEORGE WYTHE RANDOLPH (grandson of Jefferson), FELIX K. ZOLLICOFFER, FITZHUGH LEE, NATHANIEL F. CHEAIRS, JESSE JAMES, FRANK JAMES, ROBERT BRANK VANCE, CHARLES SIDNEY WINDER, JOHN W. MCGAVOCK, CARRIE (WINDER) MCGAVOCK, DAVID HARDING MCGAVOCK, LYSANDER MCGAVOCK, JAMES RANDAL MCGAVOCK, RANDAL WILLIAM MCGAVOCK, FRANCIS MCGAVOCK, EMILY MCGAVOCK, WILLIAM HENRY F. LEE, LUCIUS E.

POLK, MINOR MERIWETHER (husband of noted pro-South author Elizabeth Avery Meriwether), ELLEN BOURNE TYNES (wife of Forrest's chief of artillery, Captain John W. Morton), South Carolina Senators PRESTON SMITH BROOKS and ANDREW PICKENS BUTLER, and famed South Carolina diarist MARY CHESNUT.

Seabrook's modern day cousins include: PATRICK J. BUCHANAN (conservative author), REBECCA GAYHEART (Kentucky-born actress), SHELBY LEE ADAMS (Letcher County, Kentucky, portrait photographer), BERTRAM THOMAS COMBS (Kentucky's fiftieth governor), EDITH BOLLING (wife of President Woodrow Wilson), and actors ROBERT DUVALL, REESE WITHERSPOON, LEE MARVIN, and TOM CRUISE.

Born with music in his blood, Seabrook is an award-winning, multi-genre, BMI-Nashville songwriter and lyricist who has composed some 3,000 songs (250 albums), and whose original music has been heard on TV and radio worldwide. A musician, producer, multi-instrumentalist, and renown performer—whose keyboard work has been variously compared to pianists from HARGUS ROBBINS and VINCE GUARALDI to ELTON JOHN and LEONARD BERNSTEIN—Seabrook has opened for groups such as the EARL SCRUGGS REVIEW, TED NUGENT, and BOB SEGER, and has performed privately for such public figures as President RONALD REAGAN, BURT REYNOLDS, and Senator EDWARD W. BROOKE.

Seabrook's cousins in the music business include: JOHNNY CASH, ELVIS PRESLEY, BILLY RAY and MILEY CYRUS, PATTY LOVELESS, TIM MCGRAW, LEE ANN WOMACK, DOLLY PARTON, PAT BOONE, NAOMI, WYNONNA, and ASHLEY JUDD, RICKY SKAGGS, the SUNSHINE SISTERS, MARTHA CARSON, and CHET ATKINS.

Seabrook lives with his wife and family in historic Middle Tennessee, the heart of Forrest country and the Confederacy, where his conservative Southern ancestors fought valiantly against liberal Lincoln and the progressive North in defense of Jeffersonianism, constitutional government, and personal liberty.

# MEET THE FOREWORD WRITER

NELSON WYMAN CALVIN WINBUSH is the grandson of Louis Napoleon
Nelson, a Confederate African-American soldier who served under General
Nathan Bedford Forrest, the author's cousin, at the Battles of Fort Pillow,
Shiloh, and Brice's Cross Roads. (Louis also fought at the Battles of
Vicksburg and Lookout Mountain.)

Mr. Winbush, born in Ripley, Tennessee, in 1929, is a graduate of
Tennessee State University and a former assistant principle. A veteran of the
Korean War (1951-1953), a husband, father, and grandfather, he is a life
member of the Veterans of Foreign Wars and the Florida Retired Educators
Association.

He is also a life member of the Sons of Confederate Veterans, member
of the Florida Division, the Louis Napoleon Nelson Brigade and Jacob Summerlin
Camp #1516. Ancestor: Private Louis Napoleon Nelson, Company M, 7th
Cavalry Tennessee.

Mr. Winbush received Commander in Chief's Award 1995,
Commander in Chief's Citation for Distinguished Service in 1996, the
Commander in Chief's Citation for Distinguished Service in 1997, and the
Commander in Chief's Citation for Distinguished Service for 1998.

In 1997 and 1998 he received a Certificate of Appreciation from the
Army of Tennessee, Department of Sons of Confederate Veterans. Received
commission as Commander Emeritus Louis Napoleon Brigade, Sons of
Confederate Veterans March 7, 1998. Received Certificate of Appreciation from
the Heritage Preservation Association August 1998. Received Certificate of
Loyalty and Appreciation from the Jacob Summerlin Camp December 2000.
Received the SCV's Private Charles Ulmer Award (Florida Division) for
outstanding service in 2005.

Mr. Winbush travels to Sons of Confederate Veterans Camps and other
events in the State of Florida, as well as other states, to speak about his
grandfather's escapades during the War for Southern Independence.

> "I am proud to be a *real grandson*, having in my possession the
> Confederate Battle Flag that draped my grandfather's coffin, a
> reunion jacket and cap, numerous newspaper articles and reunion
> pictures. I was five when he passed and I still remember war
> stories as told me by my grandfather." — Nelson W. Winbush

Louis Napoleon Nelson (left) with his grandson Nelson W. Winbush (right), circa mid 1930s, Memphis, Tennessee, train station. Louis was on his way to one of the thirty-nine Confederate reunions he attended, this one in Nashville. Photo © courtesy Nelson W. Winbush.

# HOW YOU CAN HELP PRESERVE THE SOUTH

If after reading this book you feel inspired to do something to aid in the preservation of America's most beautiful, special, and unique region, please consider joining a pro-South organization. All are devoted, in one way or another, to conserving Dixie and to protecting her from the nefarious processes of Northernization, liberalization, Yankeefication, and scallywagfication.

Among the many pro-South groups you might consider:

FOR MEN
1. Sons of Confederate Veterans (SCV): www.scv.org
2. Military Order of the Stars and Bars (MOSB): www.mosbihq.org

FOR WOMEN
3. United Daughters of the Confederacy (UDC): www.hqudc.org
4. Order of the Confederate Rose (OCR): www.confederate-rose.org

FOR ALL
5. League of the South (LS): www.dixienet.org
6. Southern National Congress (SNC): www.southernnationalcongress.org
7. Southern Legal Resource Center (SLRC): www.slrc-csa.org
8. The Southern Party: www.southernparty.org

EDUCATION
9. The Abbeville Institute: www.abbevilleinstitute.org
10. The Stephen Dill Lee Institute: www.stephendleeinstitute.com
11. The 1861 Athenaeum Girls' School: www.athenaeumrectory.com

> IMPORTANT NOTE: Many of these fine organizations have been labeled "racist" by the uninformed. Don't be taken in by this absurd anti-South accusation, one intended to create racial discord and further humiliate, degrade, and subjugate Dixie. Not only do their constitutions contain anti-racism clauses, but the founders and leaders, as well as their members, strongly denounce racism in all its forms, and membership is open to all races, creeds, and colors. The fact is that individual racists can be found in all organizations, whatever their focus or mission. But this unfortunate reality does not make the organization to which they belong racist as well. An entire group should never be condemned for the bigoted views of a few of its misguided members.

April is Confederate History Month all across the U.S. Celebrate it by displaying one of the many beautiful Confederate flags and educating your loved ones, friends, and neighbors as to the Truth about the South and the Confederacy. Future generations will thank you.

If you enjoyed Mr. Seabrook's
*Everything You Were Taught About the Civil War is Wrong, Ask a Southerner!*
you will be interested in his other Civil War titles, such as:

*A REBEL BORN: A DEFENSE OF NATHAN BEDFORD FORREST*
*ABRAHAM LINCOLN: THE SOUTHERN VIEW*
*THE QUOTABLE JEFFERSON DAVIS*
*THE OLD REBEL: ROBERT E. LEE AS HE WAS SEEN BY HIS CONTEMPORARIES*

Available from Sea Raven Press and wherever fine books are sold.

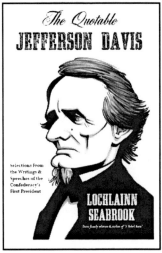

.

CPSIA information can be obtained at www.ICGtesting.com
Printed in the USA
LVOW061948020512

280085LV00001B/176/P